Disciplinary Approaches to Aging

General Editor

Donna Lind Infeld, Ph. D.
George Washington Univesity

A ROUTLEDGE SERIES

Contents of the Collection

Volume 1
Biology of Aging

Volume 2
Psychology of Aging

Volume 3
Sociology of Aging

Volume 4
Anthropology of Aging

Volume 5
Economics of Aging

Volume 6
Political Science, Public Policy, and Aging

Disciplinary Approaches to Aging

Volume 5
Economics of Aging

Edited with introductions by

Donna Lind Infeld, Ph. D.
George Washington University

ROUTLEDGE
New York/London

Published in 2002 by
Routledge
29 West 35th Street
New York, NY 10001

Published in Great Britain by
Routledge
11 New Fetter Lane
London EC4P 4EE

Routledge is an imprint of the Taylor & Francis Group.
Copyright © 2002 by Routledge

Printed in the United States of America on acid-free paper.

10 9 8 7 6 5 4 3 2 1

Library of Congress Cataloging-in-Publication Data

Disciplinary approaches toward aging / edited with introductions by Donna Lind
Infeld.
    p. cm.
    Includes bibliographical references.
    Contents: v. 1. Biology of aging—v. 2. Psychology of aging—v. 3. Sociology of
aging—v. 4. Anthropology of aging—v. 5. Economics of aging—v. 6. Politics, policy, aging.
    ISBN 0-415-93895-3 (set : alk paper)—ISBN 0-415-93896-1 (vol. 1 : alk. paper)
-— ISBN 0-415-93897-X (vol. 2 : alk. paper)—ISBN 0-415-93898-8 (vol. 3 : alk.
paper)—ISBN 0-415-93899-6 (vol. 4 : alk. paper)—ISBN 0-415-93900-3 (vol. 5 :
alk. paper)—ISBN 0-415-93901-1 (vol. 6 : alk. paper)
    1. Gerontology. 2. Aged. 3. Aging. I. Infeld, Donna Lind.
HQ1061.D557 2002
305.26—dc21   2002020627

Contents

v

Retirement and Labor Force Participation

Housing and Consumer Economics

Health and Medical Economics

Series Introduction

Life expectancy around the world has been increasing dramatically over the last several decades. Global average life expectancy has now reached 66 years (U.N. 2000). This trend has resulted in a large, and still growing, elderly population. There are currently well over 550 million people in the world who are over age 60, and this number is expected to approach 1.2 billion by 2025 (AoA 1998).

Increasing longevity is a result of numerous factors. Chief among them are improved nutrition and sanitation, higher levels of healthy behaviors (e.g., reduced smoking), and improved medical care. Underlying these changes at the population level are higher levels of education, income, and knowledge about health, trends that are continuing to spread throughout the world.

However, this lengthening life expectancy and increasing size of the older population is not occurring evenly. In more developed regions of the world, including Europe, Northern America, Australia/New Zealand and Japan, the 14 percent of the population that was 65 or older in 2000 is expected to increase to 19 percent by 2020 (U.N. 2001). Life expectancy in the United States, now 76.9 years, is almost 30 years longer than it was in 1900 (AoA 2001). The age group 65 and over makes up over 12 percent U.S. of the population and is expected to increase to 20 percent by 2030 (Ibid). One way I like to represent this proportion to students is to compare it to the current 17.6 percent of the population of Florida that is age 65 and older. In other words, there will be a greater proportion of older people throughout the United States than currently live in Florida. If you have ever visited Florida, you will understand why this is hard to comprehend.

In less developed regions of the world, including Africa, Asia (excluding Japan), Latin America, the Caribbean, Melanesia, Micronesia and Polynesia, the growth rate of the elderly population is even greater than it is in more developed regions. The projected increase of people over age 60 is from 5 percent in 2000 to over 7 percent by 2020 (ibid.). This is increase of two percentage points represents a faster rate of growth than that occurring in the more developed parts of the world.

In addition to the growth of the older population, the older population itself is getting older. The oldest old population (age 80 and older) is growing at an even faster rate than the young-old (age 60–79), with an increase of the 60 and older age group worldwide from 11 percent to 19 percent projected for 2050 (U.N. 2000).

These numbers are so large and changing so rapidly that the consequences to societies and to individuals' lives are almost impossible to comprehend. Gerontology, the study of aging, is the field that attempts to undertake this daunting task. Further extension of the life span, and more importantly adding quality to the added years, will be based on our knowledge of the multi-faceted components of aging. These components include new levels of understanding and intervention in the normal processes of aging (biology), mood, morale, and life-satisfaction (psychology), productive and rewarding roles in retirement and widowhood (sociology), cultural norms and supports for aging members of communities (anthropology), distribution of resources, particularly income opportunities for retired persons (economics) and the ability to shape public policy to assure equity of access to public resources (political science). These challenges are at the core of the disciplines that contribute to the field of gerontology.

GERONTOLOGY

The term gerontology is based on the Greek word *geron*, which means old men. It is the field that involves the study of the many dimensions of aging. It is a relatively young field. The Gerontological Society of America, the primary American organization devoted to promoting the scientific study of aging, was founded in 1945, and the behavioral and social sciences section was established in 1956 (www.geron.org/history.htm). Since the 1960s, the study of aging has grown dramatically and there has been extensive theoretical development and growing research applying a wide range of disciplinary approaches to examining the phenomenon of aging.

Gerontology is a multidisciplinary field. Numerous disciplines are interested in and make unique contributions to understanding aging. What is less clear is the extent to which gerontology can be considered interdisciplinary, that is reflecting integration among disciplines in the study of aging. While some studies have interdisciplinary research questions and methods, most research on age-related topics continues to be either disciplinary or multidisciplinary. In other words, research is generally grounded in a single discipline or else involves a team of researchers exploring a range of discipline-based issues. However, in some cases it achieves significant integration of theoretical concepts and approaches within an individual study.

I come from a multidisciplinary gerontological background. My aging career started with support from the Administration on Aging as an undergraduate trainee at Portland State University. My degree was in Psychology with a minor in Sociology. My doctoral work at the Florence Heller

Graduate School for Advanced Studies of Social Welfare at Brandeis University continued this multidisciplinary approach involving coursework in economics and political science as well as continued work in gerontology.

In the twenty-five years since completing my formal education, my professional positions have involved teaching aging courses to students in the applied fields of health services management and policy, public health, and public administration. As a result of this education and these academic settings, I view my background as strong on breadth and short on depth in the basic disciplines that contribute to understanding aging. This lack of depth was a motivating factor for creating this anthology. In preparing for classes in my gerontology overview course I found myself trying to stay up to date with the latest disciplinary work in numerous fields. It was my goal to produce a set of publications to help faculty members and other professionals in the field of aging to keep abreast of these developments.

DEVELOPMENT OF THE ANTHOLOGY

The series is designed to provide an integrated set of foundational articles from the primary disciplines interested in the study of aging. Each volume includes articles that provide an historical overview of theoretical perspectives in that discipline. Each volume also explores major concepts and issues within the discipline, highlights recent research findings, and provides directions for future research

I decided to organize this anthology along traditional disciplinary lines for two reasons. First, most academic training in gerontology continues to be organized along disciplinary lines. Thus, disciplinary-based readings can be more easily integrated into courses and training. Second, despite the inter/multidisciplinary nature of much research in aging, most theoretical developments continue to emerge from disciplinary homes.

University courses and textbooks about aging can be found in all major academic disciplines. According to the Association for Gerontology in Higher Education, there are more than 500 campuses in the United States that offer aging courses in more than 30 disciplines and fields of study (www.aghe.org/natdbase.htm). For example, The University of Southern California, arguably among the most extensive gerontology programs in the United States, offers 37 undergraduate and 35 graduate courses thorough its Leonard Davis School of Gerontology. Disciplines represented include biology, physiology, psychology, sociology, demography, policy, and ethics (www.usc.edu/dept/gero/ldsg/index.htm).

In addition to these traditional disciplinary approaches, numerous professional fields offer courses related to aging, many of which are grounded on disciplinary theories and applied research. Training in fields such as social work, nursing, counseling, recreation therapy, and health care administration depend on the multi-disciplinary literature on aging. Further, international attention to aging is expanding rapidly. As a result there is broad and growing demand for accessible and coherent gerontological literature.

This six-volume anthology on Disciplinary Approaches to Aging is designed to help respond to the need for more gerontological literature. The volumes include 1) Biology, 2) Psychology, 3) Anthropology, 4) Sociology, 5) Economics, and 6) Political Science. The series draws from a wide array of published sources from the United States and around the world. While most articles were selected from academic journals, a broad range of sources was reviewed including professional publications, book chapters, web sites and government reports and documents.

The process of searching for articles was complex and varied across the disciplines. The criteria I used in making selections were:

Overview or review articles rather than reports of single research studies

My goal was to provide articles that would bring readers up to date with current developments in each discipline. Review articles were easier to identify in biology because several medical literature databases provide a search option for them. In each of the other disciplines I had to look through hundreds of abstracts and articles to identify those that provide a broad overview of the topic or field.

Recent publication

Almost all of the articles were published within the last five years, with the large majority less than two years old. Recent publication supports the anthology's objective of focusing on *current* developments in each discipline.

Broadest possible array of authors and publications

In several disciplines I could have produced a whole volume from articles published in a single journal or written by a single author. However, my objective was to represent the widest possible range of publications that address issues of aging. Therefore, no authors or publications have more than one article in any volume of the anthology.

Inclusion of publications from around the world

Priority was given to articles that contribute to the understanding of current *international* theoretical and research developments contributing to disciplinary approaches to aging as part of the effort to represent the breadth of the field.

With these criteria in mind, I applied multiple search engines and databases, focusing first on the academic and professional journals they catalogue. I started with broad terms (e.g., anthropology and aging/old age/aged/elderly) but also searched a range of subtopics (culture, ethnography, etc.). For some of the volumes there was ample material identified using these steps. Next I had to make difficult choices, again using the criteria identified above. For several volumes the initial search processes did not provide adequate coverage of work in the discipline. I then turned to other sources such as the web and book chapters to round out the coverage.

Despite these efforts, I know that there are some gaps in the selections included here. When I was overwhelmed with the choices and decisions, I tried to keep in mind the overall goal of creating a resource for faculty and other professionals to use to provide the basis for developing and updating lectures in a wide range of aging-related courses. To supplement the readings, a list of additional references is provided in each volume to direct readers to additional resources and recent examples of research conducted in that field.

The multi-disciplinary nature of aging research and theory presented a particular challenge when sorting and organizing the articles into discipline-specific volumes. Not only do many major research studies include, for example, psychological as well as sociological and economic data, but concepts often cut across disciplinary lines as well. Concepts such as norms and roles, whose homes are in sociology, are also prevalent in psychological and anthropological research. Further, it was not always easy to decide where to place an article when a sociologist was publishing in an anthropological journal or visa versa. And, of course, research in social psychology belongs in both sociology and psychology. The most significant area of overlap was between economics and political science, more specifically, public policy. In fact much of the economic research on aging could have been just as appropriately considered to be public policy research. Despite these challenges, I feel the resulting compilation meets the goal of being a collection of articles that captures the major issues, concepts, and research directions of each disciplinary field.

As I struggled with making the many decisions involved in producing this anthology, it became painfully clear that knowledge simply does not fit into neat and distinct boxes. Thanks to Mark Georgiev, Associate Editor at Routledge, who reminded me that there is no perfect anthology. Without his support, encouragement, and prompting this project would not have been completed. My thanks also go to Lauren Block who tried to make the product as perfect as possible. Her help was invaluable throughout every step. Thanks also to Marcel and Amanda for their never-ending love and support. In the end, producing *Disciplinary Approaches to Aging* was an education for me and I hope it will be a useful resource for my colleagues around the world.

Donna Lind Infeld, Ph.D.

REFERENCES

Administration on Aging (November 9, 1998). International Activities of the Administration on Aging. Retrieved March 4, 2002 from *http://www.aoa.gov/Factsheets/international.html*.

Administration on Aging (December 21, 2001). A Profile of Older Americans: 2001. Retrieved March 4, 2002, from *http://www.aoa.gov/aoa/STATS/profile/profile.pdf*.

Association for Gerontology in Higher Education. Retrieved April 1, 2002, from *http://www.aghe.org/natdbase.thm*.

Gerontological Society of America. Retrieved April 1, 2002, from *http://www.geron.org/history.htm*.

United Nations/Division for Social Policy Development, (May 24, 2000). The Aging of the World Population. Retrieved March 4, 2002, from *http://www.un.org/esa/socdev/ageing/agewpop.htm*.

United Nations, Population Division (2001). Population Division of the Department of Economic and Social Affairs of the United Nations Secretariat, World Population Prospects: The 2000 Revision. Retrieved March 4, 2002, from *http://esa.un.org/unpp/index.asp?Panel=3*

University of Southern California. Leonard Davis School of Gerontology. Retrieved April 2, 2002, from *http://usc.edu/dept/gero/ldsg/index.htm*.

Volume Introduction

Economics comes from the Greek words "oikos" and "nomos." Oikos means household or family estate, and nomos means rules or laws. Thus, the literal meaning of economics is the management of one's estate. The social science of economics deals with the production, distribution, and consumption of resources (goods and services), at both the personal and societal levels. Economics is divided into two components, microeconomics and macroeconomics. Microeconomics considers individual markets and individual economic decisions. That is, microeconomics is the study of how individual people and businesses make decisions about what to produce, distribute, and use. Macroeconomics involves the study of the economy as a whole, the aggregate of all individual economic decisions.

ECONOMIC THEORY

Economics, as a discipline, is heavily theory driven, with theories emanating from various economic doctrines or schools. These doctrines include, for example, Classical Economics, Keynesian Economics, Neo-Keynsian or Neo-Classical Economics, Monetarist Economics, New Classical Economics, and Marxist Economics. These doctrines vary in terms of the extent to which they apply microeconomic analysis versus macroeconomic analysis and the role of the market.

Several microeconomic theories have direct relevance to economic decisions made by individuals over their life course. For example, in microeconomics, purchasing decisions are seen as based on individuals' decisions to maximize the level of satisfaction they expect to receive from purchasing one good versus another and from present versus future consumption of these goods and services. Decisions to consume are influenced by expectations about future income, interest rates, and result in decisions to invest or save for future uncertainty (a rainy day) or for future income (retirement). One article in this volume, "Reverse mortgage choices: a theoretical and empirical analysis of the borrowing decisions of elderly homeowners" (Fratantoni 1999) is a very specific example of an age-related purchasing decision potentially made by older people.

Many economic models are based on the concept of utility maximization. That is, people are viewed as making rational decisions about buying goods and services with the goal of maximizing their overall satisfaction.

There are several assumptions underlying this model. People are assumed to be able to rank their preferences for various goods and services. Further, they are assumed to make rational economic decisions about the tradeoff between working versus leisure, which affects their decision to work overtime, to take vacations, and to retire. Several articles in this volume examine retirement trends and labor force participation of older people.

Macroeconomic theories and principles apply to economic decisions made by societies, focusing on aggregate demand for goods and services and distribution of resources. Of particular interest in macroeconomics are issues of income for unemployed and other disenfranchised groups. Thus, decisions about retirement income support are within the realm of macroeconomics. In the United States, the design and solvency of the Social Security program are of immediate concern. However, articles selected for the volume were chosen in an effort to address issues of general applicability rather than specific single-country concerns. For example, a topic of more general interest is the relationship between the existence of public retirement programs and the likelihood that people will save for retirement during their working years. Increased levels of savings are important because savings is seen as being directly related to economic growth. However, some argue that investment generates savings, not the other way around (Schulz 1999). A series of articles in this volume examine these general issues related to Social Security, pensions, and savings in greater depth.

In general, the models and theories in economics explain how things should operate given ideal circumstances. However, market imperfections and externalities interfere with the operation of markets. Market imperfections include, for example, the lack of perfect information about available products and services. Externalities result when prices of goods do not reflect the true cost to society of their production, due to, for example, the creation of pollution. These factors result in the need for a welfare economics approach that aims to maximize the utility or well being of the community. Welfare economics involves examining the social desirability of various patterns of resource allocation. Its goal is to identify the optimal situation, that is one in which no individual can be made better off without making someone else worse off.

Related to welfare economics is health economics. What level of economic resources, both individual and societal, should be devoted to health, and what are the benefits from spending on health? These issues are addressed in two articles included in this volume (Smith 1994, VanZon and Muysken 2001).

In sum, economic theories and concepts provide us with tools to examine how population (macro) and individual (micro) aging affects the production, distribution, and consumptions of goods and services and the costs and benefits associated with various patterns of resource distribution in a society.

ECONOMICS AND AGING

Most of the literature on the economics of aging focuses on descriptions of how societies distribute income to older (retired) persons and how older people allocate their resources (spending versus saving). Decisions about the allocation of resources at a societal level are significantly influenced by political processes rather than being purely economic decisions. Thus, economics and politics are strongly related. "Economics ... might be described as the 'math' of politics which results largely from the distribution and movement of wealth and its power among people. Thus, economics is closely related to, and intertwined with, the social science of politics. Some say that politics *is* economics, or the result of economics" (Richmond 2002). As a result, many of the articles in the volume on Political Science, Politics, and Public Policy are also relevant to the economics of aging.

Economics chapters in gerontology textbooks are often organized according to micro-and macroeconomic issues. They typically include a chapter addressing individual economic circumstances of older people (e.g., employment, retirement, and individual income) and another dealing with the overall economy (e.g., income maintenance policies and patterns of economic well-being among the elderly). While these topics build on the distinction between macro- and microeconomics, that is they separate out individual and societal economic concerns, they are generally not theory-based.

The lack of age-specific (or age-applied) economic theory does not imply that the field has not progressed. Jim Schulz (1995), in the first article in this volume, identifies several areas in which our understanding of the economic well-being of older people has advanced in the past 30 years. There is now better data and more analysis that differentiates the economic circumstances of various elderly subgroups, more and better longitudinal data sets, and significant analysis and evaluation of Medicare and Medicaid as part of the general issues of health care. Schulz also identifies several areas in which only limited progress has been made. They are, most notably, gathering more information on economic issues and programs affecting people in old age, research on the use of time over the life span, and research on the economics of population aging.

In regard to population aging, Schulz was concerned about the lack of attention to the aging of the baby boom. However, since 1995, this topic has received growing attention. Several articles in this volume focus on population aging. They include: Paying for an aging population (Aaron and Reischauer 1999)," "The impact of population aging on the socially optimal rate of national saving (Guest 2001)," "Social Security financing policies and rapidly aging populations" (Ron 1998), "The consequences of

population aging on private pension fund saving and asset markets"
(Schieber and Shoven 1997), and "Population aging in Canada and Japan"
(Venne 2001). It is clear that economists, as well as politicians, are now
well aware that the baby boom is coming.

Another important topic included in this volume is comparative economics. As with other volumes in this anthology, every effort was made to
present international approaches to the discipline. Selected papers repre-
senting economic realities around the world include an article from the
European Economic Review focusing on distributive implications of aging
in the industrialized world (von Weizsacker 1996) and a discussion paper
from a World Bank conference, addressing social security financing
throughout Asia (Ron 1998). Additionally, attention is given specifically to
Japan (Yashiro), the Netherlands (Broer 2001), and China (Benjamin et al.
2000). Comparisons across countries include Australia and Japan (Guest
2001), Canada and Japan (Venne 2001), and the U.S., Great Britain and
Japan (Barton 1995). Finally, Clark et al (1999) examine economic development and labor force participation using national data from 134 countries.

CONCLUSION

Whether focusing on aging in the United States, Japan, or elsewhere
around the world, the articles in this volume represent topics of global
interest. Productivity and retirement among older people, national savings
rates and individual borrowing decisions, and health economics are issues
that all nations are facing or preparing to face. Because some of the more
developed countries are also those with the oldest populations, their successes and failures at preparing for an aging population should provide
valuable lessons for the other countries of the world.

REFERENCES

Richmond, A. Business, Economics, and Wealth. Economics. Accessed
    March 7, 2002, retrieved from, *http://www.encyclozine.com/humani-
    ties/economics/*.
Schulz, J. H. "Saving, Growth, and Social Security: Fighting Our Children
    Over Shares of the Future Economic Pie?" in Butler, R. N., L. K.
    Grossman, and M. R. Oberlink (Eds.) *Life in an Older America.* NY:
    The Century Foundation Press.

Additional References

Baker, M., & Benjamin, D. (1999). Early retirement provisions and the
    labor force behavior of older men: Evidence from Canada. *Journal of
    Labor Economics,* 17(4), 724–756.

Barth, M. C. (2000). An aging workforce in an increasingly global world. *Journal of Aging & Social Policy,* 11(2–3), 83–88.

Bosworth, B and G. T. Burtless. (1998). *Aging Societies: The Global Dimension.* Washington, D.C.: The Brookings Institution.

Budetti, P. P., R. V. Burkauser, J. Gregory. (2001). *Ensuring Health and Income Security for an Aging Workforce.* Conference of the National Academy of Social Insurance. Kalamazoo: W. E. Upjohn Institute for Employment Research.

Burkhauser, R. V., Couch, K. A., & Phillips, J. W. (1996). Who takes early Social Security benefits? The economic and health characteristics of early beneficiaries. *Gerontologist,* 36(6), 789–799.

Butler, M., & Kirchsteiger, G. (1999). Aging anxiety: Much ado about nothing?, *Tilburg Center for Economic Research Discussion Paper.*

Cameron, L. A. (2000). Poverty and inequality in Java: Examining the impact of the changing age, educational and industrial structure. *Journal of Development Economics,* 62(1), 149–180.

Choi, N. G. (2000). Determinants of engagement in paid work following social security benefit receipt among older women. *Journal of Women and Aging,* 12(3/4), 133–154.

Costa, D.L. (1998). *The Evolution of Retirement: An American Economic History 1880–1990.* NBER Series on Long-Term Factors in Economic Development. Chicago: University of Chicago Press.

Crystal, S., & Waehrer, K. (1996). Later-life economic ineqaulity in longitudinal perspective. *Journals of Gerontology (B),* 51(6), S307.

Daniels, N. (1998). Does economics provide a unified account of aging behavior and aging policy? *Ethics,* 108(3), 569–585.

Deaton, A. S., & Paxson, C.H. (1998). Aging and inequality in income and health. *American Economic Review,* 88(2), 248–253.

Disney, R. (1998). *Frontiers in the economics of aging.* Chicago:University of Chicago Press.

England, R. S. (2002). *The Fiscal Challenge of an Aging Industrial World.* Washington, D.C.: Center for Strategic and International Studies.

Ezrati, M. (1997). Japan's aging economics. *Foreign Affairs,* 76(3), 96–104.

Favreault, M., Ratcliffe, C., & Toder, E. (1999). Labor force participation of older workers: Prospective changes and potential policy responses. *National Tax Journal,* 52(3), 483–503.

Frey, D. E. (1997). Advances in the economics of aging. *Southern Economic Journal,* 64(1), 336–337.

Funakoshi, T. (1996). A Problem of the aging society—Including the economics of medical treatment. *Nippon Seikeigeka Gakkai zasshi (Journal of Japanese Orthopaedic Assn),* 70(3), S504.

Futagami, K., & Nakajima, T. (2001). Population aging and economic growth. *Journal of Macroeconomics,* 23(1), 31–44.

Gokhale, J., & Raffelhuschen, B. (2000). Population aging and fiscal policy in Europe and the United States: Erratum. *Federal Reserve Bank of Cleveland Economic Review,* 36(2), 38.

Goldberg, B. (2000). *Age Works: What Corporate America Must do to Survive the Graying of the Workforce.* Free Press.

Gregg, J. (1997). Social Security: Keeping our promise to prosperity. *Vital Speeches of the Day,* 63(21), 642–644.

Harris, A. R., Evans, W. N., & Schwab, R. M. (2001). Education spending in an aging America. *Journal of Public Economics,* 81(3), 449–472.

Hurd, M. D. (1997). The economics of individual aging. In M. R. Rosenzweig, & Stark, Oded (Ed.), *Handbook of population and family economics* (Vol. 1B, pp. 891–966). Handbooks in Economics, vol. 14. Amsterdam: Elsevier Science North-Holland.

Jones, F. (1999). Seniors who volunteer. *Perspectives on Labour and Income,* 11(3), 9–17.

Jones, L. D. (1997). The tenure transition decision for elderly homeowners. *Journal of Urban Economics,* 41(2), 243–263.

Krause, N. (1997). Anticipated support, received support, and economic stress among older adults. *Journals of Gerontology (B),* 52(6), P284–P293.

Kutty, N. K. (2000). The production of functionality by the elderly: A household production function approach. *Applied Economics,* 32(10), 1269–1280.

Luth, E. (2001). *Private Intergenerational Transfers and Population Aging: The German Case.* NY: Physica Verlag.

Martikainen, G. M. P., Stansfeld, S. A., Brunner, E. J., Fuhrer, R., & Marmot, M. G. (2000). Predictors of early retirement in British civil servants. *Age and Ageing,* 29(6), 529–536.

Miller, N. J., Kim, S., & Schofield-Tomschin, S. (1998). The effects of activity and aging on rural community living and consuming. *The Journal of Consumer Affairs,* 32(2), 343–368.

Ogura, S, T. Tachibanaki, D. A. Wise (Eds.) (2001). *Aging Issues in the United States and Japan.* National Bureau of Economic Research Conference Report. Chicago: University of Chicago Press.

Ono, H., & Stafford, F. (2001). Till death do us part or I get my pension? Wives' pension holding and marital dissolution in the United States. *Scandinavian Journal of Economics,* 103(3), 525–544.

Ono, T., & Maeda, Y. (2001). Is aging harmful to the environment. *Environmental and Resource Economics,* 20(2), 113–127.

Oster, S. M., & Hamermesh, D. S. (1998). Aging and productivity among economists. *The Review of Economics and Statistics,* 80(1), 154–156.

Payne, B. (2001). Making sense of the private finance initiative. Developing public-private partnerships. *Age and Ageing*, 30(1), 97–98.

Poterba, J. M., Venti, S. F., & Wise, D. A. (1998). Implications of rising personal retirement saving. In D. A. Wise (Ed.), *Frontiers in the economics of aging* (pp. 125–167). NBER Project Report. Chicago and London: University of Chicago Press.

Randel, J., T. German and D. Ewing (Eds.) (2000). *The Aging and Development Report: Poverty, Independence and the World's Older People*. London: Earthscan Publishers Ltd.

Savishinsky, J. S. (2000). Breaking the watch: The meanings of retirement in America. *Ithaca* (Cornell University Press).

Schulz, J.H. (2001). *The Economics of Aging*. Seventh Edition. Westport, CT: Auburn House Publishing.

Shields, M., Stallmann, J. I., & Deller, S. C. (1999). Stimulating the economic and fiscal impacts of high- and low-income elderly on a small rural region. *Review of Regional Studies*, 29(2), 175–196.

Sicker, M. (2002). *The Political Economy of Work in the 21st Century: Implications for an Aging American Workforce*. Westport, CT: Quorum Books.

Thogersen, O. (2001). Reforming Social Security: Assessing the effects of alternative funding strategies. *Applied Economics*, 33(12), 1531–1540.

Topinkova, E., & Callahan, D. (1999). Culture, economics, and Alzheimer's disease: Social determinants of resource allocation. *Journal of Applied Gerontology*, 18(4), 411–422.

Weil, D. N. (1997). The economics of population aging. In M. R. Rosenzweig & O. Stark (Eds.), *Handbook of population and family economics* (Vol. 1B, pp. 967–1014). Handbooks in Economics, vol. 14. Amsterdam: Elsevier Science North-Holland.

Whaples, R. M. (2001). The Economics of aging. *Choice*, 38(11/12), 2007.

Wigger, B. U. (2001). Productivity Growth and the Political Economy of Social Security. *Public Choice*, 106(1–2), 53–76.

Wise, D.A. (Ed.) (2001). *Themes in the Economics of Aging*. (National Bureau of Economic Project Report). Chicago: University of Chicago Press.

Yabiku, S. Y. (2000). Family history and pensions: The relationships between marriage, divorce, children and private pension coverage. *Journal of Aging Studies*, 14(3), 293–312.

Zweifel, P., Felder, S., & Meiers, M. (1999). Ageing of population and health care expenditures: A Red Herring? *Health Economics*, 8(6), 485–496.

Journal of Gerontology: SOCIAL SCIENCES
1995, Vol. 50B, No. 5, S271-S273

> *Editor's Note:* The following essay is one of a series appearing in Volume 50 to mark a half-century of social science research in gerontology.

What We Have Learned About the Economics of Aging: "Ratings" for Past Years of Research

James H. Schulz

Florence Heller Graduate School, Brandeis University.

IN 1969, *The Gerontologist* published a report by a special committee of the GSA chaired by Robert J. Havighurst (1969). The committee's charge was to survey existing research in social gerontology that was particularly relevant to social policy and practice and then to recommend research priorities. I was hired by the committee to address the economics of aging area. Looking back with a quarter-century perspective related to the field, I find that if we use the recommendations of the 1969 report as a benchmark, progress to date has indeed been significant.

The economic well-being of people in old age has been a major concern over the years. It has been an important issue in every major inquiry into the aged's general welfare. For example, economic questions have figured prominently in the various White House Conferences on Aging. And the "economics of aging" is at the heart of the battle currently raging with regard to the role of government in the 21st century and what government programs voters are willing to pay for.

To what extent has research furthered our understanding of the economic aspects of aging? Not surprisingly, the answer depends on the specific questions or issues that are addressed. In many areas, we have learned a great deal; in other key areas, we have learned relatively little. Perhaps more important is the fact that economic policy decisions related to aging are still driven more by stereotypical notions than by scientific knowledge.

One example of the latter point will be familiar to all readers. When I first entered the field as a young economist, everyone talked about the elderly as the group that lives on "fixed incomes." Still today, almost everyone describes the elderly that way, despite the fact that *almost no older person today lives on a fixed income.* Major sources of income in old age are now indexed to compensate partly or fully for inflation (OASDI, government employee and military pensions, SSI, and food stamps). Others are adjusted partially or fully by ad hoc decisions (wages and some private employer-sponsored pensions). And, income from assets adjusts upward or downward, depending on the nature of the asset, market forces, economic conditions, and monetary/fiscal policy.

Little or no additional research is needed to refute the "fixed income stereotype." However, suppose one asks the question: To what extent are the income and assets of various elderly subgroups eroded by inflation and is this erosion greater or less than that experienced by other age groups? Relatively little research on this question has been done, and, as a result, we can say very little that is definitive. Fortunately, that is not true for other areas of economics relating to the elderly. Much has been accomplished.

This is not the place for an exhaustive and scholarly review of those research accomplishments — especially since the various editions of *The Economics of Aging* chronicle my summaries of our changing knowledge base (Schulz, 1976, 1995). Instead, to summarize progress to date, I am going to use a very unscholarly style common to hotel, restaurant, and movie reviews — one- to four-star ratings — to summarize progress to date. Everyone knows that they may hate a movie that receives a four-star rating from some expert. Likewise, this "expert" does not claim that his views are "correct," only that they are based on nearly three decades of doing research related to the economics of aging.

Have we done (are we doing) useful research on the welfare and economic well-being of older people? Let's start with the list of research issues raised in the 1969 GSA report.

1. **Better data and more analysis to differentiate the economic circumstances of various elderly subgroups.** While the media and many policy makers continue to discuss all "the elderly" as one group, researchers have long ago, in rich detail, shown the dramatic differences that exist in this heterogeneous population. Major problems are an obsolete poverty index, inadequate alternatives to that index, and a general lack of consensus on appropriate indicators of economic well-being. ★★★★

2. **Simulation projections of future elderly income and assets.** The invention of computers permitted the development of an important new methodological tool for policy analysis — stochastic simulation modeling. Simulations utilizing the new technology have produced important insights into the extent to which economic circumstances will change as new cohorts enter old age. But development costs

for these complex models, data limitations, and a lack of basic research on many behavioral issues have limited the number of researchers, reduced the number of operational simulation models, and prevented a rigorous assessment of findings from these models. ★★

3. **The development of longitudinal data sets to supplement prevailing cross-sectional data.** There has been a dramatic increase in longitudinal surveys funded by the federal government. Key data sources have been the Retirement History Survey, the national longitudinal surveys, and the current Health and Retirement Survey. Studies using the resulting data have been commonplace for many years. For example, economists and others have used these surveys to produce important insights regarding changes in the dynamics of the retirement decision, the changing economic circumstances of older people, and the role of various income sources for people at different ages. ★★★★

4. **Gathering more information on opinions and attitudes regarding economic issues and programs affecting people in old age.** Over the years there have been many public opinion surveys monitoring changing views regarding old age and the elderly. For example, these surveys identified the "loss of confidence" surrounding Social Security financing that surfaced in the late 1970s. In most cases, however, surveys have been very superficial and offered limited insight into understanding important economic issues. Only recently have focus groups and other approaches been used to get more comprehensive information and to promote greater understanding. ★

5. **Research to determine and understand both employer and worker actions relating to the employment of older workers.** Based on a large body of research, we now have a good understanding of the retirement decision from the employees' perspective. However, we have a very poor understanding of issues related to the productivity of older workers and its relationship to wage and pension costs. And while recent research has given us excellent insights into how employer-sponsored pension plans have been used to influence work/retirement decisions, there is still relatively little research on other employment issues (job discrimination, health care costs, retraining, reentry by women, etc.). ★★

6. **Studies of the effects of Social Security on individuals and the economy and analyses of proposed changes in the system.** We now know the distribution of Social Security benefits, the level and adequacy of benefits, and who finances the system. Research findings are highly suggestive but not conclusive on how Social Security affects labor force participation, personal saving, and distributional equity. And despite numerous studies and projections of Social Security payments and revenues, there is still major debate about the nature and extent of future Social Security financing concerns and also about the extent to which future retirees will get their "money's worth." ★★★

7. **Research to determine the levels, adequacy, and distribution of employer-sponsored pensions, the effect of these pensions on the economy, and the impact of pension trends on future benefits.** For many years, employer-sponsored pensions were virtually ignored. Even today research is limited to a few economists. The result is

that the potential, limitations, and impact of this huge American industry are still not understood very well. ★★

8. **Comparative studies of developments and experiences in other countries, to give us perspective and insights into the American situation.** There is now a relatively large comparative literature on issues related to pensions and the economic situation of older persons. The research shows big differences between the United States and most other industrialized countries — in terms of public and private pensions, aged poverty, labor force participation among older workers, and concerns about the future. The aged are generally better off in other industrialized countries, although it is difficult to generalize. At the same time, concerns about the "crisis" in Social Security financing, intergenerational conflict, and the "greedy geezers" have been found to be uniquely American, with only marginal cutbacks in the "welfare states" created in most other countries. ★★★

9. **Analysis and evaluation of Medicare and Medicaid as part of the general issue of providing and financing health care.** As the cost of health care has risen dramatically, so too has there been a big increase in research on the quality and cost of health care for the elderly. Failure to reduce rapidly growing costs in this area is not due primarily to our lack of understanding of the economic issues involved, although much research remains to be done. ★★★★

From my *current* perspective, some areas need to be added to the 1969 list:

10. **Research on the use of time over the life span.** A member of the 1969 GSA committee and a pioneer in the economics of aging, Juanita Kreps did much of the early work to lay out the issues involved in the "work-leisure choice" area. Relatively little has been done since then with regard to how individuals prefer to distribute their leisure over the life span, part-time versus full-time work, flexible retirement and education/retraining. We know (mostly from sociological and psychological research) that most older workers want to retire as soon as it is financially feasible and that, once retired, usually adjust well to their new situation. However, "retirement" means different things to different workers, with recent research showing the complexity of "exit routes" and the interests of many so-called retired individuals in continuing to "work" — often in jobs very different from their lifetime jobs. Also, we have not yet resolved the seeming contradictions between longer hours in the working years, lengthening life expectancy, continued early retirement rates, and the rising costs of retirement. ★

11. **The adequacy and equity of the safety net for elders who "fall through the cracks."** We have done a reasonably good job of identifying the numbers and characteristics of the poor elderly, but we need to do much more to understand and evaluate the operation and impact of social assistance programs. ★★

12. **Research on the special economic problems of older women and ethnic minorities.** For many years, researchers were faced with data sets that had serious limitations for those seeking to understand the special problems of women and minorities. As the data have improved, we have seen a growing amount of research — documenting, among

other things, the serious economic problems of many older women and the non-White elderly. We have also made some progress in understanding the underlying causes of various problems and in evaluating proposed options for reform. This is especially true for older women. Unfortunately, the research on ethnic minorities is still dominated by descriptive analyses. ★★

13. **Research on the economics of population aging.** Everyone is concerned about what will happen when the "baby boom" cohort retires. Unfortunately, there has been insufficient economic research to assess the now common cries of doomsday ahead and, alternatively, the less common assertions that we should not worry. ★

When I did my graduate work in economics in the 1960s, my dissertation encompassed the areas of aging, Social Security, and private pensions (using simulation modeling). It was about as far out of the mainstream of economics as one could go. Today, the young economist who becomes interested in the aging field is still out of the economists' mainstream but certainly not as far. And the fact remains that there are now many more economists doing research on the economics of aging — mainstream or not.

The reasons for the increased interest and research are many: the growing number of dollars involved in aging programs; the increased availability (and accessibility) of longitudinal surveys, program data, and other types of information; the growth of policy research by economists hired in schools of social and public policy; research funds made available by the federal government; and the attention created by serious concerns raised by the polity, sometimes quite dramatically in the form of "aged bashing."

The Gerontological Society of America can also take some credit. The Society has sponsored many activities and projects over the years that have encouraged economists to work in aging. GSA's publications also deserve a lot of credit. The first article I ever published appeared in *The Gerontologist* (Schulz, 1967). In the early years, when the discipline of economics (and its journals) had almost no interest in the area, the GSA publications provided a publishing opportunity and an audience interested in the economics of aging for me and other economists. And they continue to do so 25 to 50 years later.

ACKNOWLEDGMENTS

On the occasion of writing this celebratory essay, I would like to acknowledge Clark Tibbitts (who got me interested in aging), Juanita Kreps (who encouraged my interest in the economics of aging when few others did), Richard Ruggles and Guy Orcutt (who opened my eyes to the potentials of microsimulation for policy analysis), Robert Morris and Robert Binstock (role models for bridging the worlds of research, policy, and practice), and my wife, former students, and readers of *The Economics of Aging* (who provided important incentives when the going got rough). Also, I wish to express my sincere thanks to Joe Quinn, another pioneer in the economics of aging, for his very helpful reactions to a draft of this essay.

Address correspondence to Dr. James H. Schulz, Florence Heller School, Brandeis University, Waltham, MA 02254.

REFERENCES

Havighurst, Robert J. 1969. "Research and Development Goals in Social Gerontology — A Report of a Special Committee of the Gerontological Society." *The Gerontologist* 9:1–90.
Schulz, James H. 1967. "Some Economics of Aged Home Ownership." *The Gerontologist* 7:73–74, 80.
Schulz, James H. 1976. *The Economics of Aging* (1st ed.). Belmont, CA: Wadsworth.
Schulz, James H. 1995. *The Economics of Aging* (6th ed.) New York: Auburn House.

HENRY J. AARON
ROBERT D. REISCHAUER

6

Paying for an Aging Population

Unlike most projections of future developments, the aging of the American population can be forecast with near certainty. Barring calamity, the population age 62 and over will more than double (from 41 million to approximately 86 million) between the years 2000 and 2040; the population over age 85 will more than triple. The elderly, who make up about 13 percent of the population today, will constitute about 20 percent of the population by 2040. The precise fraction will depend on birth rates, immigration, advances in medical science, and personal behavior (including how little Americans exercise and how much they kill one another and themselves with guns, automobiles, and cigarettes). But the overall trend is inescapable—the American population will age rapidly during the next four decades.

Almost everyone is aware of this demographic fact. Americans also understand that, as the population ages, the elderly will consume an increasing share of the nation's output. But widespread confusion persists about what an aging population means for the two largest government programs serving the elderly (social security and medicare),

The authors would like to thank Jeanne M. Lambrew, Jeffery Lemieux, Edward Lorenzen, and Joshua M. Wiener for their comments on sections of this chapter. Shanna Rose and James Sly provided exemplary research assistance.

for the living standards of working Americans, and for private and government budgets. Hyperbole abounds. Young workers of today won't
receive any social security benefits! Medicare will go bust within two
decades! The burden of supporting the baby boomers when they retire
will leave the working population in sackcloth! Government budgets
again will be awash in red ink! Though sobering, the reality is not apoc-
alyptic, particularly if government and individuals take measured steps
now to prepare for this inevitable demographic change.

This chapter begins with a brief review of the demographic trends.
This review introduces two concepts that need to be kept distinct for a
full understanding of the economic consequences of population aging:
the government budget costs of rising obligations for social security,
medicare, and other programs serving the aged, and the impact of those
costs on household budgets and living standards. The chapter then ana-
lyzes the principal alternative approaches that have been suggested to
help prepare social security and medicare for their coming burdens. It
concludes with a brief examination of medicaid, a third major program
that the aging of the population will significantly affect.

Darling, We Are Growing Older

In 2008, the oldest of the baby boomers, the group born between 1946
and 1964, will turn 62 and become eligible for social security retirement
benefits. Three years later, they will turn 65 and start receiving medicare
benefits. Millions of them will already have been receiving social security disability and survivor benefits. In the decades that follow, increasing numbers of baby boomers will become eligible for the nation's
means-tested programs. Some who earned little during their working
years and who don't have a spouse's pension to rely on will have to turn
for support to the food stamp program and Supplemental Security
Income (SSI)—the means-tested cash assistance program for the aged,
blind, and disabled. As age and infirmities overwhelm their bodies and
medical expenses deplete their savings, many baby boomers will have to
depend on medicaid to help pay for their acute and long-term health
care needs. Elderly veterans, whose ranks will peak in the year 2000
and remain high for the next few decades, will draw increasing amounts

of assistance from veterans' disability compensation, pensions, and medical benefits.

By 2040 when all the baby boomers are of retirement age, nearly one-fourth of the U.S. population will be over age 62. The major change will be among those age 75 and older. Their ranks will have increased sharply to 11.4 percent of the population, as large as the share that was over age 62 in 1960 (figure 6-1). The young elderly—those between the ages of 62 and 74—will constitute only a modestly larger share of the population in 2040 than in 1990.

The Economic Burden of Dependents

All consumption—that of the elderly and the nonelderly—comes from the goods and services produced by current workers. The burden that workers bear to produce for others depends on the proportion of the population that is not working—the retired elderly, children, and non-working adults. As figure 6-2 shows, the proportion of the population that is economically inactive will reach a low point around the turn of the century. The reason is that children have constituted a steadily smaller proportion of the population since 1964 because birth rates fell after the baby boom. Despite a continuing drop in the proportion of children in the population, the share of the population that is economically inactive is projected to rise after 2000 because the proportion of retirees will increase, and adult (20 to 62) labor force participation rates will drift down as the average age of those in this group increases. On balance, the number of people each worker will have to support will rise about 6 percent between 2000 and 2040, and the number of adults each worker will have to support will rise by 14 percent.

Broad demographic trends do not adequately capture the economic effects of population aging because the size and distribution of the burdens imposed by different groups among the economically inactive population differ. For the most part, parents bear the daily living expenses of children. Their educational costs are mostly borne by state and local government. The health and income support costs of poor children are shared by the states and the federal government. In contrast, large portions of the income support and health costs of the

7

Figure 6-1. *Percentage of Population, 62 and over, 1950–2040*

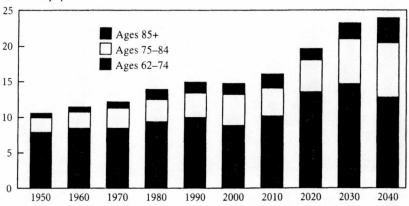

Percent of population

Source: Bureau of the Census.

elderly are borne by the federal government through the social security, SSI, and medicare programs. In addition, more than half of medicaid expenditures on behalf of the elderly and disabled with low incomes is paid out of the federal budget; the remainder comes from the states. Thus, as the population ages, the fiscal responsibility of sup-

Figure 6-2. *Ratio of Total and Adult Populations to the Labor Force*

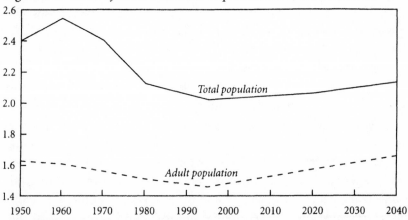

Source: Authors' calculations based on data from Office of the Actuary, Social Security Administration.

porting the economically inactive population shifts from families to governments and, within the public sector, from states and localities to the federal government. The anticipated difficulties of these fiscal redistributions, as much as the higher costs of the elderly relative to children, lie behind concerns about the aging of the American population.

Public Budgets

Whether a government program is financed by general revenues or earmarked taxes has profound political consequences. Policymakers concern themselves more strenuously with the long-run financial viability of entitlement programs supported by earmarked taxes than with entitlements financed through general revenues, even if the costs of such programs rise just as fast.

Earmarked payroll taxes are the primary receipts used to support both social security and the hospital insurance (HI) portion of medicare.[1] Receipts from these payroll taxes are deposited in trust funds from which program expenses are paid. If the balances are depleted, policymakers must raise taxes, cut benefits, or change the program's financing structure.

Almost since their inceptions, the social security and medicare actuaries have made long-term projections of the programs' expected revenues and expenditures. While both programs are currently running cash flow surpluses, the actuaries' projections reveal significant financial shortfalls between earmarked revenues and outlays that will grow over the long run. In the case of social security, earmarked tax receipts are expected to exceed the cost of benefits and program administration through 2013; total receipts, including interest earnings on the trust fund reserves, are projected to exceed program outlays through 2021, when reserves reach $4.5 trillion. Current projections indicate that social security will then have to begin drawing down its reserves to supplement program receipts in order to pay promised benefits.

1. The social security and medicare HI trust funds also receive income tax revenues attributable to including social security benefits in taxable income, interest earnings on trust fund balances, and other small general revenue payments as compensation for providing benefits to several small categories of beneficiaries who otherwise would not be eligible.

The financial pressures facing the hospital insurance component of medicare are more immediate. While social security's average cash surpluses are projected to exceed $100 billion a year over the next two decades, medicare is expected to run surpluses only through 2006, averaging less than $5 billion a year. The HI trust fund reserves are projected to peak at $155 billion at the end of 2006 and will be depleted by 2015 when expenditures will exceed revenues by a whopping 16 percent, and the gap will be growing fast. Adjustments will have to be made in the program's financing or expenditures several years before that date if large tax increases or abrupt benefit cuts are to be avoided.

The projected imbalances between the earmarked revenues that support social security and the HI portion of medicare and those programs' projected expenditures have generated concern and a vigorous debate over policies to strengthen the finances of these two programs or to change their structure. Although it is vital that the nation address the projected imbalances facing social security and medicare soon, the challenges elsewhere in the budget should not be overlooked. The costs of other entitlement programs, also of importance to the elderly—such as medicaid, SSI, food stamps, and veterans' programs—are also expected to rise rapidly over the next four decades. These programs also deserve attention even if projections of insolvent trust funds do not highlight their costs.

Although social security and medicare are both entitlement programs that serve the aged and the disabled, and both face projected long-term deficits, they differ markedly in nearly every other respect. Not surprisingly, the nation's options for strengthening these two programs for the future have little in common.

Social Security

Social security annually pays retirement, disability, and survivors benefits to 44 million elderly and disabled people. Monthly retirement benefits, which averaged $894 in 1998 for male workers, are based on each worker's highest thirty-five years of earnings. Benefits are financed largely by a payroll tax levied at the rate of 12.4 percent—half paid by workers, half by employers—on earnings up to a limit. The taxable wage ceiling, $72,600 in 1999, is raised each year at the same rate as the increase in average earnings. In addition, a small share of social security's income comes from income tax revenues on a portion of social security benefits received by middle- and upper-income beneficiaries that is included in taxable income.

Social security benefits have four distinguishing characteristics. First, they depend on each worker's earnings history, not on prices of financial market assets. As a result, older workers know with virtual certainty what their retirement pensions will be. Second, benefits are progressive. They replace a larger fraction of earnings for those whose average lifetime earnings were low than for those whose earnings were high, and they provide special benefits to workers' spouses and former spouses who have had limited or no participation in the paid labor force. Third, benefits are fully protected against erosion by inflation. And fourth, benefits are provided as joint-survivor annuities, which provide payments guaranteed to last as long as retirees and their spouses live.

By law, social security reserves—which are projected to reach $887 billion at the end of 1999—are invested only in assets guaranteed by the federal government. Most are held in safe but low-yielding Treasury securities.[2] Even at their projected maximum, in 2021, reserves will be much smaller than the amount that would have accumulated if each worker's payroll taxes had been deposited in a reserve and invested until the worker claimed benefits. The reason is that successive Congresses and presidents have used the reserves to provide those who retired during the program's first few decades with vastly larger benefits than their payroll taxes could have supported even if those contributions had been invested at market rates. If benefits had been limited to the value of taxes paid and interest earned on those taxes, poverty among the elderly

---

2. Social security reserves may also be invested in bonds of government agencies that are guaranteed by the federal government. Issues of eligible agencies include the Government National Mortgage Association, Export-Import Bank, Farmers Housing Administration, General Services Administration, Maritime Administration, Small Business Administration, Commodity Credit Corporation, Rural Electrification Administration, Rural Telephone Bank, and the Washington Metropolitan Area Transit Authority. The special issues in which nearly all social security reserves are invested carry the average interest rate on government bonds with a maturity of four years or more at the time the special issues are created. Special issues cannot be traded publicly but may be resold to the Treasury at par before they mature, if the social security trustees find that they need the funds.

would have been much higher than it was for decades after social security was enacted, and many more of the elderly and disabled would have been forced to turn to welfare programs for support. Whether the decision to pay generous social security benefits was wise or foolish, it cannot be undone. It has generated the so-called unfunded liability—benefit obligations to current workers and retirees that exceed accumulated reserves. This unfunded liability is the source of the projected deficit in social security, and all proposed reforms must come to terms with it one way or another.

The social security actuary has projected that revenues will fall short of expenditures by 2.07 percent of taxable earnings during the next seventy-five years. In other words, an immediate increase in the payroll tax rate or cuts in benefits equivalent to 2.07 percent of taxable payroll would be sufficient to close the gap between revenues and outlays projected over this period.[3] But neither a tax increase nor a benefit cut of this magnitude, which some might regard as modest, would be a viable solution to the program's long-run problem. These policies would result in larger surpluses and an even more significant buildup in reserves over the next few decades. But in 2075 reserves would be exhausted and expenditures would exceed revenues by more than 4 percent of payroll. Truly complete reform would not only eliminate the deficit as projected over the next seventy-five years but also leave the system's revenues and expenditures in rough balance at the end of that period and provide an adequate contingency reserve to deal with a temporary revenue shortfall that might accompany a recession.

While social security is not projected to face cash flow deficits for at least twenty years, there are two reasons why it is not too soon to address the long-run imbalance facing the program. First, any significant changes to the program will have to be phased in over a decade or two. Because most retirees and near retirees have a limited ability to

---

3. These estimates are based on the actuary's intermediate economic and demographic assumptions. Under more optimistic economic and demographic assumptions, the system remains in surplus indefinitely. Under more pessimistic assumptions the deficit is more than twice as large, and reserves would be exhausted in 2020. The terms "optimistic" and "pessimistic" refer to effects on the trust fund only. Paradoxically, higher inflation and shorter life expectancies are part of the "optimistic" assumptions because they improve the balance between revenues and expenditures.

adjust their lifestyles to accommodate reduced benefits, Congress has been appropriately loathe to enact benefit cuts affecting older workers or retirees. Younger workers will need fair warning that the rules of the game have changed. Unless needed to meet some immediate crisis, tax hikes are best introduced in small bites as they have been over the program's first sixty-five years during which two-thirds have been smaller than 0.2 percentage point. Second, demographic, economic, and budgetary conditions are almost certainly more conducive to reform today than they were in the past or will be in the future. In less than a decade, the fraction of the population receiving social security benefits will begin to climb, and the political constituency resistant to change will become ever more influential. With the economy strong, the unified budget in surplus, and the surpluses projected for the non-social security portion of the budget as yet uncommitted, the fiscal environment is unusually favorable for the consideration of a wide range of reform options.

What Are the Choices?

Proposed reforms fall into three broad categories: those that would replace the current system in whole or in part with mandatory, individually owned savings accounts modeled on Individual Retirement Accounts (the IRA option); those that would replace the current system in whole or in part with mandatory, individually owned savings accounts modeled on 401(k) accounts (the 401(k) option); and those that would fix the current system without reliance on individual accounts (fix the current system option).

THE IRA OPTION. Under this approach, the government would require individuals to establish and make deposits into special retirement savings accounts.[4] These deposits would be funded in one of three ways: by diverting a portion of the current payroll tax from financing social security (a carve out); by increased payroll taxes (an add on); or by tapping general revenues (drawing on the projected budget surpluses). Account holders would select their own fund managers and be free to invest in

4. An example of this approach is the Personal Securities Accounts plan put forward by five members of the Advisory Council on Social Security (1997, pp. 30–58).

13

stocks, bonds, mutual funds, insurance policies, real estate, or other approved assets. Social security benefits would be scaled back and, under some plans, eventually eliminated. Upon reaching retirement, people would withdraw funds from their accounts or, under some plans, would be required to convert the balances into an annuity. Most IRA-type plans would leave the basic framework of social security disability and survivors insurance in place but would scale back these benefits.

Advocates of this approach emphasize that people would own their accounts and would be free to invest the balances as they saw fit. These attributes, it is held, would spark workers' interest in saving for retirement, and private ownership would ensure that additions to the accounts increase national saving. Many claim that establishing personal accounts would raise the returns workers receive on their payroll taxes because the yield on the private securities in which the account balances would be invested is much higher than the low and declining implicit return workers will receive on their social security payroll tax contributions. As we explain later in this chapter, this assertion is incorrect.

Critics of the IRA option are concerned that many people would make poor investment choices and that administrative costs would be excessive. Those who invest unwisely or are merely unlucky in financial markets might be left with balances at retirement that are insufficient to support an adequate pension. Administrative and annuitization costs could reduce returns on investments significantly, undermining pension adequacy. Under the IRA-type system in Britain, for example, these costs are estimated to absorb an average of 43 percent of potential balances.[5]

THE 401(K) OPTION. Those who find the arguments advanced on behalf of personal accounts convincing yet harbor concerns about the IRA approach endorse the 401(k) option, which seeks to reduce these problems.[6] Under this approach, people would be required to invest their contributions in a few approved index mutual funds that would be heavily regulated or directly managed by the government. Pensions

5. Murthi, Orszag, and Orszag (1999).
6. An example of this approach is the Individual Accounts plan favored by two members of the 1994–96 Advisory Council on Social Security. See Advisory Council on Social Security (1997, pp. 30–34).

would be less variable across account holders than under the IRA option because the investment returns on all accounts would track broad financial market averages. Centralized management and passive investment would make administrative costs much lower than under the IRA option, although they would remain well above the estimated 0.9 percent administrative cost under social security. Most 401(k) type plans require that workers use their account balances to purchase annuities of at least a minimum size upon retirement.

FIXING THE CURRENT SYSTEM. Fixing the current system requires some combination of benefit cuts, payroll tax increases, higher returns on trust fund investments, or infusions of new revenues from other taxes.[7] Advocates of fixing the current system claim that personal accounts cannot reliably fulfill social security's primary purpose—providing ensured basic income to retirees and their spouses and dependents. The value of personal accounts would fluctuate with asset prices and each worker's investment decisions. The normal swings in financial markets will cause the account balances of new cohorts of retirees to vary considerably over relatively short periods even when all contributions are invested in index funds. For example, if the nation had had a personal account system in which all balances were invested in a total stock market index fund, workers retiring in 1977 would have received benefits that—measured as a share of average lifetime earnings—were less than half those of workers retiring in 1969.[8] If workers may select freely among assets, the

7. An example of this approach is the Maintain Benefits plan favored by six members of the 1994–96 Advisory Council on Social Security. See Advisory Council on Social Security (1997, pp. 59–97). See also Aaron and Reischauer (1998).

8. This calculation, provided by Gary Burtless, is based on simulations of working histories and pension fund contributions for average male workers who enter the labor force at age 22 and work for forty years. The text refers to workers who entered the labor force in 1937 and 1929. Workers experience the age earnings profile of employed men in 1995. Economywide real earnings grow 2 percent a year. Each worker saves 6 percent of earnings and invests those savings in a mixture of common stocks that yields the average dividend and capital gain of all listed securities in that year. The worker reinvests all dividends, which are free of individual tax when paid. At age 62, the worker converts his accumulated savings into an annuity based on the expected mortality experience of American men in 1995 and the interest rate on six-month commercial paper in the year when the annuity is purchased. All insurance company fees are ignored.

15

variations would be even larger. People whose accounts proved insufficient could become an added burden on welfare programs; cohorts whose pensions proved significantly smaller than the pensions received by those a bit older or younger would probably pressure government to compensate them for the market's poor performance.

Furthermore, if forced to rely on the balances in personal accounts, many people might outlive their assets and be forced to turn to SSI and food stamps for support. All would be exposed to inflation risk that would erode the value of their pensions as they grew older. The only way to avoid these risks would be for the government to require that personal account balances be converted at retirement into inflation-protected annuities similar to those provided by the current social security program. But this requirement would preclude leaving balances to heirs, one of the attributes of private accounts that proponents find most attractive.

Advocates of strengthening the current system point out that the claim made by some proponents of individual accounts—that returns would be higher if the nation switched from collective management of pension plans to private accounts—is simply wrong.[9] The pension returns that workers receive for their payroll taxes depend on three considerations: whether the pension plan builds reserves, what assets the reserves are invested in, and how cheaply the reserves are managed. On the first point, reserves can be accumulated in the social security trust fund just as well as in personal accounts. On the second issue, reserves held in the social security trust fund could be invested in assets similar to those that would be held by individual accounts if the restrictions on trust fund investment were relaxed. If the size of the reserves and the investment patterns were similar, reserve accumulation in the trust fund and in individual accounts would have similar *average* rates of return before administrative costs are deducted. Thus the claim that private accounts will boost returns must rest on the belief that the management costs of individual accounts would be lower than those of a centrally managed trust fund. In fact, however, administrative costs entailed in having private sector firms or the government manage more than 150 million individual accounts would be higher—possibly much

9. Geanakoplos, Mitchell, and Zeldes (1998).

higher—than those of managing the collective investment of a single social security trust fund account. The costs of managing individual accounts could range from .15 to 1.50 percent of account balances, while collective investment has been estimated to cost only .01 percent.

The Clinton Budget Initiative

In his January 1999 state of the union address President Bill Clinton proposed that bonds and other resources equal to 57 percent of the unified budget surpluses projected for the 2000–14 period be given to the trust fund to bolster social security's financial situation. This proposal was greeted with considerable criticism, in part because it appeared to credit the trust fund twice for a portion of the program's surpluses. In the mid-session review of the budget, the administration revised its approach and proposed that the social security surpluses be reserved to pay down the federal government's publicly held debt. To enforce this policy, the administration suggested that Congress adopt procedural restraints that would make it more difficult for Congress to pass tax or spending legislation that caused the non-social security accounts to be in deficit. The administration estimated that by the end of 2014, social security surpluses would be responsible for paying down $3.067 trillion of the $3.653 trillion public debt outstanding at the start of 2000.

The president also proposed that a portion of the surpluses projected for the non-social security budget accounts be credited to the social security trust fund after 2010. The amount transferred to the trust fund each year would be set to equal the projected interest savings the Treasury enjoyed as a result of the reduction in the public debt attributable to social security's surpluses. Over the 2011 to 2014 period, the administration estimates that these transfers, which represent general revenue support for social security, would amount to roughly $543 billion.

The additional resources provided to social security would be used to purchase equities for the trust fund until such holdings constituted about 15 percent of the trust fund's reserves. Thereafter, resources not needed to maintain that level of equity holdings would be invested in government securities similar to those traditionally held by the fund. The president recommended a number of institutional safeguards to allay widespread concerns that such stock market investment could lead to inappropriate government influence over private companies or politically motivated investment policies. He called for the creation of an independent board consisting of members with lengthy, staggered terms to oversee the private investment of reserves. The board would hire private fund managers, each of whom would invest a portion of the reserves passively in the broadest of stock index funds. The private managers would vote the trust fund's shares so as to maximize their long-run economic returns. These safeguards, the president believes, would insulate the trust fund's private sector investment activities from political influence.

Administration estimates suggest that the additional funds provided to the trust fund and the higher returns expected on equity investments would delay the trust fund insolvency from 2034 to 2053. These changes would close a bit more than two-thirds of social security's projected long-term deficit (table 6-1). Other measures—benefit cuts, increases in earmarked taxes, or additional general revenues—would be required to close the rest of the projected deficit. Although the president indicated his willingness to discuss such changes with congressional leaders, he did not make specific recommendations. The following changes are a few of the many possible ones that, when combined with policies presented in the mid-session review, would close the entire projected long-term deficit while keeping social security in its current form (table 6-1).

—Increase payroll tax base. The limit on earnings subject to social security payroll tax—currently $72,600 and indexed to the growth of average wages—could be raised. The current level encompasses roughly 86 percent of all earnings. Setting the limit at a level that covered 90 percent of earnings—$108,600 in 1999—would reduce social security's long-run deficit by more than one-quarter.[10]

—Accelerate increase in the "full benefits age" and raise this age along with increased life expectancy. The age at which retirees can obtain unreduced benefits will increase from 65 to 65 and 2 months for those turning 62 in 2000. This will be repeated in each of the next five years until the age reaches 66 for those turning 62 in 2005. After a twelve-year hiatus, the whole process will be repeated with the age at

10. Information supplied by Bill Piatt, Social Security Administration, August 1999.

Table 6-1. *Estimated Social Security Imbalance and Impact of the Clinton Plan and Selected Other Changes*

Percent of taxable payroll

Item	Trust fund balance, 75-year projection
Deficit projection in 1999 Trustees Report	−2.07
President Clinton's plan:	
Transfer of bonds to social security reserves and investment of 15 percent of reserves in equities	1.48[a]
Deficit remaining if Clinton plan is implemented	−0.59
Other possible changes	
Increase payroll tax base	0.57
Accelerate increase in "full benefits age" and index for increased life expectancy	0.49
Extend coverage to all newly hired state and local workers	0.21
Increase "averaging period"	0.25

a. This number reflects the administration's January 1999 estimates. It does not include adjustments made in the 1999 mid-session review.

which unreduced benefits are available for those turning age 62 after 2021 reaching 67. About 24 percent of the deficit could be eliminated if the increase to age 67 were accomplished by 2011—that is, by dropping the hiatus—and if this age were then increased gradually along with improvements in adult life expectancy.

—Extend coverage to all newly hired state and local workers. Roughly one-quarter of state and local government workers are not covered by social security payroll taxes, although most receive benefits upon retirement as the spouse of a covered worker or as a result of employment in covered jobs either before or after their state or local service. If all newly hired state and local workers were covered by social security, roughly 10 percent of the program's long-term deficit would be closed.

—Increase "averaging period." Retirement benefits are currently based on the average of each worker's highest thirty-five years of covered earnings. If the highest thirty-eight years of earnings were used to calculate benefits, benefits for future retirees would be cut by an average

19

of 3.1 percent for male and 3.9 percent for female workers, reducing the program's long-run deficit by about 12 percent.

Other Measures to Encourage Retirement Saving

Social Security was designed to provide a secure source of basic retirement income that would be supplemented by employer- and union-sponsored pension plans and personal saving. The tax system has been used to encourage group pension plans since 1921 and individual retirement saving since 1962.[11] Businesses and individuals have made massive use of these saving incentives. Qualified employer pension plans hold assets totaling $7.5 trillion, and tax-favored individual accounts held balances of more than $2 trillion at the end of 1998.

In his fiscal year 2000 budget, President Clinton proposed to further encourage retirement saving by creating Universal Savings Accounts or "USA" accounts funded from part of the projected budget surpluses. While the president explicitly distinguished the USA accounts initiative from his social security reforms, his proposal is important for the debate over the future of social security because the USA accounts are similar to the personal accounts that are an integral component of many reform plans crafted by members of Congress.

Under the president's plan, the government would provide to eligible people—beginning in 2003—a refundable tax credit that would have to be deposited in a retirement saving account (USA account). When fully phased in, this credit would have a maximum value of $400 per person and would be available to those individuals and couples with at least $5,000 in earnings. The credit would phase out completely at incomes of $40,000 for individuals and $80,000 for couples.[12] In addition, starting in 2005 the government would match workers' voluntary contributions to their accounts. The match would be dollar-for-dollar, up to a limit of $325 in 2005, $300 in 2006–08, and $550 in 2009 and

---

11. Although the legislation and debate surrounding the first two of these provisions have stressed saving for retirement, balances in all tax-sheltered individual savings accounts are available at any time to people who are willing to pay ordinary income tax on withdrawals and a 10 percentage point penalty tax and without the penalty tax if certain conditions are met.

12. There would be no income limit for those lacking access to an employer-sponsored pension plan.

thereafter, for voluntary contributions made by low- and middle-income participants; lower match rates would apply to those with higher incomes.[13]

The investment options available for the USA accounts would be limited to a few broad-based funds similar to those offered to government employees in their Thrift Saving Plan. Withdrawals could not begin until the account holder reached the age of 65 but would otherwise be unrestricted. The maximum government transfer to a low- or middle-income couple that contributed voluntarily an additional $1,100 would be $1,900 a year—two $400 grants plus $1,100 in government matching payments. A couple who received the $800 annual grant starting at age 25, but made no voluntary contributions, would accumulate approximately $102,500 in 1999 dollars by age 65 if the account balance earned an average return of 5 percent a year (above inflation). If the same couple made the maximum voluntary contribution, their total balance would amount to approximately $380,500 by 65 years of age.

The Alternatives

Members of Congress have developed many social security reform proposals. One of the most prominent of these is the Social Security Guarantee (SSG) plan crafted by Bill Archer (R-Tex.), chairman of the Committee on Ways and Means, and Clay Shaw (R-Fla.), chairman of that committee's social security subcommittee. Under the SSG plan workers would be given a refundable tax credit equal to 2 percent of their earnings subject to the social security payroll tax. These credits would be deposited in qualified mutual funds whose portfolios would be 60 percent invested in stock index funds and 40 percent in corporate bonds. Annual fund administrative costs would be limited to .25 percent of account balances. Individuals would receive the higher of the benefits promised by social security or the annuity that could be supported from their SSG account balances. If the benefits promised by social security were higher, which would be true for virtually all workers, the SSG account annuity would be remitted in full to social

13. The president's plan would count deposits into 401(k) plans as contributions to USA accounts. The intent of this provision is to ensure that workers did not cut back on contributions to their employer-sponsored plans to gain the tax credit.

security, thereby bolstering the program's resources. Account balances of workers who died before reaching entitlement would be transferred to the accounts of their spouses, former spouses, or dependent children. If there were no potential social security liabilities of this sort, the balance would go, tax free, into the worker's estate.

Deposits in the SSG accounts would be funded from general revenues. While the social security actuary has estimated that the SSG plan would eliminate the program's long-run deficit under reasonable economic assumptions, the plan would subject the unified budget balance to something of a roller coaster ride. The plan would absorb virtually all of the surpluses projected over the next decade and then push the budget back into deficit. With time, the average SSG account balance would grow and an increasing fraction of the social security benefits paid to retirees would be offset by annuity remittances paid from the individual accounts to the trust fund. Toward the middle of the next century, the budget situation would turn around as a result of sharply growing offsets, permitting a payroll tax rate cut of 2.5 percentage points in 2050 and a further 1 percentage point in 2060.

The 21st Century Retirement Security Act (21st Century plan), another prominent proposal, has bipartisan support.[14] Under this "carve-out" plan, 2 percentage points of the current payroll tax would be diverted to support new Individual Security Accounts (ISAs). Workers could invest their account balances in a limited number of index funds that held stocks, bonds, or government securities. To keep administrative costs low, these funds would be managed in a fashion similar to the federal employees' Thrift Saving Plan. The government would contribute an extra $150 to the accounts of workers with low and modest earnings who voluntarily contributed at least $1 to their accounts and would match, on a one for two basis, these voluntary contributions up to $600 a year. All workers, no matter how high their incomes, would be permitted to make unmatched voluntary contribu-

14. The origins of this plan are to be found in the recommendations of the National Commission on Retirement Policy, a group that included members of Congress from both parties, leaders from the private sector, and policy analysts. Representatives Charles Stenholm (D-Tex.) and Jim Kolbe (R-Ariz.) have introduced H.R. 1793 in the House of Representatives. A similar, although not identical bill, has been introduced in the Senate by Judd Gregg (R-N.H.) and John Breaux (D-La.) as S. 1383.

tions of up to $2,000 a year. Owners of ISAs could withdraw their balances in a variety of ways when they retired or became disabled. Those choosing to withdraw the balance in a lump sum would have to use enough of the proceeds to purchase an inflation-indexed annuity that, when combined with the worker's reduced social security benefit, would at least equal the poverty threshold.

To close the long-run social security deficit—which the diversion of a portion of the payroll tax to fund ISAs would increase—the 21st Century plan would cut the benefits most for high earners but not at all for the lowest earners.[15] Furthermore, benefits would be calculated by dividing workers' total lifetime earnings over as many years as the worker had earnings by forty, rather than averaging workers' highest thirty-five years of earnings. Benefits would be cut across the board by accelerating the scheduled increase in the age at which unreduced benefits are paid and further raising the age at which unreduced benefits are paid to reflect improved life expectancy. The cost-of-living adjustment that protects benefits from erosion by inflation would be reduced to compensate for the upward bias assumed to be present in the consumer price index. Together, these changes would reduce social security benefits for the average wage worker retiring in 2040 at age 65 by roughly 39 percent. If, on average, future market returns are similar to those of the past, most participants will be able to offset these reductions with resources from their ISAs. The inevitable broad swings that characterize financial markets would mean that, at times, ISA pensions would not offset cuts in social security benefits for most workers.

To ensure that the reductions in social security's defined benefit do not impose undue hardship, the 21st Century plan would establish a new minimum benefit. Workers with twenty years of earnings would be guaranteed a social security benefit of 60 percent of the poverty level. This guarantee would rise for each year of work beyond twenty, reaching 100 percent of the poverty level for those with forty or more years of earnings.

15. Specifically, the Primary Insurance Amount (PIA) would be reduced gradually over the 2012–44 period, and the 32 percent and 15 percent PIA formula factors would be reduced gradually between 2006 and 2030 until they were 19.8 and 9.3 percent respectively. Stephen C. Goss and Alice H. Wade, "Estimated Long-Range OASDI Financial Effects of the 21st Century Retirement Security Act," memorandum to Harry C. Ballantyne, May 25, 1999.

The 21st Century plan would fully close social security's long-term deficit. While it would use projected budget surpluses to cover a portion of the transition costs, its reliance on surpluses would be small compared with that of the SSG plan. Moreover, because the plan would extend the temporary reduction in the COLA to the tax code and to most other indexed benefits, the non-social security surpluses would be augmented sufficiently to fully cover the transfers.

The Choices Ahead

With his 1998 state of the union pledge to "save social security first"— that is, to delay committing future budget surpluses to tax cuts or to increases in other government spending until measures were enacted to shore up social security's finances—President Clinton energized the debate over how best to reform social security and stimulated the development of many reform proposals. The most recent plans crafted by leading policymakers have shared several common themes. Foremost has been an increased willingness to use general revenues to support retirement pensions. Nevertheless, the nature and extent of the commitment of general revenues differs greatly from plan to plan. In addition, most reform proposals would create some type of individual account through which workers would save for their retirement. Under the president's approach, these accounts would be separate from the social security system; under most of the plans crafted by members of Congress, these accounts would be an integral component of a reformed social security program. In addition, recent proposals exhibit a growing reluctance to reduce benefits or raise taxes now or in the future. Some would guarantee retirement benefits no smaller than those provided under social security while others call for increased benefits.

Sharp substantive and political differences remain. Compromise will be difficult when there is no immediate crisis forcing legislative action and when legislative missteps could tip the balance of political power in the 2000 elections. Neither political party is likely to risk a blunder on an issue like social security that could give the other party a significant advantage for years to come.

The president and members of Congress elected in 2000 do not *have to* address the social security problem. Revenues are projected to cover currently promised benefits for more than two decades beyond the end of their terms. But the nation will be poorly served if its elected officials procrastinate. Options narrow as deficits become imminent because elected officials are properly reluctant to cut benefits or make other changes that would adversely affect people nearing retirement.

One fundamental choice before policymakers involves the extent to which projected budget surpluses should be used to strengthen the financing of the nation's mandatory pension system. The primary advantage of using general revenues to shore up social security is that this step would reduce the need to cut benefits or boost payroll taxes. However, general revenue financing might erode the contributory social insurance base of the program, which is a major reason for its overwhelming popularity. Furthermore, surpluses devoted to saving social security will not be available for other high-priority purposes, such as medicare, education, medical research, defense, and tax cuts.

The most fundamental decision facing policymakers is whether to replace, in whole or in part, the current defined benefit system—which provides progressive, fully inflation-protected benefits that do not fluctuate in value with asset prices—with a system of personal accounts that will inevitably lack some or all of those attributes but that will give people a heightened sense of ownership and control. A move to personal accounts will almost certainly affect the future distribution of retirement income and the political dynamic that sustains the mandatory pension system.

Who Gains? Who Loses?

Individual accounts, whether financed from the surplus or from carving out a portion of the payroll tax, raise the distributional question: what groups should benefit most? Under the president's approach, general revenues deposited in USA accounts would flow primarily to low and moderate earners. Under proposals that call for deposits proportional to earnings up to the social security earnings ceiling, a larger share of deposits would flow to upper-middle and upper-income workers. Under both approaches, high earners are likely to earn larger returns than low earners, because people with low incomes traditionally invest conservatively in relatively low-yielding assets such as bonds and money market instruments, while high earners invest proportionately more in higher-yielding assets such as common stocks. Such caution among low earners is understandable, because they usually have few assets, meager private pension coverage, and little experience with financial markets. But it means that unless deposits are progressive (as they would be in the president's plan and, to a lesser extent, in the 21st Century plan) or investment opportunities are severely constrained (as they would be in the SSG plan), the balances in the individual accounts of high earners at retirement are likely to be larger relative to their earnings than those in the accounts of low earners. If pensions from individual accounts replace, in whole or in part, the progressive benefits of the social security system, the net benefit to high earners will be even greater.

Policymakers should also consider the political dynamic that personal accounts will create as part of the government-mandated pension system. If workers are told that these accounts are their property, they are likely to demand control over investment decisions and disposition of account balances. The history of existing tax-sheltered individual savings accounts suggests that Congress would readily grant people permission to draw on these funds before retirement—for example, for college tuition, to buy a first home, to pay for medical care, or upon leaving a job. Similar pressures can be expected under any new system of personal accounts whether they are outside of the social security structure like President Clinton's USA accounts, or integral to a reformed system, like the SSG accounts. If account holders are given increased flexibility to control their account balances, some will dissipate their retirement assets through misfortune or misjudgment. Unless ensured retirement income—like social security's defined benefit— remains adequate, the number of people who find themselves with inadequate retirement incomes will grow.

Personal accounts could also create a political dynamic that erodes support for social security. As balances build up in personal accounts, people would come to rely less and less on social security. Many workers, particularly high earners, would compare the seemingly small returns on payroll taxes with the seemingly larger returns on personal accounts and conclude that they could do better if only social security were scaled back and their payroll taxes were transferred to their personal accounts. Support for social security among such workers would erode, putting in jeopardy the relatively generous benefits provided to low earners. If this process went far, even a guarantee that benefits would be as high as those promised currently by social security would become progressively harder to sustain.

The American public has before it two sharply different visions of government's role in supporting retirement income. The traditional view has been that ensuring basic income during retirement is a shared responsibility, one in which the inevitable risks should be broadly spread across all workers, and benefits should be distributed progressively. The alternative vision would give people ownership and control of their retirement accounts in return for agreeing to bear increased risk and to accept a less progressive distribution of benefits.

A critical question for both approaches concerns the wisdom of increasing transfers to the elderly at the very time when retirement of the baby boom generation threatens sharply increased budget costs not only for pensions but also for acute and long-term health care benefits. The apparent unwillingness to propose even modest benefit cuts means that future payroll and income tax payers will have to bear the full burden of supporting the growing ranks of the economically inactive elderly population.

Medicare

Medicare provides basic health insurance protection for the elderly and disabled. The program has two components: hospital insurance (HI, also known as part A) and supplemental medical insurance (SMI, also known as part B). Those who are eligible for social security disability benefits and those who are eligible for retirement benefits and are at least 65 years old are entitled to part A benefits, which cover inpatient hospital services, some skilled nursing facility and home health costs, and hospice care. Part A, which accounted for about 63 percent of total medicare spending in 1999, is financed largely by a 2.9 percent payroll tax paid—half by employees, half by employers—on all earned income. Tax receipts are deposited in a trust fund, and program expenditures can not exceed the balances in the fund.

Part A participants have the option of enrolling in part B, which covers physician visits, laboratory fees, outpatient hospital services, durable medical equipment, preventive services, some home health care, and other medical services. Because this insurance is highly subsidized, almost everyone chooses to enroll. Participants pay a monthly premium—$45.50 in 1999—that covers about one-quarter of the program's costs. General revenues cover the balance.

Most medicare beneficiaries receive care on a fee-for-service basis. Besides paying part B premiums, participants in fee-for-service medicare are responsible for a part B deductible of $100, a deductible for inpatient hospital services set at the cost of an average day in the hospital ($768 in 1999), and coinsurance on some part A and B services. Approximately one in six participants has chosen to receive care through one of the roughly 350 Medicare+Choice (M+C) health plans, (almost three-quarters of beneficiaries live in counties where these plans are available). While other plan types are permitted, almost all of these are managed care plans, such as health maintenance organizations (HMOs), independent practice associations (IPAs), or preferred provider organizations (PPOs). M+C plans are paid a fixed amount per month per enrollee that, subject to certain limits, is related to a blend of per beneficiary fee-for-service expenditures in the service area and in the nation, and the characteristics (age, sex, health risk, welfare status) of the enrollee. Most of these plans give their members, at no additional cost, benefits—such as routine physical exams, immunization, prescription drugs, vision and hearing care, and low cost sharing—that supplement medicare benefits.

Nearly all providers participate in medicare, thereby giving the elderly and disabled unfettered access to mainstream medical care. The fee-for-service component pays participating providers according to legislated fee schedules; providers serving members of M+C plans negotiate payment rates with the individual plans with which they contract. Both to ward off HI trust fund insolvency and to help balance the federal budget, Congress has periodically reduced the fee-for-service payment schedules. The most recent example of such legislation was the Balanced Budget Act of 1997 (BBA97), which at the time of passage was estimated to reduce the growth of medicare spending by $116 billion, or by about 9 percent, over the 1998–2002 period.

Medicare has been a great success but suffers from several deficiencies, which policymakers should address soon so that reforms can be implemented before retirement of the baby boomers creates additional strains. Foremost is the tendency for program costs to grow disturbingly fast. This problem is not unique to medicare. During the past two decades, per capita medicare spending has risen at roughly the same pace as health care spending for the nonelderly, nondisabled population. Nevertheless, as the capabilities of modern medicine expand and new and expensive diagnostic techniques and therapeutic procedures are introduced, cost pressures will increase. These pressures are likely to be especially intense among those, like the elderly and disabled, with chronic conditions and, for medicare, they will be compounded by the demographic stress of the aging baby boomers. Even after assuming that a substantial slowdown will occur in the historic rate of growth of per beneficiary medicare costs, the medicare actuary projects that spending will rise from 2.55 percent of GDP in 1999 to 5.25 percent in 2040; this 2.7 percentage point increase is even larger than the 2.43 percentage point rise forecast for social security. Under these projections, the HI trust fund will be depleted by 2015, and an ever-increasing fraction of general revenues will be needed to support part B.

A second problem facing medicare is that its benefits are outdated. Medicare offers benefits similar to those provided by employers in the mid-1960s. It does not cover outpatient prescription drugs, an ever more important and expensive component of modern health care. Nor does it provide protection against catastrophic costs, and therefore the deductibles, copayments, and costs arising from limits on coverage can easily become crushing. Medicare provides very circumscribed coverage for nursing home services, which, as the number of frail elderly with chronic conditions grows, will become an increasing concern. Finally, many believe that the bifurcated structure through which medicare benefits are provided makes little sense and offers undesirable opportunities for financial gaming. The division of services between parts A and B followed the distinction that employer-sponsored insurance of the 1960s made between hospital and medical services insurance, a distinction that has all but disappeared in the private sector. Because it persists in medicare, the program retains a confusing hodgepodge of deductibles and coinsurance rules. Furthermore, policymakers have been able to delay trust fund insolvency by shifting benefits from part A, where expenditures are limited by the trust fund balances, to part B, where there is an unlimited draw on general revenues.

The inadequacies of the basic medicare package have led almost all participants to seek supplementary coverage. In 1996, 30 percent received additional insurance through a former employer. Another 29 percent bought supplemental protection through so-called medigap policies. Medicaid filled in medicare's holes for an additional 16 percent. Eleven percent got additional benefits through an M+C plan.[16] Only 12 percent lacked some type of supplemental coverage.[17] The system of dual coverage through multiple types of supplemental policies is complex, confusing, inequitable, and costly both for providers and participants. If medicare beneficiaries received coverage through a single, more comprehensive policy, administrative costs would be reduced. Service costs would also be lower, because many supplementary policies provide first-dollar coverage that increases utilization, some of which is of marginal worth.

A third weakness is that fee-for-service medicare provides only limited encouragement for efficiency. Neither providers, who are paid on a per episode or service basis, nor participants, many of whom are shielded from cost considerations by supplemental insurance, face strong incentives to limit care to that which is cost effective. In addition, in many market areas, medicare pays more for durable medical equipment, laboratory, oxygen, and ambulance services than do other large insurers because these payments are set administratively rather than through market forces.

Finally, the availability and cost of medical services are becoming increasingly variable across geographic areas and among medicare participants. In some metropolitan areas, beneficiaries can choose between fee-for-service care and any of half a dozen or more M+C plans offering extra benefits. In others, participants may have only one or two M+C alternatives, or none at all. Those with supplemental policies provided by a former employer generally have extensive coverage at a limited cost, but this group is shrinking as employers curtail this fringe benefit. Those who must depend on a medigap policy face significant pre-

16. The importance of capitated plans—now called M+C plans—has increased since 1996. As of June 1999, 18 percent of enrollees were covered by such plans. Probably, the prevalance of employer-sponsored insurance has declined since 1996.

17. Most enrollees in M+C plans receive coverage in addition to the basic medicare package. These percentages reflect this fact.

miums—often around $1,500 a year—that are rising rapidly for much less comprehensive coverage.

The Alternative Approaches

Three broad approaches to medicare reform have emerged. The first is to strengthen and modernize the existing medicare program while preserving its basic structure. The benefit package would be extended to include outpatient prescription drug coverage, an out-of-pocket catastrophic expenditure limit, lower cost sharing for certain services, and broader coverage of preventive care—a package comparable to what most employers offer workers and their dependents. Such an expansion would reduce the importance of supplemental insurance, simplifying the system and lowering overall costs. To slow the growth of expenditures, medicare would let the prices it pays for lab services, oxygen, durable medical equipment, and similar items be set by competitive market forces rather than by administrative mechanisms. In addition, the restraints imposed on the growth of hospital and physician fees by the BBA97 would be extended when the current restrictions expire at the end of 2002, just as they have many times in the past.

Advocates stress that this approach would build on proven success and not subject a vulnerable population to risk or disruptive change. They also argue that strengthening the current structure does not depend on sophisticated new institutional arrangements and operational mechanisms that reforms described in the following pages would require.

Critics feel that under this approach cost growth will not be dampened, and inefficiencies and inequities will persist. Accordingly, two other reform approaches have emerged.

Under one approach—known as premium support or the competitive defined benefit approach—the government would contribute up to a maximum amount related to the cost of fee-for-service medicare, the cost of the average plan, or some other benchmark. Medicare fee-for-service and M+C plans would compete with one another. All would be required to offer a more adequate benefit package than provided currently. Participants selecting plans that charged less than the maximum amount offered by the government would pay reduced premiums, while those joining more expensive plans would be required to pay additional amounts. To hold down costs in fee-for-service medicare, the various cost-reducing measures encompassed in the previous approach would be adopted.

Advocates believe that this structure, which is similar to the federal employees' health benefit system, will lead participants to demand and plans to offer cost-effective, high-quality care and that competitive forces will slow cost growth. Opponents of this approach fear that the government will be unable to adjust payments it will make to plans to accurately reflect the differential health risks of their participants. If younger, healthier beneficiaries gravitated to a few low-cost plans and older, less-healthy ones joined other plans, the chronically ill might end up facing higher costs than they now confront. If the chronically ill chose fee-for-service medicare because it offered the widest and least constrained choice of providers, they might face relatively high costs, both for their basic medicare coverage and for their supplemental medigap policies. Opponents also question whether the benefits of competitive markets can be realized in the health sector. They believe that competition will result in lower quality and, possibly, deny needed services to those in low-cost plans. Furthermore, critics point out that a well-functioning premium support model requires adequate mechanisms not only to adjust plan payments for the differential health risks of their members but also to measure the quality of the different plans and to inform beneficiaries of the choices available to them.

The third approach involves prefunding future medicare benefits through individual or group accounts similar to those promoted by some social security reform proposals.[18] Medicare payroll taxes would be deposited in personal or group accounts for people of a given age cohort that would be invested in a mix of private and government assets. The tax rate for each cohort would be adjusted periodically to generate an account sufficient to buy insurance when the cohort reached retirement age. Government would make contributions on behalf of nonworkers and supplement the payments made by those with low earnings. Upon retirement, individuals would be required to purchase adequate insurance in a regulated individual insurance market. At a minimum, this coverage would consist of a catastrophic policy.

18. Gramm, Rettenmaier, and Saving (1998).

Advocates argue that it would make beneficiaries and providers more price conscious; that it would eventually eliminate medicare's unfunded liability; and that, by increasing saving, it would increase investment and economic growth. Skeptics see this approach as unworkable. To function efficiently, the individual insurance market would have to be reformed to ensure that plans could not discriminate against unhealthy persons. Mechanisms would have to be developed to pool or share risk so that plans that found themselves with disproportionate numbers of participants with expensive illnesses were not unfairly disadvantaged. Furthermore, large tax rate adjustments could become necessary if poor investment outcomes deplete account values or if advances in medical technology boost costs as a cohort nears retirement age.

The Bipartisan Commission on the Future of Medicare

The Balanced Budget Act of 1997 established a seventeen-member commission to analyze the problems facing medicare and report any findings and recommendations that at least eleven commissioners endorsed. The chairman, Senator John Breaux (D-La.), and the vice chairman, Representative William Thomas (R-Calif.), fell one vote short of the number required to make a plan that they crafted the official commission recommendation. Nevertheless, this proposal has considerable congressional support and represents a comprehensive, if somewhat skeletal, description of the sorts of changes that would be required to strengthen medicare for the long term. The Breaux-Thomas plan adopted a version of the premium support approach, under which the government's maximum contribution would be tied to the average price charged by all competing plans—both M+C plans and fee-for-service medicare. Participants who enrolled in an average-priced plan would pay a premium that covered 12 percent of the plan's costs—about the fraction of total medicare costs that part B premiums will cover in the future. Participants joining less expensive plans would face lower premiums, with no premium charged to those enrolling in plans charging 85 percent or less of the average. Those joining plans whose price exceeded the average would pay all the additional costs.

All plans would be required to offer both a standard and a high-option benefit package. The standard option would cover medicare's current mandated benefits although plans could, with approval of a newly established medicare board, vary benefits and cost-sharing requirements within specified limits. The high option would include a prescription drug benefit as well as a cap on catastrophic out-of-pocket spending. Those with incomes over 135 percent of the poverty line would bear the full additional cost if they chose this richer package. The federal government would, however, pay the high-option premium for those with incomes below this threshold if they joined plans whose costs were less than or equal to 85 percent of the national average of all high-option plans.[19]

The Breaux-Thomas proposal would unify parts A and B into a single trust fund, establish a single deductible that would be indexed to the growth of medicare costs, and impose 10 percent coinsurance on those services (except the first sixty days of inpatient hospital care and preventive care) for which no or lower coinsurance requirements currently are in force. The proposal also recommended that the age of eligibility for medicare be raised gradually along with the already scheduled increase in the age at which unreduced social security benefits will be paid. Those over 64 but below the higher eligibility age would be allowed to purchase medicare coverage without subsidy. Medicare would require additional resources over the long run even if the commission's modifications were adopted. However, the commission left unresolved whether the needed resources should come from higher payroll taxes, general revenues, or premiums.

Criticism of the Breaux-Thomas proposal focused on the recommended increase in the age of eligibility, which could expand the number of uninsured retirees, the possibility that fee-for-service medicare would have above-average costs forcing those who wanted to remain in this program to pay higher premiums, and concern that the high-option plans would be very costly and possibly unsustainable because, with voluntary participation, they would attract largely less healthy participants.

The President's Medicare Initiative

As part of the mid-session review of the fiscal year 2000 budget proposal, President Clinton unveiled a major four-pronged initiative to

---

19. If no such plan is available in an area, the government would pay the premium for the cheapest available high-option plan.

strengthen and reform medicare. The initiative included a premium support structure for private plans, a new prescription drug benefit, measures to modernize and restrain costs in the fee-for-service program, and an infusion of general revenues from the projected budget surplus to bolster the HI trust fund. Under the president's "competitive defined benefit" approach, those choosing the traditional fee-for-service medicare would continue to pay part B premiums. Participants in M+C plans that charged less than 96 percent of the cost of fee-for-service medicare would pay reduced premiums; those joining plans that charged 80 percent or less of the fee-for-service costs would pay no part B premium, a saving estimated to be $60 a month in 2003 when the competitive structure would be implemented.[20] Participants joining plans with costs over 96 percent of fee-for-service costs would pay the part B premium plus all costs above that threshold.

All plans would be required to submit bids based on their costs of providing the standard medicare benefit package, although M+C plans could price into their bids reduced cost-sharing requirements. The standard medicare benefit package would be modified to eliminate cost sharing on preventive services such as mammography screening, impose 20 percent coinsurance on clinical laboratory services, and increase the $100 part B deductible annually with inflation. M+C plans would be able to offer additional benefits, but they would have to market and price these supplements separately.

The prescription drug benefit proposed by the president is modest and, like the Breaux-Thomas approach, voluntary. Participants would face no deductible but would have to pay 50 percent coinsurance and a monthly premium (about $53 when fully phased in) set to cover half of program costs. The government would pick up both the premium and coinsurance costs for those with incomes below 135 percent of the

20. The actual reduction in part B premiums would be 75 percent of the difference between 96 percent of the cost of fee-for-service medicare and price charged by the plan. The government would take the remaining 25 percent as savings. Under current estimates of fee-for-service costs, the part B premium would be canceled at 80 percent of fee-for-service costs. If the estimates for total fee-for-service costs and part B costs are higher or lower than current estimates, the point at which the part B premium was absolved could be a bit higher or lower than 80 percent. National Economic Council (1999).

poverty line; those with incomes between 135 percent and 150 percent of poverty would face reduced premiums. The maximum annual benefit would be limited to $1,000 in 2002, the program's first year, and grow to $2,500 in 2008 when fully implemented.

All plans would have to offer as a high option the standard medicare package with the prescription drug benefit. Participants in M+C plans would receive their benefits through their plans, whereas those in fee-for-service medicare would receive benefits through a pharmacy benefits manager (PBM) or other private sector entity selected competitively in each region to provide this service. The PBMs could establish formularies and incentives to encourage the use of generic or less expensive drugs but "beneficiaries would be guaranteed access to off-formulary drugs when medically necessary."[21]

Although roughly 65 percent of medicare beneficiaries have some prescription drug coverage, virtually all beneficiaries would take up, directly or indirectly, the president's prescription drug option because it would be highly subsidized—half of the costs being paid by the government. Participation would also be spurred by the restrictions that would be placed on enrollment; beneficiaries could join only during their first year of medicare eligibility or when they lost coverage provided by their or their spouse's employer or former employer. Unsure what their prescription drug needs may be in the future, even the disabled and seniors with no current pharmaceutical expenditures would likely join. A partial government subsidy to employers that offer their retirees more generous prescription drug benefits would encourage these firms to continue coverage, rather than redesign their plans to offer only wrap-around benefits.

The president's proposal also includes measures designed to modernize fee-for-service medicare and restrain its costs. Medicare would be permitted to adopt techniques that private plans have used to restrain costs and improve care: incentives for participants to seek treatment for complex problems at institutions with proven track records of high-quality, cost-effective care; payment bundling for groups of services; a preferred provider option; encouragement of primary care case management and disease management; and arrangements to set pay-

---

21. National Economic Council (1999, p. 21).

ments through competitive bidding and negotiated prices. In addition, some of the payment restraints imposed by the BBA97 would be extended through 2009.

The president proposes to strengthen the HI trust fund with an infusion of general revenues from projected non-social security surpluses. Specifically, over the 2000 to 2009 period, the Treasury would issue to the trust fund $328 billion in special government securities in addition to those purchased with fund surpluses. Like the transfers made to the social security fund after 2010, these infusions would occur whether or not the surpluses materialize; that is, whether or not debt is actually retired. They will give the HI trust fund a claim on future general revenues and push off the date of insolvency to 2027.

Critics of the president's proposal point out that it would add a new and expensive benefit to an entitlement program that already faces insolvency. They also charge that it gives the Health Care Financing Administration (HCFA) too much flexibility, cuts payments to providers too deeply, and is unfair to M+C plans. The president's plan could also be criticized for being too timid in forgoing the simplification and efficiencies that could be realized from adopting a more adequate benefit package and an out-of-pocket expenditure cap—changes that would eliminate, for many, the need for supplementary insurance.

The Future

The future of medicare is more uncertain than that of social security. Both face retirement of the baby boom, but medicare must also cope with the uncertainties of advancing medical technology. Today's laboratory experiments and clinical trials will become tomorrow's routine care. These developments could conveivably lower costs but are far more likely to add—perhaps greatly—to tomorrow's medical bills.

Uncertainty surrounds not only medicare costs but also the institutional setting in which the program will operate. During the past decade and a half, new ways of providing coverage have emerged. Indemnity or fee-for-service care, which was the dominant form of insurance in the mid-1980s, has been replaced everywhere but in medicare by the bewildering acronyms of managed care—HMOs, HMOs with the option of service outside the HMO (so-called points of service plans), IPAs, and PPOs. Administrators are implementing measures of plan quality and encouraging evidence-based medical practice—concepts that were nothing more than the playthings of policy analysts a decade ago. Per service, cost-based provider payments have given way to prospective payment systems, bundled fee schedules, and capitation. Providers, such as hospitals, nursing homes, and physicians, have begun to consolidate into chains and ever larger group practices. Because the situation is so fluid and medicare, which accounts for nearly 20 percent of health expenditures, can strongly influence the direction in which this institutional environment evolves, policymakers should reform medicare in ways that preserve flexibility and are reversible if developments warrant.

The similarities between the Breaux-Thomas proposal and the president's initiative suggest that a consensus may be developing over the general form of structural reforms needed to strengthen medicare. Both would rely on a premium support approach to determine payments to plans and would have fee-for-service medicare and the M+C plans compete. Both would provide fee-for-service medicare with added flexibility to enhance efficiency and extend BBA97 payment restraints. Both would expand medicare's benefit package although neither would establish a sufficiently comprehensive benefit package. Comprehensive benefits are essential for real reform because without a package that the vast majority of beneficiaries regards as sufficient, supplementary policies will remain widespread, and the overall system of coverage will remain needlessly complex, confusing, costly, and inequitable. Under the president's approach, beneficiaries would continue to need supplementary protection both from high out-of-pocket costs associated with the traditional services and the coinsurance required by the pharmaceutical benefit and any expenditures above $5,000. The voluntary and unsubsidized nature of the Breaux-Thomas high-option package could produce the same result, because those who anticipate significant medical expenses would be more likely to enroll in the high-benefit option, thus making it unaffordable for many. The problem could be solved under the president's structure if a $3,500 to $4,500 cap on total (drug, hospital, and other) out-of-pocket expenditures were added.

However, policymakers wishing to make medicare's benefit package adequate face a dilemma resulting from increased costs. If beneficiaries are required to pay significantly higher premiums for the added benefits, those who already have such coverage through a supplemental policy provided at little or no cost by a former employer will, understandably, be upset. Deep subsidies can neutralize such opposition, but they would boost government costs and provide windfall relief to employers and individuals paying medigap premiums.

In the future, as in the past, medicare will face the challenge of cost control. But medicare's costs cannot be held down if per capita expenditures for the nonelderly, nondisabled population are soaring unless lawmakers are willing to impose heavy burdens on beneficiaries or cut provider payments to the point that few will be willing to participate and access will become a problem, as it is in medicaid. In the past, these responses have been mitigated by cross subsidies — that is, providers have been willing to accept lower payments from medicare and medicaid as long as commercial insurers paid higher fees. But in the new competitive environment, commercial insurers are increasingly unwilling to pay more than is required to cover the services used by their participants, all but eliminating the public sector's ability to hold down its program costs when systemwide costs are exploding.

The dirty secret of the medicare debate — which none of the participants has yet acknowledged — is that financing problems cannot be solved unless payroll taxes are greatly increased, premiums and cost sharing raised dramatically, or general revenue support sharply expanded. The choice among these financing approaches will determine who pays for the inevitable growth of medicare costs.

Beneficiaries could be required to contribute more for their coverage in one of three ways. Cost sharing (copayments and deductibles) could be raised. This would place most of the burden on those in the poorest health, who are also likely to have relatively low incomes and few assets. Alternatively, premiums could be raised across the board. While the part B premium is now set to cover one-quarter of that component's costs, when the program was established premiums covered one-half of part B costs. Across-the-board premium increases would hit sick and well, rich and poor alike. Of course, a $20 a month increase in premiums means much more to an elderly widow trying to make ends meet on only a $650 social security check, than to a couple whose private pension, social security, and dividend income amount to $3,000 a month. For this reason, many have proposed that only middle- and upper-income medicare beneficiaries be asked to pay higher premiums. When the president and the chairs of the bipartisan commission explored this approach, they met strong opposition from both members of Congress and interest groups. Many remembered the highly unpopular income-related premium imposed by the Catastrophic Care Act of 1988 which, in part because of this premium, was repealed eighteen months after enactment. Opponents argue that income-related premiums would subtly convert medicare into a means-tested welfare program and that upper-income people are already paying more than their share because the HI payroll tax is imposed on earnings without limit.

As premiums for medicare and supplementary insurance and out-of-pocket costs rise, policymakers must ensure that low- and moderate-income beneficiaries are not burdened excessively, relegated to second-class care, or denied access. During the past several decades, a loosely structured system has evolved to protect the low-income elderly and disabled. Medicare beneficiaries with very low incomes are eligible for medicaid, which supplements medicare with its much more comprehensive coverage. Those with incomes too high for medicaid eligibility but below the poverty threshold can have their part B premiums and cost sharing picked up by medicaid's Qualified Medicare Beneficiaries (QMB) program. Medicaid's Specified Low-income Medicare Beneficiaries (SLMB) program will pay the part B premiums of those with incomes between the poverty line and 135 percent of that level and the Qualified Individual (QI) provisions will cover a small portion of these premiums for those with incomes up to 175 percent of the poverty level. Some fourteen states have established programs that provide prescription drug coverage to low-income elderly.

For a variety of reasons, a substantial fraction of those who are thought to be eligible do not participate in these programs.[22] The stigma associated with welfare, the complexity of the application and recertification processes, and the failure of the HCFA and the states to inform seniors adequately about these options are some of the possi-

---

22. For estimates of participation rates see O'Brien, Rowland, and Keenan (1999, p. 9).

ble explanations for limited participation. As medicare reform increases the financial burden on beneficiaries, as it almost certainly must do over the next decades, the system for assisting low- and moderate-income participants must be rationalized and simplified. The subsidy schemes proposed in the Breaux-Thomas high-option and the president's drug benefit represent structures that, if expanded, could adequately address this problem.

Medicaid

Most people view medicaid as the program that pays for the acute health care needs of poor children and their parents. In fact, roughly 70 percent of medicaid beneficiaries fall into these categories. But medicaid outlays go primarily to support acute and long-term health care for the low-income elderly and disabled (including the blind). Although the elderly and disabled make up only 29 percent of beneficiaries, 73 percent of medicaid's vendor payments are made for their care. Of this total, acute care accounts for roughly 42 percent and long-term care, the balance.[23] Medicaid's acute care expenditures, for the most part, supplement medicare's benefits and pick up medicare's deductibles, coinsurance, and premium amounts.

Medicaid pays 40 percent of the nation's long-term care costs compared with 18 percent by medicare and 29 percent by individuals directly.[24] Private long-term care insurance pays only 7 percent of the total. Medicaid is the primary payer for more than two-thirds of nursing home residents and provides nursing homes with about half of their revenues.[25]

Medicaid is particularly important the very old. More than one-third of those 85 years old and over receive acute or long-term care benefits from medicaid. An estimated 43 percent of those who turned 65 in 1990 are expected to use some nursing home care before they die.[26] As the

23. U.S. House of Representatives (1998, p. 983).
24. Health Care Financing Administration, National Health Expenditure Projections 1998–2008 (http://www.hcfa.gov/stats/nhe-proj/proj1998/tables/default.htm [September 16, 1999]).
25. Komisar, Lambrew, and Feder (1996).
26. HCFA tables; Kemper and Murtaugh (1991, pp. 595–600).

population ages, the medicaid-dependent population will grow rapidly, straining federal and state budgets and highlighting the program's inequities.

States administer the program but pay only a fraction of the program's costs that varies with each state's per capita income—from 23 percent (in Mississippi) to 50 percent (in ten states) in fiscal year 2000.[27] The federal government pays the rest. Federal law sets minimum benefit and eligibility conditions, but states have wide latitude in setting provider payments, determining eligibility, and supplementing federally mandated benefits. As a result, long-term care expenditures per elderly beneficiary varied in 1994 from $17,776 in Connecticut to $3,267 in Mississippi, and acute care spending per elderly beneficiary varied from $3,914 in Rhode Island to $1,365 in Wyoming.[28] To limit their financial exposure for long-term care costs, states have restricted the growth of nursing home beds, held down medicaid reimbursement rates, and encouraged home and community-based care, which is sometimes less expensive than nursing home care on a per person basis.[29]

The fraction of the low-income elderly and disabled population eligible for medicaid benefits also varies greatly from state to state. Federal rules require that SSI recipients be covered. Some states also offer eligibility to the "medically needy," those aged and disabled whose resources and incomes are too high to make them categorically eligible but who meet higher state-set income and asset thresholds after their medical expenditures are taken into consideration. The other states make use of "special needs caps" under which nursing home residents with incomes up to a state-set limit that cannot exceed 300 percent of the SSI eligibility level can have medicaid pay for their care once they "spent down" to medicaid eligibility, which means that they have used all of their income except for a small personal needs allowance.

For those faced with lengthy stays in a nursing home, which cost roughly $50,000 on an annual basis, these options are important. Very high-income households can afford to pay long-term care costs them-

27. *Federal Register*, vol. 64, January 12, 1999.
28. Liska and others (1996, pp. 41, 58, 64).
29. Wiener and Stevenson (1998, pp. 81–100); and Coleman (1997).

selves and the persistently poor, who receive SSI benefits, can rely on medicaid. But most households retire with modest incomes and have assets that are sufficient to disqualify them from medicaid coverage but lack the resources to pay for more than a very short stay in a nursing home. Such families face agonizing financial choices when independent living is no longer physically possible. Some try to divest assets so that they qualify for medicaid. Others quickly deplete their income and assets and become eligible for medicaid. Of those first entering a nursing home as private pay residents, some 31 percent eventually end up with medicaid paying the bills.[30]

The deficiencies of the current system of paying for long-term care will become more apparent as the number of seniors grows. The population age 85 and older, one-quarter of whom are in nursing homes, will triple in size over the next four decades.[31] States with strong economies and robust revenue structures may be able to keep up with the need, but many states will find themselves overwhelmed and will take steps to reduce their financial exposure, possibly exacerbating existing interstate disparities in the availability of long-term care. More important than state fiscal pressures, however, is the personal anguish that families will suffer as assets shrink and the need to apply for means-tested benefits looms.

For years, policymakers have recognized the deficiencies of the current system of financing long-term care. They have not, however, agreed on a solution. Should policy encourage people to save when young so that most will be able to pay directly for their own long-term care should they need it? Or should people be encouraged to buy long-term insurance when they are a bit older by regulating and subsidizing the market for long-term care policies? Or should the nation develop a broad, publicly financed social insurance program like medicare that would help everyone obtain the long-term care they need? Or should policy build on the current system by improving the assistance available to households with incomes somewhat above current medicaid limits?

Even if policymakers agreed on the broad approach to take, disagreements would occur over the focus of any public subsidies and

30. Weiner, Sullivan, and Skaggs (1996).
31. Komisar, Lambrew, and Feder (1996, p. 11).

other details that would make legislative action difficult. For example, shallow public subsidies could be given to all those in need of long-term care, most of whom have needs that last a relatively short time. Or deeper support could be provided only to the minority with longer stays who have exhausted their own savings. Among the many details that would have to be resolved are the extent to which the systems of support for long-term and acute care should be integrated, the division of fiscal responsibility between the federal and state governments, and the relative emphasis placed on home and community-based versus institutional care.

Another inhibition to legislation is cost. Ensuring access to long-term care for a growing population of the very old would be expensive. Under a continuation of current policies, the total cost of all long-term care—home and community-based as well as institutional care—for the elderly is projected to increase from $123 billion in 2000 to $346 billion in 2040 in inflation-adjusted 2000 dollars.[32] Costs will be still higher if age-specific rates of disability do not decline 1.1 percent annually over the forty-year period, as currently assumed.

Any change in the current structure of paying for long-term care could cause a much more rapid growth in costs. Family, relatives, friends, and religious organizations now provide at home, without charge, much of the care the frail and the functionally impaired require. One estimate suggests that donated care amounts to 63 percent of the value of all care given.[33] If reforms made institutional care and formal home-health services affordable and widely accessible, many who are receiving informal care or are not receiving needed assistance, formal or informal, would increase their use of paid care.

Few lawmakers are currently advocating full-fledged social insurance for long-term care. Legislative proposals have been largely confined to using the tax code to encourage the purchase of long-term care insurance and to provide support to informal caregivers. The president, in his fiscal year 2000 budget, proposed a nonrefundable $1,000 tax credit for those with chronic conditions or the care giver with whom

32. Congressional Budget Office (1999).
33. Arno, Levine, and Memmott (1999). For another estimate, see U. S. Department of Health and Human Services (1998).

they live. The tax bill passed by Congress in August 1999 would permit taxpayers to deduct from their taxable incomes the medical care component of premiums paid for long-term care insurance if such insurance was not provided by their employer, allow employers to offer long-term care insurance as an option in their "cafeteria" benefit plans, and provide an extra personal exemption to taxpayers who provide informal care to a related member of their household.

Even if enacted, such measures would accomplish little. The credits and deductions are relatively small and would be of no value to the many who have no tax liability. Less than half of all elderly households have any income tax liability.[34] Deductions for long-term care insurance premiums would provide a significant benefit only to those with the highest incomes who face the highest marginal tax rates. Such households are likely to have the resources needed to pay out-of-pocket for adequate long-term care. In any case, very few people choose to take out such insurance policies, which typically are written for a maximum daily benefit amount with a corresponding lifetime limit. While premiums are modest if the policy is written when the beneficiary is 55 years old, few middle-aged individuals regard protection against the costs of long-term care as an immediate or pressing problem. When the need becomes palpable, say around 65, premiums become quite expensive—around $2,500 for a healthy individual.[35] Moreover, insurers will not write policies for people of any age who exhibit signs of a significant health risk.[36] In addition, consumers are dissuaded from purchasing this insurance by the complexity and variation in the product and the uncertainty that surrounds their access to benefits, which involves difficult judgement calls by the insurer.[37]

Conclusion

Helping families deal with the financial burden of long-term care will become increasingly urgent over the next several decades. However,

34. Burman, Gale, and Weiner (1998, p. 642).
35. Coronel (1998).
36. Employee Benefit Research Institute (1995).
37. Lewin-VHI and Brookings Institution (1996); Alecxih and Lutzky (1996).

the lack of consensus about the best approach to the long-term care problem, combined with the high cost of certain options, places this issue well behind restoring financial balance to social security and medicare. Nevertheless, all are important elements of retirement security. The current economic, budget, and demographic environments present lawmakers with an unusual window of opportunity during which they should begin to address these problems that, left unresolved, will force themselves onto tomorrow's policy agenda, generating social and political conflict.

References

Aaron, Henry J., and Robert D. Reischauer. 1998. *Countdown to Reform: The Great Social Security Debate.* Century Foundation.

Advisory Council on Social Security. 1997. *Report of the 1994–96 Advisory Council on Social Security, vol. 1: Findings and Recommendations.* Washington.

Alecxih, Lisa Maria B., and Steven Lutzky. 1996. "How Do Alternative Eligibility Triggers Affect Access to Private Long-Term Care Insurance?" Washington: AARP Public Policy Institute (August).

Arno, Peter S., Carol Levine, and Margaret M. Memmott. 1999. "The Economic Value of Informal Caregiving." *Health Affairs* 18 (March–April): 182–88.

Burman, Leonard E., William G. Gale, and David Weiner. 1998. "Six Tax Laws Later: How Individuals' Marginal Federal Income Tax Rates Changed between 1980 and 1995." *National Tax Journal* 51 (September): 637–52.

Coleman, Barbara. 1997. "New Directions for State Long-Term Care Systems: Volume 4: Limiting State Medicaid Spending on Nursing Home Care." Washington: AARP Public Policy Institute (April).

Congressional Budget Office. 1999. "Projections of Expenditures for Long-Term Care Services for the Elderly" (March).

Coronel, Susan. 1998. *Long-Term Care Insurance in 1996.* Washington: Health Insurance Association of America.

Employee Benefit Research Institute. 1995. *Long-Term Care and the Private Insurance Market.* Washington (July).

Geanakoplos, John, Olivia S. Mitchell, and Stephen P. Zeldes. 1998. "Would a Privatized Social Security System Really Pay a Higher Rate of Return?" In *Framing the Social Security Debate: Values, Politics, and Economics,* edited by R. Douglas Arnold, Michael J. Graetz, and Alicia Munnell, 137–57. Washington: National Academy of Social Insurance.

Gramm, Phil, Andrew J. Rettenmaier, and Thomas R. Saving. 1998. "Medicare Policy for Future Generations—A Search for a Permanent Solution." *New England Journal of Medicine* 338 (April 30): 307–10.

Health Care Financing Administration. 1999. *National Health Expenditures Projections 1998–2008.* Washington.

Kemper, Peter, and Christopher M. Murtaugh. 1991. "Lifetime Use of Nursing Home Care." *New England Journal of Medicine* 324 (February 28): 595–600.

Komisar, Harriet L., Jeanne M. Lambrew, and Judith Feder. 1996. *Long-Term Care for the Elderly: A Chart Book.* New York: Commonwealth Fund (December).

Lewin-VHI and Brookings Institution. 1996. "Key Issues for Long-Term Care Insurance: Ensuring Quality Products, Increasing Access to Coverage, and Enabling Consumer Choice." Draft Final Report, Contract 500-89-0047 (February).

Liska, David, and others. 1996. *Medicaid Expenditures and Beneficiaries: National and State Profiles and Trends, 1988–94,* 2d ed. Washington: Kaiser Commission on the Future of Medicaid (November).

Murthi, Mamta, J. Michael Orszag, and Peter R. Orszag. 1999. "The Change Ratio on Individual Accounts: Lessons from the U.K. Experience." Discussion Paper. University of London, Birbeck College, Department of Economics (March).

National Economic Council. 1999. *The President's Plan to Modernize and Strengthen Medicare for the 21st Century,* detailed description. Washington.

O'Brien, Ellen, Diane Rowland, and Patricia Keenan. 1999. "Medicare and Medicaid for the Elderly and Disabled Poor." Washington: Kaiser Commission on Medicaid and the Uninsured (May).

U.S. Department of Health and Human Services. Office of the Assistant Secretary for Planning and Evaluation, Administration on Aging, 1998. *Informal Caregiving: Compassion in Action* (June).

U.S. House of Representatives. Committee on Ways and Means. *1998 Green Book.* Government Printing Office (May).

Weiner, Joshua M., and David G. Stevenson. 1998. "State Policy on Long-Term Care for the Elderly." *Health Affairs* 17 (May–June): 81–100.

Wiener, Joshua M., Catherine M. Sullivan, and Jason Skaggs. 1996. "Spending Down to Medicaid: New Data on the Role of Medicaid in Paying for Nursing Home Care." Washington: AARP Public Policy Institute (June).

OVERVIEW

Emergence of the Third Age:
Toward a Productive Aging Society

Scott A. Bass, PhD

*University of Maryland
Baltimore County*

KEYWORDS. Productive aging, aging baby boomers, future aging policy, local aspects of aging policy

A possible future scenario of the policy context for older people in the United States that may unfold in the next decade will be explored in this essay. The challenges facing policymakers as we head toward 2010 will also

Scott A. Bass is Dean of the Graduate School and Vice Provost for Research at the University of Maryland Baltimore County (UMBC) and Distinguished Professor of Sociology and Policy Sciences. He has published extensively in the area of aging and social policy, including a 1995 edited volume supported by the Commonwealth Fund, *Older and Active* (Yale University Press). Dr. Bass was Founding Director of the Gerontology Institute and Center at the University of Massachusetts Boston. He can be contacted care of the Graduate School, University of Maryland Baltimore County, 1000 Hilltop Circle, Baltimore, MD 21250 (E-mail: bass@umbc.edu).

[Haworth co-indexing entry note]: "Emergence of the Third Age: Toward a Productive Aging Society." Bass, Scott A. Co-published simultaneously in *Journal of Aging & Social Policy* (The Haworth Press, Inc.) Vol. 11, No. 2/3, 2000, pp. 7-17; and: *Advancing Aging Policy as the 21st Century Begins* (ed: Francis G. Caro, Robert Morris, and Jill R. Norton) The Haworth Press, Inc., 2000, pp. 7-17. Single or multiple copies of this article are available for a fee from The Haworth Document Delivery Service [1-800-342-9678, 9:00 a.m. - 5:00 p.m. (EST). E-mail address: getinfo@haworthpressinc.com].

be considered. Aging policy as we know it, I believe, will need to undergo a substantial transition as we prepare for the entrance of elder baby boomers into the realm of senior citizenship. The political, economic, and lifestyle changes we have witnessed since the emergence of the baby boom in 1946 have been considerable. Based on the continuation of these trends, we can expect that their influences will have a significant effect on the way we think of aging and the aging society in the future (Rostow, 1998; Roszak, 1998; Torres-Gil, 1992).

Coupled with the expectations of the baby-boom generation, much of our policy context and many of our options will be influenced by the strength of our national economy. The working and spending habits of baby boomers are likely to sustain national economic growth which, in turn, will have unprecedented implications for public policy and public programs. It is further argued here that a sustained pattern of diminution of federal government involvement will intensify new issues at the state and local levels.

EMERGENCE OF THE THIRD AGE

The concept of the Third Age, a time period in one's lifetime between the completion of the primary family and traditional career responsibilities and old age and frailty, is being both defined and extended (Weiss & Bass, in press). The elements which better define the Third Age are emerging as we enter the new century. Pioneers among today's elderly are extending the frontiers of human potential in terms of their physical and intellectual activity in later life. Adults well into their seventies, eighties, and beyond are climbing mountains, exploring space, running marathons, writing books, managing corporations, building homes, and farming the land (Moody, 1988). Previously, retirement was considered to be a time of withdrawal, to make room for a younger and better-prepared generation, and of subsequent physical decline (Haber & Gratton, 1994; Riley, Kahn, & Foner, 1994). While leaders among today's elderly are beginning to question that concept, evidence is mounting that tomorrow's elderly will surely follow a different path.

Nevertheless, the Third Age is not just an extension of middle age or the sustained active engagement of those who were once considered the old. It is far more a transition of the institutions, norms, and opportunities afforded to older people as well; and, it is this larger societal transition—to new kinds of businesses, organizations, and enterprises—that the next decade will begin to foster. Matilda White Riley and her associates have been quite prolific about the structural lag of our institutions in their response to changing social behaviors (Riley & Riley, 1994). During the next decade, we will embark on this structural transition.

50

ECONOMIC GROWTH

Few people would have speculated 10 years ago that the start of the new century would be a time when the federal and state governments would be faced with decisions regarding budget surpluses–a time in which inflation would be nearly nonexistent, unemployment low, and welfare roles cut in half. Could they have imagined even the glimmer of reducing the federal debt, let alone any capacity for eliminating it? With the sustained economic expansion of the 1990s, such fantasies may become realities. Surely, our unprecedented economic growth may slow or even reverse itself; nonetheless, it does raise new ways to consider some of the concerns and fears associated with the costs of goods and services for the aging of the baby-boom generation.

If we had known in the 1930s of the huge birth spike between 1946 and 1964 that would cost the nation millions of dollars in hospital and health care and require new school construction, thousands of new teachers, and huge infrastructure costs, we would have said it was impossible for the nation to absorb such costs. From the perspective of a Depression era analyst, it would have been seen as a drain on federal, state, and local treasuries that would cripple the nation. In some ways, our lens on the demographic imperative–looking forward to the period 2020 to 2040, and very large numbers of older people–may be as imprecise. For the most part, the nation and its economy have successfully absorbed the early baby-boom era, most of which was expansionist. The dire consequences prognosticated regarding a growing, aging society may be just as unrealistic as it would have been in 1932 to forecast the economic consequences of the fertility boom that occurred from 1946 to 1964.

Much of our forecasting and planning for the aging society is based on a series of economic assumptions. These economic assumptions are largely accepted without critical examination. But, what if these historic middle-series assumptions are too conservative and actual growth exceeds projections, as witnessed at the end of the 20th century? What might the consequences be for the coming aging society and what are the implications for public policy? The Hudson Institute, a conservative think tank, in its report *Workforce 2020: Work and Workers in the 21st Century* explores a very different scenario for the future of aging than that of mainstream policymakers (Judy & D'Amico, 1997). For example, the Bureau of Labor Statistics projects that between 1996 and 2005, the United States will experience a one-percent-per-year labor-force growth rate (between 1996 and 1999, growth has exceeded those projections). This growth rate is lower, but is based on the actual 1.1% growth in the labor force experienced in America from 1982 through 1993. Rather than accepting this middle series projection, the Hudson Institute report asks us to consider the implications of a slightly higher growth rate–say, 1.3% between 1996 and 2020, rather than 1% (Judy & D'Amico, 1997).

The consequences of a 1.3% growth rate would result in a demand for 11.5 million additional workers. Such a demand for labor would allow older workers, if they chose, to remain in the workforce and it would provide increased opportunity for other heretofore-surplus labor groups. Accompanying a growth in job opportunities, workers would have more money to spend, fueling economic growth and tax revenues while reducing the demand for public spending, including that on Social Security. According to the report, "Even if productivity does not accelerate, those millions of additional experienced workers could produce approximately half a trillion dollars of additional goods and services (in 1997 dollars) beyond what the national economy would otherwise produce" (Judy & D'Amico, 1997, p. 101). But, as we have seen in the economic cycles of the 1980s and 1990s, it is possible to have continued growth for long stretches that includes job expansion and increased productivity. Such growth creates considerable added wealth that fosters increased consumer spending. Economists refer to this phenomenon as the "wealth effect," in which people feel richer, have greater confidence in the future, and spend more. Active consumer spending, which constitutes nearly two thirds of the GDP, stimulates economic growth.

In the projected cycle of economic growth, the nation would be faced with rising tax revenues, revenues of $1 trillion beyond Congressional and Executive branch expectations, over the next 15 years. This $1 trillion surplus is based on a projected GDP growth rate of 2.4%. Between 1996 and 1999, the growth rate has been 4%. The rate of reduction of the nation's $3.7 trillion debt could be faster than projected, and the surplus could be even larger. By eliminating the national debt, interest rates would fall, allowing companies to borrow at favorable rates, and fuel further growth. With little or no debt by 2015, the United States, if it wanted to, could borrow to cover the costs associated with the aging baby boomers and once again retire the debt when the much smaller cohort of elders follows the passage of the baby-boom generation.

The same kind of calculations can be extrapolated to Social Security (OASDI Trustees Report, 1999). Most discussions about the Social Security Trust Fund are based on the intermediate estimate of GDP growth at 1.2% rather than the current 4%. As a result of this conservative estimate, it is projected that the surplus will disappear in 2034 and, at around 2014, Social Security will be paying out more in benefits than it receives in payroll taxes, requiring it to withdraw monies from the Trust Fund to make up the difference. An even more conservative estimate of growth reveals a dwindling Trust Fund by 2024. Nevertheless, there is a third estimate available that is less frequently discussed which anticipates a growth rate of 2.1%. Should growth be sustained at this level, there would be sufficient funds in Social Security to meet all obligations through 2075 without any alterations.

No one really knows what will happen with the economy, and it is important to develop cautious figures in planning for the future. It *is* possible that the economy could maintain the growth evidenced over the past 75 years, however; if so, the nation could afford an elderly society whose behavior in retirement is like that of previous cohorts. But, this essay argues that the upcoming cohort of elders will *not* behave like previous cohorts; and, as a consequence of the market behavior of the baby boomers, policy issues facing the ascendancy of the Third Age will be different from those of today.

BABY BOOMER BEHAVIOR

In national surveys conducted by the American Association of Retired Persons, baby boomers indicated that over three quarters of their cohort anticipate retiring by age 65 (Startch, 1998). This would leave a somewhat larger percentage working longer in their career jobs than people of the same age today. While many baby boomers may plan on retiring from their primary career jobs, a 1998 AARP/Roper survey indicated that four out of five boomer retirees plan to work during retirement (Startch, 1998); that is, after retiring from their lifetime career jobs, they intend to become engaged in some form of paid labor. The expectation of work after retirement is quite different than the expectations of today's retirees–fewer than one out of five individuals over age 65 is employed (Schulz, 1992). Indeed, the ravages of time may present another story; nevertheless, tomorrow's retirees are indicating that their retirement will be different than that of the previous generation. Over one third of the baby boomers in the AARP/Roper survey indicated they wanted to work part-time after retirement, primarily for interest or enjoyment.

Adults of the baby-boom generation are for the most part healthier, better educated, and wealthier than any previous American generation. The Congressional Budget Office compared real incomes (adjusted for inflation) and household size between baby boomers and their parents' generation. Depending on the age of the baby boomers, the income advantage (aggregate income and assets) of the boomers over their parents' generation at the same age ranged between 75% and 82% (Manchester, 1994). Even among lower-income baby boomers, their relative income was greater than the poor of their parents' generation. Still, among baby boomers, income inequality–the distance between affluence and poverty–is quite profound and, according to U.S. Bureau of Census figures, incomes in 1995 among baby boomers are more disparate than among the same age group 20 years earlier (AARP, 1998; Frey, 1999).

With more money and better education for the vast majority of baby boomers, baby boomers have had a significant effect on styles, fashions, and trends throughout their adult experience. From the sheer standpoint of economics and the capacity to spend, baby boomers should continue this behavior well into their retirement years.

For example, advertising in popular magazines is targeted at improving, masking, or altering the appearance of an aging body. Ads for "contouring facial lifts," removal of "wrinkles and brown spots," and vitamins to add vigor are already routine, and we have not yet entered the period of transition for baby boomers to the Third Age when all of this will accelerate.

Cosmetic surgery, once an exclusive choice of celebrities, has expanded dramatically. People are reconstructing entire bodies including noses, waistlines, breasts, eyes, and skin. In 1984, 477,700 plastic surgeries took place in America. This grew to 825,000 operations a decade later and continues to grow each year, driven by the demands of aging baby boomers. Interestingly, 65% of cosmetic operations were performed on individuals whose family income was below $50,000 (Sharlet, 1999).

Boomers will spend to look good and feel good despite their years; sometimes the products they buy will be fairly priced and of high quality and, at other times, they will not be. New pharmaceuticals will be developed and marketed to retard the maladies associated with human aging. Some book titles already attracting attention include: *Live Now, Age Later: Proven Ways to Slow Down the Clock, Immortality: How Science Is Extending Your Life Span–and Changing the World*, and *Living to 100: Lessons in Living to Your Maximum Potential at Any Age*. Unfortunately, many individuals fear their own aging and the implications of inching toward mortality. Rather than embracing the natural aging process, some older people will search for a fountain of youth at any cost.

Baby boomers will have more available in combined assets, pensions, and Social Security with which to retire than any previous generation; some will also experience financial windfalls in the form of inheritances. With about three quarters of the current population age 65 and older now owning their homes and 83% of these homes being fully paid for, baby boomers are most likely in line to inherit those properties. In 1987, the median value of all owner-occupied elderly housing was $58,900 (U. S. Bureau of the Census, 1990); this value has risen over the past decade. It is estimated that between 1990 and 2030, baby boomers will inherit $9 trillion (AARP, 1998). This windfall will help baby boomers continue their spending, which in turn will help the economy to grow, and sustain continuation of their social needs from the federal and state largess.

PUBLIC POLICY IN THE THIRD AGE

As we shift to an aging society in which 20% of the population is 65 or older, many of today's pressing issues of health care and Social Security may recede from the headlines to be replaced by new and different issues that focus on other work-related, invested interests of the able elderly. As the AARP Public Policy Institute (1998) notes, "Productivity gains, more than demographic changes, are key to the future economic prospects for boomers" (p. 58). The policy of the Federal Reserve Board and the behavior of the economy are crucial to the successful future of the baby-boom generation. Low interest rates and modest growth create demands for older workers; low unemployment with low inflation (a difficult balance) stimulates consumption that fuels the economy; a growing economy generates tax revenues to help pay for expansion of human services. A cycle of economic productivity that includes older people as part of the expanding economy is one in which the entire society benefits and one that can support the health and services needs of its dependent population.

Many issues other than health care and economic security will be determined outside of Washington, DC in the future. While we frequently think of Congress when considering public policy, many salient policy issues are of a state or local nature. In addition, the current conservative Supreme Court is proactive in asserting the independence of state governments and the reduction of federal authority. Two examples occurred recently. First, the Court ruled that a person who has a physical disability that can be corrected by medicines or devices is not disabled and therefore is not protected by federal law from discrimination; and second, the Court voted 5 to 4 to restrict Congress' authority to allow individuals to sue a state in state court to enforce their rights under federal law. In a time of shrinking federal power and a highly partisan Congress, public policy will continue to be made in the 50 state capitals and in local jurisdictions.

Some of the issues that older baby boomers will confront on a local level include land use, tax structure, transportation, environmental matters, workforce training, career counseling, volunteer programs, and housing. As boomers consider downsizing their residences, issues may be raised about the continued residential spread into rural communities, forcing the expansion of regional services and costly infrastructure. Alternatively, if baby boomers stay where they now live or consider moving closer to the urban core, greater environmental sustainability will be achieved. Discussion at the local level on regional policy in an aging society is a topic that will move to the forefront.

Indeed, concern about the housing patterns of retiring baby boomers may be a serious local issue. In his paper "Beyond Social Security: The Local Aspects of Aging America," William H. Frey examines the implications of a large, economically mobile, older population of baby boomers who are able to select the most desirable living environments, leaving city and county governments with uneven distributions of economically well-off elders and pockets of poor, older baby boomers in need of extensive public services. The current division between poorer-urban and more affluent-suburban neighborhoods will be revised; as a consequence of aging-in-place, large numbers of older people, unable to afford relocation, may become a strain on surrounding suburban neighborhoods. According to Frey (1999), "Concentrations of 'demographically disadvantaged' boomer elderly will arise within suburban communities that will not be prepared to deal with [their] social services, health care, and transportation needs . . ." (p. 3). With a larger elderly society that is more affluent and potentially less concerned about the needs of the poor, it may be that much more difficult to garner public support for programs at a federal level designed to mitigate these economic inequalities.

In the future, in a society in which older people will have a wide array of options and many will have the economic means to make choices, questions will arise as to the competitiveness and viability of many of the traditional, local aging organizations, such as the senior center. Senior centers, begun under the Older Americans Act of 1965 (OAA), now reflect a nationwide network of community agencies (Gelfand, 1999). These organizations face new competitors in the marketplace for older people's time and energy, including fitness centers, community colleges, restaurants, bookstores, and dedicated programs such as Elderhostel or lifelong learning centers. Created in a very different era, the OAA needs some retooling to reflect the needs of the aging society and to keep current with the changing interests and demands of older boomers. Two areas in need of immediate attention are (1) defining the role OAA can play in assessing and planning for flexible employment options for older people, and (2) providing incentives for OAA programs to upgrade their facilities, enhance their programs, explore partnering with the private sector, and revitalize their mission. Without these changes, the senior center and other allied OAA activities run the risk of becoming mere shadows of what they once were.

OAA was designed to serve all older people, regardless of income. With the greater choices afforded affluent elders and the speed with which the private sector can respond to fads for market segments, nonprofit or universal government programs may have a hard time competing for market share. Cumbersome rules and regulations may make these programs an option of last resort. Political support for OAA programs may decline, leaving only a core of constituents of modest economic means with modest services. Well-connected elders may focus their political clout on their own needs, which will be much more marketplace- and investment-oriented and less focused toward traditional, social welfare programs.

CONCLUSION

The next decade will be a period of transition wherein our society will move from policy directed at aging individuals to policies aimed at cultivating an aging society. Central to our aging society will be the nurturing of the nation's economy. A growing economy spells good years ahead for older baby boomers. Rather than being seen as liabilities, older baby boomers will be deemed assets with an important role in sustaining economic growth (see Roszak, 1998). If policies are crafted that tap the potential of baby boomers in the workforce, then it is likely we will experience unprecedented economic expansion. That is not to say, however, that there will not be poor and dependent elders; for there will be.

The experiences of a lifetime of low earnings are compounded for the aged through poor health, inadequate nutrition, poor dental hygiene, and the incapacity to solve situational financial problems. For these unfortunate elders, private charities and government funded organizations are the best hope. Government programs become their lifeline and support. Unfortunately, funding from these programs is likely to be modest. With a potential reduction in federal anti-poverty efforts, very poor and vulnerable elderly will be dependent on the services available in their immediate communities. Some elders will go without as considerable political clout will reside with more affluent elders. As pioneers of the aging society, attention will be given to the needs of these more organized and influential elders. In all likelihood, the vulnerable elderly will be dispersed geographically throughout suburban and urban areas and, for those who have aged in place in areas without a history of services, the capacity of those communities to meet their needs will be strained.

Despite the evidence of growing inequality, public policy will be driven by the economic interests of baby boomers. Most likely, legislation will be introduced that provides financial advantages to baby boomers. Bills will be focused on reductions in estate taxes, capital gains taxes, and mechanisms for older people to retain equity earned in their homes. Also, tax incentives will be proposed to provide long-term care insurance and mechanisms to foster individual solutions to high-cost health or long-term care expenses. These schemes will more likely follow the tax assistance historically provided to families for child care, with direct subsidies for long-term care for the very poor.

In the next decade, we will see new kinds of organizations, industries, and services to respond to the needs and desires of aging baby boomers. These new enterprises will require some regulatory and governmental oversight to ensure that consumers will not be defrauded or exploited. Public policy will be needed to develop regulations that are responsive, but not overly constraining, to these new industries. In a time of growing states' rights and shrinking federal authority, local decision making will be important to older baby boomers. Larger numbers of older people will require more cooperation among local jurisdictions to ensure coordination of local services. Regional planners will need to examine policies and programs to encourage housing and transportation patterns that are affordable and workable for local communities.

Finally, the OAA and the organizations it fosters will need to be updated to be responsive to the interests and habits of baby boomers. Areas in need of expansion and revision include local career training and employment options for the able elderly. Also, incentives will be needed to upgrade senior center facilities and provide activities that are more consistent and competitive with those found in the private sector.

The next decade will only usher in the transitional elements; the actual changes in organizations, structures, and initiatives will take place as the baby boomers move closer to traditional retirement ages in the second decade of the 21st century. Most important will be a sustained growth of the economy. Through continued economic growth, the country's middle-class aging baby boomers will experience a time of unprecedented prosperity.

REFERENCES

AARP (1998). *Boomers approaching midlife: How secure a future?* Washington, DC: AARP Public Policy Institute.

Bass, S. A., Kutza, E. A., & Torres-Gil, F.M. (1990). *Diversity in aging: Challenges facing planners & policymakers in the 1990s.* Glenview, IL: Scott, Foresman and Company.

Frey, W. H. (1999). *Beyond social security: The local aspects of an aging America.* Washington, DC: The Brookings Institution.

Gelfand, D. E. (1999). *The aging network: Programs and services.* New York: Springer Publishing Company.

Haber, C., & Gratton, B. (1994). *Old age and the search for security.* Bloomington, IN: Indiana University Press.

Judy, R.W., & D'Amico, C. (1997). *Workforce 2020: Work and workers in the 21st century.* Indianapolis, IN: Hudson Institute.

Manchester, J. (1994). *Baby boomers in retirement: An early perspective.* Washington, DC: Congressional Budget Office.

Moody, R. (1988). *Abundance of life: Human development policies for an aging society.* New York: Columbia University Press.

OASDI Trustees Report (1999). *1999 OASDI trustees report.* Washington, DC: Social Security Administration.

Riley, M. W., Kahn, R. L., & Foner. A. (Eds.). (1994). *Age and structural lag.* New York: John Wiley & Sons, Inc.

Riley, M.W., & Riley, J. W., Jr. (1994). Structural lag: Past and future. In M. W. Riley, R. L. Kahn, & A. Foner (Eds.). *Age and structural lag* (pp. 15-36). New York: John Wiley & Sons, Inc.

Rostow, W. W. (1998). *The great population spike and after.* New York: Oxford University Press.

Roszak, T. (1998). *America the wise: The longevity revolution and the true wealth of nations.* Boston: Houghton Mifflin Company.

Schulz, J.H. (1992). *The economics of aging* (5th edition). New York: Auburn House.

Sharlet, J. (1999, July 2). Beholding beauty: Scholars nip and tuck at our quest for physical perfection. *The Chronicle of Higher Education.* A15-A16.

Startch, R. (1998). *Boomers look toward retirement.* Washington, DC: AARP.

Torres-Gil, F.M. (1992). *The new aging: Politics and change in America.* New York: Auburn House.

U.S. Bureau of the Census. (1990). *Home ownership trends in the 1980s.* Current Housing Reports Series H-121, No. 2. Washington, DC: U.S. Government Printing Office.

Weiss, R.S., & Bass, S.A. (Eds.). (In press). *Challenges of the third age: Meaning and purpose in later life.* New York: Oxford University Press.

NBER WORKING PAPER SERIES

THE FINANCIAL PROBLEMS OF THE ELDERLY: A HOLISTIC APPROACH

Victor R. Fuchs

Working Paper 8236
http://www.nber.org/papers/w8236

NATIONAL BUREAU OF ECONOMIC RESEARCH
1050 Massachusetts Avenue
Cambridge, MA 02138
April 2001

This paper was prepared for the Policies For An Aging Society: Confronting the Economic and Political Challenges Conference, sponsored by the Council on the Economic Impact of Health System Change, Schneider Institute for Health Policy, Brandeis University, October 1999. I am indebted to the Robert Wood Johnson Foundation and the Kaiser Family Foundation for financial support. The research assistance of Sarah Rosen is also gratefully acknowledged. The views expressed herein are those of the author and not necessarily those of the National Bureau of Economic Research.

The Financial Problems of the Elderly: A Holistic Approach
Victor R. Fuchs
NBER Working Paper No. 8236
April 2001
JEL No. J14, I10

ABSTRACT

A holistic approach to the financial problems of the elderly focuses simultaneously on their expenditures that are self financed as well as those that are financed by transfers from the young (under age65). It also focuses simultaneously on paying for health care and paying for other goods and services. The "full income" of the elderly, defined as the sum of personal income and health care expenditures not paid from personal income, provides a useful framework for empirical application of the holistic approach . In 1997, approximately 35 percent of the elderly's full income was devoted to health care; 65 percent to other goods and services. Approximately 56 percent of full income was provided by transfers from the young and 44 percent by the elderly themselves. The paper shows how these percentages might change under alternative assumptions about the growth of health care relative to other goods and services and the effect of these changes on the need for more saving and more work prior to retirement.

Victor R. Fuchs
NBER
30 Alta Road
Stanford, CA 94305
fuchs@newage3.stanford.edu

Financial Problems of the Elderly:

A Holistic Approach"

"Grow old along with me! The best is yet to be," wrote Robert Browning in his poem, *Rabbi Ben Ezra*. A century later Robert Butler, a former Director of the National Institute of Aging, took a more dismal view of aging, epitomized in the title of his book, *Why Survive? Being Old in America*.[1] Why the change in perspective? One possible reason is that an elderly person was a rarity in Browning's time, but as the 20th century drew to a close, mortality tables showed that three out of four Americans would reach the biblical "three score and ten". Just being old no longer carries any special distinction.

A Japanese statesman-scholar, Wataru Hiraizumi, has recently provided a provocative insight into the effect of an increase in the proportion of the elderly in a society. Recalling his first few weeks in France in the 1950s, he says, "I suddenly saw the reason for a singular uneasiness...it was the presence of a seemingly inordinate number of old people...they looked vigilant, severe, and vaguely ill-tempered."[2] He attributed this to the fact

that in France, at that time, more than 11 percent of the population was

over 65, whereas in the Japan he had recently left, the elderly were barely 5

percent of the population.

Probably an even more important reason for the change from

Browning to Butler is that improvements in the material condition of

America's elderly have been surpassed by rapidly rising expectations.

Although today's elderly are on average healthier and wealthier than any

previous generation in the nation's history, their desires and expectations

regarding life in retirement are outpacing the ability of society to fulfill them.

Nowhere is this more evident than with respect to health and medical care.

Recent decades have witnessed an unprecedented number of advances

in medical technology that, albeit costly, have contributed to longer, better

quality lives for many older Americans. Ten of the most important are

shown in Table 17.1.[3] Thanks in part to such innovations, (and in part to

declines in cigarette smoking), the overall age-adjusted death rate has fallen

by 20 percent since 1980. But some major causes of death, such as cancer and diabetes, show little or no decline in mortality. When medical care could do little to extend life for anyone, not much was expected of it. In an era of great progress, however, expectations of further gains accelerate. The more medical care does to keep people alive and healthier, the more is demanded of it.

Moreover, despite the gains in health and wealth, many Americans still experience a troubled old age. In addition to the inevitable loss of family and friends, diminution of status, and existential concerns, many elderly face two potentially serious financial problems: lower income and greater expenditures for medical care. Physiological changes are the primary cause of both lower earnings and poorer health. Earnings are also affected adversely by obsolescence of skills and knowledge, and by public and private policies that reduce the incentives of older persons to continue working and increase the cost to employers of employing older workers.

These financial problems have been widely discussed in recent years; the papers in this volume provide additional food for thought. Unfortunately, most policy discussions of the financial problems of the elderly tend to focus on only one program at a time. Thus, there is a plethora of papers on Social

Security, Medicare, Medicaid, employment-based pensions, Medigap

insurance, and so on. Sometimes these sharply focused studies are required

by legislative or administrative exigencies, but I believe a holistic view is a

necessary complement to such fragmented analyses.

A Holistic View

A holistic view focuses simultaneously on the financing of health care

and the financing of other goods and services. It also focuses on the

expenditures of the elderly that are self-financed as well as on those that are

financed by transfers from the young. A holistic view cautions against policy

proposals that claim we can patch existing public programs for the elderly

without major changes in policies and behavior. These limited proposals

usually include means testing benefits, subsidies, modest increases in taxes,

and various administrative maneuvers. When they are examined one

program at a time, they may seem reasonable and feasible. The entire

package, however, applied to all programs for the elderly, is likely to create

large disincentives for work and saving prior to retirement and require huge transfers that will ultimately be rejected by taxpayers. This is what

happened with welfare. Each additional program and subsidy seemed

desirable by itself, but the cumulative effect was a bipartisan revolt against

"welfare as we know it."

At one time it was reasonable to treat the problem of earnings

replacement separate from the problem of paying for health care. Health

care expenditures of the elderly were small relative to expenditures on other

goods and services and a holistic approach was not essential. Now,

however, health care expenditures equal or exceed expenditures for all other

goods and services for many elderly, and given the trends of recent decades,

this may be true for the elderly as a whole within 20 years.

Artificial separation of the problem of earnings replacement from that

of health care payment ignores the fact that there are often trade-offs

between the two. Money is money, and for most of the elderly there is

never enough to go around. This is self-evident where private funds are

concerned. Low-income elderly, for example, frequently must choose

between prescription drugs and an adequate diet. For middle-income elderly the choice may be between more expensive medigap insurance and an airplane trip to a grandchild's wedding. Difficult choices are also apparent with respect to public funds. The same tax receipts that could be used to maintain or increase retirement benefits could be used to fund additional health care, and vice versa. Policy analysts who fail to understand that a large increase in Medicare spending will jeopardize the government's ability to fulfill its Social Security commitments ignore the realities of economics and politics.

A holistic approach not only requires analyses that encompass different government programs but also must involve examination of the two-way interactions between changes in the private sector and public programs. For instance, from 1993 to 2000 the share of employers providing health insurance for retirees declined from 40 to less than 25 percent.[4] This change may suggest that government provision of health insurance for retirees should expand, but such expansion could result in further decreases in private coverage.

Another significant trend in the private sector that has major implications for the future financial problems of the elderly is the shift

in private pensions from defined benefits to defined contributions. This

change works well for retirees when the stock market is rising briskly, but

looks less attractive when the stock market flattens or goes into decline.

Moreover, the 401-K plans and IRAs that have supplanted the traditional

retirement plans typically do not call for automatic annuitization upon

retirement. This can be advantageous to retirees who would like access to

their money, but can be problematic for them and for taxpayers if they lose

their retirement savings in bad investments or spend them at too rapid a

rate. Furthermore, if annuitization is voluntary, the terms available are

likely to suffer from the problem of adverse selection. Hurd and McCarry

have shown that the ability of individuals to predict their longevity is

significantly greater than could be expected from chance.[5] For this reason,

some compulsory annuitization is probably as necessary as some compulsory

enrollment in health insurance.

<u>"Full Income"</u>

To provide a holistic framework for addressing the financial problems of the elderly, it is useful to think of the "full income" (or its equivalent, "full consumption") of the elderly. I define "full income" as the sum of personal income and health care expenditures not paid from personal income. Two critical questions can be addressed within this framework: 1) How much of the elderly's full income is devoted to health care and how much to other goods and services? 2) How much of the elderly's full income is provided by transfers from the population under age 65 (social security retirement payments, Medicare, and similar programs) and how much is provided by the elderly themselves (earnings, pensions, income from savings, and the like)?

Using data from the Current Population Survey, the Medicare Current Beneficiary Survey and other sources, with adjustments for under reporting, I estimate that 35 percent of the elderly's full income in 1997 was devoted to health care and 65 percent to other goods and services (see the right-hand column of Table 17.2). I also estimate that 56 percent of full income was provided by transfers from the "young" and 44 percent by the elderly themselves (see the bottom row of Table 17.2).

Probably the most important information in Table 17.2 is the disaggregation of full income by use and source found in the interior of Table 17.2. We see that the elderly are much more dependent on transfers for health care expenditures than for other goods and services. Of the 35 percent of full income that goes for health care, more than three-fourths (27 divided by 35) is provided by the young, as opposed to less than half (29 divided by 65) for other goods and services. This fact combined with the tendency for spending on health care to grow more rapidly than for other goods and services will pose major problems for policy makers and the elderly within two decades.

Table 17.3 shows what the uses and sources of full income would be in 2020 if the generations under 65 continue to bear the same share of health care and "other" as in 1997. If health care spending does not grow more rapidly than "other" (the first column of Table 17.3), the shares of uses and sources will be identical to those shown in Table 17.2. On the other hand, if health grows 3 percent per annum more rapidly than "other" (the last column in Table 17.3), we see that the health share of full income would jump from 35 to 52 percent and the young would provide 62 percent of full

income instead of the 56 percent provided in 1997. These calculations are

all per capita; that is, they do not take into account the fact that the ratio of

elderly to those under age 65 will be higher in 2020 than it was in 1997.

Thus, the figures in Table 3 underestimate the potential increased

dependency of the elderly on transfers from the young.

Will spending on health for the elderly grow faster than spending on

other goods and services? This question cannot be answered with certainty,

but it would be prudent to assume that it will. Over the period 1970-2000,

Medicare expenditures per elderly enrollee grew approximately 2.8 percent

per annum faster than GDP per capita (excluding health care expenditures).

The growth of the non-health economy is an indicator of the rate at which

expenditures on "other" could grow. The "gap" of 2.8 percent per annum is

attributable primarily to technological advances such as those listed in Table

17.1. Will the pace of technological advance in medicine slow down in the

next two decades? Not likely. There are currently 700 new drugs in

development for the diseases of aging, and, as the elderly's share of the health care market increases, the share of medical R&D focused on the elderly is likely to grow.

In theory, advances in medical technology do not necessarily lead to higher expenditures, but in practice that is usually the way it works. The last major exception to this rule occurred a half century ago with the introduction and rapid diffusion of antibiotics. But antibiotics were a very special kind of medical advance. They were given to patients who had life threatening infections, most of whom who were in otherwise good health. Many beneficiaries were children and young adults who, once the infection was cured, went on to live many years without requiring major medical intervention. By contrast, advances in medical technology that extend life or improve quality of life for older Americans do not offer that same prospect of reducing overall utilization of medical care. Indeed, many expensive interventions such as open-heart surgery will only be undertaken on patients who are otherwise in reasonably good health. Moreover, antibiotics were very inexpensive to produce and dispense. By contrast, many of the products currently under development in the biotech and bioengineering laboratories are likely to be expensive to produce and implement.

<u>Implications For Policy</u>

The coming increase in the absolute and relative number of elderly will unquestionably increase the burden on the working population and require an increase in taxes. But if the scenario sketched out in Table 17.3 materializes, that is, if health care expenditures for the elderly grow 2 to 3 percent per annum more rapidly than expenditures on other goods and services, the burden on the young is likely to be unbearable. There seems to be only two possible escapes from this bleak scenario: Slow the rate of growth of health care expenditures or require the elderly to assume more of the responsibility for paying for their health care.

Slowing the growth of health care expenditures may not be feasible, and even if it is feasible, it may not be desirable. Although advances in technology are the driving force behind the growth of medical expenditures, many of these advances contribute significantly to longer, better quality lives. Politicians in both parties strongly support increased spending for medical research, and private decision makers in the drug and biotech industries are betting tens of billions of dollars each year that the money to pay for advances in medical technology will be forthcoming. Many economists now assert that the advances of recent decades, albeit expensive, are "good buys" and see no reason why that will not be true of future advances as well.

If health care expenditures for the elderly continue to grow rapidly, however, and if the ability to finance these expenditures by transfers from the young reaches its limit, the only alternative is for the elderly to pick up a larger share of the bill. If these payments must come from incomes that grow at only a modest pace, the elderly will become increasingly "health care poor." Indeed, many are already in that unhappy condition. While eligible for MRIs, angiograms, bypass surgery, and other high tech diagnostic and surgical interventions, they do not have the resources to purchase a new mattress, to heat their house to a comfortable temperature in winter, to take a taxi to the doctor, or to access other goods and services that would make life more bearable.

To prevent more and more elderly becoming "health care poor," they must have additional personal income. They need more income from savings (including pensions and investments) and from earnings, which means they will have to work more both before and after age 65. Why do millions of Americans reach age 65 so heavily dependent on transfers from the young? One possibility is that their income over the life cycle was so low that they could barely meet everyday expenses let alone save for retirement. This explanation is undoubtedly correct for some low income elderly, but analyses of longitudinal data by Venti and Wise[6] show that inequality in savings for retirement varies greatly even among those with the same earnings prior to retirement. This conclusion holds after adjustments for special factors that affect the ability to save and for differences in investment returns.

An examination of CPS data on sources of income provides additional evidence concerning the question of the relation between saving and income. To obtain the statistics shown in Figure 17.1, everyone 65 and over was sorted into deciles based on their Social Security income, an ordering which is probably similar to one based on lifetime earnings.[7] Within each decile individuals were sorted by savings income (pensions, interest, dividends, and rent) and the 25th, 50th, and 75th percentiles were indentified. The results reveal that while savings income tends to be positively correlated with Social Security income, there is great variation within each decile. Many elderly in the lower deciles have substantial savings income while many in the higher deciles have very little. Consider the striking differences among workers in the middle range of income, that is, Social Security deciles 5 and 6. Those are the quintessential "average workers." At least one-fourth of them have virtually no savings income; on the other hand one-fourth have savings income of over $8000 per year. It is clear from these data that when saving is voluntary, many individuals do not save. To provide higher income for future elderly, and to reduce inequality among them, it will be necessary to introduce some form of compulsory saving.

The other major potential source of increase in income for the elderly is more paid work. In the late 1990s, mean hours of work per man age 60 was only 1495 per year, at age 65 only 701 hours, and at age 70, only 338 hours.[8] The comparable figures for women were 926, 423, and 150 hours per year respectively. Given that most Americans at these ages are in reasonably good health and suffer from fewer physical limitations than earlier cohorts, there seems to be ample potential for more work.

Since 1975, life expectancy at age 65 has risen appreciably, especially for men. This change, unfortunately, has not been accompanied by any increase in paid work by older men and only a small increase for women. Thus, the number of years when income must come from sources other than employment has grown, and employment's share of total income was less in 1995 than in 1975. Table 4 provides a useful summary of how work has failed to keep pace with increases in life expectancy.

The first row of Table 17.4 presents life expectancy at age 65, a familiar statistic calculated from age-specific mortality rates in the year indicated. It is the mean years of life remaining for the cohort that reached age 65 (in, say, 1995) if it experienced the age-specific mortality that prevailed in 1995. Expected years of work is conceptually similar; it is obtained by combining age-specific rates of work with age-specific survival rates. It shows the years of work that the cohort that reached age 65 (in, say, 1995) would experience if the age-specific work rate and the mortality that prevailed in 1995 continued through the lifetime of that cohort. The expected years of work are not forecast, anymore than the life expectancies are forecast. The values could be used for forecasting purposes, however, by making assumptions about future trends in age-specific mortality and in age-specific work rates.

Inspection of Table 17.4 reveals that years of life expected at age 65 increased at a rapid pace from 1975 to 1995, more rapidly for men than for women, although the latter still enjoyed a 4.3 year advantage over men in 1995. In contrast to life expectancy, expected years of work remained relatively constant, at about 2 years for men and 1 year for women (full time equivalents). The number of years *not* at work (row 1 minus row 2) rose appreciably for men from 11.7 in 1975 to 13.7 in 1995. Women also show an increase in years *not* at work, from 17.3 to 17.8 years. Health care and consumption of other goods and services in these years not at work must be financed by the accumulated savings of the elderly or by transfers from the young.

In order to make paid work for older Americans more attractive there must be a reexamination of all policies that create high implicit marginal tax rates on earnings and employment as well as a review of employment laws that often make it more costly for employers to hire or retain older workers. In addition to providing more income, there could be additional benefits to the elderly from making work more feasible and desirable. Work often provides satisfaction, identity, and an opportunity to maintain or develop relationships. Moreover, staying active usually contributes to better health. We should recall the words of another English poet, Alfred Tennyson, who in contemplating Ulysses in retirement has the aging hero say, "How dull it is to pause, to make an end, to rust unburnished, not to shine in use! As though to breathe were life."

"The Financial Problems of the Elderly: A Holistic Approach"

Endnotes

1.   Butler, R. N. 1975. *Why Survive? Being Old in America*, New York: Harper and Row.

2.   Hiraizumi, W. 2000. Mass Longevity Transforms Our Society. *Proceedings of the American Philosophical Society* 144(4):361-383.

3.   Fuchs, V. R. and Sox, Jr., H.C. 2001. Physicians' Views of The Relative Importance to Patients of Medical Innovations: A Survey of Leading General Internists, NBER, in progress.

4.   Freudenheim, M. 2000. *New York Times*, December 31:38.

5.   Hurd, M.D. and McCarry, K.. 1997. The Predictive Validity of Subjective Probabilities of Survival. Mimeo.

6.   Venti, S.F. and David A. Wise. 1998. The Cause of Wealth Dispersion at Retirement: Choice or Chance? *American Economic Review* 88(2):185-91.

7.   All household income was assumed to be shared equally among the members of the household.

8.   These figures were calculated from the 1996-98 Current Population

Surveys. They reflect the total annual hours worked for each age-sex

group divided by the total number in the group regardless of labor

force status.

"The Financial Problems of the Elderly: A Holistic Approach"

References

Butler, R.N. 1975. *Why Survive? Being Old in America*. New York: Harper and Row.

Freudenheim, M. 2000. *New York Time*, December 31: 38.

Fuchs, V.R. and Sox, Jr., H.C. 2001. Physicians' Views of the Relative Importance to Patients of Medical Innovations: A Survey of Leading General Internists. NBER, in progress.

Hiraizumi, W. 2000. Mass Longevity Transforms Our Society. *Proceedings of the American Philosophical Society* 144(4): 361-383.

Hurd, M.D., and McCarry, K. 1997. The Predictive Validity of Subjective Probabilities of Survival. Mimeo.

Venti, S.F., and Wise, D.A. 1998. The Cause of Wealth Dispersion at Retirement: Choice or Chance? *American Economic Review* 88(2): 185-91.

Table 1

Ten Major Advances in Medical Technology During Past 30 Years

Balloon angioplasty with stents

Blood pressure lowering drugs

Cataract extraction with lens implant

Cholesterol lowering drugs

Coronary artery bypass graft

Hip and knee replacement

MRI and CT scanning

Mammography

New drugs for depression

New drugs for ulcers and acid reflux

Table 2
Americans 65 and Over, Sources and Uses
of "Full Income" in 1997 (percent distribution)

Uses	Sources		Total
	Under age 65	Age 65 and over	
Health care	27	8	35
Other	29	36	65
Total	56	44	100

Table 3
Projected Uses and Sources of "Full Income" in 2020
Under Alternate Assumptions about Gap between
Growth of Health and Other

	Percent per annum gap			
	0	**1**	**2**	**3**
Uses				
Health	35	40	46	52
Other	65	60	54	48
Sources				
< 65	56	58	60	62
≥ 65	44	42	40	38

Note: Assuming that the share of Health and the
share of Other provided by < 65 remain constant.

Table 4
Expected at Age 65 [a]

Expected	Men			Women		
	1975	1985	1995	1975	1985	1995
Years of life	13.7	14.6	15.6	18.0	18.6	18.9
Years of work (f-t-e) [b]	2.0	1.7	1.9	0.7	0.7	1.1
Years not at work	11.7	12.9	13.7	17.3	17.9	17.8

a. Based on age-specific mortality and employment rates in the year indicated.
b. Assuming a fulltime work year of 2000 hours.

Figure 1

Savings Income by Social Security Income Decile, Americans Ages 65 and Over, 1997

Savings income

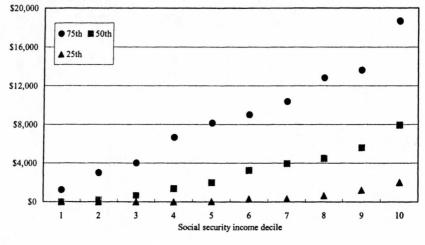

Social security income decile

EUROPEAN
ECONOMIC
REVIEW

ELSEVIER   European Economic Review 40 (1996) 729–746

Distributive implications of an aging society

Robert K. von Weizsäcker

Department of Economics, University of Mannheim, D-68131 Mannheim, Germany
CEPR, London, UK

Abstract

The paper reviews recent research on the impact of an aging population on the distribution of income. After briefly discussing the demographic conditions responsible for population aging, a short account is given of demographic trends in the industrialized world. In order to disentangle the many potential channels by which an aging society affects the dispersion of income, several levels of aggregation are distinguished. The paper differentiates between intra- and intergenerational issues, between direct and indirect demographic inequality effects, and between the distribution of current and lifetime income. It emphasizes the critical role of age-related redistributive tax-transfer systems, like public pension schemes and health care systems. Sources of distributional policy conflicts are identified at both the cross-section level and the lifetime level of income inequality. The institutional design of intergenerational burden sharing, individual disincentive reactions, shifts in age–income profiles related to cohort size, and politico-economic repercussions are shown to drive the relation between population aging and income distribution in distinct and partially opposite ways.

JEL classification: D31; H55; J18

Keywords: Income distribution; Population aging; Fiscal-demographic policy conflicts; Social policy design

1. Introduction

"Does an aging society increase inequality?" This question is posed by policymakers in many industrialized countries today. A main message of the research presented below is that this question is ill-defined to have any simple answer.

Though most economists and demographers may have expected the vagueness, they nevertheless tend to know little about why they are having this expectation. The general insight into the demo-economic complexities involved is still neither large nor undisputed. This is not primarily due to the complex issue of defining and measuring inequality, but relates to the intricate demo-economic causes of changes in fertility and mortality, the consequences for the financing of demographically sensitive public expenditures, and its combined impact on the distribution of income.

Any economic variable or decision having an age or life-cycle aspect bears upon this interrelation. Moreover, numerous demographic variables come into play. [1] In order to isolate at least some of the most basic effects, the analysis has to be rather restrictive. Once a few first results have been established, further factors may be introduced. Most of the extensions, however, prove to be analytically untractable. Empirically supported numerical simulations constitute fairly quickly the only possibility to gain further insight into the distributive consequences of an aging population. It turns out to be a thorny path to introduce some transparency to the policy debate.

After a conceptual clarification in the next section, some demographic facts and projections are presented in Section 3. The question of how an aging society might affect the dispersion of income will be taken up in Section 4. Using a highly stylized framework, the many potential interrelations are reduced to four separately treated, though of course related issues: Compositional effects, fiscal and institutional repercussions, optimizing responses and cohort-size effects, and current versus lifetime incidence. Section 5 concludes.

2. Population growth versus population aging

As opposed to the distributive repercussions of an aging population, the relation between population *growth* and income distribution constitutes an old issue in the economics literature. Classical writers like Malthus, Smith, and Ricardo were concerned with the depressing effect of rapid population growth on relative wages. Long theoretical debates tackled the question of how population growth might influence factor shares, and many empirical efforts have been undertaken to investigate the conjectured effects. [2] From today's perspective, this line of research has to overcome two problems before being able to say something about our focus of interest: the *inequality* of income. First, the studies are typically keyed to the distribution among factors of production; despite considerable research efforts, it is still a long way from shares of factors to the distribution of

---

[1] See the general surveys by Lam (1987, Lam (1992), Birdsall (1988), and Pestieau (1989).

[2] The interested reader is referred to the reviews of Rodgers (1978, Rodgers (1983), Kuznets (1980), Lee (1987), Lam (1987, Lam (1992), or Heerink (1994).

income among persons. Secondly, population growth alters the distribution in two ways: It changes relative wages, at the same time, however, it changes the composition of the population. The ensuing difficulty of separating pure compositional from real welfare effects is a standard problem in this area. As will be shown below, it is also of central importance when considering the distributive implications of an aging population.

From a worldwide perspective, population growth (related to poverty and hunger) may be considered to be the more pressing issue. In the developed countries, however, it is population *aging* that has become a dominant policy issue.[3] What is the difference? Doesn't slower population growth imply an older age structure, thus linking the two concepts in a consistent way? Though there are demographic constellations where this is true, the alleged relation between population growth and population aging is not, in general, that simple.

The stable population model has been the main device to gain insight into the determinants of population aging. Focusing on long-term impacts it turns out that fertility and mortality have rather divergent effects on the age composition. Fertility shows a pivoting pattern, having a large positive effect on the shares of the very young age groups and a declining impact on less young age groups, turning to a negative effect from (about) previous mean age onwards. The impact of mortality on the age structure is more intricate due to its combined effects on the stable rate of natural increase and the survival rates, starting with a negative impact on very young age groups that changes its strength and direction in a non-linear way at higher ages.[4]

Thus, whether slower population growth is caused by a decline of fertility or an increase of mortality makes quite a difference for the age structure. Moreover, as pointed out by Lam (1986) and Lam (1987), once you allow for differential fertility rates across income groups, a reduction in the fertility of high-income groups will have a very different effect on age composition and income inequality from a general fertility decline for all income groups that produces the same change in the population growth rate. It becomes clear from these observations that there can be no simple mapping of the population growth rate onto changes in the age distribution, or vice versa.

A further misunderstanding may also be noted here. Population aging cannot, in general, be attributed to high or low *levels* of fertility or mortality. As long as the demographic regimes have been in place long enough (a span of two or three generations is typically sufficient), the age composition of a population will be fixed whatever levels of fertility or mortality apply. This classic lesson[5] is

---

[3] See the large number of NBER-studies in the economics of aging edited by David A. Wise, e.g. (Wise, 1994).

[4] See Heerink (1994, Ch. 6) and, for the non-stable case, Preston et al. (1989) for further details.

[5] Euler (1760), Lotka (1907), Lotka (1922).

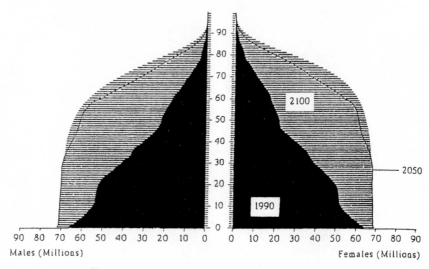

Fig. 1. Age structure of world population 1990, 2050, 2100.

Assumptions:
- Target year for replacement fertility level: (total fertility rate = 2.13) 2050
- Form of fertility decline: Hyperbolic
- Mortality level: Medium
Source: Birg (1995).

overlooked by those who assume that populations with below-replacement fertility are necessarily aging populations. Persistent *deceleration* in the rate of growth of births is required to produce an older population.

By the same token, when discussing the possible age structure impact of immigration, [6] it is not immigration per se that affects population aging, rather it is *changes* in immigration rates. A large inflow of younger people will not affect the rate of population aging, unless it is a new event; but, the disappearance of what had been a persistent influx of younger people will increase the rate of population aging.

3. Demographic facts and projections

In many regions of the world – a notable exception is Africa – the populations are growing older (United Nations, 1985; OECD, 1995). Fig. 1 depicts the age structure of the world population in 1990, 2050, and 2100, manifesting the

---

[6] This is an important issue, e.g., in Germany; see the interesting paper by Steinmann (1993).

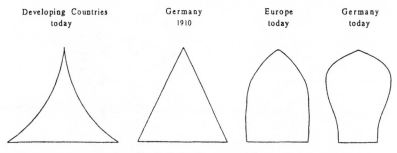

Fig. 2. Stylized age pyramids.

enormous momentum of overall population development and the implied expected changes in the shares of all age groups. [7]

The impressive aggregate demographic picture disguises regional differences which are large and important for the fiscal and distributional implications of an aging society. A stylized representation of the aging process, pointing at some relation between population growth, population aging, and economic development, is given in Fig. 2. The age pyramid of today's developing countries is thus characterized by a broad basis (high fertility) and concave flanks (relatively low life expectancy). An increasing life expectancy with no change in fertility will fill the flanks until a triangular form is reached. A continuation of this process will lead to a bell-shaped age composition. Once fertility starts declining, as is the case in the industrialized world, the pyramid constricts at the basis and becomes urn-shaped (low fertility and high life expectancy), as projected for, e.g., Germany. The prospective shift in the age structure of the German population constitutes a drastic example indeed of a shrinking and aging society – see Fig. 3. [8]

Tables 1 and 2 present some aggregate indicators for the major seven OECD countries. All of these countries will experience a rapid aging of the population during the first half of the next century. The combined impact of increased life expectancy and declined fertility will raise the proportion of the population aged 65 and over from 12.2 percent in 1990 to 19.5 percent in 2030 in the US, from 11.4 percent (1990) to 20 percent (2030) in Japan, and from 15.5 percent (1990) to 25.8 percent (2030) in Germany. At the same time, sharp falls are projected for the share of the working-age population in the course of the next three decades in Japan, Germany, and Italy, and moderate falls in France, the United Kingdom, and Canada. Moreover, the labour force itself will also be aging.

---

[7] The figure is taken from Birg (1995) and is based on a 'medium' projection variant. See in addition, United Nations (1993) and World Bank (1994).

[8] According to Birg and Flöthmann (1993, p. 97), allowing for immigration will render the demographic change in Germany only slightly less dramatic.

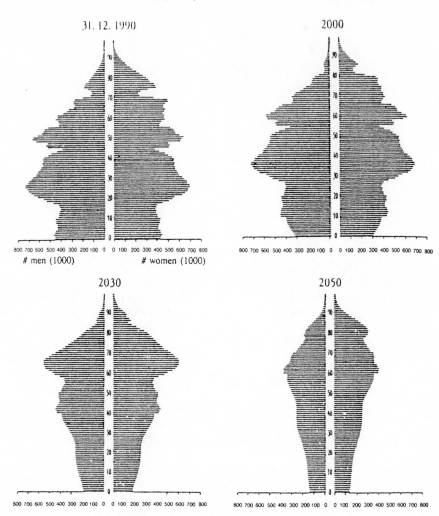

Fig. 3. Population age structure in Germany, 1990–2050.

Assumption: Fertility and mortality constant at 1990 level.
Source: Birg (1994).

Old-age dependency ratios will climb up to 0.44 (Germany), and elderly dependency ratios [9] are expected almost to double by around 2030 to 2040 before stabilizing or falling slightly. In Japan, Germany, and France, elderly dependency ratios are projected to peak at 0.6 and in Italy at over 0.7, while the peak for the

---

[9] Here, the working-age population is defined as from age 20 to legislated retirement age (as opposed to the standard definition of 15–64 years).

Table 1
Population aged 65 and over

	(%)			
	1900	1950	1990	2030
Canada	5.1	7.7	11.4	22.4
France	8.2	11.4	13.8	21.8
Germany	4.9	9.4	15.5	25.8
Italy	–	8.0	13.8	21.9
Japan	–	5.2	11.4	20.0
United Kingdom	4.7	10.7	15.1	19.2
United States	4.1	8.1	12.2	19.5

Source: OECD (1988, OECD (1995).

United States, the United Kingdom, and Canada will be around 0.4 to 0.5. [10] Note that the prospective change in the ratio of retirees to workers, a ratio that is closer to the fiscal problems entailed by the aging process, is even worse, particularly in Germany where it is expected to approach 1 by 2030.

4. Age composition and income inequality

4.1. Intra- versus intergenerational incidence: Compositional effects

The effects of a changing age structure on the current distribution of income have been studied by a number of authors. [11] The empirical findings underline the importance of the demographic shift. However, the results have been mixed in one important respect: there is quite a confusion regarding the *overall* distributional impact of an aging society. The following stylized set-up gives a first indication why this may be so.

Consider a population consisting of two groups: workers and pensioners. Net earnings of worker j, Y_j, are given by

$$Y_j = (1 - c) A_j, \quad 0 < c < 1, A_j > 0, \tag{1}$$

where c denotes the rate of contributions to the state pension fund [12] and A_j

---

[10] OECD (1995).

[11] Lydall (1968) stressed the importance of age composition, but it was the empirical work of Paglin (1975), not undisputed, that set off a series of studies. See, e.g., Danziger et al. (1977), Winegarden (1978), Repetto (1978), Blinder (1980), Morley (1981), Schultz (1981), Mookherjee and Shorrocks (1982), Cowell (1984), Lam (1987, Lam (1992), Formby et al. (1989), von Weizsäcker (1989), Heerink (1994), Klevmarken (1994), Ermisch (1994), and Jenkins (1994).

[12] For expositional reasons, other redistribution systems are ignored.

Table 2
Old-age dependency ratios

| | Population aged 65 + /Population aged 15–64 | | |
	1990	2010	2030
Canada	16.8	21.4	37.3
France	20.9	24.5	35.8
Germany	22.3	30.6	43.6
Italy	20.1	25.7	35.3
Japan	16.2	29.5	31.9
United Kingdom	23.0	22.3	31.1
United States	18.5	18.8	31.7

Source: OECD (1988, 1995).

marks gross earnings of worker j. Pensioner i's retirement income, P_i, is specified as

$$P_i = p\mu_A L_i, \quad 0 < p < 1, \ L_i > 0, \tag{2}$$

where p is the retirement benefit rate, μ_A the average gross earnings of the working population, and L_i the pension claim basis for retiree i (which is typically linked to his earnings history and his number of insurance years). Eq. (2) is based on pension formulas currently used in a number of nations. In particular, it reflects the built-in flexibility of state pensions increasing in line with gross earnings per worker.

To move from the micro level characterized by (1) and (2) to the macro level, i.e. to the population as a whole and thus to the *distribution* of individual incomes, we have to aggregate across all j's and i's. For illustrative purposes, the present study concentrates on the first two central moments, indicating per capita income (μ) and the variance of income (σ^2). The latter may be expressed as [13]

$$\sigma^2 = \underbrace{x\sigma_Y^2 + (1-x)\sigma_P^2}_{\text{intra}} + \underbrace{x(1-x)(\mu_Y - \mu_P)^2}_{\text{inter}}. \tag{3}$$

The distributional influence of an aging population is captured by $x: = E/(E+R)$ $= 1/(1+\theta)$, which is a monotonically decreasing function of the *old-age dependency ratio* $\theta: = R/E$, the ratio of the number of retirees R to the number of active workers E. The dispersion of income of the total population is thus

---

[13] Note that (3) [or (5)] is based on a moment aggregation over *population subgroups*, which is not to be confounded with a moment calculation of the sum of correlated random variables as met, e.g., in an inequality decomposition by *income components* [like (10)]. See Theil (1967, Ch. 4.A), Shorrocks (1980), Shorrocks (1984), or Lam (1986).

decomposed in an intra- and intergenerational component. The impact of an older age structure is obtained as

$$
\frac{d\sigma^2}{d\theta} = \underbrace{(\sigma_Y^2 - \sigma_P^2)\frac{dx}{d\theta}}_{\text{intra-effect } (<0)} + \underbrace{(1 - 2x)(\mu_Y - \mu_P)^2\frac{dx}{d\theta}}_{\text{inter-effect } (>0)}.
$$

$$(4)$$

If the number of workers exceeds the number of retirees, i.e. $E > R \geq 0$ (or $\frac{1}{2} < x \leq 1$), and provided that the variance of net earnings of the working population is greater than the variance of retirement incomes, i.e. $\sigma_Y^2 > \sigma_P^2$ – an empirical constellation met in most industrialized countries – then an aging society yields two *conflicting* signals: The *intra*generational component of income dispersion goes down, and the *inter*generational component goes up. This constitutes one of the sources of confusion. Others will be identified in the next sections. The reader may already envisage here the problems of drawing firm conclusions about the distributive role of a shifting age structure.

Opposing demographic effects of this kind are also revealed by measures of *relative* dispersion, i.e. by measures of inequality. In fact, as long as the specific inequality-indicator at hand is a member of the Generalized Entropy family [14] and hence, among other things, additively decomposable by population subgroups, it is possible, in principle, to derive analytical results similar to (4).

From the first two moments μ and σ^2 one may determine the squared coefficient of variation $V^2 := \sigma^2/\mu^2$, for example, which is a member of that family, and check for the conditions of a well-defined *overall* sign. From

$$
V^2 = V_{\text{intra}}^2 + V_{\text{inter}}^2 ,
$$

$$
V_{\text{intra}}^2 = x\frac{\mu_Y^2}{\mu^2}V_Y^2 + (1 - x)\frac{\mu_P^2}{\mu^2}V_P^2 ,
$$

$$
V_{\text{inter}}^2 = \frac{x(1 - x)}{\mu^2}(\mu_Y - \mu_P)^2
$$

$$(5)$$

it can be shown that $E > R$ and $\mu_Y \geq (1 + 1/x)\mu_P$ is a sufficient – and in many cases empirically corroborated – condition for the overall effect to be positive, i.e. for $dV^2/d\theta > 0$. [15] Thus, under fairly weak conditions, aging *increases* inequality.

Note that the change in aggregate dispersion is caused by a pure *compositional* effect; all economic variables have been held fixed. This has to be borne in mind when trying to draw any normative inferences from the empirical evidence.

---

[14] Cf. Bourguignon (1979), Cowell (1980, Cowell (1995), Shorrocks (1980), and Shorrocks (1984). See also Jenkins (1991).

[15] See von Weizsäcker (1995) for further details.

4.2. Fiscal and institutional repercussions: Budget incidence

There is more to come beyond simple compositional shifts. Indeed, an aging society does not only affect relative population shares, it also changes *relative incomes*. Regarding the latter, one important channel is created by the demographically sensitive government budget.

In all industrialized countries projected population aging is likely to put significant fiscal pressure on public old-age insurance and health-care systems. According to a recent OECD study, future demographic changes are indeed the major source of generational imbalances. [16] Restricting our attention to the demographic incidence of the pension budget, we may continue our stylized investigation by stating the standard accounting equation for a pay-as-you-go financed state pension scheme:

$$\sum_{j=1}^{E} cA_j = \sum_{i=1}^{R} P_i.$$ (6)

For (6) to hold in light of an aging society, the two principal policy options are raising the contribution rate, or lowering pension payments. Both kind of adjustments induce *indirect* demographic inequality effects which distort the cross-sectional picture above and beyond the direct impact depicted in the previous section. These effects may be critical to the conclusions drawn.

If the pension budget is balanced by a variation of the contribution rate c, this will be endogenously determined by $c_{BB} = \theta \mu_P / \mu_A$, so that $V_{BB}^2 = V^2 [\theta, c_{BB}(\theta)]$. The incidence of an increasing population share of retirees is then captured by

$$\frac{dV_{BB}^2}{d\theta} = \underbrace{\frac{\partial V^2}{\partial \theta}}_{>0} + \underbrace{\underbrace{\frac{\partial V^2}{\partial c_{BB}}}_{<0} \underbrace{\frac{dc_{BB}}{d\theta}}_{>0}}_{<0}.$$ (7)

If, on the other hand, the retirement benefit rate is adapted, we have $p_{BB} = (1/\theta)$ $\cdot (c/\mu_L)$ and $V_{BB}^2 = V^2 [\theta, p_{BB}(\theta)]$, such that

$$\frac{dV_{BB}^2}{d\theta} = \underbrace{\frac{\partial V^2}{\partial \theta}}_{>0} + \underbrace{\underbrace{\frac{\partial V^2}{\partial p_{BB}}}_{<0} \underbrace{\frac{dp_{BB}}{d\theta}}_{<0}}_{>0} > 0.$$ (8)

---

[16] OECD (1995). As for the German economy, featuring one of the most rapid aging processes in the world, see in particular the profound paper by Börsch-Supan (1994).

The additional aging effects in (7) and (8) have *opposite* signs. Whether the indirect effect in (7) is strong enough to produce an overall negative sign is an empirical question. [17] For Germany, e.g., these conditions are clearly met, i.e. we have $dV_{BB}^2/d\theta < 0$ for a contribution rate adjustment, and $dV_{BB}^2/d\theta > 0$ for a benefit rate adjustment.

In other words, fundamental policy decisions responding to the solvency problems caused by an aging population may induce *contrary* demographic inequality effects. Note that, whichever adjustment policy is chosen, the additional inequality impact results from a purely *fiscal* reaction to disturbances of budget equilibrium, not from any redistributional reaction to changes in the personal distribution of incomes. This constitutes another obstacle to a meaningful interpretation of the empirical evidence.

The institutional design of the pension formula decisively drives the relation between demographics and inequality. This insight offers some intriguing *politico-economic* aspects. As long as the question of intergenerational burden division has no well-founded basis, the political need for redistribution, as derived typically from cross-sectional information (adequate longitudinal data are still missing and, above all, the lifetime view does not seem politically viable as a standard of distributional analysis [18]), is subject to the whim and will of policymakers, since the empirical inequality picture can be manipulated in both directions through the continuous transition from a contribution to a benefit rate adjustment. If the current distribution is an important determinant of reelection strategies, then demographic incidence effects like (7) or (8) may prejudice plans for an overdue old-age insurance reform. Moreover, the fact that an aging society changes not only the financial relations of a state pension scheme (or public health-care system) but also the relative number of votes cast by workers and pensioners, may put conventional conclusions drawn from simple accounting equations in a different light. Factors like political power distribution enter the stage, alongside population aging and institutional constraints.

4.3. Optimizing responses and cohort-size effects

There is another kind of demographically caused fiscal repercussion: *disincentive reactions* of income- or utility-maximizing individuals. Given our exploratory framework, potential implications for the distribution of income may be illustrated as follows.

Allowing for optimizing responses makes labour income A_j an endogenous variable: $A_j = A_j(c)$. Considering the usual case of contribution rate adjustment

---

[17] Precise conditions are given in von Weizsäcker (1995).
[18] Cf. Barthold (1993).

entails in budgetary equilibrium: $A_{j,BB} = A_j[c_{BB}(\theta)]$, or $Y_{j,BB} = [1 - c_{BB}(\theta)] \cdot A_j[c_{BB}(\theta)]$. Taking into account the institutional dynamics of retirement incomes [μ_A in (2)], we also have $P_{i,BB} = P_i[c_{BB}(\theta)]$. Given these feedbacks, intricate additional demo-economic inequality effects result (for illustrative purposes and to simplify matters, we stick to the variance decomposition):

$$
\frac{d\sigma^2_{BB}}{d\theta} = \left[\sigma^2_{Y,BB} - \sigma^2_{P,BB} + x \underbrace{\frac{\partial \sigma^2_{Y,BB}}{\partial c_{BB}} \frac{dc_{BB}}{dx}}_{>0} + (1-x) \underbrace{\frac{\partial \sigma^2_{P,BB}}{\partial c_{BB}} \frac{dc_{BB}}{dx}}_{>0} \right] \underbrace{\frac{dx}{d\theta}}_{<0}
$$

$$
+ \left[(1 - 2x)(\mu_{Y,BB} - \mu_{P,BB})^2 + 2x(1 - x)(\mu_{Y,BB} - \mu_{P,BB}) \right.
$$

$$
\left. \times \left(\underbrace{\frac{\partial \mu_{Y,BB}}{\partial c_{BB}} \frac{dc_{BB}}{dx}}_{>0} - \underbrace{\frac{\partial \mu_{P,BB}}{\partial c_{BB}} \frac{dc_{BB}}{dx}}_{>0} \right) \right] \underbrace{\frac{dx}{d\theta}}_{<0} . \tag{9}
$$

$$
\underbrace{}_{>0 \text{ (for most cases)}}
$$

Since disincentive reactions involve modifications not only of the distribution of net incomes but also of gross incomes, all moments in (3) are affected. An aging society ($\theta \uparrow$) causes c_{BB} to rise, which in turn lowers gross and net incomes so that the additional terms [as compared to (4)] of the intra- [first line of (9)] and intergenerational effects [second and third line of (9)] tend to be *negative*. This identifies an interesting *demographic-fiscal* channel of maximizing responses which is quite different in character and sign from the usual result in the theory of personal income distribution that optimizing reactions tend to *increase* inequality. [19]

Another important demographic impact on relative incomes results from *cohort-size effects*. A number of empirical investigations have indeed revealed that individual age-income profiles are not independent of the age composition of the population – apparently because younger and older workers are imperfect substitutes in production. [20] What does this imply for the overall incidence of an aging society?

An alteration of individual age-income profiles triggered by changes in the

---

[19] See von Weizsäcker (1993, Ch. IV.2) and von Weizsäcker (1994) for further details.

[20] See, e.g., Freeman (1979), Stapleton and Young (1984), Dooley and Gottschalk (1984), Berger (1985, Berger (1989), Ben-Porath (1988), Lam (1989), Burtless (1990), Katz and Murphy (1992), and Klevmarken (1993).

population age structure entails a direct demographic effect on income dispersion since aggregation is based on individual life cycles. At the same time, this effect retroacts upon the micro level by its impact on government budget equilibrium: Fiscal instruments become functions of the mean slope of individual income profiles *as well as* functions of demographic variables related to the working-age distribution; allowing for incentive reactions, this involves modifications not only of the distribution of net incomes but also of gross incomes. Thus, demographic shifts again interfere with the process of income formation, opening up yet another channel of demographic disparity bearings. Except for highly stylized cases, the additional complexities caused by the sensitivity of age-specific incomes to the relative sizes of age groups force a resort to numerical simulations. [21] No *general* cross-section result can be given. For future research, this suggests a closer demo-economic examination of the life-cycle profile of within-cohort inequality, i.e. a truly dynamic cohort approach. [22]

The interactions outlined above may even go one step further when considering the findings of the *endogenous fertility* literature, [23] rendering the age structure itself an economically determined variable $[\rightarrow \theta = \theta(c)]$. Conceptually, this complication undermines any positive or normative conclusion drawn so far.

4.4. Current versus lifetime income incidence

What about the *lifetime* perspective? Does this level of aggregation avoid the demographic interference encountered in the preceding sections?

Contrary to the widely held belief that the distribution of lifetime income (as opposed to the distribution of current income) remains largely unaffected by changes in the population age structure, the mechanism of the pension formula as well as optimizing responses by workers and/or the government – to give just two forces – lead to demographic distortions also of lifetime inequality.

Implementing the lifetime approach requires making some stringent assumptions, of course. Going on from the above descriptive set-up and ignoring discounting, lifetime income W of individual j may be expressed as: $W_j = Y_j + P_j$, where $Y_j = (1 - c)A_j$ and $P_j = p\mu_{A_+}L_j$ (μ_{A_+} indicates average gross earnings one

---

[21] Cf. von Weizsäcker (1993). It may nevertheless be noted that empirical studies for the *U.S.* suggest that labour supply effects associated with fluctuations in age composition play a substantial role for the increase in earnings inequality during the 1980's (though shifts in labour demand seem to have played an even bigger one) – see Levy and Murnane (1992), and Danziger and Gottschalk (1993).

[22] See in this context the promising work of Deaton and Paxson (1994a), Deaton and Paxson (1994b).

[23] See, e.g., Nerlove et al. (1987), Becker (1988) or Becker and Barro (1988). Cf. also the stimulating work of Lam (1986), Lam (1987), and Lam (1992).

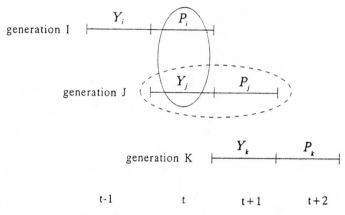

Fig. 4. Current versus lifetime perspective.

period up); see also Fig. 4. Again considering the squared coefficient of variation for purposes of illustration, we arrive at

$$V_W^2 = \frac{\sigma_W^2}{\mu_W^2} = z^2 V_Y^2 + (1 - z)^2 V_P^2 + 2z(1 - z)V_Y V_P \varrho_{YP}, \tag{10}$$

where

$$z = \frac{(1 - c)\mu_A}{(1 - c)\mu_A + p\mu_{A_+}\mu_L},$$

and $\varrho_{YP}(> 0)$ denotes the correlation coefficient of net labour and retirement incomes. The old-age dependency ratio θ – and hence the demographic change – enters z via the contribution rate c or the benefit rate p, depending on the prevailing pension formula. Though the direct effect of shifting relative population shares, i.e. the pure compositional effect of an aging society indeed disappears: $dV_W^2/d\theta = 0$, all other demo-economic channels known from the preceding deliberations survive to the lifetime level: $dV_{W,BB}^2/d\theta \neq 0$.

A final remark in this context. Changes in the age composition also play a decisive part in an important *inconsistency* issue: As mentioned before, due to scarce empirical information on lifetime income disparity and due to politico-economic reasons, policy measures designed for achieving a more even distribution of income are typically oriented towards the current distribution. The crucial question then is whether distributional policy decisions made on this basis are generally compatible with those which would have been made on the basis of the distribution of lifetime income (which may be considered as the normatively superior incidence level). The answer is no, for there can be situations where a certain policy action successfully reduces current inequality, while at the same time it alters the allocation plans of optimizing individuals in such a way that lifetime inequality systematically rises. The main reason for this inconsistency is to be found in the aggregation function of the population age structure, assigning to each intra-cohort policy effect (across all income levels) its relative weight in the aggregate policy impact on current inequality. [24]

5. Conclusion

The main objective of this paper has been to sketch some of the potential effects of an aging society on economic inequality. Given the complex nature of demographic incidence, there seems to be no easy answer to the starting question: "Does an aging population increase inequality?" Policymakers face a difficult problem when trying to interpret the empirical evidence. An aging society produces simultaneous shifts in both population shares and relative incomes, interacting in numerous intricate ways. The available data today are too limited within and across generations for a refined multivariate analysis that could provide the required disentangling information.

To understand at least partially how the observed relationships may have been generated, a highly stylized framework has been applied for the identification of some basic demo-economic interactions. The analysis reveals that even at this level of structural simplicity there is a substantial danger of *underrating* the distributional significance of an aging population. Without a proper understanding of the demographic component, however, no normative inferences can be drawn from changing inequality and no meaningful policy recommendation can be given. Theoretical and, in particular, intensive empirical research into the distributive repercussions of an aging society (including a careful collection of appropriate data) is very much needed.

Acknowledgements

Portions of this paper were presented at the Universities of Bonn, Halle, Mannheim, and Munich, the London School of Economics, the University of Bergen, Tilburg University, the European Science Foundation Conference 'Economics of Aging' in Barcelona, and the EEA Congress in Prague. I am grateful to the participants for helpful suggestions and to the German National Science Foundation for financial support.

---

[24] See von Weizsäcker (1994).

References

Barthold, T.A., 1993, How should we measure distribution?, National Tax Journal 46, 291-299.

Becker, G.S., 1988, Family economics and macro behavior, American Economic Review 78, 1-13.

Becker, G.S. and R.J. Barro, 1988, A reformulation of the economic theory of fertility, Quarterly Journal of Economics 103, 1-25.

Ben-Porath, Y., 1988, Market, government, and Israel's muted baby boom, in: R.D. Lee et al., eds., Economics of changing age distributions in developed countries (Clarendon Press, Oxford) 12-38.

Berger, M.C., 1985, The effect of cohort size on earnings growth: A reexamination of the evidence, Journal of Political Economy 93, 561-573.

Berger, M.C., 1989, Demographic cycles, cohort size, and earnings, Demography 26, 311-321.

Birdsall, N., 1988, Economic approaches to population growth, in: H. Chenery and T.N. Srinivasan, eds., Handbook of development economics (North-Holland, Amsterdam) 478-542.

Birg, H., 1994, Perspektiven des globalen Bevölkerungswachstums: Ursachen, Folgen, Handlungskonsequenzen, in: F. Nuscheler and E. Fürlinger, eds., Weniger Menschen durch weniger Armut? (Verlag Anton Pustet, München).

Birg, H., 1995, World population projections for the 21st century: Theoretical interpretations and quantitative simulations (St. Martins Press, New York).

Birg, H. and E.-J. Flöthmann, 1993, Entwicklung der Familienstrukturen und ihre Auswirkungen auf die Belastungs- bzw. Transferquotienten zwischen den Generationen (Institut für Bevölkerungsforschung, Universität Bielefeld, Bielefeld).

Blinder, A.S., 1980, The level and distribution of economic well-being, in: M. Feldstein, ed., The American economy in transition (University of Chicago Press, Chicago, IL) Ch. 6.

Börsch-Supan, A., 1994, The consequences of population aging for growth and savings, in: A.L. Bovenberg and C. van Ewijk, eds., Lecture notes on pensions and aging, Forthcoming.

Bourguignon, F., 1979, Decomposable income inequality measures, Econometrica 47, 901-920.

Burtless, G., 1990, Earnings inequality over the business and demographic cycles, in: G. Burtless, ed., A future of lousy jobs? (The Brookings Institution, Washington, DC) 77-122.

Cowell, F.A., 1980, On the structure of additive inequality measures, Review of Economic Studies 47, 521-531.

Cowell, F.A., 1984, The structure of American income inequality, Review of Income and Wealth 30, 351-375.

Cowell, F.A., 1995, Measuring inequality, 2nd edition (Prentice Hall, London).

Danziger, S., R. Haveman and E. Smolensky, 1977, The measurement and trend of inequality: Comment, American Economic Review 67, 505-512.

Danziger, S. and P. Gottschalk, eds., 1993, Uneven tides: Rising inequality in America (Russell Sage Foundation, New York).

Deaton, A.S. and C.H. Paxson, 1994a, Intertemporal choice and inequality, Journal of Political Economy 102, 437-467.

Deaton, A.S. and C.H. Paxson, 1994b, Saving, inequality, and aging: An East Asian perspective, Mimeo. (Princeton University, Princeton, NJ).

Dooley, M.D. and P. Gottschalk, 1984, Earnings inequality among males in the United States: Trends and the effect of labor force growth, Journal of Political Economy 92, 59-89.

Ermisch, J., 1994, Changing demography and income distribution, Mimeo. (Department of Political Economy, University of Glasgow, Glasgow).

Euler, L., 1760, Recherches générales sur la mortalité et la multiplication, Mémoires de l'Académie Royale des Sciences et Belles Lettres 16, 144-164.

Formby, J.P., T.G. Seaks and W.J. Smith, 1989, On the measurement and trend of inequality: A reconsideration, American Economic Review 79, 256-264.

Freeman, R.B., 1979, The effect of demographic factors on age-earnings profiles, Journal of Human Resources 14, 289-318.

Heerink, N., 1994, Population growth, income distribution, and economic development (Springer-Verlag, Berlin).

Jenkins, S.P., 1991, The measurement of income inequality, in: L. Osberg, ed., Economic inequality and poverty: International perspectives (M.E. Sharpe, London) 3–38.

Jenkins, S.P., 1994, Accounting for inequality trends: Decomposition analyses for the UK, 1971–86, Economica 61.

Katz, L.F. and K.M. Murphy, 1992, Changes in relative wages, 1963–1987: Supply and demand factors, Quarterly Journal of Economics 107, 35–78.

Klevmarken, N.A., 1993, Demographics and the dynamics of earnings, Journal of Population Economics 6, 105–122.

Klevmarken, N.A., 1994, The impact of demographic changes on the income distribution: Experiments in microsimulation, Mimeo. (Department of Economics, Uppsala University, Uppsala).

Kuznets, S., 1980, Recent population trends in less developed countries and implications for internal income inequality, in: R. Easterlin, ed., Population and economic change in developing countries (University of Chicago Press, Chicago, IL) 471–515.

Lam, D., 1986, The dynamics of population growth, differential fertility, and inequality, American Economic Review 76, 1103–1116.

Lam, D., 1987, Distribution issues in the relationship between population growth and economic development, in: D.G. Johnson and R.D. Lee, eds., Population growth and economic development: Issues and evidence (University of Wisconsin Press, Madison, WI) Ch. 15.

Lam, D., 1989, Population growth, age structure, and age-specific productivity, Journal of Population Economics 2, 189–210.

Lam, D., 1992, Demographic variables and income inequality, Mimeo. (University of Michigan, Ann Arbor, MI).

Lee, R.D., 1987, Population dynamics of humans and other animals, Demography 24, 443–465.

Levy, F. and R.J. Murnane, 1992, U.S. earnings levels and earnings inequality: A review of recent trends and proposed explanations, Journal of Economic Literature 30, 1333–1381.

Lotka, A.J., 1907, Relation between birth and death rates, Science, N.S. 26, 21–22.

Lotka, A.J., 1922, The stability of the normal age distribution, Proceedings of the National Academy of Sciences 8, 339–345.

Lydall, H.F., 1968, The structure of earnings (Oxford University Press, Oxford).

Mookherjee, D. and A.F. Shorrocks, 1982, A decomposition analysis of the trend in UK income inequality, Economic Journal 92, 886–902.

Morley, S.A., 1981, The effect of changes in the population on several measures of income distribution, American Economic Review 71, 285–294.

Nerlove, M., A. Razin and E. Sadka, 1987, Household and economy: Welfare economics of endogenous fertility (Academic Press, New York).

OECD, 1988, Ageing populations: The social policy implications (OECD, Paris).

OECD, 1995, Effects of ageing populations on government budgets, in: OECD Economic Outlook 57, 33–42.

Paglin, M., 1975, The measurement and trend of inequality: A basic revision, American Economic Review 65, 598–609.

Pestieau, P., 1989, The demographics of inequality, Journal of Population Economics 2, 3–24.

Preston, S.H., C. Himes and M. Eggers, 1989, Demographic conditions responsible for population aging, Demography 26, 691–704.

Repetto, R., 1978, The interaction of fertility and the size distribution of income, Journal of Development Studies 14, 22–39.

Rodgers, G.B., 1978, Demographic determinants of the distribution of income, World Development 6, 305–318.

Rodgers, G.B., 1983, Population growth, inequality, and poverty, International Labour Review 122, 443–460.

Schultz, T.P., 1981, Age of individuals and family composition as factors underlying the distribution of personal income, Discussion paper no. 383 (Department of Economics, Yale University, New Haven, CT).

Shorrocks, A.F., 1980, The class of additively decomposable inequality measures, Econometrica 48, 613–625.

Shorrocks, A.F., 1984, Inequality decomposition by population subgroups, Econometrica 52, 1369–1386.

Stapleton, D.C. and D.J. Young, 1984, The effects of demographic change on the distribution of wages, 1967–1990, Journal of Human Resources 19, 175–201.

Steinmann, G., 1993, Zusammenhang zwischen Alterungsprozeβ und Einwanderung, Mimeo. (Institut für Bevölkerungsökonomie, Universität Halle-Wittenberg, Halle).

Theil, H., 1967, Economics and information theory (North-Holland, Amsterdam).

United Nations, 1985, World population prospects: Estimates and projections as assessed in 1982, Population studies no. 86 (United Nations Publications, New York).

United Nations, 1993, World population prospects: The 1992 revision (United Nations, New York).

von Weizsäcker, R.K., 1989, Demographic change and income distribution, European Economic Review 33, 377–388.

von Weizsäcker, R.K., 1993, Bevölkerungsentwicklung, Rentenfinanzierung und Einkommensverteilung (Springer-Verlag, Berlin).

von Weizsäcker, R.K., 1994, Educational choice, lifetime earnings inequality, and conflicts of public policy, Discussion paper no. 1014 (CEPR, London).

von Weizsäcker, R.K., 1995, Public pension reform, demographics, and inequality, Journal of Population Economics 8, 205–221.

Winegarden, C.R., 1978, A simultaneous-equations model of population growth and income distribution, Applied Economics 10, 319–330.

Wise, D.A., ed., 1994, Studies in the economics of aging (University of Chicago Press, Chicago, IL).

World Bank, 1994, World population projections, 1993–94 edition (Baltimore and London).

AGING AND ECONOMICS: A COMPARATIVE EXAMINATION OF RESPONSES BY THE UNITED STATES, GREAT BRITAIN AND JAPAN

by Laurence Barton, Pennsylvania State University Graduate Center at Great Valley

Introduction

The process of aging has been called many things, but almost never is it referred to as pleasant. In large measure this is because the process of growing older is disproportionately shaped by three factors regardless of citizenship:

1. our individual quality of health

2. our financial status

3. our support mechanisms, such as children and family members.

This article focuses upon a variety of factors that influence policies for the aged in three economies, namely the United States, England and Japan. The goal is to determine where differences exist in government policies, in social programmes and in our collective ability to help those nearing or in retirement stages of life.

Comparisons

Any comparison of welfare policies for the aged in the newly industrialised economies of Asia and more mature economies is unfair because mature economies have worked for decades to develop responses to the issues discussed in this article. That does not mean they have always been successful, however. Emerging economies such as Singapore, Korea and Thailand can learn from models in the US, Britain and Japan, and these mature economies can learn from the important policy questions that are now being raised, especially in Asia where new degrees of affluence are creating the need for significant new policies for older workers. Indeed, no major economy, including highly-praised efforts in Sweden, are perfect.

Each country has problems in financing support for older persons. Most have occasional financial short- falls. And all appear to be ill-prepared for the growing size of the aging population within their borders.

Shared Characteristics: US, England and Japan

Although each of the three governments studied "headquarters" welfare programmes for the aged in different government agencies and departments, there is some commonality among the responses to the welfare policies. They are summarised below:

• Each of the governments has designated one or more agencies to study and launch welfare programmes. In the US, for example, the largest concentration of government officials who support the aged exist in the Social Security Administration. In Japan, three different agencies oversee programmes for the aged. In England, at least four agencies have such responsibilities.

None of these three countries has turned these functions over to privatised companies or sub-contractors. In large measure this is because retired persons constitute a sizeable voting influence who can sometimes elect or defeat a candidate who appears to be non-responsive to the needs of the aged. Turning welfare policies over to a private concern would probably be far more economical, but also give the appearance that government does not care about its aged. On the other hand, the fact that these governments choose to directly support programmes through the tax system makes welfare programmes highly dependent upon national economic strength (eg. trade surpluses, rates of inflation, national debt). It is somewhat interesting to note that the largest, most stable pension fund in the world is the Teachers Insurance and Annuity Association (TIAA), based in New York City, with over three trillion US dollars under management. It is rated AAA by Moody's and Dun & Bradstreet and is a private, non-government concern. Welfare managers around the world often travel to meet the TIAA managers to determine how they are so successful at launching retirement and insurance programmes.

• In all three cases, the national government conducts an annual review of the budget allocated to welfare programmes for the aged. The US Congress, British House of Commons and Japanese Diet all conduct a formal review of the effectiveness of their efforts at least annually. In the US, an independent auditing arm (The Congressional Budget Office) actually audits the Social Security Administration to insure that its previous projections and calculations were accurate and that any assistance promised to the aged has been delivered.

• All three economies have established minimum standards for what a retired person should receive in terms of a fixed monthly payment in retirement. These figures are changing as the article is being written, but the minimum payment for an American worker with ten years (40 quarters) of contributions to the Social Security Fund is about $140 per month, increasing to as much as $908 or more per month for those with more years of contribution and no other income from private savings or corporate retirement accounts.

Current Issues: United States

In the United States, an astounding 52% of all federal spending is on programmes for entitlements, as indicated in Exhibit One. Of this, almost 40% is directed to the aged through Social Security, Medicare, retirement payments to federal workers and supplemental payments to the "poorest of the poor." Senior citizens have access to a wide variety of health care needs through government-subsidised Medicare, although many do not participate because of lack of education about the programme.

Many efforts to educate the aged about their welfare benefits exist: The American Association of Retired Persons (AARP) has 33 million Americans, the largest single organisation in the nation: it has considerable political power at the local, state and federal levels.

Health care reform in the United States could require that the federal government pay 80% of premiums for retirees aged 55-64, a provision that would cost $11.6 billion for the two year period

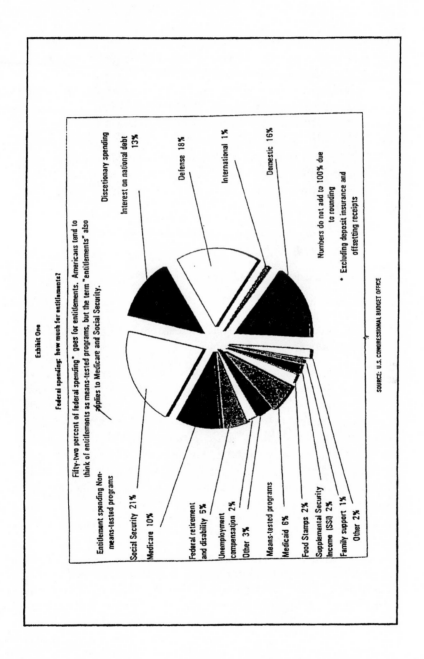

Exhibit One

Federal spending: how much for entitlements?

Fifty-two percent of federal spending* goes for entitlements. Americans tend to think of entitlements as means-tested programs, but the term "entitlements" also applies to Medicare and Social Security.

Discretionary spending

Interest on national debt 13%

Defense 18%

International 1%

Domestic 16%

Entitlement spending Non-means-tested programs

Social Security 21%

Medicare 10%

Federal retirement and disability 5%

Unemployment compensation 2%

Other 3%

Means-tested programs

Medicaid 6%

Food Stamps 2%

Supplemental Security Income (SSI) 2%

Family support 1%

Other 2%

Numbers do not add to 100% due to rounding

* Excluding deposit insurance and offsetting receipts

SOURCE: U.S. CONGRESSIONAL BUDGET OFFICE

1998-2000. The current administration has indicated that it will not change a major, popular feature of the Medicare programme which allows the aged over 65 to choose their health provider. Yet many elective surgeries costing more than $500 are not reimbursed, which drains the private savings of the aged. In 1991 the federal government set limits on fees for procedures, and many states such as New York limit doctors to not charging more than 10% above these ceilings. This poses a variety of challenges because the aged are the fastest-growing portion of the American population, the current 31 million Americans over age 65 will rise to 51 million by the year 2000. (Kline, 16)

To pay for their cost of living in retirement years, many Americans rely on three sources:

- Social Security and Medicare

- Private savings

- Retirement plans developed with employer and/or employee contributions.

The newest vehicle that has encouraged savings by the aged is the Individual Retirement Account (IRA), where each employee may contribute up to $2000 per year into a tax-deferred savings account; prudent investment in an aggressive mutual fund can earn 10-12% or more per year. In addition, "401k" plans established with employer contributions are very popular, but a new study finds that the majority of those nearing retirement have no idea how these funds are managed or even understand how they can transfer their monies. (Schachner, 5).

Great Britain

Unlike the United States and Japan, where a growing aged population is sure to strain the federal budget in the years ahead, a new study just completed in Great Britain suggests that the number of aged will actually drop and then increase only slightly after the year 2000. (Hills 5) More than 10 million British citizens are over the official retirement age (65 for men, 60 for women), constituting 18% of the population and 26% of all voters. And people are retiring earlier every year: *The Economist* (10/20/93, 66) concluded that only 54% of men aged 60-64 were still working in 1991.

The Hills study, prepared for the Joseph Rowntree Foundation, concludes that if pensions in Great Britain were linked to earnings, rather than to prices and inflation, spending on programmes for the aged would increase by five percent of the GDP over the next 40 years. Currently, retired men in Britain receive 15% of their earnings in retirement compared to 31% in the US and about 34% in Japan. The Hills report indicates that linking payments to prices will drop the British payments to just 7.5% of income but also save the national government 32 billion pounds; the alternative is to increase the basic income tax from 25 to 42%. Interestingly enough, although Great Britain probably has the most stable funding for retirement programmes in the entire Economic Community, the spending on benefits appears to be out of control, as evidenced in Exhibit Two, which includes spending for the aged unemployment and child care. These three major welfare programmes now exceed 70 billion pounds annually. In 1993, the aged were given a generous allowance in their taxes for the value-added tax on fuel, but it appears likely that the British will be required to restructure their entire funding mechanism for welfare policies for the aged in the next decade.

The British government is now close to implementing changes:

- The UK Department of Social Security seeks to raise the retirement age for women to obtain full benefits from 60 to 65; this will occur between the years 2010 and 2020.

- Employers who choose not to pay into the State Earnings Related Pension programme and instead provide a private pension may be simplified in an effort to encourage more employers to follow the American model of "401k" contributions.

- Ever since the European Court of Justice ruled on May 17, 1990 that British employers must pay equal retirement wages to men

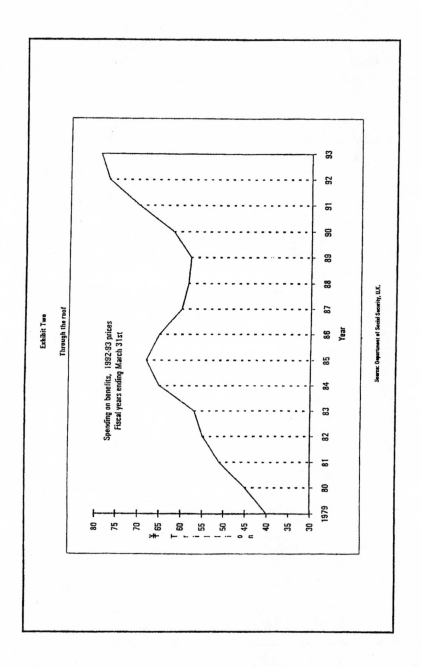

Exhibit Two

Through the roof

Spending on benefits, 1992-93 prices
Fiscal years ending March 31st

Source: Department of Social Security, U.K.

and women, a period of adjustment has created a short-fall in many pension plans.

Unlike the United States, where an incredibly large single organisation (AARP) represents the aged, more than 30 organisations exist in Great Britain: all pursue the same agenda and thus actually reduce the effectiveness of the aged to plead their agenda to government officials.

The Japanese Model is Changing, but not for the Better

The approach taken by the Japanese to assisting the aged is rapidly changing. For many generations, families were expected to support themselves in their retirement years through savings; this self-sufficiency approach triggered the single highest standard of savings in the world; whereas Americans save about 3.1% of all of their earnings, the Japanese figure is nearly double at 5.8%; the British ranking is 4.1%. Social Security expenditures in Japan have also risen at a considerable rate; Japan's skyrocketing costs are reflected in Exhibit Three. By 1989 these costs exceeded 39 trillion Yen, in 1994 they exceed 40 trillion Yen.

However, several notable changes are taking place in Japan; these changes are certain to place enormous strains on their budgetary outlook in the years ahead:

• The increase in the number of women who are demanding equal access to management positions will require that the Japanese Diet and courts change laws regarding equal compensation, which now exist in theory but which are not uniformly applied. As this change occurs, which it must because of an aging male population, women will also seek and secure access to lucrative retirement benefits.

• Only the French have a more serious demographics problem: the Japanese are getting older, more quicker, than any other industrialised nation. The percentage of Japanese over age 65 is now 16%; this increases to 26% by 2020.

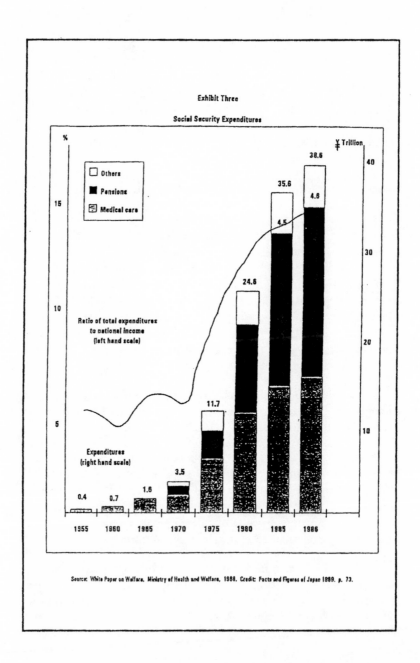

Exhibit Three

Social Security Expenditures

Source: White Paper on Welfare, Ministry of Health and Welfare, 1988. Credit: Facts and Figures of Japan 1989, p. 73.

Although 72% of Japanese workers have some monies set aside either by themselves or their employer for retirement, many of these savings are small, driving many hard-working and formally well-off aged couples to live in very small apartments with few amenities as they approach 70 years old.

The Japanese took serious steps in the 1970's to develop a fairer system for welfare for the aged: "assorted pension plans for civil servants, company employees, self-employed and others" now rank comparatively well, "but there are also schemes for those too poor, old or infirm to take care of themselves." (Woronoff, 261). Indeed, those in Japanese society who enjoy the most financial, health and social benefits in their retirement years are:

1. Government workers

2. Employees of multinational corporations (Sony, Mashushita, etc.)

3. Farm cooperative members.

Japan suffers from an inability to make up its mind: the official retirement age is 55 yet pensions begin between 60-65 years of age, a significant gap during high-risk medical years. According to government projections, the Japanese will have to increase the budget for its welfare system for the aged from about 11% of national income in 1994 to 20% in 2000 and an incredible 32% by 2025.

Indeed, in a major survey a decade ago, 66% of Japanese workers said they were worried about pensions, health care and quality living standards in their retirement years. The number held steady at 67% in 1993. (*Japan Times*, 4/8/83, 2/2/93).

This is largely because the average Japanese household has saved only about 13 million yen when retirement arrives. As the Japanese continue to live longer, the burden of health care and social programmes will continue to rise on younger workers, who are fewer and fewer. Of the three systems studied for this article, the Japanese appear to have done the least to prepare for this crisis; there is virtually no meaningful planning or budgetary projections that take into account this looming demographic crisis. Other key comparative figures are noted in Exhibit Three.

Conclusions

Vital Statistics			
	US	UK	Japan
Life Expectancy	76	77	79
Population Growth	.09%	.06%	0.4%
People Per Doctor	420	570	610
Savings, % of GDP	15%	16%	34%

Although one would assume that the established economies have been effective at planning for the welfare needs of their aged, that is not the case. Clearly, as the citizens of these three countries have become more industrialised, they have become more collectively dependent upon government to care for them in order years: the era of the independent farmer setting aside a little money each month for retirement has given way to tens of millions in each of these three countries who have little or no savings and who will need direct government subsidies in the decades ahead. The current tax structures of the US, UK and Japan and are not currently sufficient to meet these growing demands, and organisations such as the World Bank, UNESCO and ILO have only begun to ask serious questions about the future of these workers and their families.

The lessons for newly industrialised countries are enormous, because they have the opportunity to learn from the mistakes of these three nations and to take active steps now to plan for programmes that give their citizens a healthy, dignified retirement:

1. Public education efforts should encourage private savings by all workers, emphasising that employees should not expect substantial support from the government in their retirement.

2.   Government systems must strongly integrate demographics,
     population projections and cooperative research ventures with
     all major and mid-sized employers to determine the level of
     benefits promised to and expected by workers.

3.   Tax programmes should encourage savings for retirement, such
     as the very successful Individual Retirement Account (IRA) in
     the US. Workers may set aside up to $2000 US each year;
     earnings on this money are not taxed until retirement, which
     tax brackets are much lower. To date over 52 million Americans
     have contributed to IRA accounts.

4.   Banks and other financial institutions should aggressively pro-
     mote government-approved retirement plans that include health
     care, nursing home and related benefits. To insure that these are
     safe, strict guidelines should be established to insure that the
     programme is administered in a safe manner.

Because health care needs for the aged are rising so dramatically
worldwide, and costs are also rising each year, this feature should be
incorporated into these "umbrella" retirement packages. For instance,
over 40 companies in the UK and US now sell "Long Term Care"
policies to workers as young as 21 years of age that will provide them
with nursing home, medical and social assistance when they turn 65
years of age.

In aggregate, the economic and social lessons learned in the
United States, Britain and Japan have been painful and certainly
expensive for taxpayers. Korea recently organised its first national
conference on policies for the aged, attracting over 700 health care,
retirement home and investment advisors at a gathering where 150
persons were expected to attend. Singapore and Thailand are in the
seminal stages of organising similar gatherings where economic and
social policies for older workers can be addressed. It is increasingly
apparent that as these economies become more sophisticated and
worker earnings increase that expectations for formal retirement
programmes and some government oversight of the legitimacy of

those programmes will proliferate. Whether the newly industrialised economies will be able to apply lessons learned from their advanced counterparts will challenge even the most talented national economists.

References

Barton, Laurence. "Introduction to the Models of Welfare Policies for the Aged: A Comparative Study," International Symposium on Welfare Facilities for the Aged, Seoul, Korea, May 1994. This article is based on that presentation and paper.

"Budget Spares UK Funds," *Pensions & Investments*, December 13, 1993.

Carlson, Eliott. "Social Security: Entitlement?" *AARP Bulletin*, April 1994.

Kline, Lillian. "Many of Us are Aiming for 100," *The Senior Advocate*, April 1994.

Livingston, Jon. *Postwar Japan: 1945 to the Present.* New York: Pantheon Books, 1973.

"Pensioners," *The Economist*, October 30, 1993.

"UK Budget Shifts Costs to Employers" *Business Insurance*, December 6, 1993.

"The Welfare State: What Crisis?" *The Economist*, November 13, 1993.

Welfare Re-Examined, *The Economist*, December 4, 1993.

Woronoff, Jon. *Japan as Anything but Number One.* Armonk, New York: M.E. Sharp Inc., 1990.

Review of Development Economics, 5(2), 312–327, 2001

The Impact of Population Aging on the Socially Optimal Rate of National Saving: A Comparison of Australia and Japan

Ross Guest and Ian McDonald*

Abstract

This paper calculates. using a representative-agent model of a small open economy, the optimal rate of national saving for Australia and Japan for the period from the middle 1990s to 2050. The calculations focus on the implications of making allowance for the aging structure of the population in both economies on employment participation. consumption demands, and labor productivity. It is found that for Australia the optimal rate of national saving increases up to the year 2011 and then decreases. For Japan the optimal national saving rate decreases from the mid-1990s until 2020. The subsequent pattern to 2050 is generally one of decrease with the exact pattern being sensitive to the weight placed on the consumption demands of old people. The contrast in these patterns between Australia and Japan is due to the fact. compared with Australia. the aging effect on the structure of population in Japan occurs sooner and will be of greater severity.

1. Introduction

Australia and Japan face a significant aging of their populations in the next three decades. This aging of their population profiles will put significant pressure on resources because the number of people in the workforce will decrease relative to the number of people demanding consumption goods and services. Added to this, very old people have higher consumption demands then younger people, mainly because of their high demands for health expenditures. In anticipation of this pressure, commentators in Australia have called for a significant increase in the level of national saving. For example, Fitzgerald (1993) recommended an increase in the rate of national saving of five percentage points of GDP to meet the increased pressure on resources from the prospective aging of the Australian population. This recommendation was made in the wake of a downward trend in national saving in Australia since the early 1970s. Japan's population is aging more rapidly than Australia's and hence the pressure on resources will be even greater.

This paper investigates for Australia and Japan the optimal response of saving to the aging profile of their populations. The paper applies a model of the socially optimal level of national saving for a small open economy developed by the authors (see especially Guest and McDonald, forthcoming).[1] To this model are incorporated predictions of the future age composition of the populations and employment levels in the respective countries. The populations and employment levels are weighted to account for the age distribution of employment rates, labor productivity, and consumption demands.

---

* Guest: Department of Economics. Monash University, 900 Dandenong Road, Caulfield East. Vic. 3145, Australia. Tel: (61)(3) 9903 2783; Fax: (61)(3) 9903 2292; E-mail: Ross.Guest@buseco.monash.edu.au. McDonald: Department of Economics, University of Melbourne, Parkville, Vic. 3052, Australia. Tel: (61)(3) 9344 5286; Fax: (61)(3) 9344 6899; E-mail: immcd.@unimelb.edu.au.

A previous analysis by Cutler et al. (1990) for the US concluded that an aging population does not imply a need to increase saving, mainly because of the reduced capital widening requirements associated with lower employment growth. Hence, both saving and investment tend to decline as a result of population aging. The same conclusions have been found for Japan using similar models of optimal saving. These results have been summarized in Yashiro and Oishi (1997). The common finding is that the prospective aging of the Japanese population calls for a gradual decline in national saving and national investment. Auerbach et al. (1989), using an overlapping-generations model, concludes that the declining population and labor supply implies a proportionate reduction in saving and investment. Noguchi (1990) arrives at the same conclusion using a Ramsey model. The Economic Planning Agency (1991) uses a multi-industry finite-horizon model and finds that saving declines gradually throughout the horizon.

While this paper focuses on the optimal response of national saving to an aging population, it is recognized that there are other mechanisms which society can and should use to deal with the pressure on resources caused by an aging population. For example, one aspect of the resource pressure is a significant increase in government outlays. Part of the response to this could arguably involve a shift to user-pays for services currently provided by the government. Such a shift will reduce the taxation burden and thus the deadweight cost of government outlays. These issues are beyond the scope of this paper but should be borne in mind in interpreting the results.

In section 2, the projected burden of the aging population is described. In section 3, a representative-agent model of optimal national saving in a small open economy is described. Section 4 describes the data and calibration required to apply this model empirically to Australia and Japan. Section 5 explains the results of simulations for the two countries. Section 6 presents the conclusions of the paper.

2. The Burden of the Aging Population

An inverse measure of the burden of the dependents on society is the support ratio, which is the ratio of employment to the total population. We use population forecasts based on ABS projections for Australia and United Nations projections for Japan. In calculating aggregate measures of employment and population, people can be weighted by age to allow for differences by age in consumption demands and in labor productivity. As will be seen, allowing for the aging of the population increases the consumption demands of the population, because very old people have high demands for health services, but also increases the productivity of the workforce, because older workers tend to be more productive than younger workers. The consumption effect tends to dominate the productivity effect, adding further to the pressure on resources generated by an aging population.

Demands for both private and public consumption vary across age groups. For example, young people consume less private consumption but more education. Older people consume more health services. To capture these relative demands for consumption we construct population figures weighted by the relative demands for consumption of different age groups. (We assumed no differences by gender.) These constructed population figures give an indication of how the changing age structure of the population over the period of projection will influence the aggregate demand for consumption over this period. In order to construct consumption weights, data are required on both private and public expenditure by age group. Such data were not readily available to us for Japan. Consequently we use a set of consumption weights based on Australian data (see Guest and McDonald, forthcoming).[2] To assess the sensitivity of our calculations of optimal national saving to these weights, we also use another set of weights based on US data (see Cutler et al., 1990). The two alternative sets of weights are given in the Appendix. The US weights, denoted U, place a higher weight on the consumption demands of old people than do the Australian weights, denoted A. Multiplying the consumption weights by the population in each age group and summing yields an aggregate population measured in consumption units.

To allow for heterogeneity in labor productivity across age groups in employment we constructed a productivity-weighted measure of employment, labeled *EMP2*. The unweighted measure of employment is labeled *EMP1*. For the years in the future, *EMP1* is constructed by multiplying the population figures for a future year for each of the nine age categories by the employment/population ratio for respective age category in 1997. For *EMP2* an additional age-related pattern was introduced; this is the variation of labor productivity across age groups. Productivity weights to capture this variation were based on relative earnings on the assumption that relative earnings reflect relative labor productivity (see the Appendix for details).[3]

Figure 1 plots the support ratios for Australia and Japan. The ratios are normalized to 1996 for Japan and 1997 for Australia. The measures of Australia's support ratio peak in the year 1999, following a trend increase from 1975. This increase reflects the baby boom generation entering the workforce. For the three decades following 2001 there is a decline in the support ratio, reflecting the movement of the baby boom generation into retirement, a decline in the mortality rate, and a decline in fertility. The measures of Japan's support ratio follow a similar pattern to those of Australia but with a difference in that they peak at approximately 1995, five years earlier than for Australia; and the decline is sharper and of a greater magnitude than for Australia. This difference will emerge as a key force driving the differences in optimal saving behavior between the two countries. The differences in the pattern of the support ratios for Japan and Australia reflect differences in their fertility rates and mortality rates. In Japan the fertility rate fell from 4.5 births per woman in 1947 to 1.5 in 1994. Australia's fertility rate has not fallen as far. It has declined from a post-war peak of 3.6 in 1961 to 1.8 in 1996. There has been a sharp fall in mortality rates in Japan which now has the longest life expectancy of all major industrial countries. Japan's life expectancy at birth rose to 76.6 (males) and 83.0 (females) in 1994. The mortality rate in Australia in 1996 was 75.2 (males) and 81.1 (females). The combination of lower fertility rates and higher life expectancy in Japan than Australia accounts for the more rapid rate of population aging in Japan and hence the more rapid decline in its support ratio.

Comparing *EMP2/CON2*(A or B) with *EMP1/CON1*, the productivity weighting in *EMP2* increases the support ratio in an aging workforce because older workers tend to have higher marginal products. However, the weighting of consumption demands in *CON2*(A or B) reduces the support ratio in an aging population. The support ratios are sensitive to the consumption weights for both Japan and Australia. For Australia beyond 1997, both of the weighted support ratios are below the unweighted ratio

© Blackwell Publishers Ltd 2001

(*EMP1/CON1*), with the gap increasing over the forecast period. This is the case for Japan only for the weighted series *EMP2/CON2*(B).

3. Model of the Socially Optimal Level of National Saving

In this section a basic model of optimal national saving is described. The model is a model of a small open economy. A social planner is assumed to maximize a social welfare function. That function is the sum of the utility levels generated from consumption by a concave utility function for a representative consumer running up to h periods in the future and from the level of wealth at the end of the h periods. This yields:

$$V = \sum_{j=1}^{h} U_C(C_j, N_j)(1 + \rho)^{1-j} + U_W(W_h, N_h)(1 + \rho)^{1-h}, \tag{1}$$

where C_j and W_j are the aggregate consumption and wealth, respectively, of N_j representative consumers at time j, ρ is the rate of time preference, and h is the consumer's finite planning horizon. The allowance for consumption demands to vary by age group discussed in section 2 is made in this paper by using the measure of population, *CON2*, for N in equation (1).

The isoelastic form is adopted for the utility function:

$$U_W(W_h, N_h) = \omega \frac{N_h}{1 - \psi} \left(\frac{W_h}{N_h} \right)^{1-\psi}, \tag{2b}$$

$$U_C(C_j, N_j) = \frac{N_j}{1 - \beta} \left(\frac{C_j}{N_j} \right)^{1-\beta}, \tag{2a}$$

where ω is a parameter which captures the weight attached to terminal wealth in generating utility.

Optimal consumption occurs when the social welfare function (1) is maximized subject to the international borrowing constraints and the production constraints of the economy. For the former, assume that in period 1 a level of overseas debt, D_0, is inherited from the past and that all debt, in whatever period contracted, is required to be repaid at the common rate, m. The use of the proportion m is a way of allowing, as an approximation, for fixed interest debt with a finite lifetime. Under these assumptions, consumption in period $j = 1, \ldots, h$ is constrained by:

$$C_j = Y_j - I_j + B_j - (m + r)(1 - m)^{j-1} D_0 - \sum_{k=1}^{j-1} (m + r)(1 - m)^{j-k-1} B_k, \tag{3}$$

where Y_j is output domestically produced in period j, I_j is investment expenditure in period j, B_j is the flow of overseas borrowing in period j, and r is the world rate of interest. We assume a perfect world capital market which implies that the interest rate is exogenous.[4] The international borrowing constraint for the time horizon h is obtained by summing (3) over C_j from j to h, see (8) below.

Output in period j is determined by a Cobb–Douglas vintage production function with "putty-clay" technology[5] of the form:

© Blackwell Publishers Ltd 2001

$$Y_j = (1-\delta)^{(j-1)}Y_1 + \sum_{k=1}^{j-1}(1-\delta)^{(j-k-1)}A_k I_k^\alpha \left(L_{k+1} - (1-\delta)L_k\right)^{1-\alpha}. \tag{4}$$

where I_k is investment expenditure in new capital stock of vintage k; δ is the rate at which capital, once installed, depreciates; L_k is employment in year k and $(L_{k+1} - (1-\delta)L_k)$ is the amount of labor available to work at time k on newly installed capital of vintage k^6; A_k is the efficiency parameter which captures technical progress. To allow for labor productivity to vary over age groups, the measure *EMP2* derived in section 2 is used for L in equation (4).

As in the standard Ramsey model, the social planner has perfect foresight about the future values of exogenous variables, and complete knowledge of the functional forms and parameter values defining the structure of the economy. A particular implication in the present context is that the social planner knows exactly the future pattern of population aging. To recognize uncertainty about the future pattern of aging (in an *ad hoc* way), we conduct a sensitivity analysis to a reasonable range of values defining the future population age structure.

Terminal wealth is the capital stock after h periods less the accumulated overseas debt after h periods. Writing K_0 for the capital stock inherited in period 1 from the past, the capital stock after h periods of accumulation is:

$$K_h = K_0(1-\delta)^h + \sum_{k=1}^{h-1} I_k(1-\delta)^{h-k}. \tag{5}$$

There is no investment in period h because, given a one-year gestation period, any investment made in period h would not generate extra output until period $h + 1$, which is after the end of the planning horizon.

The level of overseas debt after h periods is:

$$D_h = D_0(1-m)^h + \sum_{k=1}^{h} B_k(1-m)^{h-k}. \tag{6}$$

Note that overseas borrowing is possible in period h. Terminal wealth is measured at the end of period h and so can be influenced by borrowing in period h.

Given (5) and (6), terminal wealth is defined as:

$$W_h = K_h - D_h = (1-\delta)^h K_0 + \sum_{k=1}^{h-1}(1-\delta)^{h-k}I_k - (1-m)^h D_0 - \sum_{k=1}^{h}(1-m)^{h-k}B_k. \tag{7}$$

Given the specific functional forms for the utility function and the production function, the maximization problem can be written:

$$\max \Gamma \equiv \sum_{j=1}^{h}\frac{N_j}{1-\beta}\left(\frac{C_j}{N_j}\right)^{1-\beta}(1+\rho)^{1-j} + \omega\frac{N_h}{1-\psi}\left(\frac{W_h}{N_h}\right)^{1-\psi}(1+\rho)^{1-h}$$

$$(C_1 \ldots C_h)$$
$$(I_1 \ldots I_{h-1})$$
$$(W_h)$$

$$+ \sum_{j=1}^{h}\lambda_j\left[Y_j - I_j - C_j + B_j - (m+r)(1-m)^{j-1}D_0 - \sum_{k=1}^{j-1}(m+r)(1-m)^{j-k-1}B_k\right]$$

$$+ \sum_{j=2}^{h} \psi_j \left[Y_j - (1-\delta)^{(j-1)} Y_1 - \sum_{k=1}^{j-1} (1-\delta)^{(j-k-1)} A_k I_k^\alpha (L_{k+1} - (1-\delta)L_k)^{1-\alpha} \right]$$

$$+ \phi \left[(1-\delta)^h K_0 + \sum_{k=1}^{h-1} (1-\delta)^{h-k} I_k - (1-m)^h D_0 - \sum_{k=1}^{h} (1-m)^{h-k} B_k - W_h \right], \tag{8}$$

where $\lambda_j, j = 1, \ldots, h, \psi_j, j = 2, \ldots, h,$ and ϕ are Lagrange multipliers.

The First-Order Conditions

The first-order conditions for the problem (8) are the constraints (3) and (4), the definition of terminal wealth (7), and the following equations. The first-order condition for investment is:[7]

$$\frac{\partial Y_{j+1}}{\partial I_j} = \alpha A_j I_j^{\alpha-1} (L_j - (1-\delta)L_{j+1})^{1-\alpha}$$

$$= r + \delta, \quad j = 1, \ldots, h - i \tag{9}$$

The first-order condition governing the pattern of intertemporal consumption is given by:

$$\frac{\partial V / \partial C_j}{\partial V / \partial C_k} = (1+r)^{k-j}. \tag{10}$$

Using the CES functional form for the utility function given in (2), (10) can be written:

$$\frac{C_k}{C_j} = \frac{N_k}{N_j} (1+a)^{\frac{k-j}{1-\alpha}}. \tag{11}$$

The remaining first-order condition is the terminal or transversality condition:

$$\frac{\partial U_W / \partial W_h}{\partial U_C / \partial C_h} = 1. \tag{12}$$

4. Data and Calibration

All of the simulations for both Japan and Australia use the common set of parameter values listed in Table 1. They were chosen as follows. The time horizon, h, was chosen to be long enough so that the path of optimal national saving to output, S/Y, for the period up to the year 2050 is sufficiently close to the path that would obtain for an infinite horizon. The criterion for "sufficiently close" is that a further extension of the horizon would change the value of S/Y in the year 2050 by less a level of tolerance specified as 0.1 percentage points. The resulting value of h is 200 years. The values of α, the elasticity of output with respect to capital, β, the reciprocal of the reciprocal of the elasticity of intertemporal substitution, ψ, the reciprocal of the elasticity of the elasticity of substitution between terminal consumption and terminal wealth, a, the rate of technical progress, and δ, the rate of depreciation, are based on typical empirical estimates. In particular, the values of α, δ, and r are the same as those used by Barro and Sala-i-Martin (1995). The value of a (0.01) is within the range of estimates for Australia and Asia—see Guest and McDonald (1998), Young (1995), Kim and Lau (1993), and Dowling and

Table 1. Values of Parameters and Exogenous Variables

h, the planning horizon (years)	200
α, the partial elasticity of output with respect to capital	0.35
β, the reciprocal of the elasticity of intertemporal substitution	2.00
ψ, the reciprocal of the elasticity of substitution between W_h and C_h	2.00
δ, the depreciation rate	0.05
m, the proportion of debt to be repaid in each year	0.15
r, the interest rate	0.06
a, the rate of technical progress	0.01
ρ, the rate of time preference	0.03

Summers (1998); the value of a used by Barro and Sala-i-Martin (1995) is 0.013. The value of m, the proportion of debt to be repaid in each year, was set at 0.15 to approximate a 10-year loan. ω was set using the transversality condition (17) to generate a terminal value of wealth to output (W/Y) equal to the exogenously given initial value.

The value of the rate of time preference, ρ, was chosen so that the asymptotic growth rates of consumption and output are equal. In a model with zero technical progress this is the familiar restriction that consumption be constant in a steady state, which implies the restriction that $\rho = r$. In the case of positive technical progress and the Cobb–Douglas production function (4), the corresponding restriction is that consumption per unit of output, C/Y, be constant, which requires that:

$$\rho = \frac{(1+r)}{(1+a)^{\frac{1}{1-\alpha}}} - 1.$$

This method for determining the rate of time preference implies that with a positive trend growth of labor productivity, consumption per person will be increasing over time. Thus the ethical position embodied in this choice of the rate of time preference implies that people in the future will be better off than people are today. Another way of putting this is that the interests of people in the future are treated generously in the simulations in this paper; some may say too generously.

The projections of population and employment for years from 1997 (Japan) and 1998 (Australia)[8] to the year 2050 are based on the estimates by the ABS (1998) for Australia and the medium variant projections by the United Nations (1997) for Japan. For years beyond 2050, population and employment are assumed to grow at their average projected growth rates over the decade from 2041 to 2050. To indicate the sensitivity of the results to these projections, alternative simulations were run for both countries using population projections with lower long-run growth rates.[9]

5. Simulations of Optimal National Saving

Figures 1 and 2 show the patterns of optimal national saving as a rate of GDP for Australia and Japan for the periods 1997 to 2050 (Australia) and 1996 to 2050 (Japan) calculated from simulating the model of section 3. As noted above, the actual simulations went to the years 2197 and 2196 in order that the calculations up to 2050 ap-

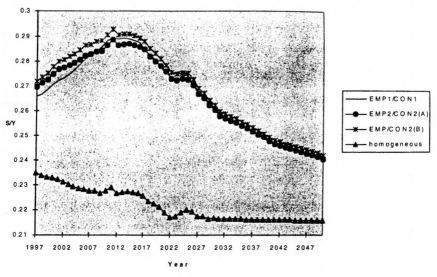

Figure 1. Australia: Impact of Aging on Optimal National Saving

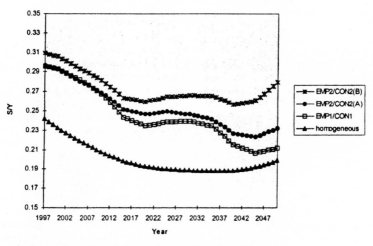

Figure 2. Japan: Impact of Aging on Optimal National Saving

proximated the optimal values if an infinite horizon was assumed. Only the years to 2050 are reported.

Consider first the simulations in Figure 1 for Australia. Three of the series show a hump-shaped pattern for optimal national saving. These three series are based on

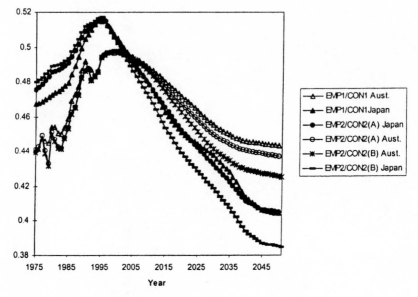

Figure 3. Support Ratios for Australia and Japan, 1975 to 2050

employment and consumption demands which allow for the effects of the aging population. The humps occur in the year 2011 for each series.[10] In anticipation of the relatively low values of the support ratio in the future (see Figure 3), especially after 2020, the optimal plan is to save at a high rate in the near future, when the support ratio is relatively high. By doing this consumption is smoothed in a way which allows for the changing age structure of the population. These three series differ in the productivity weights attached to employees and the consumption weights attached to people. For the series labelled *EMP1/CON1*, different age groups are unweighted. For the other two series, weights allow labor productivity and consumption demands to vary across age groups, as described earlier. The consumption weights B have a higher weighting on old people than consumption weights A. The striking effect is that the weights do not make a large difference to the path of the optimal national saving projection (they do tend to slightly increase optimal national saving, especially in the early years of the projection). On the other hand, allowing for the changing age structure of the population does have a large impact on the path of the optimal national saving projection. This can be seen by comparing the three series which incorporate the changing age structure of the population with the series labeled "homogenous." The latter series assumes away the changing age structure. It assumes instead that the aggregate employment/population ratio is constant at its 1997 value throughout the projection. It also assumes away any difference across age groups in productivity and consumption demands. The result is a markedly different projection of optimal national saving. Instead of a hump, optimal national saving decreases to about 2022 and from

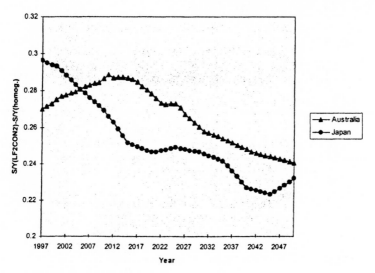

Figure 4. Comparison of Optimal Saving Rates for Australia and Japan, Using EMP2/CON(A)

then on is fairly constant. Furthermore, the homogenous projection shows that the rate of optimal national saving is much lower if aging is not allowed for. The aging structure of the Australian population increases the rate of optimal national saving by 3–6% of GDP throughout the period 1997 to 2050.[11]

For Japan the three series for optimal national saving which capture the aging structure of the Japanese population, labeled *EMP1/CON1, EMP2/CON2*(A) and *EMP2/ CON2*(B), decrease up to the 2040s. There is no hump in projected optimal national saving for Japan. Furthermore the pattern of optimal national saving for these three series is similar to the pattern for the "homogenous" projection, defined using similar assumptions for the Australia homogenous projection. (There is a slight difference. The decrease in the rate of optimal national saving ends a decade sooner if the aging structure of the Japanese population is not allowed for.) The three sets of weights for labor productivity and consumption demands by age make only a small difference to optimal national saving up to 2012, but thereafter optimal national saving becomes more sensitive to the weights chosen. Also, allowing for the aging structure does increase by a large amount, around 6% of GDP, the rate of optimal national saving throughout the period 1996 to 2050.[12]

Figure 4 compares the projections of optimal national saving for Australia and Japan. We focus on the *EMP2/CON2*(A) projections, which we believe are more realistic than *EMP2/CON2*(B). The contrast between the hump-shaped pattern for Australia and the "ski-slope" shaped pattern for Japan stands out clearly. Part of our interpretation of this difference is that Japan is further down the aging track than Australia, in that Japan is well into the period of a decreasing support ratio (an increasing dependency

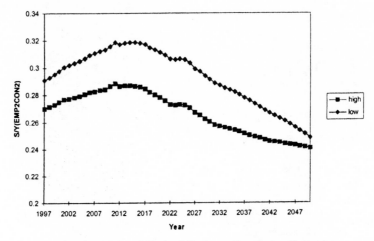

Figure 5. Australia: Sensitivity of Optimal Saving to Population Projections

ratio), while Australia has several years before its support ratio decreases significantly (see Figure 3). When Australia gets further down its aging track then the path of the optimal rate of national saving becomes a decreasing path. However, there is an additional difference which has to be taken into account in interpreting the results. This is that Japan faces a more rapidly decreasing support ratio than Australia. This more rapid decrease implies that, for optimal consumption smoothing, Japan has to be decreasing its saving rate from the beginning of the projection. The years of relative abundance, that is the years of high support ratios, are more rapidly coming to an end for Japan than for Australia.

Simulations were conducted of the sensitivity of our calculations of optimal national saving to the population projections. For both Australia and Japan two alternatives, "high" and "low," were used. High reflects less aging by assuming higher population growth, and low more population aging. For Australia we constructed a population projection assuming that the rate of immigration was zero. This projection, labeled "low," is in marked contrast to the projection used above for Australia, in which the rate of immigration was 0.54% of population per year.[13] For the purposes of the comparison we treated the latter population projection as the "high" case. The effect on the rate of optimal national saving for Australia is shown in Figure 5. The rate of optimal national saving is 2–4% of GDP greater for low compared with high. The hump-shape is not changed. For Japan, high and low are the United Nations' "high" and "low" variant projections. The effect of these alternative projections on optimal national saving for Japan is shown in Figure 6. The magnitude of the effect on optimal saving is comparable to that for Australia. Overall, these results indicate that the path of the increase in optimal national saving is quite robust to a range of alternative population projections that are within reasonable limits.[14]

How confident can we be that the optimal saving rates are an accurate guide to what should happen for socially optimal outcomes? Our calculations of optimal saving are

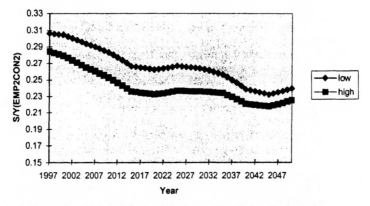

Figure 6. Japan: Sensitivity of Optimal Saving to Population Projections

based on a simple model and a particular set of parameter values. Are there reasons for thinking that the specification of the model or the choice of parameter settings bias the results in any direction? First, as pointed about above, the choice of the rate of time preference can be argued to treat future generations rather generously, in that the trend is for consumption per person to grow with labor productivity. Thus on this count our calculations of optimal rates of national saving cannot be judged as too low; indeed they could be argued to be too large. Second, note that the model ignores any adjustment costs that would be incurred in shifting resources to the export and import-substitution sectors. Insofar as there are costs of shifting resources, then the optimal plan would require smaller fluctuations in the rate of saving. The model also ignores the effect of a habitual level of consumption on people's utility. Insofar as people get used to a particular level of consumption, they will tend to favor small rather than large changes in consumption levels. Thus ignoring adjustment costs and habitual levels of consumption suggest that our calculation of the optimal rates of national saving and the current-account balances may have a greater variation than the true optimal levels. Third, for the functional forms of the model, it is not clear how more complicated functional forms would affect the optimal outcomes.

6. Conclusion

This paper has calculated, using a representative-agent model of the optimal level of national saving in a small open economy, the levels of optimal national saving for Australia and Japan for the period from the middle 1990s to 2050. The calculations have focused on the implications of making allowance for the aging structure of the population in both economies on employment participation, consumption demands, and labor productivity. It was found that for Australia the optimal national saving rate increases up to the year 2011 and then decreases. For Japan the optimal national saving rate decreases from the mid-1990s until 2020. The subsequent pattern for Japan to 2050 is generally one of decrease with the exact pattern being sensitive to the weight placed

© Blackwell Publishers Ltd 2001

on the consumption demands of old people. The hump-shape in Australia's saving profile and the absence of a saving hump for Japan reflects the fact that Japan is further along its aging path than Australia and is also on a path of more rapid aging than is Australia. Australia has a period of relative abundance, that is a period of a relatively high support ratio, the ratio of employment to population, during which the socially optimal plan is to add to wealth in order to bolster consumption in the future. The aging profile faced by Japan does not give her this opportunity. Sensitivity analysis shows that these profiles are robust with respect to variations in consumption demands and labor productivity by age, and to variations in population growth. Earlier papers which used an optimizing approach, in particular Auerbach et al. (1989), Noguchi (1990), and the Economic Planning Agency (1991), have also found that the saving rate for Japan will tend to decrease in the coming decades.

The contrast made in this paper between Australia and Japan illustrates the complex relationship between population aging and optimal saving. In particular, prospective aging of the population should be met by a period of an increasing rate of saving only if it is preceded by a period of little or no aging, such as is the case for Australia. For Japan, which has already entered a period of rapid aging, the optimal pattern of saving is one of decrease.

Appendix

This appendix describes the method of determining the consumption weights for Australia and the labor productivity weights for Australia and Japan. Consumption weights were not calculated for Japanese data. However, to test the sensitivity of the results to the consumption weights chosen, the weights used by Cutler et al. (1990) were used as an alternative set of weights. Hence, $CON(A)$ and $CON(B)$ refer to the consumption-demands-weighted population levels for the Australian set of weights and the Cutler et al. weights, respectively. Labor productivity weights were calculated for both Australian data and Japanese data.

The consumption weights for Australian data were determined as follows. We distinguished between private consumption expenditures and government social expenditures on health and education. For private consumption levels, using the household expenditure survey for 1993/94 (ABS cat. no. 6530.0) and assuming, following the equivalence scale approach in Bradbury and Saunders (1990), that a young person consumes half the private consumption of a working-age adult, the weights for private consumption on young, working-age adults and old adults are 0.5, 1.0, and 0.75. For government-provided consumption, we used the detailed survey Commonwealth and state social expenditure per person by age group for education and health by the Commonwealth Department of Community Services and Health (1990). This survey was based on a division of the population into nine age groups. Combining the private consumption expenditures with the government consumption expenditures yielded the consumption weights for the nine age groups given in Table A1. Further details are in Guest and McDonald (1998). This method followed Cutler et al. (1990)'s method for the US. The main reason why Cutler et al. calculate a higher weight for older people is that they assume a weight of 1.0 for the private consumption of older people, compared with our weight of 0.75. They give no basis for their figure of 1.0. The estimates of Schultz and Borowski (1991, p. 97) for the US imply a weighting for the private consumption of older people of 0.85. In our view the

Table A1. Consumption Weights by Age Group

	0–15	16–24	25–39	40–49	50–59	60–64	65–69	70–74	75+
Weights A	0.68	0.89	1.00	0.98	1.00	1.05	0.87	0.95	1.19
Weights U	0.72	0.72	1.00	1.00	1.00	1.00	1.27	1.27	1.27

Table A2. Employment Productivity Weights by Age Group

	0–19	20–24	25–29	30–34	35–39	40–44	45–49	50–54	55–59	60–64	65+
Japan	0.603	0.802	0.935	1.076	1.170	1.222	1.261	1.284	1.199	0.970	0.897
Aust	0.502	0.842	1.094	1.094	1.210	1.210	1.208	1.208	1.112	1.032	1.032

Cutler et al. (1990) weights place too high a weight on the consumption demands of old people, even for the US.

The productivity weights used in the calculation of the weighted employment, EMP2, were calculated on the assumption that the age distribution of earnings reflects the age distribution of labor productivity. For Australia the earnings distribution was measured by the distribution of mean weekly earnings of full-time employees in their main job in 1997. The source is ABS catalogue 6310.0, "Weekly Earnings of Employees," published in August 1997. For Japan, the indicator of the earnings distribution was given by the distribution of monthly contract earnings of regular employees by age group for 1996. The source is the Ministry of Labour (Japan) and the data are published in the *Statistical Yearbook of Japan 1998*. Table A2 gives the weights for Australia and Japan.

References

Auerbach, A. J., L. J. Kotlikoff, R. P. Hagemann, and G. Nicoletti, "The Economic Dynamics of an Aging Population: The Case of Four OECD Countries," *OECD Economic Studies* 12 (spring 1989):28–9.

Australian Bureau of Statistics, "Weekly Earnings of Employees," Catalogue 6310.0 (1997).

———, "Projections of the Populations of Australian States and Territories, 1995–2051," Catalogue 3222.0 (1998).

Barro, R. J. and X. Sala-i-Martin, *Economic Growth*, New York: McGraw-Hill (1995).

Bradbury, B. and P. Saunders, "How Reliable are Estimates of Poverty in Australia? Some Sensitivity Tests for the Period 1981–82 to 1985–86," *Australian Economic Papers* (December 1990):154–81.

Commonwealth Department of Community Services and Health, "The Impact of Population Aging on Commonwealth and State Social Outlays 1987–88," Policy Development Division, Canberra (1990).

Cutler, D. M., J. M. Poterba, L. M. Sheiner, and L. H. Summers, "An Aging Society: Opportunity or Challenge?" *Brookings Papers on Economic Activity* 1 (1990):1–74.

Dowling, M. and P. M. Summers, "Total Factor Productivity and Economic Growth: Issues for Asia," mimeo, University of Melbourne (1998).

Economic Planning Agency, "Simulation of the Industry and Economy in 2010," Tokyo: Government Printing Office (1991).

Fitzgerald, V., *National Saving: A Report to the Treasurer*, Canberra: AGPS (1993).

Guest, R. S. and I. M. McDonald, "The Socially Optimal Level of Saving in Australia, 1960–61 to 1994–95," *Australian Economic Papers*, 37(3) (1998):213–35.

———, "Ageing, Immigration and Optimal National Saving in Australia," *Economic Record*, 77(237) forthcoming.

Kim, J. and J. L. Lau, "The Sources of Economic Growth of the East Asian Newly Industrialised Countries," Paper presented at EMBA Training Course on Productivity Measurement, Sydney, 21–3 August (1994).

Noguchi, Y., "The Age Structure of the Population and Saving/Investment: An Analysis Based on Cross-Country Comparisons," *Financial Review* (Institute of Fiscal and Monetary Policy, Ministry of Finance) 17 (August 1990):39–50.

OECD, "Japan Population Aging," *OECD Observer* 209 (1997):34–5.

Olekalns, N., "What a Drag it is getting Old. Aging and Government Expenditure in the OECD," Department of Economics, University of Melbourne (1999).

Schultz, J. and A. Borowski, "Estimating the Economic 'Burden' of the Aged in the United States," in *The Economics of Population Aging: The Greying of Australia, Japan and the United States*, Westport, CN: PB Greenwood (1991).

Statistical Yearbook of Japan, Japan Statistical Association (1998).

United Nations, "The Sex and Age Distribution of the World's Populations: The 1996 Revision," New York (1997).

Yashiro, N. and A. S. Oishi, "Population Aging and the Savings–Investment Balance in Japan," in M. D. Hurd and N. Yashiro (eds.), *The Economic Effects of Aging in the United States and Japan*, Chicago: University of Chicago Press for the NBER (1997).

Young, A., "The Tyranny of Numbers: Confronting the Statistical Realities of the East Asian Growth Experience," *Quarterly Journal of Economics* 110 (1995):641–80.

Notes

1. The analysis is normative in the sense that the model determines socially optimal outcomes. There are a number of reasons why privately optimal outcomes may not be socially optimal, including myopia, taxes, market power, and time-inconsistent consumer preferences.

2. Olekalns (1999) suggests that the consumption weights are very similar across countries (at least for the OECD), in which case adopting Australian as proxies for Asian countries' weights is defensible.

3. A referee has pointed out that the method of calculating the consumption and productivity weights confounds age and cohort effects. However, the small effect of alternative values of the weights on optimal national saving shown below suggests that trying to correct for this would make little difference to the results.

4. The assumption of an exogenous interest rate for Japan can be questioned. We adopt this assumption for Japan for analytical tractability. An exogenous interest rate implies that the level of investment is determined independently of the level of consumption.

5. A vintage production function with putty-clay technology is chosen because it captures more realism than the case of malleable capital. It assumes that each vintage of capital has a fixed labor requirement until it is scrapped. This is more realistic than the malleable capital case, which assumes substitutability of an unchanged degree between machines and labor before and after the machines are installed. An implication of the vintage technology is to impose a pattern of dynamic adjustment on the capital stock that is more gradual than with malleable capital, unless special assumptions are made in the latter case, and has an economic basis. This gradual adjustment yields more reasonable patterns of investment; see Guest and McDonald, forthcoming.

6. This lag between expenditure on investment and production from the investment goods is a one-period gestation period.

7. The one-period difference in the time subscripts in the definition of the derivative in (9) reflects the one-period gestation period of investment. Note that with putty-clay technology, after installation the marginal product of investment simply declines at rate δ.

8. The starting year for the Australian simulations is 1997, but 1996 for Japan owing to limited availability of 1997 data for Japan.

9. The reason for choosing a lower long-run growth rate is that, for Australia, the baseline series has a higher long-run growth rate (but not short-run) than all of the other series constructed by the ABS.

10. The timing of this peak is not changed by moving the starting date of the simulation back in time. For example in another simulation, not reported, which began in 1961 and used actual population data for the period up to 1997 with the weights and assumptions used in $EMP2/CON2$(A), the peak in optimal saving occurs around 2011.

11. For the saving–investment balance, or current-account balance, we confine our comments to $EMP2/CON2$(A). The simulation with $EMP2/CON2$(B) gives a similar pattern. The reduction in employment caused by the aging population tends to reduce investment. However, the optimal consumption path requires a build-up of wealth in the early years of the plan. A current-account surplus is run through the entire period 1997 to 2050. This surplus increases to 6% of GDP by 2015 and then decreases, reaching 1% of GDP by the year 2050. The wealth to GDP ratio rises throughout the period 1997 to 2050. 2050 is the peak for W/Y. Thereafter it declines to the exogenously imposed level of 2.12 in 2197.

12. For Japan, Yashiro and Oishi (1997) have made projections of actual saving rates up to 2025 using simulations of an estimated model of saving behavior. Their estimated model allows for the impact on saving of the aging structure of the Japanese population. Although their focus is different from ours, being an actual saving and not socially optimal saving, a comparison of the results is of interest. Their simulations suggest, as do ours, a uniform decrease in the saving rate from the 1990s to 2025. However, the size of the decrease over this period in their calculations is much greater than the decrease in our calculations, being in the order of 25 percentage points of GDP, compared with one to three percentage points, depending on the consumption and productivity weights, in our calculations.

13. For "low," population in Australia is projected to be 19.5 million in 2051 and for high 29.3 million in 2051. The population in 1997 is 18.5 million.

14. For the saving–investment balance, or current-account balance, we, as for Australia, confine our comments to $EMP2/CON2$(A). The simulation with $EMP2/CON2$(B) gives a similar pattern. The reduction in employment caused by the aging population tends to reduce investment and this reduction is to lower levels than Australia, reflecting the greater reduction in employment. The optimal consumption path requires a build-up of wealth in the early years of the plan. A current-account surplus is run through the entire period 1997 to 2050. This surplus is generally larger than that of Australia, being between 8 and 9% of GDP up to 2020 and then declining to 3% of GDP by the year 2050. The wealth to GDP ratio rises throughout the period 1997 to 2050. The peak for W/Y is in 2197, later than for Australia. Thereafter it declines to the exogenously imposed level of 3.14 in 2197.

4   The Economic Position of the Elderly in Japan

Naohiro Yashiro

Japan's economy and society face a rapid aging of the population. The proportion of the elderly (defined here as those 65 years of age or older) in the total population, which was 4.9 percent in 1950—very low by international standards—rose to 14.8 percent in 1995. The ratio is projected to rise further, to over 25 percent by 2020, which would make it among the highest in the major OECD countries.[1] The rapid aging of the Japanese population reflects the high rate of economic growth during the postwar period and associated structural changes in industry and society, particularly in family structure.

This paper focuses on the economic status of the elderly, with specific reference to their family relationships. First, the transformation of the Japanese household structure in the postwar period is reviewed. Second, the income of elderly households under both conventional and alternative definitions is compared with that of average households for a better understanding of their relative economic status. The distribution of the income and wealth of elderly households is a major concern here. Third, the high proportion of the elderly living with their children, though declining steadily over time, has been a particular characteristic of the Japanese family. Major factors determining the coresidence of the elderly with their children are analyzed based on cross-sectional data by prefecture. Finally, we arrive at some policy conclusions from the above discussions.

Naohiro Yashiro is professor of economics at the Institute of International Relations, Sophia University.

Financial support from the Japan Foundation Center for Global Partnership and technical assistance from the Japan Center for Economic Research are gratefully acknowledged.

1. The relatively fast aging process in Japan is evident when we compare the time required to double the share of the elderly from 7 percent to 14 percent in various countries. In Japan, this doubling is projected to take only 25 years, compared with 70 years in the United States, and 130 years in France. For an overview of the economic aspects of the aging of the Japanese population, see OECD (1990) and Takayama (1992).

89

4.1   Changes in Living Arrangements of the Elderly

The aging of the Japanese population has been due largely to the gradual aging of the postwar baby boom cohort (born between 1947 and 1949), which will become elderly toward the year 2020. The rapidity of the aging is due mainly to the continuous decline of the birthrate, from 4.5 in 1947 to 1.43 in 1995. In addition, an increase in life expectancy has contributed to an increase in the average age of the population; the average life expectancy of those reaching age 65 rose from 11.5 years in 1950 to 16.7 years in 1994 for males and from 13.9 years to 21.0 years for females. This extension of life expectancy has greatly affected the living arrangements of the elderly in Japan. In 1990, 85 percent of elderly men lived with their wives (including those who also lived with other family members), while only 42 percent of elderly women lived with their husbands, reflecting the large difference in life expectancies and the low divorce rate.[2]

A major characteristic of Japan's family structure is the high proportion of the elderly who live with their children or other relatives, indicating the important role of extended families in securing a comfortable life for the retired elderly. For example, only 15 percent of all elderly women in Japan lived alone in 1989—much lower than the 41 percent in the United States (table 4.1).[3] In addition, the more aged the elderly become, the more likely they are to live with their extended families.

Moreover, the likelihood of coresidence of elderly women is relatively high; 62 percent of "very elderly" (those aged 75 or over) men and 77 percent of very elderly women live with their families in Japan, compared to 9 and 22 percent in the United States, respectively. While the greater likelihood for women is partly due to the fact that elderly women are on average older than elderly men, the incidence of elderly women living with their children is consistently higher than that of elderly men in the same age groups; for example, over 80 percent of Japanese women aged 80 or over live with their children, compared with 70 percent of men in the same age group. This high rate of coresidence of elderly women with their children helps to reduce the incidence of poverty among the elderly in Japan.

The living arrangements of the elderly, which have important implications for their economic position, have continuously changed over time. The share of the elderly who live with and are supported by their children in the total number of elderly declined from 56 percent in 1977 to 39 percent in 1991, consistent with the decline in the share of extended families in total house-

---

2. In 1993, Japan's divorce rate (the number of divorces per 1,000 population) was 1.53. This compares with 1990 divorce rates of 4.73 in the United States, 2.88 in the United Kingdom, and 2.20 in Sweden.

3. These figures do not include the elderly who are institutionalized. According to the Census of the Population in 1990, 4.3 percent of the total elderly population was institutionalized.

Table 4.1   Distribution of Living Arrangements of the Elderly (percent)

Age	Men					Women				
	With Spouse	Alone	All Relatives	Children's Family	Nonrelatives	With Spouse	Alone	All Relatives	Children's Family	Nonrelatives
Age 65+										
Japan	37	5	57	36	0	18	15	67	47	0
United States	75	16	7	–	2	40	41	17	–	2
Age 65–74										
Japan	41	5	54	31	0	24	16	60	39	0
United States	80	13	5	–	2	51	33	14	–	2
Age 75+										
Japan	32	6	62	45	0	8	15	77	58	0
United States	67	22	9	–	2	24	51	22	–	3

Sources: For Japan, Ministry of Health and Welfare (1989); for the United States, Hurd (1990).

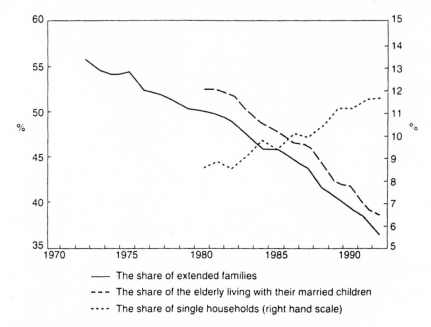

- The share of extended families
- - - The share of the elderly living with their married children
···· The share of single households (right hand scale)

Fig. 4.1   Historical development of living arrangements of the elderly
Source: Ministry of Health and Welfare (1989).

holds. At the same time, the share of the elderly living alone rose from 8 percent to 12 percent (fig. 4.1).

Various signs suggest that this trend is likely to continue in the coming decades. First, the share of extended families in total households in rural areas is consistently higher than the share in urban areas and is inversely related to the size of the city; the share of extended family households in small cities is twice as large as that in large cities. Second, nearly half of farming households are extended families, in both urban and rural areas; this share is much higher than the shares among nonfarm self-employed and employee households (fig. 4.2). Both continued urbanization—migration from rural to urban areas, particularly large cities—and the associated contraction of the agricultural sector as it is replaced by the manufacturing and service sectors should contribute to a further decrease in the share of extended family households and an increase in the incidence of single elderly households.

Improvements in the social security and welfare systems have also contributed to the increased incidence of the elderly living alone and have allowed for other, diversified living arrangements. Instead of the traditional type of extended family in which household members' incomes are pooled, the elderly can live economically independent from their children while sharing the house

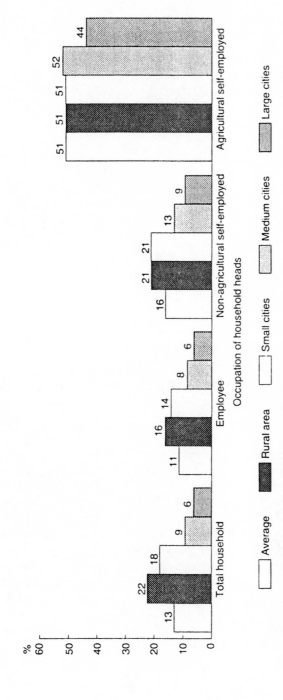

Fig. 4.2 Extended families as a fraction of total households, 1989
Source: Ministry of Health and Welfare (1989).

143

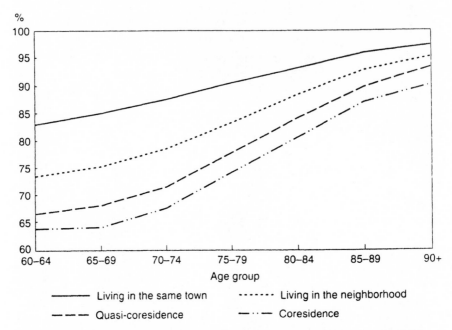

Fig. 4.3   Incidence of various types of living arrangements of the elderly, 1989 (accumulated basis)
Source: Ministry of Health and Welfare (1989).

or housing space ("quasi coresidence"),[4] or they can live alone in either the same neighborhood or the same town as their children. Indeed, the pattern of living arrangements evolves from the elderly living apart from their children but in the same neighborhood toward coresidence as they age. As a result, the accumulated level of the various types of elderly living arrangements (fig. 4.3, *solid line*) is flatter than the closer coresidence type (i.e., living together in the same house) across various age groups (fig. 4.3).

The wide divergence in the living arrangements of the elderly between Japan and the United States and how these arrangements have evolved over time has various analytical and policy implications. In an extended family, the economic independence of household members varies with age: Of males aged 40–59, over 90 percent earn the largest incomes in the household; they are normally heads of household. However, the ratio declines steadily with age, to 23 percent of males aged 80 or over; the remainder are economically dependent on their children.

4. In typical examples of quasi coresidence the child's family lives in a small house built in what was a yard next to the parents' house, or the extended family occupies a multilevel dwelling in which parents and children maintain separate households by living on different floors of the same building.

4.2   Income, Consumption, and Wealth of the Elderly

4.2.1   Income of the Elderly

The economic status of the elderly vis-à-vis the nonelderly has important implications for social policy and the system of transfers from the nonelderly to the elderly. Comparing ordinary household income (excluding single households) by age of household head indicates that elderly households (defined here as those 70 years of age or older) have incomes equivalent to 79 percent of average household income (table 4.2). If we exclude the self-employed, whose reported incomes are less accurate than those of salaried employees, the relative income of the elderly household falls further, to 60 percent of the income of the average employee household. The incomes of single elderly households, which usually belong to the poor group, were approximately 60 and 70 percent of the average, for males and females, respectively.

The large income difference between households headed by the elderly and average households, however, is subject to the following qualifications: First, elderly households are smaller; the average number of members in elderly households was 2.9 compared with 3.8 in all households in 1989. Accounting for the difference in family size, the per capita income and consumption of the elderly household exceeded those of the average household, though scale economies of household consumption should be accounted for.[5] Second, self-employed incomes may not be fully declared, particularly by farming households. Elderly workers are found most often in the self-employed sector; close to 60 percent of elderly workers are self-employed, though self-employed workers account for less than 30 percent of all workers. This high incidence of self-employment among elderly workers may well lead to an underestimation of average elderly income.

Finally, the income gap between the elderly and the nonelderly would be even smaller if imputed incomes from nonmonetary sources were accounted for as follows: First, the ratio of homeownership for elderly households is generally higher than the national average (80 percent vs. 60 percent in 1989). In addition, elderly people who bought their houses in the past have more unrealized capital gains from continuous land price hikes. Both factors result in larger housing and land assets for the elderly, on average two times those of the nonelderly (see table 4.2). Second, the elderly are intensive users of medical benefits, and most such use takes the form of in-kind transfers from the government; the average per capita medical expenses of the elderly are approximately five times as large as those of the nonelderly. Accounting for these

5. To compare per capita household income and consumption by family size, a family of two has 5 percent lower per capita income than a single person and 12 percent lower per capita consumption, implying a scale merit of household consumption of 7 percent. A family of four has 30 percent lower per capita income than a single person and 49 percent lower per capita consumption (Ministry of Health and Welfare 1989).

Table 4.2 **Relative Economic Position of the Elderly (average household = 100)**

Age	Total Ordinary Household			Total Excluding Self-Employed		
	Annual Income	Consumption	Housing Assets	Annual Income	Consumption	Housing Assets
Age 60–69	92.3	91.8	140.9	82.7	90.8	142.5
(per capita)	(112.2)	(111.7)		(113.3)	(124.3)	
Age 70+	79.1	77.2	183.1	59.7	66.9	179.1
(per capita)	(102.9)	(100.4)		(93.9)	(105.2)	

	Single Household					
	Males			Females		
	Annual Income	Consumption	Housing Assets	Annual Income	Consumption	Housing Assets
Age 60–69	73.8	81.2	487.6	94.6	91.3	110.3
Age 70+	60.5	76.3	201.6	72.3	91.0	235.3

Source: Ministry of Health and Welfare (1989).

sources of imputed income would significantly improve the relative economic position of the elderly.

4.2.2   Distribution of Income and Wealth of the Elderly

The comparison of income and wealth between the elderly and the nonelderly indicates that the economic position of the *average* elderly household is no less advantageous than that of the average nonelderly household. However, as in other industrial countries, the income and wealth of the elderly appear to be less equally distributed than those of the nonelderly (Tachibanaki 1989). While the elderly head 18 percent of households, 35 percent of elderly households are in the lowest income quartile, compared with 13 percent of nonelderly households. Moreover, the income distribution of the elderly is U-shaped, contrary to the traditional normal distribution pattern (fig. 4.4).

There are various reasons why income distribution among the elderly is inequitable in Japan. First, while public pensions account for nearly half of average elderly income, labor income still accounts for one-quarter, implying that whether one can continue working beyond retirement age, subject to health as well as employment opportunities, is an important factor (table 4.3). Second, under the seniority-based wage structure prevalent in the Japanese labor market, not only does the average wage of employees grow with age but the dispersion of wages in the same age group becomes wider. Because the size of the firm pension or lump-sum severance payment is proportional to a person's wage at the time of retirement from the firm, differences in wages continue to be reflected in income differentials after retirement. Third, because many elderly women were either homemakers or unpaid family workers, their eco-

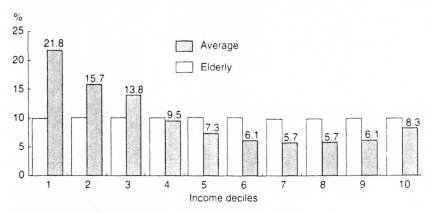

Fig. 4.4   Distribution of elderly household incomes, 1989
Source: Management and Coordination Agency (1989).

nomic positions often depend on family situations, such as whether they live with their extended families, with their spouses, or alone. In 1989, the average income of an elderly man living alone was 40 percent of that of an elderly couple (without children), while that of an elderly woman living alone was 36 percent that of an elderly couple.[6]

Housing assets are even less equitably distributed than household income. While housing and land assets account for much of the wealth of the elderly, the value depends on accumulated potential capital gains in previous periods. The median housing asset of the elderly (those 70 years of age or older) is 50 percent larger than that of the average household, and the gap widens in the third quartile to 150 percent, indicating that the housing asset distribution by age group is wider in the higher asset-holding class. In addition, even among the elderly, the distribution of housing assets varies across regions, particularly between large cities and rural areas. For example, the average value of housing of the elderly in the Tokyo area was twice the national average in 1989 (Management and Coordination Agency 1989).

4.2.3   Savings of the Elderly

One of the major issues concerning Japanese household behavior is how to explain its high rate of savings. Numerous studies have been published giving possible reasons for the difference in the average rate of savings between Japan and the United States.[7] One of the factors that raises average Japanese household savings is the relatively high rate of savings of the elderly, who are ex-

6. Here, the single elderly are defined to be those aged 60 or over, and elderly couples are defined to be those families in which the husband is aged 65 or over and the wife is aged 60 or over (Ministry of Health and Welfare 1989).

7. See Horioka (1990b) for a survey of the major literature on Japan's high savings rate.

Table 4.3   International Comparison of Major Sources of the Elderly[a] Income (percent)

Major Sources of Income	Japan			United States			United Kingdom		Korea	
	1981	1986	1990	1981	1986	1990	1981	1990	1981	1990
Wages	31.3	24.5	23.8	15.2	14.1	10.7	6.5	5.5	16.2	31.9
Public pension	34.9	53.4	54.3	53.9	53.0	55.2	64.0	68.8	0.8	2.5
Private pension	3.8	1.9	1.9	10.0	10.4	13.6	13.5	18.0	0.0	0.3
Deposit	2.1	2.2	2.0	1.7	1.8	1.8	1.6	1.3	2.2	1.9
Other wealth income	5.3	5.6	4.0	14.5	17.4	11.0	2.2	1.9	3.3	4.6
Support from children	15.6	9.0	5.7	0.3	0.2	0.7	0.5	0.1	72.4	54.8
Income maintenance	1.2	1.1	0.9	0.7	0.4	1.4	3.1	2.3	1.2	2.2
Others	3.1	1.9	1.8	3.5	2.4	2.7	2.6	0.9	3.2	1.6
None of the above	2.7	0.4	5.7	0.2	0.3	3.0	6.1	1.3	0.6	0.2

Source: Management and Coordination Agency, *Life and View of the Elderly* (in Japanese; Tokyo; Government Printing Office, 1992).

[a]Age 60 or older.

pected to be dissavers. Major explanations for the high rate of elderly household savings in Japan are later retirement from the labor market, greater incentive to leave bequests to their children, significant imputed incomes, and absorption of the poor elderly into their children's households (Horioka 1990a).

First, the life-cycle theory states that people start to dissave after retirement. A simple explanation of the high savings rate of the Japanese elderly is that many of them continue to work after normal retirement age. Though labor force participation rates of the male elderly fall with age, the decline at age 60—the normal retirement age from a company—is relatively small, and beyond age 60 the participation rate falls only gradually; the average participation rates for those aged 60–64 and 65–69 in 1992 were 72 and 59 percent, respectively (fig. 4.5). Moreover, declining labor force participation rates bottomed out and then rose from 1988 to 1992, partly reflecting tightening labor market conditions. If this new trend toward later retirement continues, it may have a significant impact on Japanese household savings.

If Japanese household savings rates are examined by age group in employee household data (the most readily available and thus the most often cited statistic), elderly household savings rates are found to be as high as 50 percent (fig. 4.6). This surprisingly high rate of savings is attributable to the fact that only the rich elderly remain employed while continuing to be household heads; they accounted for 15 percent of those aged 65–69 and only 5 percent of those aged 70 or older. On the other hand, the retired elderly (those who do not work) do dissave in Japan as the life-cycle theory predicts. Combining these employee and retired households results in a falling savings rate for elderly households,

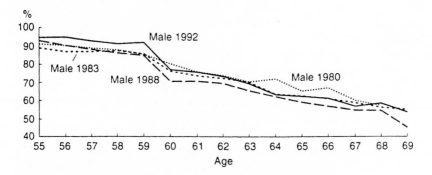

Fig. 4.5   Labor force participation of the elderly by age, 1992
Source: Ministry of Labor, *Basic Survey on the Elderly's Employment* (Tokyo, 1992).

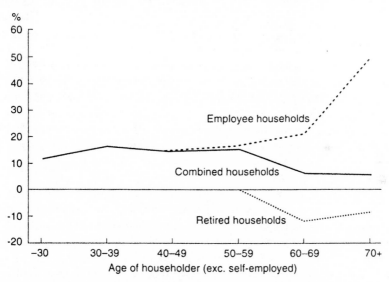

Fig. 4.6   Household savings rates (employee vs. retired households)
Source: Management and Coordination Agency (1989).

though not to a negative level, which is similar to what occurs in the United States.

A principal factor behind longer retirement life is the continuous extension of Japanese life expectancy; expected life remaining at age 65 increased by 4.9 years for males and 6.7 years for females between 1950 and 1993. This increase forces the elderly to save more in order to finance their longer lives. Another factor accounting for the large aggregate household savings (National Account basis) is the large fraction in the elderly labor force of the self-employed,[8] whose business profits are often mixed with household savings and for whom retirement is quite flexible, unlike the case of employees subject to mandatory retirement.[9]

Second, the desire of the Japanese elderly to leave bequests to their children is also important in explaining their later retirement and relatively high rate of savings. A survey by the Bank of Japan in 1990 indicated that the majority of Japanese parents who have financial and real assets want to leave bequests to their children. The share is higher among the older generation and among self-employed, particularly farming, households. The bequest motive, however, can be altruistic or strategic. While 60 percent of the elderly responded that they would leave the bequest unconditionally, the remainder said that they would do so only if their children agreed to take care of them in their retired life (Management and Coordination Agency 1992).

Third, the significant imputed income of the elderly raises their savings rate as conventionally measured. When we account for estimated imputed income and consumption from housing and land, as well as medical benefits, the savings rate of the elderly falls, resulting in a consumption pattern resembling the life-cycle pattern. In addition, if household expenditure for education, which is conventionally defined as consumption, is reclassified as savings for human capital investment in the family, it raises the savings rate of the nonelderly, while having little effect on the rate for the elderly. Also, by so doing, the mysterious decline in the household savings rate for those aged 40–49 (when the household's burden of educational expenditure is largest) disappears, and we are left with a smooth life-cycle pattern of savings in Japan (fig. 4.7).

4.2.4   Age Selectivity Bias

The sharp decline in the economic independence of the Japanese elderly as they age is a major source of the "age selectivity bias" in Japanese household statistics concerning the income and savings of the elderly that makes it difficult to compare the economic position of the elderly in Japan with that of the elderly in the United States. The extent of this age selectivity bias can be approximated by the gap between the age composition of the population and the age composition of heads of households. For example, 70-year-olds account for 13.2 percent of the population above age 30, but only 7.8 percent of household heads (table 4.4). This age composition gap is much smaller in the United States.

The likelihood that the Japanese elderly will be economically dependent on

---

8. The rates of labor force participation of the male elderly (those aged 65 years or older) in self-employed and employee households in 1991 were 72 and 40 percent, respectively. However, with a declining self-employed elderly population, mainly concentrated in agriculture, the average labor force participation rate of the elderly is likely to fall in the long run.

9. The age of mandatory retirement from a firm practicing long-term employment is set on a firm-by-firm basis. In 1991, over 90 percent of Japanese firms had this system, and half of them set retirement age at 60 or older. Unlike in the United States, this mandatory retirement system is a perfectly legal practice in Japan.

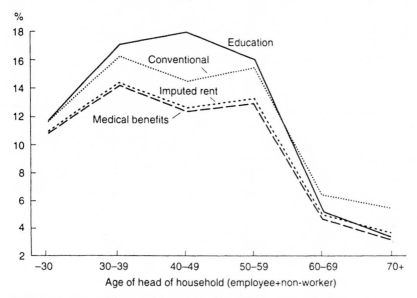

Fig. 4.7   Alternative definitions of household savings rates (excluding the self-employed)
Source: Management and Coordination Agency (1989).

Table 4.4   **Comparison of Age Compositions of the Population and of Heads of Households between Japan and the United States, 1989**

	Japan			United States	
Age	Population	Households	Age	Population	Households
30–39	22.7	27.0	25–34	27.9	23.9
40–49	26.6	29.3	35–44	23.1	22.9
50–59	21.4	21.2	45–54	15.8	16.0
60–69	16.0	14.7	55–64	13.7	14.6
70+	13.2	7.8	65–74	11.5	13.3
			75+	8.1	9.3
Total	100.0	100.0	Total	100.0	100.0

Sources: For Japan, Management and Coordination Agency (1989); for the United States, U.S. Bureau of the Census, *Current Population Reports* (Washington, D.C., 1989).

their children or relatives, and will thus be omitted from statistics compiled on a household basis, is closely related to their income level. Three-quarters of the elderly who have annual incomes of less than 400,000 yen live with their children, which results in an *upward* bias in the perceived elderly household income because it is the relatively rich elderly who can afford to remain heads of households. However, the negative correlation between elderly individual

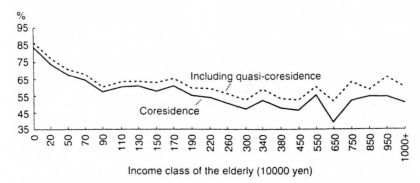

Fig. 4.8 Incidence of coresidence of the elderly (percentage of the total elderly population)
Source: Ministry of Health and Welfare (1989).

income level and incidence of coresidence with children disappears when income level exceeds 2 million yen, implying that the decision of the elderly to live with their children may be independent of their income level unless their income is so low that they have few choices. There is even a positive correlation between elderly income level and incidence of quasi coresidence (shown by the gap between the two lines in fig. 4.8). Thus, while coresidence is more prominent for the poor elderly, quasi coresidence, which assures privacy while maintaining the benefits of coresidence, is more associated with the rich elderly.

There are various ways to cope with this age selectivity bias (Ando, Yamashita, and Murayama 1986; Hayashi 1986). Hayashi (1986) estimated the income and consumption of the elderly living with their children as the difference between the income and consumption of extended families taking care of elderly members and those of nuclear families. We basically follow this method with various modifications, such as estimating the savings rate of the "hypothetical" elderly group, who are actually absorbed in their children's families, by equating the age compositions of the population and of household heads (Yashiro and Maeda 1994).[10] With this adjustment, the savings rate of elderly households (aged 70 or older) is estimated to be −93 percent—that is, they consume nearly twice their own incomes. The large negative savings of the elderly living with their children is not surprising, given their low incomes.[11]

10. This assumes that the elderly who depend economically on their children are statistically independent household heads. Including these hypothetical household heads with low savings greatly lowers the average elderly household savings rate.
11. The large negative savings rate of the elderly living with their children is consistent with the following estimates of a loglinear equation based on the income and consumption data of nonearning households in 1989 (Yashiro and Maeda 1994):

This result has two implications. First, the savings behavior of the Japanese elderly is not necessarily different from that of the U.S. elderly, but the large gap in rates of coresidence with children tends to overstate the difference. Second, the falling incidence of coresidence with children among the Japanese elderly is likely to lower their savings rate in household-based statistics and thus narrow the gap with the United States.

4.3   Determinants of Living Arrangements of the Elderly

The living arrangements of the elderly play a key role in determining their economic position as well as their household savings. We already observed in section 4.1 that the percentage of the elderly who live with their children rises with age. Also, the percentage of coresidence is higher for women, those who are without a spouse, those in farming households, and those living in rural areas; since the very old are more likely to be women and spouseless, these variables are not mutually exclusive.

Various studies indicate that the effect of economic factors, particularly the income level of the elderly, on their living arrangements is indecisive. Many previous studies attribute the increasing ratio of elderly persons living alone to their rising income level. According to this view, the poor elderly must live with their children for financial reasons, even though they do not wish to do so. In contrast, the school of the strategic bequest motive argues that many adult children live with their elderly parents for financial reasons—they cannot afford to buy their own homes. In return, the elderly parents expect in-kind services as well as monetary support from their adult children. For this reason, it may well be the rising income of children that will lower the likelihood of shared living arrangements.

4.3.1   Review of Previous Studies

Kotlikoff and Morris (1988) presented a model of family living arrangements in which the joint utility maximization between elderly parents and their adult children was explored. In the model, the economic gain from shared housing was compared with its disutility in determining whether the parent and child would live together. For example, when parents would like to coreside, but their children would not, the parents were able to bribe their children to coreside if their income, including housing services, was high enough relative to their children's income. A major conclusion of this study was that nonmonetary characteristics of children (such as gender and education) are

---

$$\ln \text{PTC} = 3.63 - 0.282 \ln \text{DI}, \qquad R^2 = 0.791,$$
$$\quad (41.03) \quad (5.50)$$

where PTC is propensity to consume, DI is disposable income, and figures in parentheses are t-values.

more important than income differences as determinants of living arrangements.

With specific reference to Japan, Ando et al. (1986) compared the behavior of extended nonelderly families and nuclear nonelderly families. Their conclusion was that the larger the assets of the elderly, the lower their probability of living with their children, because the rich elderly tended to live alone. In contrast, Otake (1991) indicated that both the assets and the income of elderly parents increased the probability of coresidence with their children, mainly because of the parents' strategic bequest motive. The implications of these two results differ widely: Ando et al. implied that the current tendency of elderly incomes to rise, partly as the result of improved social security benefits, would lower the probability of coresidence, while Otake's conclusion was exactly the opposite.

4.3.2   Empirical Specification

The living arrangements of the elderly are explained by the incomes of the elderly and their adult children, housing services, and other family characteristics. The source of the data examined in this paper is the Basic Survey on the People's Life (BSPL), which was conducted nationwide by stratified random sampling in 1986 and 1989 by the Japanese Ministry of Health and Welfare. The 1986 and 1989 BSPL were based on about 40,000 randomly selected households. Because microdata were not available, the pooled data for 47 prefectures in 1986 and 1989 were used instead.

Table 4.5 shows the estimates of the living arrangements of the elderly. The dependent variable is the ratio of the elderly living with their married children and sharing income and consumption to the total elderly.[12] The elderly living with unmarried children were removed from the sample to eliminate cases of unmarried youths living with their parents until marriage. Elderly people living with their married children are classified by age group. Almost 30 percent of the elderly (those 65 years of age or older) in 1990 were self-employed. Since self-employment incomes are difficult to measure, household consumption is used as a proxy for permanent income. Consumption in households where the head is aged 40–49 is used as a proxy for children's income. Housing services are represented by the area of the house divided by the number of "tatami" mats (about 1.7 square meters each) per household member.

Major findings are the following: First, the higher the income (approximated by household consumption) of the elderly, the greater the probability of coresidence, which is consistent with the result obtained by Otake (1991). The extent of this income effect, however, declines with age, implying that the effect of

---

12. This is the narrowest definition of coresidence and is different from quasi coresidence (i.e., living together in the same living unit but maintaining independent family budgets) used in Otake (1991).

Table 4.5   **Determinants of Coresidence**[a]

Age Group	Constant	Consumption of the Eldrely	Consumption of Supporters[b]	Housing Spaces[c]	1989 Dummy	R^2
60–69	−5.187	2.984	−2.31	1.564	−0.345	0.583
	(0.293)	(5.446)	(−3.580)	(4.540)	(−5.32)	
70+	0.315	1.263	−0.89	0.648	−0.201	0.718
	(0.130)	(8.034)	(−3.983)	(4.032)	(−5.349)	

Sources: Ministry of Health and Welfare (1989).
Note: Figures in parentheses ate *t*-values.
[a]The ratio of the elderly living with children to the total number of elderly having children.
[b]Average consumption of the age group 40–49 (10,000 yen per month).
[c]1.7 m² per household number.

higher elderly income used to bribe children into coresidence diminishes with age, mainly because elderly income levels fall with age. Second, the higher the children's income, the *lower* the probability of their living with parents, which is consistent with what Kotlikoff and Morris (1988) implied. The greater independence of children with higher incomes would encourage their living alone, particularly in present-day Japan, where values differ widely between generations, in part, because of the vastly different societies in which the generations grew up. However, the extent of this negative income effect also declines with the age of the elderly, partly because the deteriorating health of a parent may depress economic incentives. Finally, better housing services, measured by larger space per household member, result in less congestion and more privacy, thereby stimulating coresidence. The effect again becomes relatively small as the age of the elderly increases.

The conclusion, based on prefectural data, that higher income of the elderly raises the probability of coresidence with their children could be subject to sample selection bias because the elderly who are economically independent tend to be richer in prefectures with a higher incidence of coresidence. However, the level of elderly consumption by prefecture is negatively correlated with the ratio of elderly household heads to the total elderly population.[13] This effect is mainly due to the fact that prefectures with a relatively high ratio of elderly household heads are generally poor regions in Japan, indicating that this sample selection bias is not necessarily significant when prefectural data are used.

13. Consumption of elderly households (C) is explained by the ratio of elderly household heads to total elderly (H) using data from 47 prefectures in both 1989 and 1990 as follows:

$$\ln C = 4.012 - 0.262 \ln H - 0.100 D, \qquad R^2 = 0.183,$$
$$(32.10) \quad (4.38) \qquad (3.37)$$

where D is a dummy for the year 1990. Figures in parentheses are *t*-values.

4.5   Summary and Conclusion

The pattern of Japanese family structure has been marked by a high number of extended families living together. This characteristic indicates that the role of the family in securing a comfortable retired life for the elderly is quite important in Japan and is a major source of "age selectivity bias" in household-based statistics. The economic position of the elderly and their savings rate as conventionally measured are largely overstated because these data tend to exclude the poor elderly who are economically dependent members of their children's families. This not only explains why the savings rate of the Japanese elderly is so much higher than that of the U.S. elderly but also predicts a decline in savings rate in the near future given the persistent increase in elderly persons living alone.

The economic position of the Japanese elderly on average is almost equivalent to that of the nonelderly. In addition, accounting for imputed income further narrows the gap between the elderly and the nonelderly. While the income of the majority of households headed by the elderly may be low, their asset level is significant, thanks to past asset inflation in Japan, so that the elderly may persuade their children to live with them by offering rich housing services. Empirical estimates suggest that this strategic bequest motive may well be important in determining the living arrangements of the elderly, despite their children's feelings about shared living.

Finally, the income and wealth distribution of the elderly is much wider than that of the nonelderly and is more concentrated in the lower income classes. This implies that welfare policy targeting the elderly *per se* would be inefficient, particularly given increasing fiscal constraints. The policy of concentrating welfare resources on the *poor* elderly, rather than on the elderly population as a whole, would be effective.

References

Ando, A., M. Yamashita, and J. Murayama. 1986. An analysis of consumption and saving behavior based on the life-cycle hypothesis (in Japanese). *Keizai Bunseki,* no. 101: 25–139.

Hayashi, Fumio. 1986. An extension of the permanent income hypothesis and the examination (in Japanese). *Keizei Bunseki,* no. 101: 1–23.

Horioka, Charles Y. 1990a. The importance of life-cycle saving in Japan. Discussion Paper no. 225. Osaka: Osaka University, Institute of Social and Economic Research.

———. 1990b. Why is Japan's household saving rate so high? A literature survey. *Journal of the Japanese and International Economies* 4 (1): 49–92.

Hurd, Michael D. 1990. Research on the elderly: Economic status, retirement, and consumption and saving. *Journal of Economic Literature* 28: 565–637.

Kotlikoff, Laurence J., and John Morris. 1988. Why don't the elderly live with their children? A new look. NBER Working Paper no. 2734. Cambridge, Mass.: National Bureau of Economic Research.

Management and Coordination Agency. 1989. *National survey of family income and expenditure.* Tokyo: Government Printing Office.

————. 1992. *National survey of family income and expenditure.* Tokyo: Government Printing Office.

Ministry of Health and Welfare. 1989. *Basic survey on people's life.* Tokyo: Ministry of Health and Welfare.

OECD (Organisation for Economic Cooperation and Development). 1990. *The economic survey on Japan 1989/1990.* Paris: Organisation for Economic Cooperation and Development.

Otake, Fumio. 1991. Bequest motives of aged households in Japan. *Ricerche Economiche* 45 (2–3): 283–306.

Tachibanaki, Toshiaki. 1989. Japan's new policy agenda: Coping with unequal asset distribution. *Journal of Japanese Studies* 15 (2): 345–69.

Takayama, Noriyuki. 1992. *The graying of Japan: An economic perspective on public pensions.* Tokyo: Kinokuniya; New York: Oxford University Press.

Yashiro, Naohiro, and Yoshiaki Maeda. 1994. Applicability of the life-cycle hypothesis in Japan (in Japanese). *JCER Economic Journal* 27: 57–76.

Social Security Financing Policies and Rapidly Aging Populations

Aviva Ron

By 2025, 58 percent of the world's projected 1.2 billion people over 60 will be in Asia (ILO 1997). Among this group, 11 percent are expected to be over 80. Thus Asia can expect to have nearly 700 million elderly persons, of whom about 77 million will be over 80. This population will contain more women than men. These projections should be at the core of the region's long-term approach to social protection for the elderly.

Challenges of an Aging Population

The paper covers developments in pension and health care benefits within the framework of social security. Since health care can account for a significant portion of household spending in old age, income security and insurance-supported access to health care are closely linked.

Inadequate social security coverage

In most Asian countries social security coverage is restricted to workers in the public and private (formal) sectors. Most of the working-age population who will become elderly by 2025 are now in their 40s and 50s. Not taking life expectancy differences by income level into account, most of these individuals are not formal workers. Under current arrangements they are unlikely to have social protection for income or health care in old age, whether through national social security schemes, community initiatives, or private commercial insurance.

The situation is particularly difficult for women, who are more likely to be engaged in informal economic activity or employed as domestic workers without social protection in their own right and without the protection they may be afforded as dependents of insured workers. For most of their lives, the elderly women of the early 21st century will have borne major burdens without remuneration in household tasks and in the provision of livelihood means. In any event, a smaller portion of elderly women than men is likely to be covered by social security systems.

Strained living arrangements and personal care

Another set of issues that will become more prominent are living arrangements and personal care of the elderly. Today most elderly men and women in Asia live with their adult children. For example, in 1994, 92 percent of the old people in the Philippines lived in households with relatives. In Singapore it was 81 percent and in Indonesia, 81 percent (Association of Southeast Asian Nations data). This situation will change dramatically by 2025, when there will be fewer older children for parents to live with. Increasing urbanization could force elderly rural residents who require assistance with daily living to move to cities to live with fewer or even lone adult children.

These adult children and their spouses may be extremely busy workers, away from home for most of the day, or themselves already over 60. Thus it may be unrealistic to expect a significant portion of the elderly to live with adult children in the coming decades. In terms of financing policy for social protection, the concept of basic services for the elderly may need to be broadened to deal with housing and personal care.

Aviva Ron is senior specialist on social security on the South-East Asia and Pacific Multidisciplinary Advisory Team at the International Labour Organization in Manila.

A third element relates to the nature and scope of the benefits to be covered under the broad objective of providing old age security. Defining these benefits raises issues of need, demand, cultural values, and perceptions and expectations. Some people aspire to live in luxurious retirement, without any barriers to seeking high-quality medical care. Most older people, however, simply want to live with dignity and to enjoy good health, without getting themselves or their children into debt when medical services and changes in living arrangements are required.

When trying to define what type of social protection is needed, we may find that from middle age, people will seek protection from the lack of cash resources during retirement, a period of much lower or no income. Many are aware of the changing economic factors that may reduce the value of cash or other assets accumulated during their working lives. They may also be confused by reports on the future viability and value of savings, pensions, or provident funds. Most elderly will essentially seek protection from poverty.

Among those who have accumulated savings, some may be irrational in using money for health care. They may delay seeking care in the early stages of disease or avoid obtaining basic services that they have always considered a low priority, such as clean water and sanitation. The elderly often do not pay sufficient attention to the hazards of ill health, including those prompted by a lack of cash resources for adequate nutrition, shelter, and mobility. The vast majority of the elderly see these goods within a general context of available cash resources, rather than as necessary for their health. Yet when the longstanding chronic condition of an individual or spouse becomes life-threatening, life savings can be wiped out in a short time by just a few high-cost medical treatments—without significant health benefits.

The approach to social protection should be basic, allowing all funding partners to provide benefits within an affordable spending limit, regardless of the sources of revenue. But defining basic levels of income, housing, and health benefits can be extremely difficult and delay the development of appropriate social security schemes. Both consumers and policymakers need to change some of their perceptions and expectations to ensure a higher-quality and more productive old age. Many elderly populations perceive that

deterioration of vision to eventual blindness is part of growing old. Access to health care that removes a cataract to retain sight may be beyond the expectations of many. A similar situation applies to mobility. There is little awareness of the improvement in the mobility of the elderly that can be attained with simple aids and physical changes in and around the home. Safe water and sanitation in the household make a significant difference in the functioning of an older person with motor difficulties. These utilities are not just public health concerns but also personal preventive measures. Broadening the nature and scope of basic benefits ensures a higher-quality old age by adding preventive and rehabilitative services. Moreover, reduced dependency in old age is generally cost-effective.

Recent Changes in Social Security Financing

Gruat (1997), in a review of trends in social security systems, identifies three main reasons for social security reform around the world. The first is to make the systems responsive to social needs by targeting the benefits to populations with the greatest needs. Reform may, for example, seek to cover informal workers, including those engaged in irregular economic activity and with unstable incomes. Social protection schemes can be developed by extending formal sector schemes through legislation that implements national social protection policies—as in Japan, the Republic of Korea, the Philippines, and Vietnam.

Recent years have seen sporadic growth in schemes for the informal sector, in some cases ahead of national policy or when the implementation of national policy has been too slow to achieve local goals. These schemes may be implemented using innovative approaches—for example, by operating through cooperatives, introducing new contractual agreements with providers of benefits, or cooperating with nongovernmental organizations (Ron 1997).

Informal sector initiatives usually start with short-term benefits, such as health care. Though the move toward such systems is positive, the list of problems to be dealt with is long, particularly if long-term benefits are included. Because the schemes are likely to start with voluntary affiliation, there may be adverse selection, and therefore a need for stringent monitoring of eligibility to prevent abuse. The concept of insurance, or prepayment for services that may not be used, is difficult for some people to comprehend. A multitude of schemes may result that lack sufficient commonality in basic conditions and benefits and do not offer portability of entitlement. While it is neither realistic nor desirable to plan for unified systems in all countries, in pluralistic systems the unguided growth of such schemes may show many cases of failure.

The second reason for social security reform is the increasing prominence of economic over social concerns. Reforms seek greater targeting efficiency by changing the conditions of entitlement and the method of calculating benefits and reimbursements. This approach appears to divert the social security system to financial activities outside its basic objectives, such as promoting capital markets. There may be a risk of neglecting membership and benefit objectives, and of undermining the social security scheme's responsiveness to changing needs.

The third reason for reform is to promote individual options. Changing supply and demand factors, including privatization, encourage reform that allows for individual preferences. The scope of this reform is enormous, from the addition of voluntary, supplementary insurance options above the basic benefits (through both public and private initiatives) to the development of purely private insurance systems for specific groups. The opening of social protection mechanisms to market forces need not necessarily mean a transfer to private for-profit insurance entrepreneurs, as often seems to be the case in discussions of social security reform. Constructive competition involving both the public and private sectors could cater to the demand for individual preferences. For example, health insurance schemes can generate competition between public and private health care providers. Thus improvements can be made without destroying equity and with due regard for international standards on social security.

Although these reforms have extended coverage and made benefits more compatible with needs, there have also been some unforeseen consequences. Collective financing is less common. Diverse, separate schemes do not offer the benefits of core principles and practices to ensure equal treatment under the various schemes, portability between them, and some minimal redistribution of funding resources. Conditions of entitlement are more likely to have means-tested benefits and limitations, leading many to wonder whether the new forms are social insurance or social assistance. And though there are new social partners, there are not yet effective mechanisms for holding them accountable in social insurance schemes.

The reform process

The development and implementation of reforms are part of a process that is not always coherent. More attention tends to be paid to stating objectives and identifying stages than to developing workable definitions of the benefits to target populations and specifying the responsibilities of each partner in funding, management, and financial control. Defining "basic" benefits is often a major stumbling block in the reform process, or even a way to delay the extension of coverage to new target populations.

To better understand the process, consider the relationship between social development and social security systems. Social development is dynamic, and Asia's pace appears to be comparatively rapid. Social security systems can be based on the principles embodied in International Labour Organization (ILO) conventions and ratified by most ILO member states. But each scheme has its own history and own pace of responding to change. In general, social security systems tend to be slow in dealing with changing needs linked to shifting demographics, employment, and globalization, and the related health hazards. Reforms that are meaningful beyond policy declarations must cover all these changes.

Thus we must define both old and new benefits over a longer lifespan, covering new populations with unstable sources of income (such as the self-employed or informal workers) or populations with changing locations for the provision of benefits (such as migrant workers). The spectrum of health care traditionally covered by social insurance mechanisms is being challenged as it becomes increasingly clear that preventive and rehabilitative components are essential not only for the health of the insured populations but also for the health of the funds. In addition, early return to productive work means a return to contributory status for an insured person, who in turn contributes to economic growth.

The nature of social security systems explains part of the delay in responding to needs. These systems may be governed by national legislation that can be amended only when certain political circumstances prevail, requiring a lengthy process under the best conditions. The regulations for operation of the law may be misused and even abused. And even when social security systems have a quasi-autonomous administrative structure, their daily management may be more political than professional.

Thus it is important to be realistic when planning, legislating, and implementing reform, and to ensure that at least five essential areas are covered: administrative structure, benefits, contributions or sources of revenue, target populations, and relationships with social partners. In addition, it is important to bear in mind that extending coverage and benefits to self-employed, informal, and migrant workers could quickly double or triple the number of insured persons. Some new social partners have less experience with planning and negotiations, as they are indeed new to social security.

Shifts in the burden of responsibility for social protection

The reform of social security systems is also shifting the burden of responsibility. One type of shift is from government responsibility for financing services, such as health care, to consumer responsibility. Another is from enterprise or employer liability for reimbursement or provision of benefits to a contributory and cost-sharing approach through regular prepayment of a defined contribution or percentage of wages by workers, employers, and sometimes governments.

Some countries have retained government responsibility for direct financing by legislating that it must pay a defined part of the contribution. Such was the case in Thailand, where the first Social Security Law, passed in 1990, stipulated government responsibility for one-third of the contribution for salaried workers in the private sector. Given Thailand's current economic crisis, government participation is now being questioned, particularly for the contribution to pensions scheduled to start in 1998. Although many successful national pension schemes do not depend on government contributions, Thailand's current political climate does not facilitate amending the law—providing an example of the problems faced in social security reform.

In transition economies such as China and Vietnam, social security reforms reflect a shift in the burden of responsibil-

ity for financing from enterprises (including state enterprises) to employees and employers. China's social security reform for public and private sector salaried workers is raising salaries to compensate for the employee contribution, even for the 1 percent employee contribution toward health insurance. In the reform of rural medical cooperatives in China, local governments can add to the contributions of the rural insured population at will. In practice, local governments add a flat amount per insured person that reflects their financial situation each year (Carrin and others 1996).

Vietnam's Health Insurance Decree of 1992 imposed compulsory health insurance for active and retired salaried workers, funded by employee and employer contributions. The same decree stipulated central government contributions for veterans or their survivors and the disabled through the Ministry of Labor, Invalids, and Social Affairs. While the operations of the health insurance system are centralized, Vietnam's Health Insurance Company encourages initiatives in voluntary affiliation through its provincial offices. One such initiative is the coverage of the elderly indigent by the People's Committee (local government) of the province of Hai Phong, through payment of the contributions of these individuals to the provincial Health Insurance Company (Ron and Carrin 1996).

The shift in responsibility for financing by no means terminates government responsibility. In fact, this transition should strengthen governments' role and responsibility in developing the optimal financing policies for social protection, enacting the required legislation, and ensuring effective implementation. The paradox is that often when government has relinquished financial responsibility and passed the necessary legislation, interest dwindles along with its financial commitment.

Pooling of funds

The pooling of funds is a basic-tenet in the concept of social security, as is the pooling or spreading of risks. In recent years renewed attention has been paid to the pooling of funds (with somewhat less attention to the pooling of risks), prompted by the trend toward establishing individual savings under or on top of pooled funds in social insurance schemes.

The elderly are a high-risk population for social protection schemes. Thus it seems that the most logical way to cost-effectively meet their needs is to share their risks with low-risk populations. Yet the population currently making contributions may not be large enough to cover its own risks over time, particularly if there is little control over how quickly funds are spent.

Who will make up future vulnerable populations? Most Asian social security schemes for public and private sector salaried workers, and for the informal sector and self-employed, cover insured persons, as retired workers, and dependents of insured persons or survivors of active and retired workers. These groups do not include most women working in family enterprises or migrant workers returning to spend their final years in their home country. Social security coverage was recently extended to overseas Filipino workers but is aimed mainly at protecting against contingencies.

In any case, many of those currently covered as workers may not be eligible for benefits in old age, either because they will not have made sufficient contributions to entitle them to old age benefits or because some benefits do not continue into retirement. Health care benefits were extended to retired workers in the Philippines only recently. In Thailand retired workers can opt to pay a flat-rate contribution to retain coverage for health care. Few countries in Asia have universal coverage through national tax-funded pension and health schemes or compulsory social security schemes. If current practices continue, the individuals now covered will not account for a significant percentage of the elderly in most of Asia by 2025.

For health care, universal coverage may be more likely through compulsory contribution schemes than through national systems funded entirely by general taxation. Once funding partners have been identified and mechanisms developed for individuals outside the system, the extension of coverage will need to be rapid. Even if the elderly are given top priority, there is no time and certainly no justification to collect contributions from them and then create funds by imposing lengthy qualifying periods. There does not seem to be any logical alternative to pooling active and retired workers, across private and public sectors and across generations, to achieve fund viability.

In this regard, consider what has happened in pluralistic systems where separate funds are operated for different groups. In the Republic of Korea active industrial workers have a well-balanced health insurance fund that runs a surplus (Lee 1995). Retirees from all labor sectors are covered by a special

fund for retired workers and their dependents. Cost-sharing levels for health care are rising for members of this fund because it the only apparent way to avoid huge deficits. Yet raising contribution rates for retirees is hardly a rational solution.

One variation being tried in the reform of social health insurance for salaried workers in China is to use pooled funds after individual accounts have been exhausted, or when high-cost services are required. The individual accounts accrue about half of the employer and employee contribution, which is based on a percentage of each employee's salary. These funds are kept in the bank to earn interest and are transferable as inheritances. Questions are now being raised on the equity and rationality of this approach in the first of 60 cities included in this experiment. Individual accounts are in fact not an insurance mechanism but compulsory savings that would otherwise be difficult to put aside.

In several of the pilot cities the individual savings are to be used for minor illness, while the pooled funds are for more costly care. Workers are reluctant to use their savings for illnesses perceived as minor, while providers have become adept at emptying the pooled funds. The neglect of minor cases often occurs at the onset of chronic disease, and the consequences of such disease further deplete pooled funds and workers' long-term capacity to work.

The trend toward privatization in transition economies must also be considered in the pooling issue. There are wide disparities in salaries and income within and between state and private enterprises. Social insurance systems that place individual savings at the base and pooled funds above put low-income workers at a double or triple disadvantage. They exhaust their smaller savings faster, possibly with a higher prevalence of health problems and with less knowledge to guide them about rational use of the system.

For all these reasons it would seem preferable and logical to continue with past social security practice. That is, pooled funds should form the base for risk sharing among all members of the insured population, and cover an essential and balanced spectrum of benefits. Individual accounts can then be used for supplementary benefits.

Pension Benefits

The rapid aging of the population in Asia is not the main reason to establish or extend pensions systems for old age.

As noted, anticipated changes in living arrangements for the elderly are prompting concern about support in old age in general. In parallel, employment and labor force factors have spurred interest in pensions as a form of support (Beattie 1997). The growth of the salaried sector has put a time dimension into the search for income replacement during retirement. Salaried employment generally involves a mandatory retirement age, after which the employee may or may not find a new job with a new employer or become self-employed.

The importance of some form of income replacement during old age is increasingly recognized, though not necessarily by most of the individuals who will be at risk in the coming decades. Awareness of the need for this form of social protection will probably grow in the near future, along with national and international activities. In the meantime, the problem of finding the optimal financing solution is compounded by projections of the population at risk, and by the length of time during which such support may be needed.

Current arrangements for financial protection in old age in most countries in Asia and the Pacific will not come close to meeting the challenges created by the expected elderly population. A small number of countries offer financial support for all their older citizens. Australia and New Zealand have statutory pension schemes funded by general taxes. Japan provides old age pensions through a contributory social security mechanism (Beattie 1997). And provident funds have developed in some countries where British influence pervaded, such as India and Malaysia.

Political and technical factors make it difficult to transform a provident fund into a pension scheme, and only recently have some countries pursued such reforms. This change has been driven by the fact that the duration of life after retirement is getting longer. The lump sum payments of provident funds are not an appropriate form of social protection for old age, particularly when this period may be more than a quarter of the lifespan. From the viewpoint of the adequacy of pension funds, a country's retirement age is crucial. The statutory retirement age may be influenced by economic recession and employment (Anderson 1994). Over the past two decades some European countries lowered the retirement age and provided incentives for early retirement. In response to largely unforeseen neg-

ative consequences, such policies are now being reversed. In Asia retirement ages are likely to rise, partly because of the increase in life expectancy.

In some systems, such as the Fiji National Provident Fund, beneficiaries can choose between lump sum and pension payments. Most members choose the lump sum, which may indicate some lack of awareness of long-term needs. Since 1995 India's Employee Provident Fund has been partially converted into a pension scheme. Employer contributions now finance a pension, while worker contributions continue to be paid into individual savings accounts.

Countries that have developed compulsory pension funds have started with salaried workers and gradually expanded to workers in small enterprises and the self-employed. But the growth in coverage of the self-employed, including individuals in high-income occupations, has been slow. Here again there may be a lack of awareness of the potential benefits of this form of social protection. Making regular contributions to a pension that will replace income in the not too immediate future may not be attractive to workers, even when the contribution is shared with employers. And employers in the salaried sector are not likely to make contributions when the capacity of pension schemes to enforce compliance with legislation is not well developed.

Throughout Asia there is increased understanding of and interest in compulsory pension schemes, and efforts are being made to extend or merge existing schemes. In Lao PDR and Vietnam schemes for civil servants are being extended to private sector workers. Since 1995 the Korean government has subsidized the administration of the pension scheme for farmers, fishers, and other rural self-employed persons as part of its efforts to implement compulsory coverage of this population. The Philippines is trying to adapt administrative mechanisms and reach reciprocal agreements with other countries for millions of migrant workers.

The continuation of entitlement to health care for retired workers and their dependents seems logical but is not always practiced. Two reasons cited are the difficulty in collecting contributions from individuals rather than from employers, and the possible unfairness of flat-rate contributions. A pension scheme enables the deduction of health care contributions at the source, simplifying matters. Where desirable, a pension scheme can also allow for a progressive contribution, based on percentage of pension, rather than a flat-rate contribution. Thus this approach deals with the criticism of cross-subsidization of health care between the elderly who have accrued significant assets and sources of income and those who depend on pensions.

Health Care and Welfare Services

Health care financing reflects the shift in government responsibility in most countries in Asia. Responsibility for both the financing and delivery of services is generally detailed in basic health laws, which stipulate free care in government facilities. While most governments have adopted the target of providing universal health care by 2000, few continue to automatically deliver free care to all but their very poorest citizens. In recent years ministries of health have introduced user fees in their health care facilities at both the national and local levels. The application of user fees has forced these ministries to develop budgeting and pricing mechanisms, leading to better financial management by governments and providers.

User fees have potential drawbacks, however (Abel-Smith 1992). Applying user fees at the time of illness can lead to irrational health behavior, first by prompting delays in seeking care and then by distorting decisions on what services to purchase beyond the initial consultation. Some old people may purchase whatever care is advised in an attempt to lengthen life, whatever the cost. Many more, however, may take a skeptical approach and do very little in terms of seeking care—particularly when it requires them to spend scarce resources.

The revenue generated by user fees, particularly if the payment is minimal in the first stage, may be less than expected and may not even justify the cost of collection. In addition, user fees can encourage patients and providers to behave unethically in seeking exemptions from payment. Health care providers quickly realize the potential for generating revenue by generating demand for care, and may start encouraging unnecessary care. In developing countries such behavior is not limited to overuse of high technology or lengthy hospital stays. More common is the large portion of patients who receive vitamins and antibiotics, often by injection.

User fees cannot become the preferred alternative to health care financing. But despite the current increase in economic activity and the potential for increases in general tax revenue, governments are not likely to return to the "free"—that is, funded through general tax revenues paid by the economically active members of society—care system. Tax collection systems are generally not well developed. And even if tax collection produced sizable revenues, other priorities (education, housing, roads, transport) would likely compete for these funds.

This analysis should take into account the effect of higher health care expenditures. For a variety of reasons, health care costs more today than ever before. People live longer, and there are more effective technologies for diagnosing and treating chronic diseases. But it is difficult to control the volume of new technology and its use, and the use of care is often driven by supply rather than demand.

These factors contribute to the reluctance of governments to return to systems in which they are responsible for securing public funds and disbursing them to finance health care for the majority of the population. Governments are also reluctant to take back the responsibility for financing health care because of current efforts to achieve a better public-private mix in resources, reduce public expenditure, and derive more resources through consumer cost sharing.

In practice, however, most of the elderly in many Asian countries fall into the "free care" category. Access to health care means being identified and possibly being given a card exempting the bearer from charges on the grounds of being an elderly indigent citizen. But utilization patterns for this population are not necessarily high, and suggest that many older persons would rather not receive care than apply for the exemption card. Where the stigma of having such a card is not an issue, it may be abused and misused.

Government responsibility after the shift

How does the change in government responsibility affect health care for the elderly? Responsibility has shifted from financing health care to finding the optimal method for financing health care, including for the elderly. If health insurance is the best option for the future elderly population, to what extent has this mechanism been developed in Asia? And what needs to be done to cover the elderly?

Social health insurance was introduced for the formal labor sector in Asian countries, as part or as a forerunner of broader social security benefits. The beneficiary population was usually defined as workers and legal dependents, though some countries opted to cover only workers. In many countries civil servants were covered by noncontributory medical benefit arrangements, with at least some benefits extended to the workers' dependents. Reflecting the small portion of the labor force in salaried employment in the public and private sectors, population coverage has remained rather low for the past decade. The proportion of the elderly covered by such schemes is even lower, as many do not offer health care benefits for retired workers.

Recent years have seen the growth of health insurance schemes as community initiatives, on a small but encouraging scale. These schemes involve economically active members of cooperatives or maybe sponsored by nongovernmental organizations, but only a small number of older people may be covered as dependent parents. Commercial for-profit insurance has grown, though on a far smaller scale and usually as a branch of large general insurance companies. The populations first covered by this type of insurance were mainly the employees of multinational companies, and the share of such schemes in national coverage is still negligible in most Asian countries. In any case, most commercial for-profit schemes do not provide coverage for people over 60 unless they have been in the scheme for many years.

The exceptions to the above are the few countries—Australia, Japan, Korea, Singapore—where legislation eventually covered all residents or citizens. Countries with universal health insurance coverage are now concerned about long-term care, mainly for the elderly. Through additional contributions, new benefits are being designed to focus on rehabilitation and long-term nursing and custodial care. The main stimulus for such schemes appears to be the increasing number of older persons living alone rather than basic concern about rehabilitation or changing morbidity in old age.

Moving toward more balanced coverage

As noted, Asia is a long way from seeing the majority of the elderly in 2025 covered by appropriate health insurance mechanisms. But rather than dealing with the problem of how coverage can be extended in terms of administrative frameworks and sources of contributions, it might be more useful to look at the optimal approach to health insurance benefits for the elderly.

Aging, as manifested by longer life expectancy, results partially from the successes of medical science and technology. In the past 50 years great strides have been made in eradicating infectious diseases and in preventing and detecting some chronic diseases. But we still lack knowledge about the value of technologies that prevent the progression of disease through complicated and costly interventions. It appears that health system development in Asia tends to promote high-cost diagnostic, pharmaceutical, and surgical interventions while neglecting other components. High-quality care is becoming synonymous with a range of diagnostic procedures and consultations, and with the private health care facilities where these have been developed.

Beyond maternal and child health care programs, governments appear to give inadequate attention to achieving a balanced spectrum of care in community, hospital, and alternative forms of inpatient care, such as hospice care. Even in countries where the elderly are covered by social health insurance, there has been little revision of benefits and conditions to promote primary health care, higher-quality care, continuity of care, or cost control. Most health insurance systems in Asia still favor inpatient care, and have done little to limit the use of high-cost technology by developing primary health care (Abel-Smith 1992). Such trends are incompatible with viable health insurance systems, in which contributions need to be affordable for the vast majority of the population. And they are certainly not compatible with achieving a balanced budget when a large portion of members is elderly.

Parallel action may be needed to achieve compatibility between the goals of extending health care coverage to the elderly and developing health systems. Governments will need to reconsider their new responsibilities and become more active in achieving balanced system development, which will have to include some control of health care resource growth. Governments will also have to support social health insurance efforts to control health care expenditures by introducing appropriate pricing mechanisms and changing provider payment mechanisms, in both public and private facilities.

Social health insurance systems will need to develop a cost-effective and cost-efficient approach to the provision of benefits for the elderly—promoting health, preventing disease, developing cost-effective measures to detect disease as early as possible, and monitoring to prevent the progression of disease. These functions are best carried out by community-based primary care providers, with referral to other types and levels of care as needed.

Alternative sites for the provision of care should also be considered. Throughout Asia, it is customary to tend to parents at home in the final stages of life. But home care at earlier stages of disease and hospice care are almost unknown beyond some recognition of their advantages for HIV/AIDS patients. Social security systems should use these approaches to enlarge the spectrum of health care benefits.

Governments and social health insurance systems will have to reach consensus on what constitutes public preventive care, provided by government, and what is included in personal preventive care, to be covered as insurance benefits. Another area requiring coordination is overall health system development. The strengthening of primary care and the inclusion of new forms or locations of care need government support, not only from ministries of health but also from ministries dealing with human resource development and welfare services. Ministries of health are clearly responsible for licensing health care practitioners and facilities. Yet in many Asian countries the development of health insurance reflects confusion about whether accreditation is the responsibility of government or the insurance scheme.

Social health insurance, together with other social insurance branches and other agencies, will also have to broaden the approach to social protection benefits beyond health care and income replacement in old age. It is extremely difficult to define what benefits will protect old people from isolation, loneliness, societal attitudes leading to discrimination, and the decline in dignity and respect that often accompanies old age.

The main difficulty is not a lack of empirical knowledge on effective services or benefits for the elderly. It is more closely related to the difficulties in changing awareness of and attitudes about these issues among policymakers and the insured population. At the level of social insurance, this means that health insurance revenues—including surpluses of contribution revenues over expenditures—could be used for less conventional purposes (for example, developing the infrastructure of health care facilities in response to members' needs). At the level of the consumer, it means that an adult son or daughter will derive more pride from purchasing a year's membership in a health insurance scheme for an elderly parent than from paying for a high-cost diagnostic procedure that may make a minimal contribution to health.

The "five D's" used as indicators of health can be used to examine the outcomes of such measures for the elderly. Ultimately Death will come, and old age will not be free of Disease. But much can be done to reduce Disability, Discomfort, and Dissatisfaction. Using such an outcome approach could help bring about changes in awareness and operations of social security systems.

Conclusion

The aging of populations does not result from medical success alone. Increased access to health and other services comes from overall economic development, including the removal of financial barriers to receiving care. Thus any adjustments should build on success, and use lessons from education, health care, and economic growth to improve the expectations for healthier, happier, and more active old age.

Healthy aging is built on a healthy childhood and working life, with appropriate social protection to cover the contingencies of the lifespan (WHO 1993). Corresponding social security mechanisms cover maternity, illness and disability, occupational injuries and diseases during the working years, and ultimately old age and death. To build on achievements, we need to consider the capacity to achieve the various forms of universal social protection.

The process to extend coverage may begin with some decisions on how to proceed in terms of structure, including the issue of unified or pluralistic systems and financing policy. Achieving universal coverage will require rapidly extending coverage to dependents of salaried workers, informal sector workers, and the self-employed. Social security does not imply one unified system, but pluralistic mechanisms to cover all citizens—using common basic standards and operated by public and nongovernmental organizations at the national and local levels. The public-private mix that satisfies basic needs and individual preferences without compromising equity should be an inherent component of this effort.

Pooling should be as broad as is politically feasible, in terms of national decentralization policies and local factors. National networks that provide guidelines and hopefully some redistribution are essential. The extension of social security does imply compulsory affiliation through contributory mechanisms by or on behalf of insured persons. Voluntary supplementary insurance, through the same scheme or through private insurance schemes, can top up nonessential benefits to enable individual preference.

The move toward universality will require more than simple changes in benefits. New beneficiary populations will need new mechanisms to calculate and collect contributions and to assure compliance. Coverage objectives could be planned in stages, beginning with new retirees if they are not currently covered, their spouses, and the dependents of active workers. In parallel, social security system management needs to be improved, not only to keep up with information technology but also to create responsiveness in the provision of benefits at each level of operation.

Until universal coverage is achieved, governments will need to provide social assistance for individuals not covered by social security schemes. Because allocations are unlikely to cover all the needy, local initiatives and nongovernmental organizations will be essential. Moreover, there should be accreditation and coordination to avoid duplication of effort and resources.

Decisionmaking and reform will be difficult, and may imply a radical shift in values and reassessment of the approach to solidarity. The approach taken should focus on value for money for the appropriate benefits for the target beneficiaries. Systems should be workable and transparent, guided by professional knowledge, compatible with economic growth objectives, and well understood and acceptable at the political level. The schemes need to be stable yet flexible, able to respond to changing circumstances without major revision of legislation.

As noted, Asia is projected to have 58 percent of the world's elderly by 2025. In most countries people over 60 will account for 10–15 percent of the population. Industrial countries with a similar percentage of elderly have problems providing appropriate services for their senior citizens. But the situation is not catastrophic in countries where a universal social protection policy has been followed and new benefits have been introduced in response to changing needs.

Some of the problems facing industrial countries developed because shifting demographics and changing employment patterns have placed the financing burden on two few workers. Other problems come from inappropriate fund management or from a period of economic instability that leads to incompatibility between the amounts that can be spent from old age funds and the real cost of services for the elderly. Yet in many cases social protection benefits have been broadened excessively to accommodate unnecessary high technology, and many payment mechanisms for providers are inefficient. If we focus on finding out what basic services are required, place more emphasis on prevention, and emphasize a primary care approach, we can foster a kinder, more respectful environment for the elderly population of 2025.

References

Abel-Smith, Brian. 1992. "Health Insurance in Developing Countries: Lessons from Experience." *Health Policy and Planning* 7(3): 215–26.

Anderson, R. 1994. "The Need to Formulate and Introduce New Measures in View of the Increasing Demand for Existing Social Security Benefits and the Consequent Growth in Social Security Expenditures." Paper presented to the International Social Security Association's European Regional Meeting on Prevention Strategies for the Different Branches of Social Security, November, Helsinki.

Beattie, Roger. 1997. "Pension Systems and Pension Reform in Asia and the Pacific." International Labour Organization Regional Office for Asia and the Pacific, East Asia Multidisciplinary Advisory Team, Bangkok.

Carrin, G., A. Ron, S.C. Wang, Le Xuesheng, and Yu Jun. 1996. "The Reform of the Rural Cooperative Medical System in the People's Republic of China." Macroeconomics, Health and Development Series 20. World Health Organization, Geneva.

Doron, H., and A. Ron. 1984. "Primary Care Promotion to Control Costs in Social Security Medical Care Systems." *International Social Security Review* 2: 150–57.

Gruat, J.V. 1997. "Trends in Social Security System Development." Paper presented at the International Seminar on Social Security Funds Management, March, Beijing.

ILO (International Labour Office). 1997. *Ageing in Asia: The Growing Need for Social Protection.* Regional Office for Asia and the Pacific, East Asia Multidiciplinary Advisory Team. Bangkok.

Lee Kyu Sik. 1995. "Health Care Reform in Korea and Its Future Issues." Paper presented at the Asian Development Bank's regional conference on Health Sector Reform in Asia, May, Manila.

Ron, A. 1997. "Community Health Care Financing Schemes." Paper presented at the international conference on health insurance in low- and middle-income countries, January 17–18, Antwerp.

Ron, A., and G. Carrin. 1996. "Health Insurance Development in Vietnam." Macroeconomics, Health and Development Series 23. World Health Organization, Geneva.

WHO (World Health Organization). 1993. "Report on Regional Seminar on National Policy Planning for Health of the Elderly." Manila.

J Popul Econ (2000) 13: 443–462

—Journal of—
Population Economics
© Springer-Verlag 2000

Social security, public education, and growth in a representative democracy

Alexander Kemnitz

University of Mannheim, Department of Economics, A5, D-68131 Mannheim, Germany
(Fax: +49-621-1811794; e-mail: kemnitz@econ.uni-mannheim.de)

Received: 05 April 1999/Accepted: 20 December 1999

Abstract. This paper studies the relationship between public education and pay-as-you-go social security in a representative democracy, where the government reacts both to voting and lobbying activities of workers and pensioners. While an intergenerational conflict prevails concerning actual social security contributions, workers may prefer public education for its positive effect on later pension benefits. Population aging diminishes the relative lobbying power of pensioners, leading to a higher contribution rate, educational expansion, and higher per capita income growth.

JEL classifications: D72, I28, J18

Key words: Pensions, education, aging

---

1. Introduction

It is well known that the continuous rise of old-age dependency ratios due to lower fertility and increased life expectancy necessitates serious adjustments in the pay-as-you-go (PAYG) pension schemes employed in most industrialized countries. Politico-economic considerations suggest that these adjustments entail higher contribution rates, for the increasing political power of the

---

All correspondence to Alexander Kemnitz. Earlier versions of this paper have been presented at the University of Mannheim, the European Public Choice Society Meeting in Lisbon, and the Congress of the International Institute of Public Finance in Moscow. I would like to thank the participants there, and Axel Brüggemann, Alessandro Cigno, Domenico da Empoli, Isidoro Mazza, Robert K. von Weizsäcker, Berthold Wigger, and an anonymous referee for valuable discussion and comments. The usual disclaimer applies. *Responsible editor:* Alessandro Cigno.

elderly precludes an appropriate cut-back of pension benefits (Preston 1984). As higher contribution rates crowd out private savings (Feldstein 1974), the growth prospects of aging economies look unfavorable at first glance: the resulting decline in physical capital accumulation depresses output growth in Romer (1986)-type endogenous growth models (Saint-Paul 1992).

This paper, however, presents an alternative picture of the effects of population aging on economic growth. It considers the fact that most societies engage not only in redistribution to the old via social security, but also to the *young* via public education. Since human capital is a generally acknowledged engine of growth (Lucas 1988), a decrease in fertility may have a positive growth effect: it allows to equip each student with a higher education level without increasing a worker's tax burden. Consequently, the development of aging economies rather hinges on how the changing population shares of students and pensioners affect the incentives to provide transfers to both groups.

In contrast to most of the literature on this topic, the present approach addresses the determination of public education and social security expenditures in a *public choice framework*. It is therefore not concerned with the question how a benevolent government *should* allocate funds for education and unfunded old-age security (Docquier and Michel 1999; Kaganovich and Zilcha 1999), but rather how policy is shaped by the attitudes and the political power of the respective living generations. The decision over both intergenerational transfers is made in a *representative democracy* where the government strives for the maximization of the political support within its constituency comprising workers and pensioners.[1] Concentrating on human capital as the source of growth, it will be shown that a politico-economic equilibrium with a *higher contribution rate* to the social security system exhibits *higher per capita income growth*. This result, which is in sharp contrast to the view outlined above, is due to the fact that the PAYG pension system creates incentives to invest in public education: higher educational expenditures raise the wage income of tomorrow's workers and so expected pension benefits. Thus, a positive future contribution rate provides a *non-altruistic incentive* to invest in the next generation's human capital.[2]

Political incentives of non-altruistic individuals to invest in the earning possibilities of succeeding generations have also been studied by Konrad (1995). He presents a *gerontocracy* where decisions over *social capital*, education being a part of it, are made exclusively by the retirees. While sharing the selfish motive for intergenerational transfers, the approach presented here allows to incorporate some important additional aspects of the political decision making on public education and old-age security. First, while the gerontocracy assumption is useful as a benchmark case, it disregards any political influence on part of the working population although this group continues to form the majority of the constituency even after the aging process has faded out. The political importance of this majority is taken account of here.

Second, in a gerontocracy benefits and costs must accrue in the same time period for public education to exist. Otherwise, the pensioners would not gain anything from transfers to the young. This is in contrast with the apparent time lag between the costs and benefits of education.[3] Konrad (1995) argues correctly that the results could be reproduced under majority voting where a worker is the median voter and the contribution rate is exogenously fixed.[4] However, fixing the contribution rate neglects ongoing pension reforms that have made social security issues almost a part of daily political business. In the model presented here, decisions over both policy instruments take place every period. Thus, the incentive to invest in the succeeding generation depends upon the *expectations* over future contribution rates, and therefore over the results of future political struggles where workers will oppose and pensioners will advocate social security. Therefore, the present approach combines the lack of intertemporal policy commitment with a realistic timing of the benefits and costs of education.

And third, the model allows for a more comprehensive investigation of the politico-demographic effects of population aging. In a gerontocracy, merely the biological interest rates of both transfers alter for all political power is concentrated among the retirees. In the representative democracy investigated here, policy is determined by both voting and interest group activities. A shift in the demographic structure affects both channels: First, the relative numbers of voters associated with both generations change. And second, as groups of different size have different incentives to invest in reaping political privilege, a changing age structure alters the political importance of both generations via their lobbying expenditures. These expenditures are explicitly derived from the group members' preferences. It is shown that a decline either in fertility or in mortality diminishes the retirees' relative lobbying influence. In the steady state equilibrium, this translates into higher per capita human capital investment and growth that is brought about by a higher contribution rate to the social security system. Thus, *population aging* leads both to a *higher contribution rate* to the social security system and to *higher per capita income growth*.

The paper is organized as follows. After a presentation of the economic environment, Sect. 3 derives the politico-economic equilibrium by considering both the government's and the interest groups' decisions. The long run equilibrium is established in Sect. 4. Section 5 reports on the effects of population aging. Section 6 concludes with some remarks on the assumptions and possible extensions of the model.

2. The economic environment

Consider a model of a small open economy with three overlapping generations. In every period, N_t individuals are born. They spend the first period of their life in a public education system and work for one period afterwards. With probability π they will survive into retirement. After this third period of life they die with certainty. Consequently, a higher π increases life expectancy and reduces mortality. The population grows from one period to the next with factor M: $N_{t+1} = M \cdot N_t$. Therefore, slower population growth due to lower fertility is captured by a decrease in M.

All individuals have an expected utility function with logarithmic per-period utility concerning consumption during work c_{t+1} and retirement z_{t+2}:[5]

$$U_t = \log c_{t+1} + \delta\pi \log z_{t+2}. \tag{1}$$

Consumption during childhood is neglected for simplicity. $\delta \leq 1$ is the individual intertemporal discount factor, determining the relative importance of old age consumption. If the individual survived into retirement with certainty, consumption during retirement would yield only δ times as much utility as consumption today. But since survival is uncertain, the probability of not dying must be considered, too. Having reached retirement, discounting of old age consumption vanishes.

Private old age security is available on a perfect annuity market. This market where benefits are only paid out if the investor is alive enables individuals to avoid accidental bequests arising from a premature death. Let a_{t+1} denote the private investment in annuities. Competition among insurers leads to the zero-profit condition $a_{t+1} \cdot N_t \cdot R = v_{t+2} \cdot \pi \cdot N_t$ with R as the world market interest factor and v_{t+2} as the amount paid out.

Consumption in both periods amounts to:

$$c_{t+1} = (1 - \tau_{t+1} - b_{t+1})h_{t+1} - a_{t+1} - x_{t+1}^w,$$

$$z_{t+2} = \frac{R}{\pi}a_{t+1} + P_{t+2} - x_{t+2}^o,$$

where τ_{t+1} is the tax rate raised to finance public education, and b_{t+1} is the contribution rate to the social security system. P_{t+2} is the pension received. x_{t+1}^w and x_{t+2}^o denote the individual's contributions to his interest group during employment (group w in $t + 1$) and retirement (group o in $t + 2$), respectively.

The human capital of a member of generation t is supplied in period $t + 1$ and is therefore denoted by h_{t+1}. It is produced in period t by educational expenditures g_t and parental human capital h_t, according to a constant-returns-to-scale production function:

$$h_{t+1} = F(g_t, h_t) = f\left(\frac{g_t}{h_t}\right)h_t.$$

Let $f(0) = 0$, $f'(0) = \infty$, $f'(\cdot) > 0$ and $f''(\cdot) < 0$. Then, educational expenditures are essential for producing human capital. The first expenditure unit yields an infinitely high increase, but further increases lead to diminishing increases in productive capabilities.

Education is entirely financed by the state, thus, g_t, the public educational expenditure per child is determined by the restriction $g_t N_t = \tau_t h_t N_{t-1}$, from which:

$$h_{t+1} = f\left(\frac{\tau_t}{M}\right)h_t \tag{2}$$

follows immediately. Therefore, the growth factor of human capital is a positive monotonous function of $g_t/h_t = \tau_t/M$, the amount of human capital a worker invests per child. We impose the restriction $\tau_t \geq 0$, i.e., it is not possible to transmit a negative human capital stock to the succeeding generation.

The social security system is of the PAYG-type and distributes its proceeds $b_t h_t N_{t-1}$ evenly among the surviving πN_{t-2} old. Budget balance then implies a pension of:

$$P_t = \frac{M b_t h_t}{\pi} \tag{3}$$

for every retiree. As mentioned above, old-age consumption can additionally be secured by investing in annuities. For a member of generation $t - 1$, the optimal investment is given by:

$$\frac{\partial U}{\partial a_t} = -\frac{1}{c_t} + \delta R \frac{\delta R}{z_{t+1}} = 0. \tag{4}$$

Considering (2)–(4), one obtains:

$$c_t = \frac{1}{1+\delta\pi} I_t, \tag{5}$$

$$z_{t+1} = \frac{\delta R}{1+\delta\pi} I_t, \tag{6}$$

with:

$$I_t = (1 - \tau_t - b_t)h_t - x_t^w + \frac{Mb_{t+1}}{R} f\left(\frac{\tau_t}{M}\right)h_t - \frac{\pi}{R}x_{t+1}^o$$

as the optimal consumption plan for a member of generation $t - 1$.

3. Political process and equilibrium

The political setting considered here is a representative democracy. A distinctive feature of this system is that political decisions are not entirely determined by election results. Rather, the government possesses some discretion, giving interest groups the ability to influence policy in their members' interest.

In this approach, we give explicit attention to the actions of these groups. However, this necessitates a formulation on how the government responds on political pressure. In the terminology of Becker (1983) an *influence function*, translating lobbying activities into political outcomes, is required. Therefore, we will derive the politico-economic equilibrium in a two-step procedure. First, we consider the government's optimal policy taking the activities of interest groups as given (Sect. 3.1). Building on the resulting influence function, the behaviour of the lobbies will be examined in section 3.2.[6] Consequently, in every period a game consisting of three subsequent stages is played. At stage 1, the lobbying groups simultaneously choose their activities. Then, at stage 2, the government sets the education tax τ_t and the social security contribution rate b_t. Finally (stage 3), workers adjust their savings a_t. As usual, the game is solved by backward-induction in order to derive a subgame-perfect equilibrium. The savings decision has already been derived in Sect. 2, (see Eq. (4)), so the analysis proceeds with the government's behaviour.

3.1. The government

The government is solely guided by its interest to stay in power. For this purpose, it strives for the highest political support it can possibly enjoy among its constituency. All decisions on education and pensions are undertaken to further this aim. As future generations including today's young cannot provide actual political support, long run consequences of today's policies are neglected. Policy simply results from balancing the interests of workers and pensioners, the two politically active generations.

The extent to which a generations' interests are followed by the government depends on various factors. One factor is the utility gain a single member experiences from governmental action. Furthermore, the relative voting power, measured by a generation's share in the constituency, and the relative strength of the lobby associated with the generations members is of importance. The latter factor is determined by X_t, the ratio of current effective influence expenditures of workers and pensioners. This variable will be discussed in detail in the next subsection, where it will turn out to be a function of the demographic structure. The precise form of the support function employed here is as follows:

$$S_t = U_{t-1} + \frac{\pi}{M} \Psi(X_t) U^t_{t-2}. \tag{7}$$

The government maximizes a politically weighted sum of the utilities – as far as they can still be influenced, see below – of the two eligible generations with the relative political weight of the pensioners amounting to $\frac{\pi}{M} \Psi(X_t)$, with $\Psi'(\cdot) > 0$, $\Psi''(\cdot) < 0$. Ceteris paribus increases in relative expenditures increase relative political power, but at an decreasing rate. To ensure interior solutions, we assume $\Psi'(0) = \infty$, $\Psi'(\infty) = 0$.

This formulation of political support draws on two branches of the political economy literature. The one branch, referring to the first factor in the relative political weight, is *probabilistic voting theory*. Coughlin (1986) shows that political competition between two parties can result in the maximization of a sum of voters' utilities, although the acquisition of power is the politicians' only aim. This model relies on uncertainty regarding individual voting decisions, with the probability to vote for a party being a continuous and concave function of the utility differentials under the policy proposals. If this function is identical for all individuals, both parties offer a utilitarian policy with equal individual weights.[7] A similar result obtains in Coughlin et al. (1990) who allow for the existence of interest groups, their decisive feature being their ideological bias in the form of the probability to vote for a certain candidate. If the distribution of these biases within groups is identical across all groups, their population shares and relative political weights will coincide. However, groups that are ideologically more homogenous than others will enjoy higher political influence.

Yet, while addressing the role of interest groups that approach neglects the active political pressure they exert on the government. Becker (1983) has developed a pioneering model of political competition with explicit *lobbying activities* like donations, threats, political advertisement, (strategic) information disclosure or personal gifts for politicians, just to name a few possibilities. In this model, all pressure groups fight simultaneously for political influence. Thus, a lobby's effectiveness is not determined by its absolute, but by its relative expenditures. This approach has been extended by various authors, e.g. Kristov et al. (1992). However, all these models explain political outcomes solely as the response to pressure groups. The political support function employed here, instead, combines the relative voting weights of Coughlin (1986) with relative lobbying expenditures, and thus allows for both voting behaviour

and pressure groups to influence policy. However, the interpretation of lobbying expenditures is not confined to political pressure in Becker's (1983)
sense. In the light of the voting approaches discussed above, interest groups
can enhance their political attractiveness by group-internal investments in responsiveness to utility differentials or ideological coherence. X_t can easily be
interpreted along these lines as the ratio of such investments.

Note, that while the worker's utility in (7) can be obtained from (1), (5)
and (6), a retiree's utility that can still be influenced in t amounts to:

$$U'_{t-2} = \log z_t = \log\left(\frac{R}{\pi}a_{t-1} + \frac{b_t M}{\pi}h_t - x_t^o\right),\tag{8}$$

since the decision over a_{t-1} can not be altered anymore.

Education tax and contribution rate are chosen by the government in
every period anew, capturing the individual uncertainty concerning especially
the development of the social security system. Because of its highly reversible
nature in our context, the contribution rate will sometimes be referred to as
the social security *tax*.

The effect an increase of the education tax has on the government's political support is as follows:

$$\frac{\partial S_t}{\partial \tau_t} = \begin{cases} -\dfrac{h_t}{c_t} : b_{t+1} \leq 0 \\[2mm] \dfrac{h_t}{c_t}\left[-1 + \dfrac{b_{t+1}}{R}f'\left(\dfrac{\tau_t}{M}\right)\right] : b_{t+1} > 0. \end{cases}\tag{9}$$

Education policy is entirely determined by the workers' preferences. The retirees are indifferent towards education, since they neither pay nor profit from
higher future human capital. The workers, however, prefer positive public
education expenditures if the future contribution rate is positive. They want a
tax rate such that the marginal gain from investing in human capital equals
the interest factor:

$$b_{t+1}f'\left(\frac{\tau_t}{M}\right) = R.\tag{10}$$

It is obvious that increases in tomorrow's contribution rate raise the marginal
return of public education and therefore lead to a higher education tax rate.
Expression (9) allows to state the condition the support-maximizing education
tax has to fulfill as:

$$\frac{h_t}{c_t}b_{t+1}\left[-R + b_{t+1}f'\left(\frac{\tau_t}{M}\right)\right] = 0,$$

where all factors are non-negative.

Still, there is no commitment possible for future contribution rates for the
government will adjust its policy in the future if this leads to higher popularity. Considering (5), (6) and (8), the contribution rate that secures maxi-

mum support in period t is determined by:

$$\frac{\partial S_t}{\partial b_t} = -\frac{1}{c_t} + \frac{\Psi(X_t)}{z_t} = 0. \tag{11}$$

From this equation, it can be seen that the pensioners profit and the workers loose unambiguously from higher social security taxes. The latter is due to the absence of any intertemporal link between the contribution rates. The workers cannot acquire any future claims by current contributions.

These conflicting interests are balanced by the government by choosing the contribution rate to the social security system such that the politically weighted marginal utilities of further increases in b_t for workers and pensioners are equalized. Put differently, the *pensioners' relative marginal utility of current consumption* $(1/z_t)/(1/c_t) = (1/z_t)/(\delta R/z_{t+1})$ equals their *relative lobbying weight* $\Psi(X_t)$. Relative marginal utility depends not only on the old age dependency ratio π/M, but also on the lifetime incomes of both generations. Via this channel the current contribution rate is partially determined by last period's human capital investment. In the same manner, the contribution rates of past and future periods enter the actual decision problem. However, the government disregards any strategic effects of today's decisions on the scope of future policies.[8]

3.2. The interest groups

Now that the government's behavior is examined, the decision of the interest groups can be derived. In fact this amounts to determining X_t, the relative political expenditures of the retirees. For further analysis, it is convenient to break this variable up into the workers' and the pensioners' total lobbying expenditures by X_t^w and X_t^o, respectively. It is obvious that $X_t = X_t^o/X_t^w$.

While it is generally acknowledged that interest groups form in order to influence policy according to the preferences of their members, their exact behavior depends upon their organizational structure. In this respect, larger groups face a disadvantage. They have to spend larger amounts to control *free-riding behavior* of its members, which is immanent to collective action (Olson 1965). Social pressure and effectiveness of individual contributions are more pronounced in smaller groups, making this problem easier to overcome.

In the present approach, these control or internal organizational costs are taken into account by stipulating that an increase in group size may not lead to an equivalent increase in total political expenditures. Formally, this means that $X_t^w = x_t^w N_{t-1}^\beta$ and $X_t^o = x_t^o (\pi N_{t-2})^\beta$ with $\beta \leq 1$. Effects of higher per capita contributions on organizational costs would not alter our results and are neglected for simplicity.

In every period, both groups decide internally about the individual obligatory contributions x_t^w and x_t^o. They decide simultaneously and thus take the expenditures of their competitor as given. All members will prefer the fee that maximizes individual utility given that it is paid by all members and considering organizational costs. Since all individuals within a generation are identical, unanimous consent over the contribution level within each lobby is ensured. The conditions for optimal per capita expenditures on part of workers and pensioners are then obtained from maximizing (1) with respect to x_t^w and

(8) with respect to x_t^o. This yields:

$$\frac{\partial U_{t-1}}{\partial x_t^w} = -\frac{db_t}{dx_t^w}h_t - 1 = 0, \tag{12}$$

and:

$$\frac{\partial U_{t-2}^l}{\partial x_t^o} = \frac{db_t}{dx_t^o}\frac{M}{\pi}h_t - 1 = 0. \tag{13}$$

Both generations equate the marginal costs of increasing lobbying expenditures with the marginal returns resulting from the reaction of b_t. This reaction can be derived from the influence function (11), the function describing the government's best response on lobbying activities. From this equation, we get:

$$\frac{db_t}{dx_t^w} = -\frac{\dfrac{1}{(1+\delta\pi)c_t^2} + \Psi'(X_t)\dfrac{X_t(N_{t-1})^\beta}{X_t^w z_t}}{\dfrac{h_t}{(1+\delta\pi)c_t^2} + \Psi(X_t)\dfrac{\pi}{M}\dfrac{h_t}{z_t^2}} < 0, \tag{14}$$

$$\frac{db_t}{dx_t^o} = \frac{\Psi'(X_t)\dfrac{(\pi N_{t-2})^\beta}{X_t^w z_t} + \Psi(X_t)\dfrac{1}{z_t^2}}{\dfrac{h_t}{(1+\delta\pi)c_t^2} + \Psi(X_t)\dfrac{\pi}{M}\dfrac{h_t}{z_t^2}} > 0. \tag{15}$$

The reaction of the social security tax to higher per capita contributions is unambiguous. It is negative for higher political spending on part of the workers, while the opposite is true for higher subscriptions from the pensioners. A closer look reveals two synchronous effects: First, higher per capita expenditures shift the relative lobbying weight in the group's favor. Second, they reduce its members' consumption possibilities and, thus, increase marginal utility.

Using (14) in (12) yields:

$$\Psi'(X_t)\frac{X_t N_{t-1}^\beta}{X_t^w} = \Psi(X_t)\frac{M}{\pi}\frac{1}{z_t}, \tag{16}$$

which gives directly a condition for the workers' optimal total expenditures stating that the shift in their lobbying weight and the pensioners' increase in marginal utility due to a higher b_t must coincide.[9] Simple, but tedious, algebra reveals that total expenditures are *ceteris paribus* the higher, the larger the own group and the higher the dependency ratio. The first statement holds because additional members allow expenditures to be spread among more shoulders. The second statement follows from the fact that the income loss a higher contribution rate incurs is the higher, the more pensioners a worker has to support. This makes retaliation more attractive. Proportional increases of the dependency ratio affect expenditures stronger than increases in group size do if the latter are associated with higher organizational costs.[10]

For the pensioners, one gets:

$$\Psi'(X_t)\frac{(\pi N_{t-2})^\beta}{X_t^w z_t} = \frac{\pi}{M}\frac{1}{(1+\delta\pi)c_t^2}, \tag{17}$$

which results from the equalization of the pensioners' marginal utility gain due to higher lobbying expenditures and the workers' loss in marginal utility due to a higher tax burden.[11] Analogous calculations show that the pensioners' expenditures are increasing in their own group size. A higher dependency ratio decreases lobbying activities, since the gains for each pensioner become smaller. The same is true for an increase in $\frac{1}{(1+\delta\pi)}$. The higher the proportion of income consumed during the working period, the stronger a worker's utility will react to a higher contribution rate, making the government less responsive to the lobbying activities of the elderly.

In equilibrium, Eqs. (16) and (17) must be compatible. Dividing and employing (11) leads to:

$$\Psi(X_t)X_t - (1+\delta\pi)\left(\frac{\pi}{M}\right)^{\beta-2} = 0, \tag{18}$$

and, consequently, to

Proposition 1. *The relative lobbying expenditures of the elderly are the lower, the smaller the workers' share within the constituency is.*

This result, which is easily established by differentiating (18) with respect to M and π:

$$\frac{dX_t}{dM} = \frac{(2-\beta)(1+\delta\pi)M^{1-\beta}\pi^{\beta-2}}{\Psi'(X_t)X_t + \Psi(X_t)} > 0, \tag{19}$$

$$\frac{dX_t}{d\pi} = \frac{[\beta-2+\delta\pi(\beta-1)]M^{2-\beta}\pi^{\beta-3}}{\Psi'(X_t)X_t + \Psi(X_t)} < 0, \tag{20}$$

is driven by the following effects: Decreasing the relative number of workers raises the dependency ratio letting the elderly reduce their expenditures according to the argumentation above. For workers themselves, there are two countervailing effects. One the one hand, the smaller group size decreases expenditures. On the other hand, the higher dependency ratio makes resistance against taxation more important. But since $\beta \leq 1$, the latter effect is always at least as strong as the first one. Therefore, the workers' contributions will never decrease and lower relative expenditures on part of the pensioners result.[12]

Yet, the strength of the reaction of lobbying expenditures depends on whether a decrease in fertility or in mortality is responsible for the workers' share in the constituency to fall. A longer life expectancy produces an additional effect on the marginal utility of workers. This holds because old age consumption in case of death is definitely zero, and therefore individuals cannot equate marginal utility of consumption in all states of nature. Consequently, a higher life expectancy increases a worker's total and depresses his marginal utility. *Ceteris paribus*, this leads to more lobbying by the old and to a less pronounced reduction of the pensioners' relative lobbying weight compared to a decrease in fertility.

Two further short remarks are in order. First, (18) gives only a condition for the pensioners' relative lobbying weight. As their relative voting weight increases with their population share, the intuitively plausible positive relation between the relative number of pensioners and their relative *political* weight is consistent with the above results. Second, the Olsonian (1965) organizational costs are not necessary to derive Proposition 1. What is crucial is that the age structure affects the rate of return of intergenerational redistribution and that both generations react rationally on changes in this rate.

This concludes the determination of the politico-economic equilibrium. To summarize: In every period, the government chooses education and social security taxes according to (9) and (11). In this decision it is lead by the activities of interest groups which according to (18) are determined by the age structure of the population.

4. The steady state

The preceeding section has demonstrated that expectations of the next period's tax rates are crucial for the determination of today's optimal policy. Incentives to invest in human capital, for example, will only prevail when workers proceed from a positive future contribution rate. Unfortunately, a proper determination of the sequence of taxes is not possible by confining the analysis to rational expectations equilibria. The choice of today's taxes depends on tomorrow's taxes which in turn depend on decisions in the period after that and so on, leading to an infinite regress. As a result, an infinite number of rationally expected time paths of education and social security tax rates are compatible with (9) and (11). However, it is possible to derive the *rational expectations steady-state equilibrium.*

In the steady state both education tax and social security tax rates are time-invariant, implying a growth rate of $f(\tau/M) - 1$ for lifetime incomes and, thus, for old age consumption due to the homothetic utility function. This modifies the conditions for a support maximum to:

$$\frac{h_t}{c_t} b \left[-R + bf'\left(\frac{\tau_t}{M}\right) \right] = 0$$

$$\frac{h_t}{z_t} \left[-\frac{\delta R}{f\left(\frac{\tau}{M}\right)} + \Psi(X) \right] = 0,$$

$$\Psi(X)X - (1 + \delta\pi)\left(\frac{\pi}{M}\right)^{\beta-2} = 0.$$

Considering these equations, we have

Proposition 2. *In addition to trivial equilibria with* $\tau = 0$ *and, consequently, a complete breakdown of the economy, there exists an equilibrium* $\tau > 0, b > 0$ *that satisfies:*

$$\Phi_\tau = -R + bf'\left(\frac{\tau}{M}\right) = 0, \tag{21}$$

$$\Phi_b = -\delta R + \Psi(X)f\left(\frac{\tau}{M}\right) = 0, \tag{22}$$

$$\Phi_X = \Psi(X)X - (1 + \delta\pi)\left(\frac{\pi}{M}\right)^{\beta-2} = 0. \tag{23}$$

It is easy to establish that both taxes must be positive. For $\tau = 0$ the second term in (22) equals 0. So (22) can only be fulfilled for $\tau > 0$. However, due to (21) this is possible only if $b > 0$. An equilibrium with $\tau = 0$ and $b \leq 0$ is therefore ruled out.

Note that in the non-trivial equilibrium the pensioners' relative marginal utility simplifies to the *per capita income growth factor*, such that the product of pensioners' relative marginal utility and lobbying weight is constant. This is due to the fact that the ratio of marginal utilities does not depend on the contribution rate. Under a constant b, lifetime incomes only differ because of a growing human capital stock. Consequently, the ratio of marginal utilities only depends on educational expenditures. Increasing the contribution rate while keeping the education tax constant affects all generations equally and does not alter the ratio of marginal utilities.

5. The effects of population aging

As alluded to in the introduction, the demographic structures of most industrialized countries are subject to significant changes: the populations age due to simultaneous decreases in fertility and mortality. In this section, we address the long-run consequences of population aging on education, social security and growth.

Basically, two politico-economic effects of demographic changes can be distinguished. On the one hand, the change in the biological interest rates affects the economic profitability of both transfers. On the other hand, the composition of the constituency alters and so does political influence. Directly, this only affects the decision on the contribution rate, since children are not endowed with political power. But an indirect effect enters the workers' calculus because public education and social security are intertwined: the social security contribution rate influences the incentives to invest in public education, and therefore the education tax, while the latter determines the ratio of lifetime incomes and so the marginal political returns and costs of higher social security payments.

With respect to the growth effects of population aging, total differentiation of the above equation system (21)–(23) yields

Proposition 3. *Population aging leads to higher per capita income growth.*

This result is easily be derived by inspecting τ/M, the amount of human capital a worker invests per child, as the per capita income growth rate is a positive monotonous function of this variable:[13]

$$\frac{d\tau/M}{dM} = \frac{\frac{d\tau}{dM}M - \tau}{M^2} = \frac{(2-\beta)(1+\delta\pi)M^{1-\beta}\pi^{\beta-2}\Psi'(X)}{\delta Rf\left(\frac{\tau}{M}\right)^2 f'\left(\frac{\tau}{M}\right)[\Psi'(X)X + \Psi(X)]} < 0,$$

$$\frac{d\tau/M}{d\pi} = \frac{\frac{d\tau}{d\pi}}{M} = -\frac{[\beta - 2 + \delta\pi(\beta-1)]M^{2-\beta}\pi^{\beta-3}\Psi'(X)}{\delta Rf\left(\frac{\tau}{M}\right)^2 f'\left(\frac{\tau}{M}\right)[\Psi'(X)X + \Psi(X)]} > 0.$$

The driving force behind this result is clarified by regarding (22) and (23). Population aging deteriorates the pensioners' relative lobbying weight. Consequently, their relative marginal utility must increase. This factor depends positively and only on the per capita-income growth factor. Put differently: The reduction of the pensioners' lobbying power admits larger differences in the lifetime incomes of both generations which in the steady state are brought about by higher per capita income growth due to educational expansion.

Comparing the growth effects of fertility and mortality, we get

Proposition 4. *The per capita income growth rate reacts less responsive to a decrease in mortality than to one in fertility.*

Comparing the respective elasticities:

$$\varepsilon_{\tau/M,\pi} = -\left(\frac{\pi}{M}\right)^{\beta-2} \cdot \frac{\beta - 2 + \delta\pi(\beta - 1)}{X[\Psi'(X)X + \Psi(X)]}$$

and:

$$-\varepsilon_{\tau/M,M} = -\left(\frac{\pi}{M}\right)^{\beta-2} \cdot \frac{(2-\beta)(1+\delta\pi)}{X[\Psi'(X)X + \Psi(X)]}$$

gives the above result:

$$\frac{\varepsilon_{\tau/M,\pi}}{-\varepsilon_{\tau/M,M}} = 1 - \frac{\delta\pi}{(2-\beta)(1+\delta\pi)} < 1.$$

It is due to the additional effect of a higher life expectancy on workers' marginal utility. The fall in the pensioners' lobbying expenditures is therefore not as pronounced as under lower fertility.

Turning to the effects of population aging on the size and structure of public spending, it can be seen that

Proposition 5. *Both a decrease in fertility and in mortality lead to a higher contribution rate to the social security system. A higher life expectancy implies*

a higher education tax. The influence of lower fertility on the education tax is ambiguous:

$$\frac{db}{dM} = \frac{bf''\left(\frac{\tau}{M}\right)}{f'\left(\frac{\tau}{M}\right)} \cdot \frac{(2-\beta)(1+\delta\pi)M^{1-\beta}\pi^{\beta-2}\Psi'(X)}{\delta R f\left(\frac{\tau}{M}\right)^2 f'\left(\frac{\tau}{M}\right)[\Psi'(X)X + \Psi(X)]} < 0,$$

$$\frac{db}{d\pi} = -\frac{bf''\left(\frac{\tau}{M}\right)}{f'\left(\frac{\tau}{M}\right)} > 0,$$

$$\frac{d\tau}{dM} = \frac{\tau}{M} - \frac{(2-\beta)(1+\delta\pi)M^{2-\beta}\pi^{\beta-2}\Psi'(X)}{\delta R f\left(\frac{\tau}{M}\right)^2 f'\left(\frac{\tau}{M}\right)[\Psi'(X)X + \Psi(X)]} \gtreqless 0,$$

$$\frac{d\tau}{d\pi} = -\frac{[\beta - 2 + \delta\pi(\beta-1)]M^{1-\beta}\pi^{\beta-3}\Psi'(X)}{\delta R f\left(\frac{\tau}{M}\right)^2 f'\left(\frac{\tau}{M}\right)[\Psi'(X)X + \Psi(X)]} > 0.$$

As shown above, population aging requires an increase in τ/M, the human capital devoted to public education per child. This increase is brought about by a higher contribution rate to the social security system, as this enhances the workers' incentives to invest in education. This is illustrated in Fig. 1.

The necessity for τ/M to increase points directly to the reason, why the education tax can react qualitatively different on changes in M and π. A support-maximizing policy adjustment does not require a change in τ, but in τ/M.

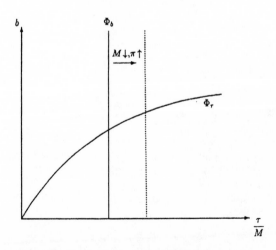

Fig. 1. Steady state effects of population aging

For lower mortality, an increase in τ/M unambiguously implies a higher τ. But for lower fertility the education tax can fall, provided it is over-compensated by the decrease in M. In that case, higher per capita educational expenditures are accompanied by a lower (education) tax burden.

6. Conclusion

This paper has investigated some driving forces of social security and public education expenditures in a representative democracy. In an environment without long term policy commitment it was shown that a social security system organized on a PAYG basis can stimulate public education expenditures. Therefore, both forms of intergenerational transfers can coexist in a setting of non-altruistic generations even when the direct beneficiaries of education do not take part in the political process.

Population aging leads to higher per capita income growth, due to the declining political success of the pensioners' lobby. This effect has been endo-genously derived in a model comprising both voting and interest group acti-vities. The effects of aging on the size and structure of intergenerational transfers are as follows: both the fraction of labor income devoted per child for educational purposes and the contribution rate to the social security system rise.

It is clear that the results of every model hinge upon its underlying as-sumptions. We will thus briefly discuss how some alternative assumptions would affect the results derived above.

It can be argued that the complete periodical reversibility of political de-cisions is a valid description of reality. Should, instead, individuals perceive today's decisions to be binding forever for some reason, the workers' marginal loss from social security financing diminishes, since now they can control their old-age benefits. If total income growth exceeds the interest rate, the inter-generational conflict may vanish because both generations profit from ex-tending the PAYG system.

The political support function employed here is well grounded in probabilistic voting theories. However, also with a more general form of the pensioners' relative political weight $\Psi\left(\dfrac{\pi}{M}, X_t\right)$, the results of Sects. 3 and 4 would remain valid. The same is true for the effects of aging as long as the pensioners' relative political weight is concave in their population share. A sufficient condition for this to hold is that the biological interest rate effect is at least as strong as the voting power effect. This is tantamount to saying that $\Psi_1\left(\dfrac{\pi}{M}, X_t\right) / \Psi\left(\dfrac{\pi}{M}, X_t\right) \cdot \pi/M$, the voting share elasticity of the pensioners' relative political weight, is not larger than one. This condition is met, for ex-ample, by any constant-elasticity-of-substitution formulation of the relative political weight function.

Although the model gives no clue for imperfections on the annuity market – the life expectancy of all individuals is publicly known –, a full protection against accidental bequests cannot be expected in the real world. If annuity markets are not perfect, the level of public education preferred by the workers will for a given social security tax be *higher* than in the model presented above. This somewhat surprising result is due to the fact that the loss of annuization depresses the marginal return of private savings, but leaves the PAYG scheme unaffected. Equalization of the marginal returns (see (10)) leads to higher education expenditures. There are also effects on the political level: In the short run the government will tend to treat income losses of the generations differently, as the distribution of wealth will vary from generation to generation.[14] But in the steady state, with a constant wealth distribution differential treatment will not be an issue anymore. So for the long-run, Eq. (22) remains unaffected from a heterogeneous wealth distribution due to accidental bequests. Therefore, the results obtained here remain valid in this alternative setting.

The analysis was undertaken within the framework of a small open economy. In a closed economy, higher contribution rates can have negative growth effects as was outlined in the introduction. It is a priori not clear whether these effects are overcome by higher human capital accumulation. Yet, as long as taxes are low and the repercussions on the real capital stock are small, the basic mechanism presented here will still retain its relevance.

Appendix

Total differentiation of (21) and (22) with respect to fertility yields:

$$\frac{\partial \Phi_\tau}{\partial \tau}\frac{d\tau}{dM} + \frac{\partial \Phi_\tau}{\partial b}\frac{db}{dM} + \frac{\partial \Phi_\tau}{\partial M} = 0,$$

$$\frac{\partial \Phi_b}{\partial \tau}\frac{d\tau}{dM} + \frac{\partial \Phi_b}{\partial \tau}\frac{db}{dM} + \frac{\partial \Phi_b}{\partial M} = 0,$$

where for ease of exposition X is directly interpreted as a function of M (Eq. (19)) and:

$$\frac{\partial \Phi_\tau}{\partial \tau} = \frac{bf''\left(\frac{\tau}{M}\right)}{M} < 0,$$

$$\frac{\partial \Phi_\tau}{\partial b} = f'\left(\frac{\tau}{M}\right) > 0,$$

$$\frac{\partial \Phi_\tau}{\partial M} = -\frac{b\tau f''\left(\frac{\tau}{M}\right)}{M^2} > 0,$$

$$\frac{\partial \Phi_b}{\partial \tau} = \frac{\delta R}{M} f\left(\frac{\tau}{M}\right)^{-2} f'\left(\frac{\tau}{M}\right) > 0,$$

$$\frac{\partial \Phi_b}{\partial b} = 0,$$

$$\frac{\partial \Phi_b}{\partial M} = -\frac{\delta R\tau}{M^2} f\left(\frac{\tau}{M}\right)^{-2} f'\left(\frac{\tau}{M}\right) + \Psi'(X)\frac{dX}{dM}.$$

From this, one obtains:

$$\frac{d\tau}{dM} = -\frac{\partial \Phi_b / \partial M}{\partial \Phi_b / \partial \tau} = -\frac{-\dfrac{\delta R\tau}{M^2} f\left(\dfrac{\tau}{M}\right)^{-2} f'\left(\dfrac{\tau}{M}\right) + \Psi'(X)\dfrac{dX}{dM}}{\dfrac{\delta R}{M} f\left(\dfrac{\tau}{M}\right)^{-2} f'\left(\dfrac{\tau}{M}\right)}$$

$$= \frac{\tau}{M} - \frac{(2-\beta)(1+\delta\pi)M^{2-\beta}\pi^{\beta-2}\Psi'(X)}{\delta R f\left(\dfrac{\tau}{M}\right)^{-2} f'\left(\dfrac{\tau}{M}\right)[\Psi'(X)X + \Psi(X)]}.$$

for the education tax rate, while for the contribution rate:

$$\frac{db}{dM} = -\frac{\partial \Phi_\tau / \partial M}{\partial \Phi_\tau^1 / \partial b} - \frac{\partial \Phi_\tau^1 / \partial \tau}{\partial \Phi_\tau^1 / \partial b}\frac{d\tau}{dM}$$

$$= \frac{\tau b f''\left(\dfrac{\tau}{M}\right)}{M^2 f'\left(\dfrac{\tau}{M}\right)} - \frac{b f''\left(\dfrac{\tau}{M}\right)}{M f'\left(\dfrac{\tau}{M}\right)}\frac{d\tau}{dM} = \frac{\tau b f''\left(\dfrac{\tau}{M}\right)}{M f'\left(\dfrac{\tau}{M}\right)}\left[\frac{\tau}{M} - \frac{d\tau}{dM}\right]$$

$$= \frac{b f''\left(\dfrac{\tau}{M}\right)}{f'\left(\dfrac{\tau}{M}\right)M} \cdot \frac{(2-\beta)(1+\delta\pi)M^{2-\beta}\pi^{\beta-2}\Psi'(X)}{\delta R f\left(\dfrac{\tau}{M}\right)^{-2} f'\left(\dfrac{\tau}{M}\right)[\Psi'(X)X + \Psi(X)]} < 0.$$

Concerning changes in mortality, an analogous system:

$$\frac{\partial \Phi_\tau}{\partial \tau}\frac{d\tau}{d\pi} + \frac{\partial \Phi_\tau}{\partial b}\frac{db}{d\pi} + \frac{\partial \Phi_\tau}{\partial \pi} = 0,$$

$$\frac{\partial \Phi_b}{\partial \tau}\frac{d\tau}{d\pi} + \frac{\partial \Phi_b}{\partial b}\frac{db}{d\pi} + \frac{\partial \Phi_b}{\partial \pi} = 0,$$

with:

$$\frac{\partial \Phi_\tau}{\partial \pi} = 0,$$

$$\frac{\partial \Phi_b}{\partial \pi} = -\Psi'(X)\frac{dX}{d\pi},$$

has to be solved. From this and (20):

$$
\frac{d\tau}{d\pi} = -\frac{\partial \Phi_b/\partial \pi}{\partial \Phi_b/\partial \tau} = \frac{\Psi'(X)\dfrac{dX}{d\pi}}{\dfrac{\delta R}{M} f\left(\dfrac{\tau}{M}\right)^{-2} f'\left(\dfrac{\tau}{M}\right)}
$$

$$
= -\frac{[\beta - 2 + \delta\pi(\beta - 1)]M^{3-\beta}\pi^{\beta-3}\Psi'(X)}{\delta R f\left(\dfrac{\tau}{M}\right)^{-2} f'\left(\dfrac{\tau}{M}\right)[\Psi'(X)X + \Psi(X)]} > 0
$$

follows, while for the contribution rate:

$$
\frac{db}{d\pi} = -\frac{\partial \Phi_\tau/\partial \tau}{\partial \Phi_\tau/\partial b}\frac{d\tau}{d\pi} = -\frac{bf''\left(\dfrac{\tau}{M}\right)}{f'\left(\dfrac{\tau}{M}\right)}\frac{d\tau}{d\pi}
$$

$$
= \frac{bf''\left(\dfrac{\tau}{M}\right)}{f'\left(\dfrac{\tau}{M}\right)} \cdot \frac{[\beta - 2 + \delta\pi(\beta - 1)]M^{3-\beta}\pi^{\beta-3}\Psi'(X)}{\delta R f\left(\dfrac{\tau}{M}\right)^{-2} f'\left(\dfrac{\tau}{M}\right)[\Psi'(X)X + \Psi(X)]} > 0.
$$

Endnotes

[1] A large number of models on the political economy of intergenerational redistribution is based on a support-maximizing government. See e.g. von Weizsäcker (1990), Verbon and Verhoeven (1992), Meijdam and Verbon (1996) and Kemnitz (1998).

[2] It is a quite common theme of the literature to explain intergenerational transfers by purely selfish motives. See Cigno (1993) for a comprehensive investigation of voluntary transfers within non-altruistic families. When intergenerational altruism is considered, further positive interrelations between education and social security can be identified: Nerlove et al. (1988) show that the introduction of social security can remove the parental problem of inefficient human capital investment in children due to non-negativity constraints on bequests. In Zhang (1995), social security changes the decision between quantity and quality of children in favor of the latter, higher per capita income growth being the result. These models, however, are concerned only with private education and take the contribution rate to the social security system as exogenous.

[3] While true for education, this objection is not relevant for all forms of social capital.

[4] In a similar spirit, Nystedt (1998) allows for simultaneous voting on education and pensions under the assumption that no-one expects voting outcomes to be revised. Under mild assumptions, the education tax rate and the social security contribution rate are positive in equilibrium.

[5] All results go through with a constant-elasticity-of-substitution (CES) utility function, where old-age consumption is essential. Note, that only CES utility is both additively separable and homothetic (Katzner 1970). Both features are necessary here: the first by the expected utility property, and the second for a steady state to exist. The requirement that old-age consumption is essential rules out the case of perfect substitutes. This is not only realistic, but also avoids a time-inconsistency problem on part of the pensioners: Otherwise, individuals might consume their whole lifetime income when working borrowing against their pension benefits, but choose not to exert any political pressure when old and thus not repay their obligations. This is precluded if consuming nothing during old age gives a lifetime utility of zero.

[6] In this respect, Verbon et al. (1998) follow a similar approach. However, their model differs in some important respects from the one presented here, a central one being their confinement to public pensions. Education is not considered.

[7] On this, see also Hettich und Winer (1988). Voters who are more responsive to utility differentials obtain a higher weight in the parties' target functions.

[8] Such effects are considered by Grossman and Helpman (1998), albeit in a model with a one-dimensional policy space.

[9] The other terms cancel out for increases in $x_t^w \cdot h_t$ and b_t cast identical effects on a worker's marginal utility.

[10] This can easily be checked by inspecting (16). Doubling N_{t-1} increases its left-hand side less than doubling the dependency ratio increases the right-hand side as long as $\beta < 1$. If organizational costs are absent both effects are equally strong.

[11] This obtains since their marginal utility is equally affected by increasing $x_t^o \cdot h_t M / \pi$ and b_t.

[12] Similar results concerning the effects of group size on lobbying expenditures have been obtained by Kristov et al. (1992) in an atemporal model.

[13] For details of the derivation of Propositions 3 and 5 see the Appendix.

[14] Schwödiauer and Wenig (1990) investigate the effects of population aging on the wealth distribution when annuity markets are absent.

References

Becker GS (1983) A theory of competition among pressure groups for political influence. *Quarterly Journal of Economics* 98:371–400

Cigno A (1993) Intergenerational transfers without altruism: family, market and state. *European Journal of Political Economy* 9:505–518

Coughlin P (1986) Elections and income redistribution. *Public Choice* 50:27–91

Coughlin P, Mueller D, Murrell P (1990) Electoral politics, interest groups, and the size of government. *Economic Inquiry* 28:682–705

Docquier F, Michel P (1999) Education subsidies, social security and growth: the implications of a demographic shock. *Scandinavian Journal of Economics* 101:425–440

Feldstein M (1974) Social security, induced retirement and aggregate capital accumulation. *Journal of Political Economy* 82:905–926

Grossman GM, Helpman E (1998) Intergenerational redistribution with short-lived governments. *Economic Journal* 108:1299–1329

Hettich W, Winer S (1988) Economic and political foundations of tax structure. *American Economic Review* 78:701–712

Kaganovich M, Zilcha I (1999) Education, social security and growth. *Journal of Public Economics* 71:289–309

Katzner DW (1970) Static demand theory. Macmillan, London

Kemnitz A (1998) Demographic structure and the political economy of education subsidies. *Public Choice* (forthcoming)

Konrad KA (1995) Social security and strategic inter-vivos transfers of social capital. *Journal of Population Economics* 8:315–326

Kristov L, Lindert P, McClelland R (1992) Pressure groups and redistribution. *Journal of Public Economics* 48:135–163

Lucas R (1988) On the mechanics of economic development. *Journal of Monetary Economics* 22:3–42

Meijdam L, Verbon H (1996) Aging and political decision making on public pensions. *Journal of Population Economics* 9:141–158

Nerlove M, Razin A, Sadka E (1988) A bequest-constrained economy: welfare analysis. *Journal of Public Economics* 37:203–220

Nystedt P (1998) A note on public education and pay-as-you-go-systems. University of Lund, mimeo

Olson M (1965) The logic of collective action. Harvard University Press, Cambridge, MA

Preston SH (1984) Children and the elderly: divergent paths for America's dependents. *Demography* 21:435–457

Romer PM (1986) Increasing returns and long-run growth. *Journal of Political Economy* 94:1002–1037

Saint-Paul G (1992) Fiscal policy in an endogenous growth model. *Quarterly Journal of Economics* 106:1243–1259

Schwödiauer G, Wenig A (1990) The impact of taxation on the distribution of wealth in an economy with changing population. *Journal of Population Economics* 3:53–71

Verbon H, Verhoeven M (1992) Decision making on pension schemes under rational expectations. *Journal of Economics* 56:71–97

Verbon H, Leers T, Meijdam L (1998) Transition towards a funded pension system: the political economy. In Siebert H (ed) *Redesigning Social Security*, pp 357–372

Weizsäcker RK von (1990) Population aging and social security: a politico-economic model of state pension financing. *Public Finance* 45:491–509

Zhang J (1995) Social security and endogenous growth. *Journal of Public Economics* 58:185–213

7   The Consequences of Population Aging on Private Pension Fund Saving and Asset Markets

Sylvester J. Schieber and
John B. Shoven

Background

In the United States the group of people born from 1946 through 1964 has come to be known as the baby boom generation. After World War II, U.S. birth rates jumped to a level significantly above long-term trends and stayed above generally expected levels until the mid-1960s, and there fore the number of people born from 1946 to 1964 constitutes an unusually large segment of the total U.S. population. Because of its size, the baby boom generation has affected various facets of the social structure more significantly during its lifetime than other comparably aged segments of the population.

For example, as the baby boomers entered the education system, they placed new demands on it. Between 1951 and 1954, the number of five- and six-year-old children in the primary education system jumped by 70%. From 1950 to 1970, when the last of the baby boomers were in primary school, enrollments jumped from 21 million to 34 million students.[1] Then, as smaller cohorts of children reached school age, school enrollments began to fall off, stabilizing to 28 million students by 1975.[2] As they came into the primary school system, the baby boomers created a fantastic demand for expanded educational services; as they exited the system, staffing positions were eliminated and schools closed as student bodies were consolidated.

Counting kindergarten, the typical primary and secondary education program in the United States takes 13 years. The leading edge of the baby boomers—those who did not immediately pursue postsecondary education—began to enter the workforce in significant numbers by 1964. The Vietnam conflict slowed the entrance of the oldest baby boom males, as many of them had a period of military service prior to entering the civilian workforce permanently. Of course, many baby boomers also pursued a college education. Thus, the baby boomers really began to enter the workforce in earnest toward the end of the 1960s and throughout the 1970s. Between 1970 and 1986, the U.S. labor force grew at a compound rate of 2.60% per year. By 1985, the youngest of the baby boomers were 21, and those who were going to enter the workforce had done so. In the latter half of the 1980s, the U.S. workforce grew at an annual rate of 0.45 percent per year.[3]

The aging process and the evolving patterns of retirement behavior among workers are predictable, thus it is possible to anticipate the baby boom generation's retirement. Because of its earlier disruptive effects on other aspects of the socioeconomic fabric, it is important to consider, as far in advance of their retirements as possible, the implications of the baby boomers' retirements on existing social and economic institutions meant to handle them. Social Security and employer-sponsored tax-qualified retirement plans provide the two largest sources of cash income for retirees today. Policymakers have focused much more attention on the Social Security system's long-term status than that of the employer-sponsored pension system.

Social Security Funding and the Baby Boom Generation

For some time, policy makers have been aware that the baby boom generation will pose particular challenges for the Social Security program, traditionally run largely on a pay-as-you-go basis. The 1983 Social Security amendments, anticipating the special burden that baby boomers' retirements would place on workers in the future, included provisions for accumulating a substantial trust fund to prefund some of the benefits promised to the boomers. In other words, the baby boom generation was expected to prefund a larger share of its own Social Security benefits than prior generations had. The amendments also reduced the benefits promised to the baby boom generation by gradually raising the age at which full benefits would be paid to age 67 after the turn of the century.

Shortly after the amendments' passage, Social Security actuaries estimated that the Old-Age, Survivors, and Disability Insurance (OASDI) trust funds would grow from around $27.5 billion in 1983 to about $20.7 trillion in 2045 (see figure 7.1). The actuaries expected the trust funds to have resources available to pay promised benefits until the youngest of the baby boomers reached 100. The first projections after the amendments' passage predicted that OASDI trust funds would be solvent until at least 2063.

Billions of dollars

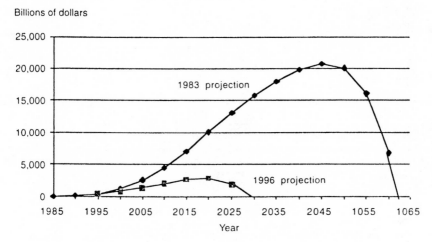

Figure 7.1
Projected OASDI trust fund accumulations (in current dollars by year of estimate)
Source: Harry C. Ballantyne, "Long-Range Projections of Social Security Trust Fund Ope-
rations in Dollars," Social Security Administration, *Actuarial Notes* (October 1983), no. 117,
p. 2, and *1996 Annual Report of the Board of Trustees of the Federal Old-Age and Survivors
Insurance and Disability Insurance Trust Funds* (June 1996), p. 180.

In almost every year since 1983, estimates of the accumulations in the
OASDI trust funds have been revised downward. The most recent projection, published in April 1996 and shown in figure 7.1, suggests the trust
funds will accumulate to only about $2.5 trillion around 2020 and then
decline to a zero balance some time during 2029. At that time baby
boomers will range in age from 65 to 83. Although their numbers will be
declining, significant numbers will still depend on their retirement benefits
to meet ongoing needs.

An alternative way to look at Social Security financing is to segment
it into periods. Table 7.1 reflects the Social Security actuaries' April 1993
long-term OASDI financing projections broken into three 25-year periods.
For the most part, the first 25-year period from 1994 to 2018 will precede
the bulk of the baby boom's claim on the program. The first baby boomers
will be eligible for early retirement benefits in 2008, and only about half
of them will have attained age 62 by 2017. In addition, if the increases in
the actuarial reductions for early retirement benefits and delayed retirement have any effect, the baby boomers will proceed into retirement
somewhat more slowly than prior generations. Even on a purely pay-as-
you-go basis, the tax revenues funding OASDI benefits are expected to

Table 7.1
Social security income and cost rates as projected under current law

Period	Income rate[a]	Cost rate[a]	Over or under (−) funding as percentage of income rate
1994–2018	12.74	12.63	0.86
2019–2043	13.10	16.89	−28.93
2044–2068	13.26	18.11	−36.58

Source: *1996 Annual Report of the Board of Trustees of the Federal Old-Age and Survivors Insurance and Disability Insurance Trust Funds* (1996), p. 22.
a. The income rate is the ratio of OASDI revenues to taxable payroll. The cost rate is the ratio of OASDI expenditures to taxable payroll.

exceed outgo as late as 2010. Over the 25-year period starting in 1994, OASDI has projected revenues about 3% above projected outlays.

As the baby boom moves fully into retirement, Social Security's financing situation is projected to turn decidedly negative. During the second 25 years reflected in table 7.1, the period when the majority of the baby boomers expect to get the majority of their lifetime benefits, projected outlays under OASDI exceed projected revenues by nearly 30%. In other words, every bit of evidence available today indicates that Social Security will not be able to provide the benefits currently being promised to the baby boom generation on the basis of existing funding legislation. Although it is impossible to anticipate exactly how OASDI projections might change over the next five or ten years, assuming no change in legislative mandates, the recent history of continual deterioration in the program's projected actuarial balances leads us to conclude the future may turn out even worse than we now anticipate.

In some regards, the challenge we face in revising our Social Security financing commitments goes beyond simply restoring the pay-as-you-go actuarial balance to the OASDI programs. During 1994, the Bipartisan Commission on Entitlement and Tax Reform looked at Social Security commitments as part of the larger total entitlement commitments embedded in current law. Figure 7.2 presents the results of their analysis. The commission found total federal revenues had been relatively constant at roughly 19% of GDP over the last 25 years or so. In 1970, approximately one-quarter of total federal revenues were devoted to entitlement programs. By 1990, their share had grown to about 10% of GDP. The commission's projections of entitlement spending under current law, however, suggested that by 2030, federal entitlement program spending would equal 20% of GDP, more than the share of GDP taxpayers have been

Percentage of GDP

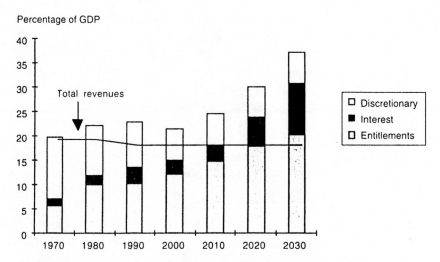

Figure 7.2
Federal outlays and revenues as a percentage of gross domestic product
Source: Bipartisan Commission on Entitlement and Tax Reform, *Interim Report to the President*
(Washington, D.C.: U.S. Government Printing Office, 1994), p. 7.
Note: Medicare and Social Security outlays follow the Medicare and Social Security Trustees'
"best estimate." Medicaid outlays are assumed to reflect demographic changes and increases
in health care costs that underlie Medicare projections. All other spending and revenues are
assumed to follow Congressional Budget Office projections through 1999 and to grow in
proportion to the overall economy thereafter.

willing to allocate to the federal government over the last 20 years.
(OASDI cash benefits account for more than one-third of current total
federal entitlement spending.) Commission projections suggest we must
not only rebalance our major entitlement programs but also significantly
constrain them from current-law levels to operate them with aggregate
budget levels the public is willing to support.

The recent history of major Social Security legislative adjustments,
specifically the 1977 and 1983 amendments, suggests that when benefit
promises exceed program revenues, at least part of the program's rebal-
ancing comes in the form of reduced benefits for retirees. Any reductions
in future benefit promises will to some degree reduce the aggregate claim
Social Security benefits will make on future economic output. Widely
varying approaches have been proposed to deal with Social Security's
funding imbalance under current law. For example, the Social Security
Advisory Council, which focused specifically on OASDI's underfunding
during their deliberations between 1994 and 1996, considered three
options to deal with the system's projected underfunding. The first would

leave the current benefit structure basically intact, restoring balance to the system by raising additional revenues to finance these benefits. The second would curtail benefits under the current system to live within the currently legislated payroll tax rates and add a second-tier mandatory savings program to be administered through the Social Security Administration. The third would significantly restructure the current system, and workers would contribute a portion of their payroll taxes to a Personal Security Account (PSA).

The PSA would be an individual account like an IRA or a 401(k), which many workers in our society already use, but it would differ from those accounts in that participation in the program would be mandatory. A portion of the worker's share of the payroll tax channeled into the accounts would finance them. This would amount to 5% of covered payroll, approximately half the current tax used to finance retirement benefits under Social Security. PSAs would be subject to some restrictions, but they would be under the sole direction of the workers who owned them. The young survivors and disability programs would be left intact and would continue to be financed and administered through Social Security.

Under the PSA proposal, the part of the payroll tax not rebated to workers for PSAs would continue to fund Social Security retirement benefits. The current benefit structure would remain in place for individuals already retired and receiving Social Security benefits or workers grandfathered under the existing system—that is, workers over age 55 at the date of transition. Ultimately the total benefits paid to retirees would come from the system's two separate tiers. The first tier would be the basic, flat benefit provided through Social Security. For individuals with a relatively full career of covered earnings, this benefit would be roughly equal to $410 in 1996 dollars, indexed by the growth in average wages for future years. In retirement, benefits would be indexed by the CPI. Accumulations in the PSA would finance the remaining benefits.[4]

A number of changes under the PSA proposal have implications for both individual and national savings. Under current law, Social Security actuaries estimate the present value of benefits that would be paid over the next 75 years is $21.3 trillion. The assets now in the trust fund plus the tax income and interest that would accrue to the OASDI trust funds over the next 75 years have an estimated value of $18.8 trillion. The problem we face in financing current-law benefits is that, in present-value terms, benefit obligations exceed the resources to pay those benefits by $2.5 trillion over the projection period. Stated alternatively, the actuaries estimate that if we had an extra $2.5 trillion in the Social Security trust funds today, at tax rates now in effect we would have sufficient resources to pay the benefits promised under current law for the next 75 years. This $2.5 trillion shortfall in Social Security funding is not carried on our government balance sheet as formal debt, although current provisions in the Social Security Act define it as a statutory obligation. It differs from formal federal debt in that Congress has reserved the right to redefine the provisions of the Social Security Act at any time. In other words, Congress can renege on the $2.5 trillion with the public having no legal recourse. The issue of political recourse, if such a prospect were to arise, is a different matter.

If the PSA proposal were enacted today, with a transition to the modified program to begin in 1998, the estimated present value of OASDI obligations over the next 75 years would drop immediately to $14.6 trillion, $6.7 trillion less than the obligations under current law. Because a portion of the payroll tax would no longer be going into the trust funds, the estimated present value of current assets plus future income for the trust funds would also fall, to $14.7 trillion. Over the 75-year period, the estimated resources to pay benefits would exceed estimated obligations by $114 billion. In other words, we would convert the $2.5 trillion present-value deficit into a $114 billion surplus.

Under this proposal, the PSA balances themselves would become a tremendous repository of national savings. In 1998, the year that the proposal calls for the modified system to be implemented, these accounts would accumulate $115 billion in today's dollars. By 2002, they would break the half-trillion-dollar mark; by 2010, the $1.5 trillion dollar mark in 1996 dollars; and by 2030, the year the current system is projected to deplete its funds, they would hold $3.5 trillion. By the end of the transition, the balances in the PSAs would equal 1.7 times gross domestic product. In other words, the PSA proposal would not only eliminate the current system's unfunded liability, it would also significantly reduce the government's overall future obligations while simultaneously increasing the wealth holdings of America's workers. To accomplish this tremendous feat, a cost must be borne by someone.

The proposed PSA transition financing mechanism would spread the cost of moving from the current Social Security system to the modified system over roughly 70 years. The transition could be accomplished in a shorter time, but a much smaller number of our citizens would bear the cost, raising serious intergenerational equity questions. Although they favor financing the transition with a consumption tax, such as a national sales tax, PSA proposal proponents, lacking the machinery to collect such a tax, have settled on an incremental, temporary payroll tax as the financing mechanism. Under the 70-year transition, the payroll tax would increase roughly 1.5 percentage points on covered earnings. Granted there is a great reluctance to increase the tax burden on anyone today, we nonetheless cannot escape the laws of arithmetic: The only way to increase saving through Social Security reform is to have workers actually put some of their money in the bank. The transition financing required to move from an unfunded retirement system to one significantly funded would let workers do just that while also letting the Social Security program pay off previously earned benefits. PSA proposal proponents believe workers will be willing to pay a 1.5% "liberty tax" on their wages if they perceive they are getting real value in return and this assures their retirement security.

Because the proposed transition from the current system to a modified system stretches over 70 years, the proposal also requires some transitional borrowing—that is, the issuance of "liberty bonds." In 2005, the amount of the borrowing would be the equivalent of 1.5% of covered payroll; by 2010 the rate of borrowing would drop to 1%. Between 2030 and 2035, we would begin to pay off the liberty bonds and completely pay them off between 2065 and 2070. In present-value terms, the liberty bonds' accumulated value in 1995 dollars would peak at slightly less than $650 billion around 2032. Critics of the proposal have characterized the potential issuance of the liberty bonds as a massive new federal borrowing program. In fact, the liberty bonds would only convert some of the current system's unfunded obligations temporarily to more formal government debt. The accumulated borrowing, at its peak, would be less than one-quarter of the unfunded obligations we face under current law. In this regard, the PSA proposal would significantly reduce total government obligations. The liberty bonds would merely be a temporary mortgage to allow the equitable elimination of existing statutory liabilities. At no time during the transition would the accumulated liberty bonds total more than 25% of the accumulated balances in the PSAs. Although the proposal would convert some statutory liabilities into more formal debt instruments, it would also create a tremendous pool of saving that could easily absorb the liberty bonds plus other expanding forms of financial investments.

To solve our country's growing entitlement dilemma, we must shrink entitlement programs, not merely balance them on some actuarial basis. Both of the Social Security Advisory Council's other proposals would also balance the program's financing and obligations. But the proposal that would maintain the current benefit structure would eliminate only a

minuscule portion of the total projected obligations under current law—
less than 1%. The proposal that would scale back the benefits provided
through the traditional program to fit within the current payroll tax rates,
supplemented with a mandatory savings program, would reduce obligations somewhat more—about 11.6% over the next 75 years. The entitlement commission's projections suggest entitlements would have to be cut
in half by 2030 to be held to the 1990 share of GDP allotted to them.
Though the PSA proposal doesn't get that far, it would reduce current-
law obligations by 31.5% over the 75-year projection period. The challenge is to find solutions to our national entitlement financing problem
that not only restore balance to these programs but also restore balance at
levels taxpayers will support.

Employer-Sponsored Retirement Plan Funding and the Baby Boom Generation

In the general context of retirement policy it is interesting that there is so
much consternation about Social Security's long-term prospects and the
potential underfunding of benefits for the baby boom generation but
hardly any concern about the funded pension system's long-term prospects. A review of the effects of recent legislation and contributions to
employer-sponsored retirement plans suggests there may be reason for
concern on the pension front as well.

Employer-sponsored retirement programs typically operate in a significantly different environment than the federal Social Security program.
Although the federal government operates its own employer-sponsored
retirement programs largely on a pay-as-you-go basis, most state and local
governments prefund retirement obligations on some basis, and ERISA
and the Internal Revenue Code (IRC) require private employers to fund
their retirement obligations on the basis of rules laid out therein.

ERISA became law in 1974. Its purpose was to provide more secure
retirement benefits for all participants in tax-qualified plans. Among other
things, ERISA established rules for including workers in plans, specified
when they had to be guaranteed a benefit, and required benefits be funded
on a schedule. For a plan to qualify for retirement plan tax preferences in
the IRC, it must meet certain requirements to assure benefits being promised are actually provided. All plans operate under fiduciary requirements
seeking to assure they prudently invest plan assets solely for the purpose of providing the benefits they promise. In addition, ERISA requires
plan trustees to disclose relevant financial and participation data to the

government periodically so the plan's ongoing viability and operation can be assured.

Defined-contribution plans have straightforward funding requirements. On the date the plan rules require a contribution, the employer must make a contribution to the plan equal to the obligation. In this case, the employer is not obligated to make any additional contributions for prior periods. The plan's ability to provide an adequate retirement benefit depends heavily on the size of the periodic contributions and the investment returns to plan assets.

Defined-benefit plans have somewhat more complicated funding require- ments because such plans promise future benefits. If a worker enters a firm at age 25, works until age 65 and is retired under the plan for 20 years before dying, his span of life under the plan is 60 years. Essentially, under ERISA funding requirements for defined-benefit plans, the employer grad- ually contributes enough to the plan so the promised benefits will be fully funded when a worker retires. An actuarial valuation of the plan's obliga- tions and assets and specific funding minimums and maximums specified in the law determine the annual contribution to the plan. The funding minimums assure that employers are laying aside money to pay promised benefits, the funding maximums that they do not make extraordinary contributions to the plan simply to avoid paying federal taxes.

Given these seemingly strong funding and disclosure requirements, it may seem odd to worry about the funding of employer-sponsored pen- sion obligations, at least those of private plan sponsors. The problem is an inherent neurosis in federal law governing pensions between the provi- sions aimed at providing retirement income security on the one hand and limiting the value of the preferences accorded pensions in the federal tax code on the other. From ERISA's passage in 1974 until the early 1980s concerns about benefit security held the upper hand in determining federal policy toward pensions. Since 1982, policies aimed at limiting tax leak- ages related to employer-sponsored retirement plans have played the dominant role. Though a number of tax law changes since 1982 have affected defined-contribution plans, they have affected defined-benefit plans somewhat more profoundly. This was especially true of OBRA87.

Defined-benefit plans have a special appeal for workers because they promise a level of benefits regardless of financial market gyrations. Over the years, such plans have had a special appeal for employers because they have provided the flexibility to fund promised benefits actuarially over their employees' working lives. Traditionally, actuarial funding allowed employers to fund in advance benefits that increase steeply at the end of workers' careers. Through 1987 employers were allowed to fund up to 100% of the projected benefits that would be paid to a worker at retirement based on his or her current tenure, age, and actuarial probabilities of qualifying for a benefit. OBRA87 dropped the full-funding limits for defined-benefit plans from 100% of ongoing plan liability to 150% of benefits accrued to date.

OBRA87's new funding limits had the effect of delaying the funding of an individual's pension benefit relative to prior law. Table 7.2 helps show the implications of the revised funding standards. For purposes of developing this example, we assumed a worker begins a job at a firm at age 25 earning $25,000 per year. We assumed the worker's pay would increase at a rate of 5.5% per year throughout his or her career. This individual participates in a defined-benefit plan that pays 1% of final average salary at age 65. We assumed accumulated plan assets would earn a return of 8% per year.

The column labeled "Projected unit credit contribution rate" shows the contribution rate, as a percentage of the worker's salary, required to fund this individual's benefit at retirement under the projected unit-credit funding method. The other four contribution rates show what effect imposing a funding limit of 150% of accrued benefits would have on workers at four different points in their careers. The column labeled "Age 25" was developed assuming the worker is covered by the more restrictive funding limit throughout his or her career. The "Age 35," "Age 45," and "Age 55" columns were developed assuming the new funding limit was not imposed until the individuals had already participated in the plan for 10, 20, and 30 years respectively.

For the worker covered by OBRA87 throughout his or her career, the full-funding limits mean that the plan sponsor's contributions to the plan during the first half of the career, until age 45, will be less than if the plan were being funded on an ongoing basis. Of course lower contributions early in the career mean that contributions in the latter half would have to be higher to fund the plan's promised benefits. In this particular example, the plan contribution rate during the worker's early to mid-50s would have to be more than twice the contribution rate under the projected unit-credit funding method.

For the worker not hit by the contribution limits until ten years into the career, the imposition of the contribution limit implies that the employer would subsequently have a nine-year contribution holiday when no contributions would be made. In this case, the accrued benefit would have to catch up with the level of funding accomplished early in the career. Again,

Table 7.2
Effects of OBRA87 full-funding limits on contribution rates for workers at ages when implemented

Age	Pay	Projected unit-credit contribution rate	Contribution rates at various ages under funding limit of 150% of accrued benefit			
			Age 25	Age 35	Age 45	Age 55
25	$ 25,000	4.2%	0.9%	4.2%	4.2%	4.2%
26	26,375	4.3	0.9	4.3	4.3	4.3
27	27,826	4.4	1.0	4.4	4.4	4.4
28	29,356	4.5	1.1	4.5	4.5	4.5
29	30,971	4.6	1.2	4.6	4.6	4.6
30	32,674	4.7	1.4	4.7	4.7	4.7
31	34,471	4.8	1.6	4.8	4.8	4.8
32	36,367	4.9	1.8	4.9	4.9	4.9
33	38,367	5.0	2.0	5.0	5.0	5.0
34	40,477	5.2	2.3	5.2	5.2	5.2
35	42,704	5.3	2.6	0.0	5.3	5.3
36	45,052	5.4	2.9	0.0	5.4	5.4
37	47,530	5.5	3.2	0.0	5.5	5.5
38	50,144	5.7	3.5	0.0	5.7	5.7
39	52,902	5.8	3.9	0.0	5.8	5.8
40	55,812	5.9	4.4	0.0	5.9	5.9
41	58,882	6.1	4.9	0.0	6.1	6.1
42	62,120	6.2	5.4	0.0	6.2	6.2
43	65,537	6.4	6.0	0.0	6.4	6.4
44	69,141	6.5	6.7	1.8	6.5	6.5
45	72,944	6.7	7.4	7.4	0.0	6.7
46	76,956	6.8	8.2	8.2	0.0	6.8
47	81,188	7.0	9.1	9.1	0.0	7.0
48	85,654	7.2	10.0	10.0	0.0	7.2
49	90,365	7.3	11.1	11.1	0.0	7.3
50	95,335	7.5	12.3	12.3	0.0	7.5
51	100,578	7.7	13.5	13.5	1.5	7.7
52	106,110	7.9	15.0	15.0	15.0	7.9
53	111,946	8.1	16.5	16.5	16.5	8.1
54	118,103	8.2	18.2	18.2	18.2	8.2
55	124,599	8.4	16.2	16.2	16.2	0.0
56	131,452	8.6	14.6	14.6	14.6	10.8
57	138,682	8.8	13.4	13.4	13.4	10.5
58	146,309	9.1	12.6	12.6	12.6	10.3
59	154,356	9.3	12.0	12.0	12.0	10.3
60	162,846	9.5	11.5	11.5	11.5	10.2

Table 7.2 (continued)

Age	Pay	Projected unit-credit contribution rate	Contribution rates at various ages under funding limit of 150% of accrued benefit			
			Age 25	Age 35	Age 45	Age 55
61	171,802	9.7	11.3	11.3	11.3	10.3
62	181,251	9.9	11.2	11.2	11.2	10.4
63	191,220	10.2	11.1	11.1	11.1	10.5
64	201,737	10.4	11.1	11.1	11.1	10.7

the contribution rate in the mid-50s would be more than twice what it was under projected unit-credit funding. For the worker not hit until age 45, the contribution holiday would be shorter, but the same general effect of delaying retirement funding would significantly increase late-career contribution requirements given the level of promised benefits. Finally, for the worker not hit until age 55 by the new funding limit, the contribution holiday would be only one year, and though contributions during the remaining career would be higher than under projected unit-credit funding, the implications would be far less significant than in the previous cases.

In 1988, when OBRA87 funding limits took effect, the leading edge of the baby boom generation was age 42. The trailing edge was age 24. OBRA87 has had the gross effect of significantly delaying the funding of the baby boom generation's defined-benefit retirement promises. Given the significant numbers of workers falling within the baby boom cohorts, OBRA87 has created an overall slowdown in pension funding. As this legislation was being considered, The Wyatt Company analyzed its 1986 survey of actuarial assumptions and funding covering 849 plans with more than 1,000 participants to estimate the effects of the new funding limits. It found 41% of the surveyed plans had an accrued benefit security level of 150% or greater. All of these plans would have been affected by the new limit had it been in effect for 1986 and could not have made deductible contributions. For a subset of 664 plans for which they could estimate the marginal effects of the new limits, 40% would be affected by the new proposal, compared with only 7% under prior limits.[5]

In its 1987 survey of actuarial assumptions and funding, The Wyatt Company reported 48% of the plans had an accrued benefit-security ratio of 150% or more. Because plans at this funding level cannot make deductible plan contributions, the percentage of plans overfunded by this measure should decline over time. In its 1992 survey, Wyatt found only 37%

Billions of 1993 dollars

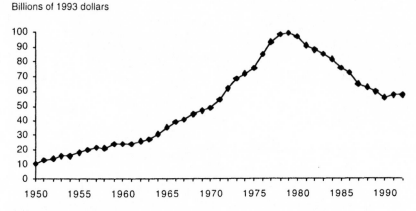

Figure 7.3
Real employer contributions to private pension and profit-sharing plans
Source: Derived by the authors from the National Income and Product Accounts.

of large defined-benefit plans had accrued benefit-security ratios of 150% or greater.[6]

OBRA87 significantly limited the funding of defined-benefit plans, but it was only one of several pieces of legislation that affected the funding of tax-qualified retirement plans after 1981. In 1982, TEFRA reduced and froze for a period of time the dollar funding and contribution limits for both defined-benefit and defined-contribution plans. TEFRA also established new discrimination tests which had the practical effect of lowering contributions for many plans. The next year's Deficit Reduction Act extended the freeze in funding and contribution limits TEFRA established. In 1986, the TRA again reduced and froze funding and contribution limits for tax-qualified plans. Finally, OBRA93 included provisions that reduced the amount of an individual employee's compensation that could be considered in funding and contributing to tax-qualified plans. OBRA93's provisions have the practical effect of further limiting the funding of employer-sponsored retirement programs.

Figure 7.3 shows the annual employer contributions to private pension and profit-sharing plans dating back to just after World War II. Contributions gradually increased through the early 1970s then escalated as ERISA was passed and implemented. But around the time the federal government started passing the various restrictive tax measures affecting employer-sponsored retirement plans, contributions began to decline. By 1990, employer nominal contributions to these plans were about 15%

below contribution levels in the early 1980s and in real terms were about 45% below the level at the end of the 1970s. On an inflation-adjusted basis, contributions in 1990 were at about the same level they had been in 1970, four years before ERISA's passage.

Most of the past decade's pension legislation has evolved within the context of short-term fiscal considerations. The need to raise revenues to reduce the federal government's deficit has delayed the funding of the baby boom generation's pension benefits with virtually no consideration of the long-term impact on benefit cost or viability. Although the Social Security Act established a board of trustees to oversee the OASDI financial operations and requires the board report to Congress on the programs' financial and actuarial status, no similar oversight body identifies pending problems with the funded pension system and warns policymakers about them. Retirement plan sponsors are individually required to disclose their plans' current funding status periodically, but the evolving policy focus pushing plan sponsors to fund for only current obligations hardly encourages individual planning for longer-term contingencies. In the aggregate, public policymakers have completely ignored tax policy's long-term implications on pension funding to minimize short-term structural imbalances underlying federal fiscal policy. In the following sections we attempt a longer-term view of pension funding.

Methodology of Current Study

This section briefly outlines the underlying methods, assumptions, and inputs used to develop the estimates presented in the next section. Projections of the U.S. pension system require a long-term projection of the population and workforce, and their respective characteristics. For purposes of this exercise, we were not interested in developing a long-term demographic and labor force projection model. To develop such a model would have been a more Herculean undertaking than we were prepared to commit to in the time available. Second, we felt the nature of our projection might lead to comparisons with the long-term Social Security projections and thought it would make sense to have the same underlying demographic and workforce characteristics as utilized in those projections. Thus we began with Social Security's 75-year projections of the U.S. population, which gave us population estimates by single-year attained ages between 0 and 99 for each of the projection years. We also started with their projections of the workforce in each year, distributed in five-year age cohorts.

From published data and our own computations developed using the Internal Revenue Service Form 5500 for pension reporting plus computations from the March 1992 CPS and the 1991 SIPP, we developed age- and sex-specific rates of participation, vesting in, and receipt of benefits from defined-benefit and defined-contribution plans. We developed age and sex-specific distributions of tenure in current job, important for projecting the vesting rates of participants in pension plans. We also developed estimates of total wages for the economy's private, state and local, and federal sectors from Bureau of Economic Analysis data published in the NIPA. Estimates of age and sex-specific pay levels were developed.

We used the IRS Form 5500 files in conjunction with data from the Employee Benefit Research Institute's *Quarterly Pension Investment Report* (QPIR) to estimate the starting total distribution of assets and contributions between defined-benefit and defined-contribution plans. We also used the QPIR data to estimate the distribution of financial assets held by plans across various forms of investments. Table 7.3 shows the resulting distribution of assets by plan type. Focusing on the private defined-benefit and defined-contribution plans in this paper, we note with interest the relatively large amount of cash and other short-term investments these pension funds hold, despite the long-run nature of the funds themselves. Equities, which have a superb track record over long holding periods, amount to only 36% to 41% of the total portfolio. Given historic returns, the pension funds would be better off with a larger stake in stocks. Table 7.3 also shows our assumed real rates of return for the different asset cat-

Table 7.3
Asset allocation of pension plans as of July 1992 (in percentage points)

Type of plan	Equities	Bonds	GICs	Real estate	Cash
Private defined benefit	36 %	33 %	0 %	15 %	16 %
Private defined contribution	41	14	13	6	26
Federal defined benefit	44	44	1	6	5
Federal defined contribution	30	70	0	0	0
State and local defined benefit	44	44	1	6	5
State and local defined contribution	33	49	5	8	5
Real return rate	5.0	2.0	1.2	2.0	0.0

Blended real rate for private defined benefit plans: 2.76
Blended real rates for private defined contribution plans: 2.65

Sources: Asset allocation: EBRI's Quarterly Pension Investment Report; rates of return: authors' assumptions.

egories. The numbers are loosely based on the information in Ibbotson 1993, although we are admittedly conservative.[7] Ibbotson reports that the geometric average real rate of return for the Standard and Poor's 500 stock portfolio over the years 1926–92 was 7.0%. The corresponding average real rate of return on long-term corporate bonds was 2.3%, while it was 0.5% for short-term Treasury bills. We have no corresponding data for GICs, which are fixed-income contracts typically issued by insurance companies and featuring a somewhat shorter maturity than long bonds. As the reader can see, we have consistently assumed rates of return somewhat below the long-run averages Ibbotson calculated.

The Social Security population projection was distributed by age, sex, and workforce participation for each year of the projection. Our analysis distributed the workforce into three separate sectors: private employment, state employment, and federal employment. The working population was further distributed by tenure and pension participation status. In each year of the projection the population and workforce were rolled forward one year with appropriate mortality decrements and workforce adjustments to account for job leavers, entrants, and changers. We made an underlying assumption there was 14% turnover of workers between jobs each year.

We developed projections separately for private-employer plans, state and local defined-benefit plans, and the federal employee thrift plan. In each case, we developed separate projections for defined-benefit and defined-contribution plans, then aggregated them. For example, in the projection for the private sector, we estimated total employer contributions to private plans were 2.8% of payroll, approximately 30% of which has been going into defined-benefit plans in recent years. We estimated employee contributions to private plans to be 1.75% of payroll, with slightly less than 2% going to defined-benefit plans. Based on Form 5500 files of plans with 100 or more participants, we estimated employer contributions to defined-contribution plans were 1.13 times employee contributions to those plans.

In the initial year, benefits were estimated from Form 5500 files and the QPIR data. Going forward, benefits were estimated on the basis of workers covered by a pension and passing into immediate retirement starting at age 54, at which age we assumed 3.7% of existing workers would retire. By age 80, we assumed all remaining workers would retire. For workers who terminated their employment under a defined-benefit plan, we assumed if they were vested they would be paid a deferred benefit at age 65. We calculated the accrual rate of the benefit formula for those working until the age of full retirement benefits to be 1.25% of final salary per year of service on average. For those receiving a deferred benefit it was 1.00% of final salary per year of service. We assumed that 40% of workers participating in a defined-contribution plan who terminated prior to retirement would take a lump sum benefit and use it for some purpose other than meeting their retirement needs. Under defined-contribution plans, benefits generally commence at retirement and are paid out as an annuity over a maximum of 30 years.

Economic assumptions in large part drive future contributions and trust fund accumulations. Our assumptions on inflation, 4.0% per year, and wage growth, 5.1% per year, correspond with those used in the Social Security projections under the second option for saving the system discussed above.

Baseline Projections for the Private Pension System

Table 7.4 shows our current combined projections for defined-benefit and defined-contribution private pension plans. Under our forecast assumptions, the total private pension system assets continue to grow in nominal terms for the next 60 years. However, this growth is slowing almost continuously. For instance, in 1993 the benefits (payouts) of the defined-benefit and defined-contribution private plans combined are 83% of total contributions. This means, of course, that there is a net inflow of funds into the total system, even without taking into account the investment return on the $3 trillion asset pool. However, by the year 2006 benefits are projected to be 102.4% of contributions, and we expect that aggregate benefits will continue to outstrip contributions for the entire remaining period through 2065. By 2025 benefits are projected to be 163% of contributions.

If inflation and asset returns match our assumptions, the value of pension assets will continue to climb, albeit at slowing rates, until peaking (in nominal terms) in 2052. In real or relative terms, however, pension assets are projected to peak and begin to fall much earlier. Our model indicates the ratio of pension assets to total payroll (at 1.25 in 1994) will climb modestly until reaching a peak of 1.36 in 2013. The ratio is projected to fall after 2014 and drop below 1.0 for the first time in 2038. Real inflation-adjusted pension assets would peak in 2024 with our baseline assumptions.

The important story from our analysis is that pensions could gradually cease to be the major engine of aggregate saving they have been for the past 20 years or more. Figure 7.4 shows the private pension system's total real saving (projected contributions less benefits plus real inflation-adjusted asset returns) relative to the economy's projected total private

Table 7.4
Combined private defined-benefit and defined-contribution projections for selected years, 1992–2065 (all dollar amounts in billions)

Year	Assets	Benefits	Contributions	Investment income	Net inflow	Real net inflow	Total payroll	Saving/ payroll
1992	2,870	86	105	181	201	86	2,313	0.037
1993	3,070	93	112	194	214	91	2,465	0.037
1994	3,284	99	120	207	228	97	2,626	0.037
1995	3,512	107	128	221	242	102	2,794	0.036
1996	3,754	116	136	236	257	107	2,971	0.036
1997	4,011	125	145	252	272	112	3,157	0.035
1998	4,283	135	154	269	288	117	3,351	0.035
1999	4,571	145	164	286	305	122	3,555	0.034
2000	4,876	154	174	304	323	128	3,771	0.034
2005	6,664	231	231	413	413	147	5,013	0.029
2010	8,913	347	303	549	505	149	6,580	0.023
2015	11,606	517	392	710	585	121	8,532	0.014
2020	14,662	751	504	891	644	57	10,993	0.005
2025	17,964	1,056	648	1,088	680	(39)	14,121	−0.003
2030	21,399	1,430	838	1,287	694	(162)	18,243	−0.009
2035	24,889	1,876	1,089	1,482	695	(300)	23,683	−0.013
2040	28,287	2,427	1,414	1,660	647	(485)	30,725	−0.016
2045	31,281	3,140	1,824	1,807	491	(760)	39,643	−0.019
2050	33,097	4,088	2,341	1,865	118	(1,206)	50,892	−0.024
2055	32,466	5,345	2,999	1,766	(580)	(1,879)	65,212	−0.029
2060	27,411	6,972	3,847	1,363	(1,762)	(2,858)	83,641	−0.034
2065	15,172	9,038	4,945	462	(3,630)	(4,237)	107,513	−0.039

Real saving/payroll

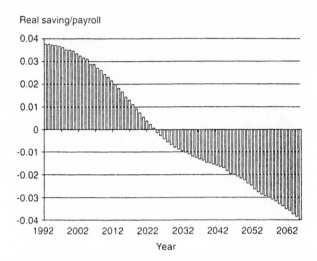

Figure 7.4
Potential real saving of private pensions relative to total private payroll for the years 1992–
2065 (assuming current plan characteristics and contribution rates persist)

payroll for 1992 to 2065. We use total payroll as the scaling factor simply because it is a readily available by-product of the Social Security forecasting operation. Figure 7.4 shows that under our assumptions the pension system would continue to generate significant investable funds for the U.S. economy for the next 20 years or so. In fact, the decline would be very minor for about the next 10 years, then would steepen considerably. By 2024, the pension system is projected to cease being a net source of saving for the economy and in fact to become from that point increasingly a net dissaver. By 2040, the net real dissaving would be more than 1.5% of payroll, and by 2065 the negative saving is projected to reach almost 4.0% of payroll. The pension system's change from a large net producer of saving to a large absorber of saving or loanable funds will likely have profound implications for interest rates, asset prices and the economy's growth rate.

It should be emphasized the prediction's timing of the change in pensions from net buyer of assets to net seller is very sensitive to our assumptions about rates of return earned on pension investments as well as to the assumed level of pension contributions. However, we feel that the pattern of figure 7.4 is almost inevitable; only the timing could be somewhat different than pictured. If investment returns exceed our fairly conservative assumptions, then the decline of pension saving will be delayed and more modest. Still, the demographic structure is such that it will by necessity occur. It is not even realistic to view this as a negative development. After all, pension assets are accumulated to provide the resources the elderly need in retirement. It is only natural that when we have an extraordinarily large number of retirees, the private pension system's real assets will shrink, and the system will at least temporarily cease being a source of new investment funds for the economy.

One concern that all this may raise is the impact on the prices of pension assets, mainly stocks and bonds. We share that concern to some degree but cannot predict the size or timing of any effect. One thing to note in this regard is that although the pension system will become a less important purchaser of securities, it will not become a net seller for quite a while. As noted earlier, our model predicts benefits will first exceed contributions in 2006. However, at that point the annual investment income (dividends, interest, and capital gains) on the $7 trillion portfolio should approximate $450 billion in nominal terms and $170 billion in real terms. There would be no reason to be net sellers of assets at that time and, in fact, we would suppose pensions will still be accumulating assets then. Under our conservative assumptions, the pension system will more likely begin to be a net seller in the early part of the next century's third decade. This could depress asset prices, particularly since the U.S. demographic structure does not differ greatly from those of Japan and Europe, which also will have large elderly populations at that time. The asset-price effect, if it occurs, would also likely affect all long-term assets. We think high real interest rates could depress the prices of stocks, bonds, land, and real estate. Although this might suggest that a good investment for this period would be short-term Treasury bills, the effect, if it occurs, is likely to be gradual and last for decades. In the 20th century, the longest stretch of time over which Treasury bills outperformed equities was about 15 years. We have little else to go on, but we certainly are not advocating that long-term investors invest in short-term instruments to ride out this demographic tidal wave. In fact, it is our opinion that far too many people invest in short-term instruments for long-term accumulations.

Under our baseline assumptions, the outlook for defined-contribution plans is relatively optimistic. Our model shows defined-contribution plan assets growing relative to economy-wide aggregates over the next 30 years or so, then stabilizing at the relatively larger level. Using total economy-wide payroll as our scaling factor, defined-contribution assets are now about 37% of one year's payroll. We project those assets to climb to 52% of payroll by 2000, to 70% by 2010, and to level out at about 85% for 2025 and beyond. The defined-ontribution system by its nature is not susceptible to running out of assets and, indeed, we do not project any such occurrence. The private defined-contribution system would be a modest net source of saving in the economy even in the period with the maximum number of baby boom retirees.

With our baseline assumptions, however, private defined-benefit plans would experience significant net outflows (dissaving). Benefits under these plans already exceed contributions; in fact, they are roughly three times contributions. The robust investment returns of the past decade or so have permitted and in fact compelled this. If investment returns drop to our conservative figures and if firms contribute a total of 2.8% of payroll to pension plans, then defined-benefit plan real assets will begin to fall immediately. Defined-benefit pension assets (now 88% of the economy's total payroll) would fall to 77% of total payroll by 2000, 66% by 2010, and 42.5% by 2025. The net flow of funds into the defined-benefit plans (or savings) would be positive, but only in nominal terms. Even nominal defined-benefit saving would become negative by 2025, and the entire stock of defined-benefit plan assets would be exhausted by 2043.

This is not a forecast of doom for the defined-benefit plans; it is simply a "what if" exercise. If by magic our rate-of-return assumptions proved to be precisely accurate, employers would be forced to increase their pension contributions above the 2.8% of aggregate payroll we have assumed or to curtail the pension benefits they offer workers. Although existing workers' vested benefits cannot be cut, certainly changes in plan design can reduce the accrual of new benefits. This tough choice of higher costs or lower pension benefits would occur long before 2043, when the model says that defined-benefit plan assets would be exhausted. Government regulators and pension actuaries would sound the alarm, decades, we hope, before the forecast could come true. The problem may become apparent, and the tough choice may have to be faced very early in the next century. We are concerned that employers may have gotten used to the very low contributions many have had to make to defined-benefit plans in recent years thanks to an extraordinary performance by financial markets and the constraints the federal regulatory environment imposes on funding. When they face their pension plans' higher long-run funding costs under more normal return realizations, they may choose to curtail the benefits they offer. It is also possible that at just about the time this is being resolved, we as a society will have to acknowledge the fact that Social Security is not in long-run equilibrium; once again, the choice will be either to raise taxes or lower benefits. In this sense, both Social Security and the funded private defined-benefit pension system will likely face cost pressure to scale back retirement benefits.

Alternative Projection Scenarios

As the discussion above suggests, the baseline scenario we have developed here is not sustainable. ERISA funding requirements would not permit the contingency of the whole private defined-benefit pension system running out of assets while accruing massive unfunded liabilities. If private employers were to face the prospect that they could not meet future benefit obligations, ERISA would require they either contribute additional funds to their plans or curtail the benefits being offered under them. Current contribution and accrual rates in the face of the workforce's demographic structure will require that contributions to plans increase or that benefits be curtailed.

A number of scenarios can be considered in terms of employers increasing contributions to cover accruing benefit obligations. In one, employers would delay increased funding for some time but ultimately would increase defined-benefit funding sufficiently to pay the benefits the current benefit structure implies. In another, employers would increase their contribution rates in the very near future to a level that would indefinitely sustain private-sector defined-benefit plans at approximately current levels of funding relative to liabilities. The former strategy would create the risk that when we reach the point where employers must increase their contributions, they will discover that they are not able or willing to make such a large commitment, and covered workers would then have very little time to adjust their personal saving to make up for the cuts in their pension benefits. The latter strategy would require such a large immediate shift in contributions to plans that employers might not be able to adjust other commitments and sustain the plans. The best strategy for minimizing the risk of benefit reductions would seem to be to increase contributions gradually to a level that would sustain the system. We developed a series of simulations to test these alternative approaches.

In recent years, private-employer contributions to defined-benefit plans have averaged about 2.8% of private-sector payroll (note that this is all private-sector pay, not just pay in covered employment). In what we

Real saving/payroll

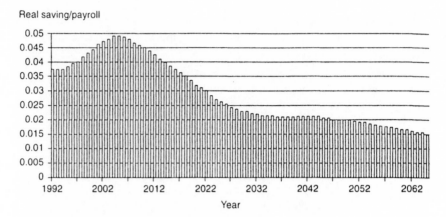

Figure 7.5
Potential real saving of private pensions relative to total private payroll for the years 1992–
2065 (assuming current plan characteristics persist and contribution rates rise)
Source: Watson Wyatt Worldwide.

consider the most likely scenario that would have employers remaining
committed to their defined-benefit plans, we assumed contributions began
to rise in 1995, increasing at a rate of 0.015% of payroll per year until the
contribution rate equaled 4.5% of payroll. Under these assumptions, the
assets in defined-benefit plans would remain at a relatively constant level
in comparison to payroll over the 75-year projection period. Figure 7.5
shows the pattern of real saving in this scenario. Under this scenario the
pattern of real pension saving to payroll would increase as employer
contributions to defined-benefit plans were increasing but would decline
over the remainder of the period, although the net real saving would be
positive in every year. In other words, private pensions would contribute
to net savings throughout the period but would take on diminished importance as the baby boomers claimed their retirement benefits.

Under this scenario, the private-sector defined-benefit pension system
would have sufficient assets to pay benefits until the baby boom generation has completely passed on. In 2065, assets relative to payroll would
be down about 4% from the current ratio and would be declining ever
so slightly. In other words, under this funding scenario private-sector
defined-benefit plan assets would make it through the baby boomers'
retirement period and last indefinitely beyond that. Over almost all of the
projection period, however, employer contributions under this scenario
would be 60% higher than they are today. The alternative would be
reduced benefits.

In the original Social Security Act in 1935 and all subsequent amendments, Congress has maintained the option of changing the law at any time, including the option to reduce benefits that might have been accrued under the definitions of prior law. Federal law does not allow employers the same flexibility in the administration of their defined-benefit programs. ERISA requires benefits accrued under a defined-benefit plan be paid unless the funds in the plan are exhausted, in which case the PBGC assumes payment of the benefits up to the guaranteed minimums under its benefit insurance program. Any discussion of employers reducing benefits to cope with the situation we have pictured here does not insinuate that employers might, at some future time, refuse to meet their legal obligations under their defined-benefit plans. We are suggesting that by reducing benefits, employers could curtail accruals under the plans, which would reduce the benefits anticipated by workers who expect their retirement plans to continue to operate in accordance with current benefit provisions.

Benefit reductions to bring plans back into balance in relation to current funding rates could occur relatively late in workers' careers, when the heaviest accrual of benefits under defined-benefit plans occurs. For example, a worker who begins a job at age 30, is covered by a defined-benefit plan, and is eligible to retire at age 60 would receive only 60% of expected benefits from the plan if it were terminated after 23 years of covered service. In the last quarter of the career, more than 40% of the benefit would be earned under the plan if it were to be continued. Stated alternatively, many plan sponsors could readily achieve the savings needed to bring benefit promises into balance with current funding rates by curtailing their defined-benefit plans when the baby boomers were within a decade of their anticipated retirement dates and substituting lower-cost defined-benefit or defined-contribution plans. Of course, baby boomers would then have less retirement income than the private pension system's current structure now implies.

Conclusions

The major finding of this chapter is that the national saving the private pension system generates can be expected to decline from current levels, gradually for about a decade, then far more steeply. With our conservative assumptions about the rate of return earned by pension assets, the pension system would cease to be a source of saving roughly in 2024. It is our opinion that this indeed will happen, although there is considerable uncertainty about the timing.

We also find the defined-benefit portion of the private pension system faces a tough choice. Our model shows the system would run out of money in 2043 if it were funded according to our assumptions and if rates of return were consistent with those we have projected. Obviously, the system will not be allowed to run out of money. However, the model is implicitly predicting that either corporate pension contributions will have to be substantially raised or pension plans scaled back. It is highly unlikely current low contribution rates, caused by the high realized rates of return on financial assets over the past decade, can be sustained.

We have briefly speculated about the impact of the pension system's reduced saving on asset prices. Even though we think the change will be less dramatic than our baseline model predicts because of adjustments in contributions and plan design, we still feel the demographic structure is such that a major change in pension saving will occur. The timing and magnitude of the effect on asset prices is impossible to determine. Capital markets are worldwide, interest rates are determined by both supply and demand, and forecasts of financial rates of return some 30 or more years into the future are futile. However, the population bulge we call the baby boom caused considerable strain on the U.S. education system in the 1950s and 1960s. Absorbing those people into the workforce was a challenge in the 1970s and early 1980s and may have been a factor in slowing the growth in worker productivity. It is probably safe to say the same numerous cohort will strain the economic system once again during their retirement years, roughly 2010 to 2050.

Notes

The authors would like to thank Dean Maki and Linda Moncrief for their valuable research assistance and Henry Aaron and Tatsua Hatta for their helpful comments. Any remaining errors are our responsibility.

1. U.S. Bureau of the Census, *Historical Statistics of the United States, Colonial Times to 1970,* (1975) Bicentennial Edition, Part 1, Washington, DC, p. 368.

2. U.S. Bureau of the Census, *Statistical Abstract of the United States* (111th edition), Washington, DC, 1991, p. 132.

3. U.S. Bureau of the Census, *Historical Statistics of the United States, Colonial Times to 1970,* (1975) Bicentennial Edition, Part 1, Washington, DC, p. 127, and *Statistical Abstract of the United States* (111th edition), Washington, DC, 1991, p. 384.

4. For a full discussion of this proposal, see Sylvester J. Schieber, "A Proposal to Establish Personal Security Accounts as an Element of Social Security Reform as Considered by the

Social Security Advisory Council," testimony before the Senate Finance Committee, Subcommittee on Social Security and Family Policy, March 25, 1996.

5. The Wyatt Company, *The Compensation and Benefits File*, Washington, DC (November 1987), vol. 3, no. 11, p. 4.

6. The Wyatt Company, *Survey of Actuarial Assumptions and Funding, 1992*, Washington, DC, 1992, p. 4.

7. Ibbotson Associates, *Stocks, Bonds, Bills and Inflation, 1993 Yearbook: Market Results for 1926–1992*, Chicago, 1993.

DE ECONOMIST 149, NO. 1, 2001

GROWTH AND WELFARE DISTRIBUTION IN AN AGEING SOCIETY: AN APPLIED GENERAL EQUILIBRIUM ANALYSIS FOR THE NETHERLANDS

BY

D. PETER BROER*

Summary

This paper studies the effects of the imminent ageing of the population on economic growth and the distribution of welfare in the Netherlands. It shows that with the current system of social security ageing leads to a substantial increase of the tax burden and an estimated welfare loss for future generations of approximately 4% of lifetime wealth. It discusses the effect of reform measures in the pay-as-you-go social security system. It shows that a cut in PAYG pensions is efficiency-improving, but hurts the lower income groups of current generations. This effect can be ameliorated by a debt-financed cut in indirect taxes.

Key words: CGE model, overlapping generations, ageing, social security, intergenerational distribution

1 INTRODUCTION

The age composition of the population in developed countries is shifting rapidly in favour of the elderly. Projections by the United Nations indicate that for the OECD area as a whole the share of the elderly (people of age 65 and over) will increase from 15% in 1990 to 22% in 2040. At the same time, the old-age dependency ratio (the ratio of the elderly to the working age population) is expected to rise from 20% to 37%. For developing countries, a similar change is expected at a later stage (United Nations (1994)). Since the last decade, it is recognized that this worldwide change in the age structure of the population will have far-reaching economic consequences.

The demographic change will generate a substantial shift in the distribution of the net financial burden of the public sector across generations, mostly as a result

* OCFEB and CPB Netherlands Bureau of Economic Policy Analysis. Address: OCFEB, Faculty of Economics, Erasmus University, P.O. Box 1738, 3000 DR Rotterdam, The Netherlands. E-mail: broer@few.eur.nl. This paper is part of the Applied General Equilibrium project on 'Tax Reform, the Functioning of Markets, and Growth in an Ageing Society' at OCFEB. I would like to thank Leon Bettendorf, Lans Bovenberg, Harry van Dalen, Johan Graafland, Ben Heijdra, Tobias Rasmussen, Harry ter Rele, Ed Westerhout, and two anonymous referees for comments on previous versions of this paper.

De Economist **149**, 81–114, 2001.

© 2001 *Kluwer Academic Publishers. Printed in the Netherlands.*

of declining labour force participation. Rising dependency ratios imply a decline in the size of the tax base that can be used to finance public expenditure and social security transfers. In addition, they will increase the outlays for health care and social security. In most OECD countries, social security is largely on a pay-as-you-go (PAYG) basis, so that the currently active population pays for the pensions of the retired population. Without a substantial cut in public expenditure programmes and transfers, ageing will therefore cause a substantial increase in the net tax burden for younger generations.

To estimate the size of the burden of future generations, Auerbach and Kotlikoff introduced the method of Generational Accounting (see Auerbach et al. (1991)). Calculations for the US show that the lifetime tax rates for future generations are expected to almost double, from around 29% to around 50%, under the current policy regime (see Gokhale et al. (1999)). Kotlikoff and Leibfritz (1999) conclude that 10 out of 17 countries in their survey have severe generational imbalances, among others the Netherlands. On the other hand, Ter Rele (1998) estimates that for the Netherlands the burden of future generations needs to be raised by only 3%, due to a future increase in labour participation and the substantial funding of Dutch pensions. Since intergenerational accounting does not include the deadweight loss of an increase in the tax burden, these estimates must be regarded as lower bounds of the intergenerational burden.

A fundamental limitation of generational accounting is its neglect of market forces that provide a counterbalance to the consequences of an increasing dependency ratio. Ageing will affect the relative scarcity of production factors. On the transition path, the decline in the labour force will cause a reduction in labour supply that also depresses investment and the demand for capital. On the other hand, during the first stage of the transition life-cycle saving will be at a maximum. Therefore, for individual OECD countries a relative scarcity of labour may be expected during the transition. To the extent that ageing is synchronized over countries, international capital flows will not be able to equalize capital returns over time, which will lead to a movement along the factor price frontier, boosting wages and depressing interest rates (see Auerbach and Kotlikoff (1987), Börsch-Supan (1996), Chauveau and Loufir (1997), and Miles (1999)). Thus relative wage increases may lead to a partial restoration of the intergenerational balance.[1]

Another counterbalance to the distributional consequences of ageing is offered by the capital deepening that results from a decline in population growth, which boosts output per capita. On this account, Cutler et al. (1990) argue that the slow-

---

1   As a caveat it may be pointed out that the life-cycle model is not generally accepted as a good description of saving by individual households. Poterba (1998) for the US and Alessie, Kapteyn and Klijn (1997) for the Netherlands show that old-age households generally dissave less than predicted by the life-cycle model. However, Miles (1999) argues that once saving through pension funds is taken into account the life cycle model is much closer to observed saving profiles. In addition, Auerbach, Cai, and Kotlikoff (1991) show that the projected macroeconomic savings rate is not sensitive to the precise model of household behaviour used.

down in population growth does not create any problems. However, it may be argued that the demographic shift not only entails a drop in fertility but also an increase in longevity that boosts the share of elderly in the population. In addition the rising excess burden of social security will have adverse supply effects on saving and labour supply that may dominate the capital deepening effect. For instance, taking these effects into account, Chauveau and Loufir (1997) predict that OECD output will fall some ten to fifteen percent below the value on a balanced growth path as a result of the increasing social security burden.

As a large part of the expected increase of the burden of future generations has to do with unfunded social security, the policy discussion focuses to a large extent on social security reform as well. PAYG social security has typically been introduced to extend the coverage of pre-existing work-related private schemes (Fabel (1994)). In the process the funded character of the original schemes was gradually abolished. This transition was motivated both by distributional considerations and by efficiency arguments. On the distributional side, the first few generations to participate in the PAYG system did not have to pay for their PAYG pensions. On the efficiency side, until the 1980s, the benefits of PAYG financing outweighed the disadvantages. As pointed out by Aaron (1966), the rate of return on PAYG social security is the population growth rate plus the real growth of wages. In the sixties and seventies, this rate of return exceeded the return on a funded social security, which is the real rate of interest. In the eighties and nineties, the real rate of interest rose and the ranking was reversed. In the next century, a lower population growth rate lowers the return on a PAYG system, making a funded system even more attractive.

Thus both distributional concerns and efficiency arguments suggest a transition to a funded system. Many proposals to switch to funding have been made in recent years, see e.g. Feldstein (1995, 1996), and Börsch-Supan (1998). Generally, these proposals aim both at a reduction in the size of the intergenerational redistribution that is caused by the PAYG system and the exploitation of the higher expected return to be achieved from a funded system.[2] However, a transition to a funded system requires that some generations pay both the PAYG contribution rate for the pensions of the currently retired, as well as the contribution to the new funded system. In a sense, these generations pay for the free lunch of the elder generations at the creation of the PAYG fund. Therefore a difference between the rates of return on a PAYG system *versus* a funded system is not in itself an indication of a possible efficiency gain from a transition.

The issue of a Pareto-improving conversion from a PAYG system to a funded system has been investigated by Raffelhüschen (1993), Breyer and Straub (1993), Broer et al. (1994), Kotlikoff (1996), and Fehr (1999). From these analyses it

---

2 If ageing also lowers the rate of return on capital, the case for funding is less clear-cut. In particular, a *transition* to a funded system would incur substantial costs in the presence of falling interest rates.

appears that such a transition is feasible if it reduces the distortion of the labour supply decision sufficiently to enable current and future generations to pay off the burden of the PAYG system from the reduced deadweight loss. A limitation of these models is that they assume that households differ only by age. Intragenerational heterogeneity is introduced by Kotlikoff et al. (1998) and by Fehr (1999). From these studies it appears that a Pareto-improving transition is more difficult to achieve if intragenerational heterogeneity is also taken into account. Different income groups are affected differently by alternative financing modes of the reform and have different tax-benefit linkages.

This paper studies the effects of population ageing on economic growth and the distribution of welfare in the Netherlands. It explicitly takes into account the effects of factor price movements and distortionary taxes on growth and intergenerational distribution. In addition, it also investigates the effects of ageing on the intragenerational distribution. It explores the possibilities to improve both efficiency and income distribution through a reform of the social security system. For this, it uses an extension of the OLG general equilibrium model of Broer, Westerhout and Bovenberg (1994). The model is calibrated on the Dutch economy as of 1994 to compute the expected time path of the Dutch economy over the next century.

Broer et al. (1994) showed that in the absence of intragenerational heterogeneity a Pareto-improving transition to a funded pension system would be possible. In this paper I take up the same issue, but with intragenerational heterogeneity included. In comparison with both our previous work and the studies by Kotlikoff et al. (1998) and Fehr (1999), I use a calibration of the model to a baseline solution that includes the projected ageing of the population, i.e. outside of the steady state. Since the demographic transition produces its own redistribution of welfare across generations, this redistribution should properly be looked at in conjunction with the redistributive effects of the social security reform. This means that a reform that in itself would harm certain generations may nevertheless be considered equitable if considered together with the distributive effects of the demographic shock. Evaluation of social security reforms are therefore not very informative if the reference scenario is a steady-state path.

The paper considers two reforms: first, a straightforward reduction in PAYG benefits, and second a combined cut in PAYG benefits and consumption taxes to compensate current old generations for the loss in income. The first option comes close to the international privatization literature, whereby PAYG saving is replaced by private life-cycle saving, but it incorporates an idiosyncrasy of the Dutch pension system that provides for a built-in compensation of existing elderly. This occurs through the supplementary occupational pension schemes that apply for most households participating in the labour market. The second option uses government debt to transfer part of the efficiency gain of the PAYG cut to current generations. This transfer is achieved by implementing a maximal sustainable cut in consumption taxes.[3]

The rest of the paper is organized as follows. Section 2 presents an overview of the model, section 3 discusses the effects of population ageing for the Dutch economy in terms of a baseline projection with a constant interest rate and the expected development of the population. Section 4 discusses some policy options to combat the adverse effects of population ageing and section 5 concludes.

2 THE MODEL

The model is basically a small open economy version of the Auerbach-Kotlikoff (1987) overlapping generations model. It consists of the following sectors: households, a private enterprise sector producing tradables, private health insurance firms, public health insurance (subdivided into two categories), health care, a pension sector (with both a basic and a supplementary pension scheme), a government sector, and a foreign sector. Four markets are distinguished, the labour market, the tradable goods market, the health care market, and the capital market. All markets clear, prices for tradables and capital are determined on world markets through arbitrage, the wage rate and the price for health care are determined on the domestic markets.

The model builds on Broer, Westerhout and Bovenberg (1994) and Broer and Westerhout (1997). It extends these studies in a number of respects, the most important of which are a disaggregation of households by productivity as well as age and a calibration on a recent, non-steady-state, demographic projection.[4] Below I give a summary description of the main characteristics of the model. A complete documentation can be found in Broer (1999).

2.1 *Firms*

The tradable goods sector uses capital, labour, and raw materials to produce goods and services that are freely traded on domestic and international markets at internationally determined prices. Investment in physical capital is subject to internal adjustment costs, which makes it internationally immobile in the short run. Firms issue debt in fixed proportion to the value of their capital, so that the marginal source of finance for investment is retained earnings. The discount rate of dividends is derived from an arbitrage relation between bonds and equity for do-

---

3 Note that a cut in consumption taxes is partly a lump sum subsidy to the accumulated wealth of existing generations.

4 Other new elements are: age-dependent wage profiles for each (productivity-defined) type of household, age-dependent demand for health care per household, a separate health insurance sector, and age-dependent government expenditure on education and social security transfers.

mestic investors. The labour input of different productivity types is perfectly substitutable, so that wages are proportional to productivity.

The health sector only uses labour to produce health care services. Different productivity types are complementary in production, so that the skill distribution in the health sector is fixed. Since health care is labour intensive, and health care demand is larger in an ageing society a sectorial shift will occur from tradable goods to health care. This shift will reinforce the labour market effects of the declining participation rate.

2.2 *Social Security*

Pension provisions are modelled as a two-tier system. The first tier is a basic PAYG scheme that pays a flat benefit to all residents of age 65 and over. This scheme is financed from a proportional levy on income.[5] Residents of age 65 and over are exempt from PAYG contributions. The PAYG contribution rate is fixed and deficits of the PAYG scheme are subsidized by the government.[6] The second tier takes the form of a supplementary occupational scheme that aims at supplementing the PAYG pension to achieve a total pension maximally equal to 70% of the wage income earned in the year before retirement, depending on the number of years workers have contributed to the fund. The supplementary character of the occupational scheme creates a franchise level so that workers with a wage income below the franchise do not currently contribute to the scheme. They do not accumulate rights for the supplementary scheme either. Contributions to the occupational scheme are deductible for both income tax and PAYG contributions but benefits are subject to income taxation. By adjusting its contribution rate, the occupational scheme tries to match its assets and its projected benefit obligations to households that are currently participating in the fund.

In the model, the form of health care insurance depends on the wage level of the household. Low-productivity households are publicly insured. The public health insurance firm levies both a proportional tax on labour income and a small, nominally fixed, contribution. It reimburses (nearly) all health care expenditures of its clients. The private health insurance sector levies a lump sum contribution on households. In the model, it reimburses a fixed proportion of the health care expenditures of its clients. Both insurance firms close their budget annually by adjusting their contribution rate.

---

5 A more extensive discussion of the model for the pension sector can be found in Broer et al. (1994).
6 Officially, only a *ceiling* has been imposed on contribution rates. In view of the expected increase in contribution rates, this amounts to the same thing. This change in the financing method of the Dutch basic pension scheme implies that it is no longer strictly pay-as-you-go if the government uses debt financing.

2.3 *Households*

Households choose their consumption of goods, health care, and leisure by maximizing expected lifetime utility subject to a lifetime budget constraint and a time constraint per period. Lifetime is uncertain and the death hazard increases with age. Households insure against this hazard by buying annuities. Preference for the consumption of leisure and health care is age-dependent. Households are free to retire when they choose, but they are eligible for old-age pensions from their 65th birthday, irrespective of their actual retirement date. Households differ both by age and by productivity (human capital). Productivity is exogenous to the individual household, but it varies by age.

Income for working age households consists of labour income, capital income, and government transfers. Households differ both by age and by productivity (human capital). Productivity is calibrated so that wages match the observed distribution over households of different ages in the base year. Households pay a proportional income tax on all forms of income. In addition, working age households contribute to the old-age social security fund and an occupational pension fund. All households are also compulsory insured with either a public health insurance fund or a private one. Households are only eligible for old-age pensions from their 65th birthday, irrespective of their actual retirement date.

Figures 1 and 2 present labour supply and wealth of households by age and position in the productivity distribution as these follow from the model for the starting year (1995).[7] The wealth accumulation profiles show that households incur some debt in the early parts of their life, to be able to smooth their consumption over the life cycle in spite of their low initial wage. The effect is most pronounced for the highest productivity type. Note that households do not dissave until high age. This is a consequence of the assumption that households insure against death by selling their assets against lifetime annuities. The return to wealth increases with age as a result of the increasing death hazard. For the median household, the wealth profile matches observed saving behaviour reasonably well. For the upper 5% of the distribution, the wealth profile after retirement is probably less realistic.

Labour supply profiles show participation rates for the base year that show a similar hump-shaped age pattern as observed participation rates. Participation rates for young low-productivity households are lower than for other types. Qualitatively, this conforms with reality. The model generates participation rates for households in their early fifties that may be too low. However, a direct compari-

---

7   E.g. type 0.48 is the household type for which 48% of households has a lower productivity at the same age.

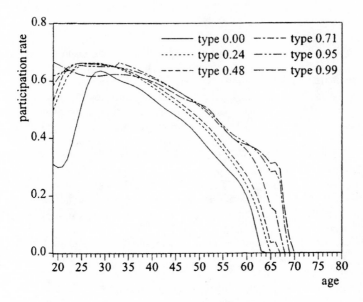

Figure 1 – Labour supply distribution by age in 1995

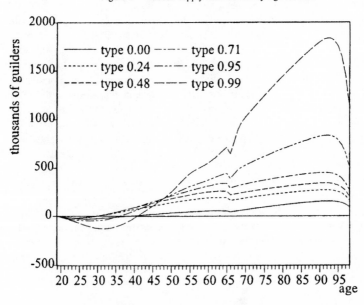

Figure 2 – Wealth distribution by age in 1995

226

son of the results with the data is hindered by the lack of observations on participation by hours worked.[8]

2.4 *Taxation*

In the model, the tax system discriminates between households in a number of ways. First, old-age households do not contribute to PAYG old-age social security or to the pension fund. Second, households with a wage below the franchise level of the occupational pension fund do not contribute to that fund nor receive a supplementary pension upon retirement. Third, households with a wage below the public health insurance threshold are compulsory insured with the public health insurance fund, while households with a wage above the threshold are privately insured.[9] So the wage level of a household determines whether it contributes to the supplementary pension scheme, and whether it is insured with the public health insurance system or with the private health insurance system.

In an ageing society, both the health insurance system and the pension system impose an increasing burden on households. The burden of the health insurance system originates primarily with the public health insurance system which raises its income through a distortionary tax on labour income. Thus, as the share of elderly in the population grows, the contribution base shrinks at the same time when demand for health care increases. This generates both a redistribution of income between generations and an increase in the tax wedge on labour. This latter effect is absent from the private health scheme. As a result, in an ageing society the tax burden of high-income households grows less than that of low income households. High-ability households escape the health insurance tax altogether, whereas medium ability households escape it over the later half of their life, when their productivity is at a maximum. The health system therefore primarily distorts labour supply decisions of young and low-ability households.

Like the public health contribution rate, the PAYG pension contribution acts as a purely distortionary tax. The expected increase of this contribution rate therefore poses similar problems. The PAYG tax does not discriminate between households of different productivity, however.[10] Since the occupational scheme is a defined-benefit system, it cannot be actuarially fair and therefore distorts labour

---

8 Observed participation rates are given in terms of persons with a job of at least 12 hours per week. These rates start declining around age 55. At age 62, participation rates are only a few percent of the available population.
9 The actual regulations are formulated in terms of *income*. The formulation chosen here neglects the effects of tax progression on labour supply.
10 In the Netherlands, PAYG contributions are levied only in the first tax bracket. The size of the PAYG contribution rate therefore does not affect the marginal income tax of high-income households. This characteristic is missing from the model, in which all taxes are proportional to their base.

supply decisions.[11] The occupational scheme discriminates between high and low-wage households on account of its franchise, so that workers with a wage income above the franchise face a larger distortion. However, the distortion created by the occupational scheme is significantly less than that of the PAYG scheme on two accounts. First, a relation between contribution and benefit does exist, so that the contribution is not a pure tax (even though it is not actuarially fair). Second, the occupational scheme is fully funded, so that it should be able to stabilize contribution rates during the demographic transition. However, since the occupational scheme is also a defined-benefit scheme, substantial redistribution between generations may still occur if interest rates or wages change.

2.5 Equilibrium

In the model, the Netherlands is described as a small open economy with an exogenous interest rate and tradable goods sold at world market prices. As a result, interactions between agents have a fairly simple structure. In the long run, when the capital stock has adjusted, the factor price frontier causes the gross wage rate to be linked one-to-one to the world interest rate. In the absence of government intervention this property effectively severs the links between the decisions of domestic households. This holds even though labour is a non-traded good. Fluctuations in labour supply, or consumption, in the long run do not feed back to the domestic economy, but are absorbed in international markets. Thus, a fall in labour supply, e.g. through population ageing, would simply lead to an equiproportional reduction in capital through a fall in investment. The presence of capital adjustment costs does not substantially alter this conclusion, because forward-looking firms will anticipate the demographic shift and reduce investment in advance to smooth fluctuations in the capital-labour ratio. As a result, the real wage will fall off slightly before ageing sets in and rise somewhat thereafter. Major inequalities in income between generations as a result of ageing can only occur through changes in the world rate of interest.[12]

In a small open economy government spending and social security provide the main link between generations. A larger share of elderly simultaneously lowers government tax receipts and boosts social security outlays. Because social security is not funded, these extra outlays inevitably raise income taxes. A rise in income taxes has several effects. First, it directly affects the intergenerational income distribution. Since the return to PAYG social security falls, young generations must pay more to maintain the living standard of the elderly. Second, it

---

11   The distortion varies over the life cycle, and may be zero for some years. It is generally largest for middle-aged households.

12   As noted in the introduction, a fall in world interest rates is not at all improbable. From a life-cycle perspective, a fully anticipated change primarily boost the return to human capital and shifts the income distribution towards high-ability households.

lowers the after-tax interest rate, which reduces the required rate of return on equity, boosts investment per capita, and increases labour productivity and gross wages. This substitution effect partially compensates households for the rise in the tax burden. Third, the increase in the tax rate also distorts labour supply decisions and saving decisions of households. The decrease in the opportunity costs of leisure induces a shift towards consumption of leisure and towards current consumption relative to future consumption. As a result, taxes and contribution rates have to rise further. This creates an efficiency loss that lowers economic growth and welfare. In the next section I attempt to provide a detailed account of the effect of ageing on welfare and economic growth over the next century.

2.6 Extensions

To put the present model into perspective, it is useful to specify a number of extensions that might affect the results presented in this paper. The presence of substantial intergenerational transfers through bequests (Kotlikoff (1988)) suggests the introduction of a bequest motive as a determinant of saving, in addition to the consumption smoothing motive used in this paper. Modelling bequests presents somewhat of a problem, however. Microeconometric studies show that little support exists for an altruistic bequest motive (Altonji et al. (1992), Wilhelm (1996)). In addition, there are some well-known theoretical difficulties with attempts to model altruism explicitly (Bernheim and Bagwell (1988)). Davies (1981) shows that observed bequests can be explained to a large part from a precautionary motive related to uncertain lifetime and imperfect insurance markets. This requires modelling of liquidity constraints and uncertainty, which is a formidable task (see e.g. Carroll (1992)).

Next to private bequest motives, social equity is another important motive for intergenerational transfers. A satisfactory treatment of uncertainty would enable consideration of public insurance motives of pensions in the form of intergenerational *risk sharing* (Gordon and Varian (1988)). The current neglect of this rationale of public pensions biases the results in the direction of efficiency considerations.

The model does not describe human capital accumulation. Differences in household productivity by age are represented through exogenous wage profiles. Modelling of human capital decisions makes it possible to study the effects of changes in the return to human capital on the accumulation decision, both in terms of schooling and on-the-job training (Heckman, Lochner, and Taber (1998)). To also model endogenous growth it is necessary to introduce a spillover of human capital between generations (Bovenberg and Van Ewijk (1997)). The effects of ageing on growth are very sensitive to the size of this spillover, whereas empirical information on this size is deficient (Fougère and Mérette (1999)).

In the present model, taxes are proportional to income. Inclusion of progressive taxation in the model would enable a better estimate of the size of the distortions created by rising tax rates and their effect on labour participation, in particular for elder workers. Combined with endogenous human capital, it would also increase the relevance of the estimates of the equity-efficiency trade-off made with the present model.

Similar remarks may be made with respect to labour market imperfections. Whereas unemployment is less of an issue in an ageing society, wage bargaining outcomes may be affected by the increase in the tax burden. In addition, if rising wage profiles over workers' lives are the result of incentive schemes in the presence of incomplete information, instead of productivity differences, a substantial increase in the share of elder workers raises labour costs.

2.7 Calibration

The calibration of the model is based on the National Accounts of 1994. The calibration uses a steady-state growth path for the values of all exogenous variables for the period after 1994, except for population growth, that is based on the so-called 'mid-range' demographic projection of the Dutch Central Statistical Office (see Figure 3).

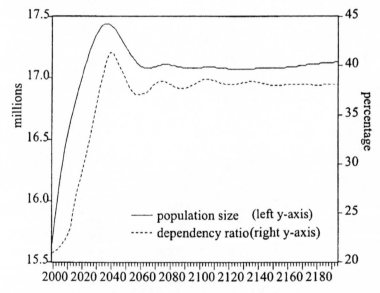

Figure 3 – Demographic projections, 2000-2194

For the household sector the scale parameters are chosen to make the model match observed aggregate labour supply, consumption of health care and of goods and services, and non-human wealth. In addition, labour participation of elderly

(> 64) is set at 2%, to conform to observed participation rates. The productivity distribution of households has been derived from a cross-sectional data set of individual wages, available by age, for 1995, by assuming that wage differences between workers in the same year are based solely on productivity differences. Steady-state price elasticities for the household sector as a whole are given in Table 4 below. The aggregate wage elasticity of labour supply is nearly zero. An increase in income taxes increases labour supply and reduces wealth accumulation (saving). In the long run, both aggregate consumption and saving respond positively to an increase in the rate of interest.

The calibration of the production sector sets the scale parameters to match the observed factor shares in the base year. For the tradable goods sector the substitution elasticities between capital and labour and between value added and the use of intermediate goods are set at 0.5. The resulting long-term price elasticities are shown in Table 5 below. These elasticities agree with the available econometric estimates for the Netherlands (see the survey in CPB (1997)). For the health care sector, it is assumed that labour is the only production factor.

3 THE EFFECTS OF AGEING ON ECONOMIC GROWTH

To evaluate the effects of ageing on economic growth, I compute a baseline projection of the development of the Dutch economy over the next two centuries. This projection assumes steady-state growth rates for all exogenous variables, except the demographics, that are taken from a recent projection by the Central Statistical Office (CSO) (see De Beer (1999)). The baseline projection deviates from a steady-state growth path both because of the demographic shift that is included and because the initial asset positions of households and government are not compatible with a steady-state growth path. However, other deviations from steady-state developments, e.g. changes in interest rates or the current government policy of debt reduction, are not taken into account. As a result, the projections presented here cannot be interpreted as forecasts of the future course of the Dutch economy, but should properly be regarded as conditional forecasts of the effects of ageing on economic growth.

Figure 3 shows the recent projection of demographics by the CSO.[13] The population is expected to grow till about 2040 (left y-axis). Extrapolating the fertility and mortality rates used by the CSO, the projection implies a small decline in the population thereafter. Shortly afterwards, the old-age dependency ratio reaches a maximum of 40% (right y-axis). This share then slightly falls off again, but it remains at almost double its present size. A sensitivity analysis reveals that, whereas the future size of the population is rather uncertain, the uncertainty in the dependency ratio remains within 2% (see Broer (1999), Figure 3). The CSO

---

13   The projections have been extended beyond 2050 by extrapolating the fertility and mortality rates for 2050 to later years.

projections also entail assumptions about immigration rates. In the model, these have been balanced with the mortality rates to obtain mortality rates that are slightly *negative* for young households.[14] Hence, immigration is assumed to continue at the rates projected for 2050.

The baseline path has been computed using the income tax rate as a closure variable for the government budget constraint and assuming that government debt as a fraction of GDP is kept constant at the calibrated value of 71%. At a steady-state growth rate of 2%, this implies a long-term government deficit of 1.4% of GDP. The (real) interest rate is assumed to remain constant at 5.5%.

In the long run, the growth rate of the economy is determined by the rate of technical progress (2%) and the growth rate of the population (-0.0%). On the transition path, the growth rate deviates from this benchmark value as a result of demographic shifts. Figure 4 shows the change in the labour market participation rate of the population. Overall participation rates fall until about 2035, to recover only partially thereafter. The end result is a fall in participation rates by about 4%-points. Obviously, this decline represents the increasing dependency ratio as a result of the ageing of the population. The endogenous part of this shift is largely captured by the participation rate of the working age population. It appears from Figure 4 that after an initial decline, this participation rate is expected to recover in the second half of the next century.

Figure 5 shows the consequences of these participation rate shifts for aggregate efficiency-corrected labour supply and labour employed in the tradable goods sector. Initially, labour supply in efficiency units grows, because the working age population grows older and, therefore, becomes more productive. From about 2010 on, these older cohorts retire, and labour supply stagnates. This effect is reinforced by the temporary decline in the participation of the working age population. The resulting fall in employment in the tradable goods sector is particularly severe. This discrepancy reflects the weight of both government labour demand and labour demand by the health care sector. Government employment is constant as a percentage of the population, and health sector employment actually increases as a result of the increasing demand for health care, due to ageing. As the health sector is labour-intensive, this sectoral shift adds to the effects of the declining participation ratio.

Since capital is immobile in the short run, the decline in labour supply creates labour scarcity in the first half of the next century, with a maximum around 2030. This scarcity does not materialize immediately, however, as employers anticipate this event, and start reducing their capital stock before the decline of labour supply sets in. Figure 6 shows that over the next decade the growth rate of the marginal product of labour lags behind the rate of labour saving technical progress.

---

14   This procedure implies that these cohorts receive a negative annuity from the life insurance fund, which effectively provides immigrants with the same assets as the resident population. Otherwise, immigrants would have to be treated separately both by year of immigration and year of birth.

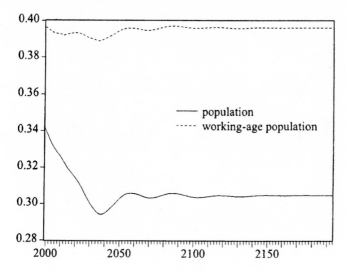

Figure 4 – Participation rates

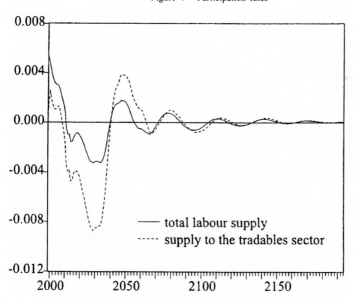

Figure 5 – Growth of labour supply

233

However, average wage rates do not show a lower growth rate because of the wage drift caused by the age composition effect. Figure 6 shows that the cumulative wage drift over the next decade is about 3 percent.

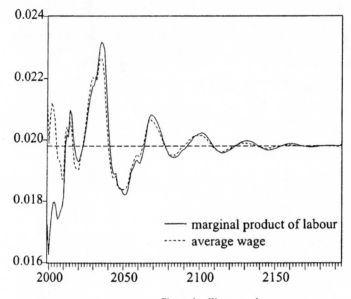

Figure 6 – Wage growth

Figure 8 decomposes the aggregate participation rate by age for a selected number of years. According to the baseline projection of the model, the labour participation of young households will decline by about 1.5%-points in the next century, whereas the labour participation of households of age 60 will increase by about 5%-points. The increase in the participation rate of households just above the statutory retirement age is even larger at 7%-points. For young households, the most important determinant of the participation change is the intratemporal substitution between time-related consumption (leisure and health care) and goods. It is negative because of the increase in the tax wedge (Figure 7).[15] Its effect is largely compensated by the wealth effect, so that only a small net negative labour supply effect remains. The single most important determinant of the increase over time in the labour market participation of older workers is the in-

15   The wedge is defined as $(1+t_c)/(1-t_l)$, where t_c denotes the consumption tax and t_l the tax and contribution rates on labour. The contribution rates consist of health insurance, AWBZ insurance, and basic pension contributions. The contributions to the FC pension fund have not been included in this measure, even though they are distortionary. The contribution to the public health care insurance has been included, even though a minority of households is privately insured.

tertemporal substitution effect. Since the after-tax wage falls, the increase in the intertemporal distortion of labour supply must be attributed exclusively to the decline in the net interest rate. The intertemporal distortion therefore originates with the increase in the rate of capital income taxation. It causes households to decrease their saving in their earlier years. When middle-aged, these households have accumulated less wealth and therefore supply more labour.

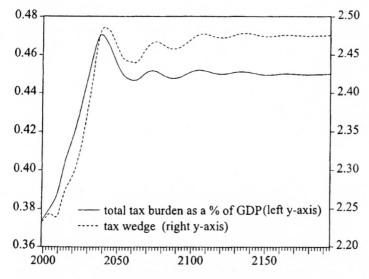

Figure 7 – Tax burdens

The preceding analysis shows that the rising tax burden is an important factor in the evolution of the labour market participation of the population. The estimated increase in the total tax burden of 7% of GDP reflects both the decline in the labour income tax base and an increase in age-related government expenditures, viz. subsidies to the PAYG fund, disability insurance, and health care subsidies (Figure 7).[16] The larger part of the rise in expenditures can be attributed to government contributions to the PAYG fund (Figure 9). The main components of government tax receipts are consumption taxes and income taxes. Consumption tax receipts rise as a consequence of an increase of 3.5% in the consumption-GDP ratio, which reflects the higher propensity of the elderly to consume. This

---

16   The estimated increase in the tax burden is much higher than the estimate of 0.7% presented in Van Ewijk and Ter Rele (1999). One reason is that they assume an exogenous upward shift in labour participation rates, due to socio-cultural factors. Another reason is that they assume that the tax increase is implemented immediately, whereas this paper uses a balanced-budget financing rule. Lastly, van Ewijk and ter Rele do not take into account the effects of the tax burden on economic activity.

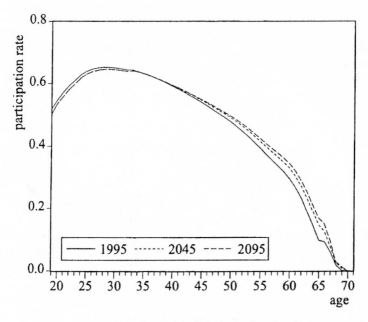

Figure 8 – Participation rates by age for selected years

rise explains 1.5%-points of the increase in the total tax burden. As a result, income tax rates need to be raised by only 3.5%-points. The increase in the marginal burden on labour is larger, due to the increase in health insurance contribution rates.[17] Health care consumption depends strongly on age, and the
increasing share of elderly will boost expenditures by about 3% of GDP (Figure
10). As private health insurance contribution rates are lump sum, high-income
households escape part of the increase in the marginal tax burden. The net result
of this development is a substantial increase in the leisure-consumption decisions
of households. Figure 7 shows a ten percent projected increase in the wedge on
labour supply for households below the public health insurance threshold.

The sharp increase in government subsidies for the PAYG fund stands in
marked contrast to the moderate 2% increase of the contribution rate for the
(funded) supplementary pension fund. This relative constancy arises from the substantial assets owned by the pension fund in the base period. By legal obligation,
these assets are sufficient to cover the accumulated pension rights by households
that are currently participating in the fund. A rise in contribution rates must therefore reflect a rise in projected benefit obligations that exceeds the current accumulation rate of the fund. This can occur because of a future acceleration in wage

17   Note that the AWBZ tax base also consists of capital income and pension benefits.

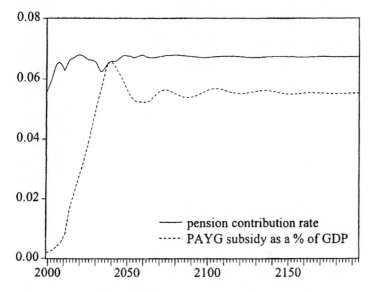

Figure 9 – Old-age social security contribution rates

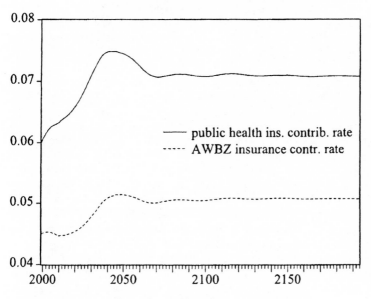

Figure 10 – Health insurance contribution rates

growth, as a result of a fall in future interest rates (that increase the present value of the obligations), or due to shifts in the age composition of the contributing members of the fund. All these events lead to intergenerational redistribution as a consequence of the lack of actuarial fairness of the pension fund. Figure 9 shows that shifts in the age composition lead to an increase in contribution rates of about 1.5%-points.

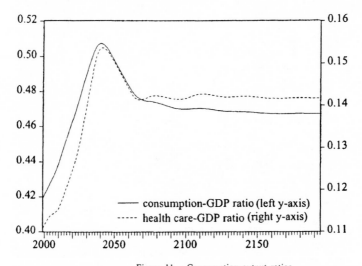

Figure 11 – Consumption-output ratios

The propensity to consume reaches a maximum a few years after the share of elderly, demonstrating the aggregate effect of the life cycle behaviour of individual households (Figure 11). Subsequently, the health care-consumption ratio declines less than the consumption ratio of other goods and services, as a result of the extreme age dependence of health care expenses. The boost of the propensity to consume is preceded by a more short-lived boost in the national savings rate. The current account reaches an all-time high of 11% of GDP around 2010, at a time when a large proportion of households are net savers, to fall back to a minimum value of 2% around 2050 because of the retirement of these large cohorts of savers. The current account remains positive however as a result of a substantial surplus on the primary factor income account. The trade balance must of course show a substantial deficit in later years.

The projected scarcity of labour has an adverse effect on investment and output growth. The fall in the investment-output ratio in the tradable goods sector leads the decline in labour supply until 2030. Output growth is half a percent below the steady-state rate over the next three decades, until the ageing process reaches its maximum. Then labour supply recovers because of both the demo-

graphic swing and the increase in the participation rate of the working age population and output growth is boosted for over a decade (see Figure 12). The net
result is a relative decline in long-run output per capita. Accumulating the deviations from the steady-state path yields an output loss of 12 percent.

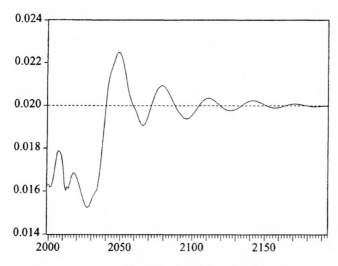

Figure 12 – Growth rate of GDP per capita

While an output loss of 12% due to ageing may seem considerable, the proper
measure of the costs of ageing is welfare, not output. In contrast to output, a
welfare indicator also takes into account the value of the consumption of leisure
and it provides a consistent discounting of future fluctuations in prices and income. The intergenerational distribution that corresponds with this baseline scenario is given in Figure 13. The distribution is defined in terms of the compensating variations required to bestow the same lifetime utility on all generations as
the 1976 generation (that enters the labour market in 1994), *corrected for technological progress*. This correction is required because, on a steady-state growth
path, successive generations will experience ever-increasing lifetime consumption
and utility. To measure the extent of intergenerational redistribution, we must
therefore compare the actual utility levels with those on a steady-state growth
path. On this growth path the correction used would result in compensating variations equal to zero. The compensating variations in Figure 13 show that, after
correction, future generations do about 4% worse than current young generations.
This is equivalent to only two years of growth, so all future generations are still
better off than the 1976 generation, despite the demographic shock. Regarding
the intragenerational distribution, high-productive households do somewhat better
than low-productive households, because they escape the increase in public health

contribution rates. The intergenerational balance worsens until about 2035 (generation 2016), when the ageing shock is maximal. This coincides with the peak in the labour tax burden (see Figure 7) and the minimum labour participation ratio (Figure 4). Afterwards, the distribution remains fairly stable.

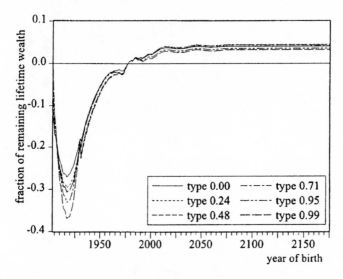

Figure 13 – Compensating variations per generation, relative to the 1976 generation

Though future generations are not much worse off than the 1976 generation, generations born before 1976 do considerably better. In Figure 13, the comparison is made in terms of remaining lifetime utility, again corrected for technical progress. Generations born around 1930 are on the brink of retirement, so they largely escape the coming rise in tax rates. In comparison with the 1976 generation, this implies a 16% higher net wage over their time in the labour force (corrected for technical progress). The remaining part of the compensating variation is largely due to a different saving profile over the life cycle. Future generations save less, because of a lower net interest rate, and so have comparatively fewer assets and lower remaining lifetime utility than current generations at the same stage in their life. The lower lifetime interest rate of future generations therefore generates an additional source of inequality.[18]

18 It is not correct, however, to conclude from Figure 13 that the elderly are up to 40% better off if evaluated over their entire life. A comparison in terms of remaining lifetime utility does not take into account past events that may have adversely affected the utility of these generations. Calvo and Obstfeld (1988) show that a time-consistent treatment of utility by a social planner requires discounting back to the birth dates of the generations involved.

4 SOCIAL SECURITY REFORM

The analysis of the effects of the demographic shock identifies several problems. In the baseline projection the main problem is the sharp rise of the tax burden, which causes generational imbalance, as shown in Figure 13. Figures 7, 9, and 10 identify the source of this problem in terms of the rise in PAYG social security contributions and health care contributions. In addition, the increasing tax rates boost the excess burden starting from an initial situation that is already characterized by high marginal rates. It is therefore attractive to try to correct both problems at once by a suitable reform of social security. Judging from the baseline projection, the obvious candidate for reform seems to be the PAYG social security system, as it contributes most to the increase in the tax burden.

To investigate the benefits of this reform, I compute the effects of three reform measures:

- an immediate reduction in PAYG benefits, compensated for by a reduction in income taxes;
- an immediate reduction in PAYG benefits, compensated for by a sustainable permanent reduction in indirect taxes;
- a gradual phasing out of PAYG benefits, compensated for by a sustainable permanent reduction in indirect taxes.

4.1 A balanced-budget reduction in PAYG benefits

A reduction in PAYG benefits aims at a decrease in the distortionary impact of the PAYG contributions on labour and capital income. The cut implies a smaller deficit of the PAYG fund, and consequently a smaller PAYG subsidy from the government. In the present scenario, income tax rates are cut to maintain a constant debt-GDP ratio. Existing old generations in the Netherlands are to some extent sheltered from the income effects of a reduction in PAYG benefits, if they are eligible to a supplementary pension. The pension fund supplements PAYG benefits to a maximum of 70% of the final wage before retirement, provided that a household has contributed to the fund during its entire working life. Households with a wage higher than the franchise threshold implied by this arrangement therefore receive a higher supplementary pension if PAYG benefits are cut.[19] All households benefit from the cut in income taxes. Table 1 below presents a summary of the macroeconomic effects of this policy measure. The welfare effects for generations and productivity types are given in Figure 14.

19 In reality, this obligation does not exist for all pension funds. For the national civil pension fund it is subject to the restriction that the pension fund has 'sufficient financial resources.'

TABLE 1 – EFFECTS OF A DECREASE OF 10% IN PAYG PENSION BENEFITS, COMPENSATED FOR BY A REDUCTION IN INCOME TAXES

	year	1	10	20	30	40	50	200
L	%	0.04	0.25	0.35	0.36	0.32	0.20	0.01
K	%	0	0.42	0.65	0.67	0.56	0.21	−0.33
c	%	−0.44	−0.24	0.01	0.32	0.63	0.90	1.80
S/GDP	D%	0.16	0.36	0.52	0.61	0.69	0.69	0.46
I/GDP	D%	0.11	0.06	0.02	−0.02	−0.08	−0.15	−0.23
TB/GDP	D%	0.03	0.21	0.23	0.15	0.07	−0.09	−0.72
A_e	%	0	−0.74	−1.87	−2.98	−4.12	−5.83	−10.4
t_y	D%	−0.27	−0.41	−0.58	−0.76	−0.95	−1.05	−1.19
w	D%	1.18	0.40	0.09	−0.05	−0.10	−0.14	−0.14
p_l	%	−0.11	−0.02	0.05	0.06	0.02	−0.09	−0.21

Legend: L is labour supply, K capital, c consumption, S/GDP saving-GDP ratio, I/GDP investment-GDP ratio, TB/GDP trade balance-GDP ratio, D/GDP Government debt-GDP ratio, A_e foreign assets, t_c indirect tax rate, t_y income tax rate, w pension contribution rate, and p_l wage rate. All variables are given either as percentage deviations from the baseline solution (%), or as absolute deviations (D%).

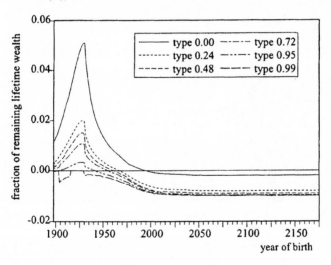

Figure 14 – Compensating variations for a 10% reduction in PAYG benefits

Equity and Efficiency

Overall, the reform is efficiency-improving. The present value of the aggregate of compensating variations is − Dfl. 40 billion, 6% of GDP. Relative to the reduction in PAYG benefits of Dfl. 148 billion, the efficiency gain is 27 cents per guilder.[20] The efficiency gain results from the decrease in distortionary income taxes and an implicit lump sum tax on the elderly. Table 1 shows that the benefit cut allows for a gradually falling income tax rate (t_y), to a final -1.2%-points. The income tax is to some extent replaced by a higher contribution rate (w) from the funded supplementary pension system, at least in the first two decades after the reform. However, this contribution is less distortionary, since it is linked to pension benefits. Efficiency also increases due to the lump sum component in the reform. Old low productivity households are not included in the supplementary pension scheme. Following the cut in PAYG benefits, they therefore receive no compensation from the supplementary pension fund, so that for them the reform operates as a lump sum tax. Young generations profit in the form of lower income taxes. Figure 14 shows that old generations of low-productivity households are indeed much worse off than households of the same age, but with higher productivity. Nonetheless, most retired households lose from the reform. Supplementary pensions are indexed on the gross wage rate, which falls as a result of the increase in labour supply of working age generations. Also, the income tax rises to compensate for the loss in tax revenue due to the decrease in consumption. Compared with younger generations, retired generations profit less from the simultaneous decrease in the income tax rate, since they do not supply labour.

Macroeconomic Effects
Labour supply increases because of the lower burden. Initially, the labour supply response is dampened by the increase in the pension contribution rate (w), which rises because the pension fund has to compensate most retired households for the fall in PAYG benefits. However, this contribution rate is less distortionary, as pension benefits are linked to hours worked. Over time, this rate declines again as the pension fund succeeds in regaining its desired coverage of future obligations. The increase in labour supply boosts investment as well, which gradually restores labour productivity and wages. The reform also stimulates savings, as the PAYG contribution also bears on capital income. This implies that consumption of young households falls initially. Consumption of retired households also falls, as a result of lower lifetime income. Since part of the increase in saving is invested abroad, this implies an initial decrease in the domestic tax base. As a result, the income tax rate initially falls by only 0.3%, less than what corresponds to the *ex ante* saving on PAYG subsidies.

The results of this analysis lead to the conclusion that a reform of old-age social security through a balanced-budget reduction in the basic PAYG pension

20 Alternatively, this outcome may be formulated as a marginal cost of funds of 27 cents per guilder for PAYG social security, if financed through income taxes. This result is at the lower end of estimates of the size of the marginal cost of funds (see Ballard and Fullerton (1992)).

benefits must hurt poor households. They cannot profit from the shelter offered by the funded pension scheme, because their income is already near the minimum level defined by the current PAYG scheme. A straightforward cut in PAYG benefits also hurts old rich generations, however. The compensation offered by the FC pension fund is incomplete, because it does not provide shelter against the general equilibrium effects of the reform, notably the fall of gross wages. These conclusions are similar to those obtained by Fehr (1999, chapter 8), for a comparable reform of the German pension system (even though that system does not provide a compensation through an FC scheme).

It is therefore improbable that the reform would enjoy sufficient political support to be feasible. A reform that makes current generations better off must compensate these generations for any implied income transfer to future generations. This can be achieved in a generic fashion through the use of debt financing.

4.2 A debt-financed cut in PAYG benefits

A simple way to implement a debt-financed cut in PAYG benefits is to combine the cut in PAYG benefits with a cut in indirect taxes that is larger than what is compatible with a balanced budget tax cut. Section 4.1 showed that the full beneficial effects materialize only in the long run. By using government debt the efficiency gain caused by the PAYG cut can be partly transferred from future generations to current generations. Table 2 presents the effects of the same 10% cut in PAYG benefits, now compensated for by a maximal sustainable cut in the indirect tax rate. The income tax rate now remains at the level of the benchmark

TABLE 2 – EFFECTS OF A DECREASE OF 10% IN PAYG PENSION BENEFITS, COMPENSATED FOR BY A SUSTAINED REDUCTION IN INDIRECT TAXES

	year	1	10	20	30	40	50	200
L	%	0.13	0.31	0.37	0.34	0.27	0.23	0.21
K	%	0	0.45	0.61	0.61	0.54	0.47	0.39
c	%	0.23	0.33	0.43	0.56	0.67	0.76	0.97
S/GDP	D%	0.16	0.36	0.42	0.45	0.41	0.37	0.31
I/GDP	D%	0.22	0.17	0.13	0.10	0.09	0.09	0.07
TB/GDP	D%	−0.13	0.08	0.13	0.06	−0.05	−0.14	−0.21
D/GDP	D%	0.62	3.28	5.43	7.86	8.83	9.18	9.89
A_e	%	0	0.17	−0.42	−0.99	−1.44	−1.90	−2.34
t_c	D%	−1.87	−1.87	−1.87	−1.87	−1.87	−1.87	−1.87
w	D%	1.17	0.40	0.10	−0.03	−0.08	−0.14	−0.15
p_1	%	−0.25	−0.11	−0.05	−0.01	−0.01	−0.02	−0.00

Legend: see Table 1.

path. This cut causes an increase in government debt and thereby transfers part of the welfare gain to current generations.

Equity and Efficiency

The present value of compensating variations is Dfl. −50 billion, 8% of current GDP. The present value of the cut in PAYG benefits is Dfl. 151 billion, so that the efficiency gain is Dfl. 0.33 per guilder. This is slightly more than the efficiency gain of the reform with balanced budget income tax compensation. As in the previous case, the efficiency gain is caused by a decrease in distortionary taxes. The indirect tax rate falls by 1.9%-points. This reduces the consumption-leisure wedge in the long term by nearly the same amount as the fall in income taxes in the preceding case. In the short-term the reduction is considerably greater, as a result of the tax smoothing. This provides a better stimulus to labour supply and generates a larger inflow of foreign capital, to finance investment. Indeed, both the capital stock and employment are larger in the long run. The larger tax base allows for lower tax rates and a smaller efficiency loss.

The reform has much more equitable intergenerational distribution effects than a balanced budget cut in PAYG benefits. Figure 15 shows that for most productivity types, almost all generations gain. Only for generations born around 1930 the majority loses. The more equitable welfare distribution results because the cut in indirect taxes operates in part as a lump sum subsidy to old households, which finance a large part of their consumption from financial wealth. This compensates for the likewise lump sum cut in PAYG benefits. Only low-productive households still suffer a substantial welfare loss. They finance most of their consumption from current income so that for them the reduction in indirect taxes does not imply a substantial lump sum subsidy. In addition they are the only type without any compensation from the FC pension fund.

The welfare loss of low-productivity households is difficult to avoid if the social security system must provide a basic income to all old households, independent of past contributions. A possible way out would be to make the PAYG benefit means-tested. This would increase the progressivity of the tax system and is beyond the present paper. Still, even for poor households the welfare losses associated with the reform are considerably less than the redistribution caused by the ageing itself. A comparison of Figures 13 and 15 shows that the combined effect of ageing and the reform is beneficial for *all* current generations. From an equity point of view, it may be argued that the effects of the shock, ageing, and the policy reform that addresses the shock should be evaluated together. Politically, the reference point is more plausibly the status quo, which includes ageing. Not surprisingly, all high-productivity households gain from the reform. All low-productivity households lose. Most intermediate types gain. From the compensating variations it appears that 62% of existing households profit from the PAYG reform, if accompanied by an appropriate debt policy.

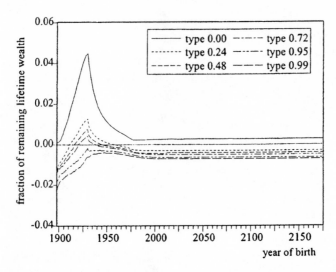

Figure 15 – Compensating variations for a 10% reduction in PAYG benefits, compensated by a 2% reduction in the consumption tax rate

Macroeconomic Effects

The macroeconomic effects of the tax-smoothed reform resemble those of the balanced budget reform discussed in the previous section with respect to their effect on labour supply. Labour supply increases more than in the previous case because the tax wedge is lower. Consumption is stimulated as a result of the tax cut. At first, this is financed through the balance of payments. In later years production increases. However, savings are lower than in the alternative case and the surplus on the trade balance remains small. As a result, income effects on labour supply in later years are also limited, and the labour supply response stays positive in the new steady-state. Government debt increases by 10% of GDP, as a consequence of the transfer of welfare between generations. Though marginal tax rates fall, the average tax burden as a percentage of GDP increases by 1.5%, as a result of the increased debt service and the increased share of non-GDP related government expenditures.[21]

4.3 Phasing Out the PAYG Pension System

In section 4.2 we saw that a reduction in PAYG benefits is welfare increasing for most current and future generations, provided that part of the welfare gain is transferred to the present through an appropriate debt policy. Even so, the reform

---

21 However, since indirect tax rates fall by 2%, the tax burden does not increase if GDP is evaluated against factor costs.

has a number of disadvantages. All low-productivity households lose from the reform, and it requires a substantial increase in FC pension contribution rates on impact to cover the sudden increase in projected benefit obligations. This curbs labour supply in the first few periods. A possible remedy to these side effects is to reduce PAYG benefits gradually. Such a policy is more in line with both the gradual expected increase in PAYG benefits and with stable FC contribution rates. This policy also resembles the actual development of PAYG benefits in the Netherlands over the past decade, where PAYG benefits were linked to contractual wage increases. PAYG beneficiaries therefore missed out on the wage drift, which amounted to about a half percent per year over that period. Since a continuing decline of PAYG benefits is incompatible with a final steady-state, I implement the policy with a reduction of a half percent per year for the next 50 years.

Equity and Efficiency
The cut results in a reduction in the present value of PAYG benefits of Dfl. 210 billion. The present value of compensating variations is −Dfl. 86 billion, 14% of current GDP. The efficiency gain is therefore 41 cents per guilder, considerably more than with the immediate cut discussed in the preceding sections. This gain indicates a steep rise in the marginal cost of funds of PAYG pensions in the future. Table 3 shows that the contribution rate to the FC pension fund rises less on impact than in the previous cases, despite the larger present value of the cut. This explains most of the extra efficiency gain. The fact that the cut in PAYG benefits is now pre-announced does not generate distortions, because the benefits are of a lump sum character. The fall in the consumption tax again serves to transfer part of the future efficiency gains to current generations. The substantial

TABLE 3 – EFFECTS OF A PHASING OUT OF PAYG PENSION BENEFITS BY 0.5% PER YEAR, COMPENSATED FOR BY A SUSTAINED REDUCTION IN INDIRECT TAXES

	year	1	10	20	30	40	50	200
L	%	0.36	0.61	0.70	0.70	0.65	0.64	0.70
K	%	0	0.80	1.12	1.21	1.24	1.31	1.31
c	%	1.09	1.11	1.07	1.01	0.97	0.96	1.14
S/GDP	D%	−0.03	0.13	0.22	0.26	0.23	0.18	0.23
I/GDP	D%	0.35	0.29	0.26	0.24	0.25	0.30	0.26
TB/GDP	D%	−0.47	−0.07	0.08	0.11	0.05	−0.02	−0.07
D/GDP	D%	0.91	8.80	19.4	29.7	37.4	42.5	43.6
A_c	%	0	1.61	1.63	1.38	1.23	1.48	1.43
t_c	D%	−2.96	−2.96	−2.96	−2.96	−2.96	−2.96	−2.96
w	D%	0.64	0.57	0.57	0.53	0.41	0.11	−0.34
p_1	%	−0.57	−0.21	−0.09	−0.04	−0.01	−0.06	−0.00

Legend: see Table 1.

increase in the debt-GDP ratio results from the gradual implementation of the cut. This implies that the efficiency gains will be postponed as well, and more debt is required to bridge the transition. Figure 16 shows that the policy succeeds better in transferring welfare gains to current generations than an immediate cut of PAYG pension benefits. As a result, the percentage of households that benefits from the reform is also higher. On the other hand, the negative welfare effects for future low-productive generations are also larger. Figure 16 shows that type 0.24 almost breaks even in the long run. This implies that slightly more that 24% of the population eventually loses from 0 to about 1.5% of lifetime wealth from the reform.

TABLE 4 – PARTIAL DEMAND ELASTICITIES FOR THE HOUSEHOLD SECTOR[22]

	c	c_{zf}	c_{zp}	c_{za}	L_s	W
wage rate	0.747	0.096	0.179	0.125	0.016	1.690
price of health care	−0.005	−0.340	−0.296	−0.325	0.007	0.031
wage tax	−1.213	−0.211	−0.296	−0.240	0.060	−3.818
PAYG contr. rate	−0.710	−0.232	−0.088	−0.183	−0.041	−2.010
pension contr. rate	−0.428	−0.042	−0.116	−0.067	0.009	−1.215
transfers	0.112	0.070	0.035	0.058	−0.082	0.298
interest rate	2.700	0.789	1.418	1.000	−0.119	22.20

Legend: c is consumption, c_{zf} consumption of public health care, c_{zp} consumption of private health care, c_{za} consumption of AWBZ health care, L_s labour supply, W wealth

TABLE 5 – PARTIAL DEMAND ELASTICITIES FOR FIRMS IN THE TRADABLE GOODS SECTOR[22]

	labour	capital	materials
wage rate	−0.281	0.219	0.219
capital user costs	0.142	−0.358	0.142
price of materials	0.139	0.139	−0.360
interest rate	0.968	−2.440	0.969

Macroeconomic Effects
Labour supply is boosted more on impact than in the previous cases. The cut in consumption taxes is larger and the FC contribution rate rises less. As a result the tax wedge on labour supply is reduced substantially. The increase in labour also stimulates investment and GDP against factor costs. GDP against market

22   The effects of taxes and the interest rate are given as the percentage response to a 1 percentage point shock.

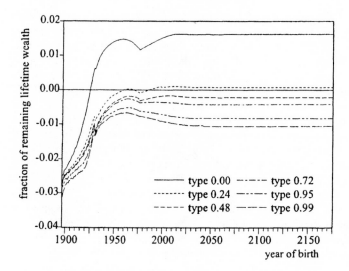

Figure 16 – Compensating variations for a phasing out of PAYG benefits by 0.5% per year, compensated for by a 3% reduction of consumption taxes

prices falls, however, which explains the initial jump in the debt ratio. Consumption is boosted more than before on impact, because the adverse consequences of the PAYG cut for the income of pensioners do not materialize right away. As a result, the trade balance turns negative initially. The increase in foreign debt is however limited, as the extra consumption is paid for from the increase in domestic production once the expansion of the capital stock has been completed.

5 CONCLUSION

This paper studies the effects of the imminent ageing of the population on economic growth and the distribution of welfare in the Netherlands. It shows that a slowdown in economic growth per capita may be expected as a result of the decrease in the participation rate and the increase in the tax wedge on labour. The slowdown results in a long-term output loss of some 12%, as compared to a steady-state growth path.

The paper identifies the PAYG social security system as the largest single distortionary influence on economic growth. The increase in PAYG benefits raises the tax burden by some 6%-points of GDP. The financing costs of public health care also contribute to an overall increase of the tax burden of 10%. This gives rise to large potential efficiency gains from a reform of social security. A balanced-budget cut in PAYG social security reduces the average excess burden over generations by 29 cents per guilder reduction and causes a redistribution of welfare towards future generations. Losses of most current generations are fairly small, as they are sheltered to some extent from the PAYG cut by the existing supplementary occupational pension schemes. Low-income groups are hit particularly hard, however, as they not only face the full size of the cut, but also an initial fall in wages to which their social security benefits are indexed.

The burden of the reform can be shifted to future generations by an appropriate use of government debt. A cut in PAYG benefits that is combined with a maximal sustainable cut in indirect taxes largely succeeds in synchronizing welfare gains and losses over generations. 62% of current generations benefit from the reform. This percentage can be raised further by implementing the cut gradually. This policy also produces the largest efficiency gains, 41 cents per guilder. However, low-productivity households still suffer a welfare loss.

The paper measures the distributional impact of the social security system on future generations in terms of a comparison of their lifetime utility. The paper shows that the main redistributive effect of ageing is not between current young generations and future generations, but between current young generations and current middle-aged and old generations. Future generations suffer the equivalent of only some 4% loss in lifetime wealth, compared to generations that currently enter the labour force. However, current young generations suffer some 30% loss in wealth in comparison with current old generations, if evaluated at the same point in their life. This is because current old generations escape the larger part of the future rise in taxes and social security contributions, in contrast to current young generations. In addition, low and mid-income groups are hit somewhat harder than high-income groups.

While the model used in this paper contains a fairly elaborate model of households, it still neglects a number of issues that are relevant for an assessment of the effects of ageing. In addition to the modelling issues discussed in section 2.6 we may consider, first, the uncertainty in both the demographic projections and the interest projections (see Broer (1999)). An equally important source of uncertainty is the projection of labour participation rates. Whereas this paper assumes that preferences for leisure do not shift between generations, labour participation rates of women have been moving upward over the past decades on account of social-cultural factors. If this trend continues, the expected decline in labour participation may be less serious than the results presented here suggest.

REFERENCES

Aaron, H.J. (1966), 'The Social Insurance Paradox,' *Canadian Journal of Economic and Political Science*, 32, pp. 371–374.

Alessie, R.J.M., A. Kapteyn, and F. Klijn (1997), 'Mandatory Pensions and Personal Savings in the Netherlands,' *De Economist*, 145, pp. 291–324.

Altonji, J.G., F. Hayashi, and L.J. Kotlikoff (1992), 'Is the Extended Family Altruistically Linked? Direct Tests Using Micro Data,' *American Economic Review*, 82, pp. 1177–1198.

Auerbach, A.J. and L.J. Kotlikoff (1987), *Dynamic Fiscal Policy*, Cambridge University Press.

Auerbach, A.J., J. Cai, and L.J. Kotlikoff (1991), 'US Demographics and Saving: Predictions of Three Saving Models,' *Carnegie-Rochester Conference Series on Public Policy*, pp. 135–165.

Ballard, C.L., and D. Fullerton (1992), 'Distortionary Taxes and the Provision of Public Goods', *Journal of Economic Perspectives*, 6, pp. 117–131.

Bernheim, B.D. and K. Bagwell (1988), 'Is Everything Neutral?,' *Journal of Political Economy*, 96, pp. 308–338.

Börsch-Supan, A. (1996), 'The Impact of Population Ageing on Savings, Investment and Growth in the OECD Area,' in: OECD, *Future Global Capital Shortages: Real Threat or Pure Fiction?*

Börsch-Supan, A. (1998), 'Germany: A Social Security System on the Verge of Collapse,' in: H. Siebert (ed.), *Redesigning Social Security*, Mohr Siebeck.

Bovenberg, A.L. and C. van Ewijk (1997), 'Progressive Taxes, Equity, and Human Capital Accumulation in an Endogenous Growth Model with Overlapping Generations,' *Journal of Public Economics*, 64, pp. 153–179.

Breyer, F. and M. Straub (1993), 'Welfare Effects of Unfunded Pension Systems when Labor Supply is Endogenous,' *Journal of Public Economics*, 50, pp. 77–91.

Broer, D.P., E.W.M.T. Westerhout, and A.L. Bovenberg (1994), 'Taxation, Pensions, and Saving in a Small Open Economy,' *Scandinavian Journal of Economics*, 96, pp. 403–424.

Broer, D.P. and E.W.M.T. Westerhout (1997), 'Pension Policies and Lifetime Uncertainty in an Applied General Equilibrium Model,' in: D.P. Broer and J. Lassila (eds.), *Pension Policies and Public Debt in Dynamic CGE Models*, Physica Verlag.

Broer, D.P. (1999), 'Growth and Welfare Distribution in an Ageing Society: An Applied General Equilibrium Analysis for the Netherlands,' *OCFEB Research Memorandum*, No. 9908, Erasmus University (downloadable from http://www.few.eur.nl/few/research/pubs/ocfeb/rm.htm).

Calvo, G.A. and M. Obstfeld (1988), 'Optimal Time-consistent Fiscal Policy with Finite Lifetimes,' *Econometrica*, 56, pp. 411–432.

Carroll, C.D. (1992), 'The Buffer Stock Theory of Saving: Some Macroeconomic Evidence,' *Brookings Papers on Economic Activity*, 2, pp. 61–135.

Chauveau, T. and R. Loufir (1997), 'The Future of Public Pensions in the Seven Major Economies,' chapter 2, in: D.P. Broer and J. Lassila (eds.), *Pension Policies and Public Debt in Dynamic CGE Models*, Physica Verlag.

CPB (1997), 'JADE, a Model for the Joint Analysis of Dynamics and Equilibrium,' *Working Paper*, No. 99, CPB Netherlands Bureau of Economic Policy Analysis.

Cutler, D.M., J.M. Poterba, L.M. Sheiner, and L.H. Summers (1990), 'An Aging Society: Opportunity or Challenge?,' *Brookings Papers on Economic Activity*, 1, pp. 1–73.

Davies, J.B. (1981), 'Uncertain Lifetime, Consumption, and Dissaving in Retirement,' *Journal of Political Economy*, 89, pp. 561–577.

Beer, J. de (1999), 'Bevolkingsprognose 1998-2050,' CBS Maandstatistiek Bevolking, January 1999, pp. 8-19 (in Dutch: Population Forecasts 1998-2050).

Fabel, O. (1994), *The Economics of Pensions and Variable Retirement Schemes*, Wiley.

Fehr, H. (1999), *Welfare Effects of Dynamic Tax Reforms*, Mohr Siebeck.

Feldstein, M. (1995), 'Would Privatizing Social Security Raise Economic Welfare?,' *NBER Working Paper*, No. 5281.

Feldstein, M. (1996), 'The Missing Piece in Policy Analysis: Social Security Reform,' *American Economic Review*, Papers and Proceedings, 86, pp. 1–14.

Fougère, M. and M. Mérette (1999), Population Ageing and Economic Growth in Seven OECD Countries, *Economic Modelling*, 16, pp. 411–427.

Gokhale, J., B.R. Page, and J.R. Sturrock (1999), 'Generational Accounts for the United States,' in: A.J. Auerbach, L.J. Kotlikoff, and W. Leibfritz (eds.), *Generational Accounting Around the World*, Chicago University Press.

Gordon, R.H. and H. Varian (1988), 'Intergenerational Risk Sharing,' *Journal of Public Economics*, 37, pp. 185–202.

Heckman, J.J., L. Lochner, and C. Taber (1998), 'Explaining Rising Wage Inequality: Explorations with a Dynamic General Equilibrium Model of Labor Earnings with Heterogeneous Agents,' *NBER Working paper*, No. 6384.

Kotlikoff, L.J. (1988), 'Intergenerational Transfers and Savings,' *Journal of Economic Perspectives*, 2, pp. 41–58.

Kotlikoff, L.J. (1996), 'Simulating the Privatization of Social Security in General Equilibrium,' *NBER Working Paper*, No. 5776.

Kotlikoff, L.J., K.A. Smetters, and J. Walliser (1998), 'The Economic Impact of Privatizing Social Security,' in: H. Siebert (ed.), *Redesigning Social Security*, Mohr Siebeck.

Kotlikoff, L.J. and W. Leibfritz (1999), 'An International Comparison of Generational Accounts,' in: A.J. Auerbach, L.J. Kotlikoff, and W. Leibfritz (eds.), *Generational Accounting Around the World*, Chicago University Press.

Miles, D. (1999), 'Modelling the Impact of Demographic Change Upon the Economy,' *Economic Journal*, 109, pp. 1–36.

Poterba, J.M. (1998), 'Population Age Structure and Asset Returns: An Empirical Investigation,' *NBER Working Paper*, No. 6774.

Raffelhüschen, B. (1993), 'Funding Social Security through Pareto-Optimal Conversion Policies,' *Journal of Economics*, 7, pp. 105–131.

Rele, H. ter (1998), 'Generational Accounts for the Dutch Public Sector,' *De Economist*, 146, pp. 555–584.

United Nations (1994), *The Sex and Age Distribution of the World Populations*, United Nations

Ewijk, C.A. van and H.J. ter Rele (1999), 'Ageing and Fiscal Policy in the Netherlands,' *De Economist*, 147, pp. 523–534.

Wilhelm, M.O. (1996), 'Bequest Behavior and the Effects of Heirs' Earnings: Testing the Altruistic Model of Bequests,' *American Economic Review*, 86, pp. 874–892.

Aging, Wellbeing, and Social Security in Rural Northern China

DWAYNE BENJAMIN
LOREN BRANDT
SCOTT ROZELLE

STEEP DECLINES IN fertility, combined with longer life expectancy, will increase the share of the elderly in the Chinese population. This aging population, with its corresponding increase in the ratio of elderly pension beneficiaries to young contributors, recently has received considerable attention. (For comprehensive discussions of these and related issues, see World Bank 1994 and 1997.) Most of the attention focuses on the present and future pension liabilities of state enterprises and the need for a more modern, financially viable public pension system for workers. Striking by its absence from the discussion, however, is the recognition that the majority of elderly Chinese not covered by formal pensions live in rural areas.[1] The inattention is rationalized on two grounds. First, family values remain strong in rural areas, and Confucian "filial piety" sustains the traditional institution of family care for the elderly. Although it may erode over time, there is already a well-functioning, deeply rooted informal old-age security system in rural areas. Second, any formal public policy response to the needs of the rural elderly may undermine the existing private arrangements. For example, state transfers to the elderly may crowd out existing transfers from younger family members. As the argument goes, it is better to leave well enough alone and focus on the urban elderly and their public pensions.

There is no empirical foundation for this view. Instead, the perceived relative strength of rural social security is based on historical impressions of filial piety and the codification of family responsibility for the elderly in existing laws (see, e.g., World Bank 1994; Fang, Wang, and Song 1992). The Marriage Law of 1950 emphasizes the duty of adult children to care for their elderly parents, and the Constitution of 1954 states that "parents have the duty to rear and educate their minor children, and the children who have come of age have the duty to support and assist their parents." More recently, the Penal Code of 1980 has established that children can be imprisoned for neglecting their parents. We can view these laws either as a reflection of the values and practices of rural society or as a response to unfulfilled social expectations.

Historically, the primary mechanism by which the young cared for the old was through shared living arrangements. Parents would live with their sons, retaining control over family assets until the father's death. Assets would then be divided among the sons, who were expected to care for their mother. But how relevant is this institution now?

The collectivization of agriculture in the early 1950s exerted an equivocal influence on family structure.[2] On the one hand, as suggested by the laws passed in the 1950s, the family institution was enshrined as the principal source of old-age security. As Goode (1963) argues, family law evolved under collectivization much as it had over the previous half-century. Furthermore, restrictions on migration and housing shortages in urban areas tended to keep families together in the same villages. On the other hand, collectivization also undermined the traditional role of the family (Selden 1993). Asset accumulation, notably of land, was curtailed, significantly reducing the bargaining power of the elderly (Davis-Friedmann 1991; Whyte 1995; Yan 1997). Moreover, the village (collective) took more responsibility for transfers to needy households, including the neglected elderly, replacing the role of the family to some degree. Davis-Friedmann (1991) argues that, on balance, the elderly probably came out ahead under collectivization, despite their weakened power within their families.

These authors are less confident of the position of the elderly since the introduction of economic reforms in the late 1970s. Some researchers suggest that the traditional family structure might restore itself in the face of increased commercialization and a diminished role of the collective. Most, however, argue that it will be further weakened (see Whyte 1992), for the following reasons. First, economic growth is usually accompanied by movement toward conjugal, in place of kinship-oriented, families (Goode 1963). With the higher incomes and lower housing prices that accompany economic reform, it is more feasible for the young and old to live separately. Second, restrictions on land ownership constrain individuals from accumulating assets for their old age. Third, village support for the elderly has been reduced to the allocation of land, which may be of little value to an elderly household with few children, a limited ability to work, and imperfectly developed factor markets. If family ties are indeed weakening, then existing transfer mechanisms may be ill-suited to supporting the elderly. Finally, attitudes of the young toward the old may be changing as the economy becomes more oriented toward satisfaction of individual needs. Yan (1997) argues that the increase in the conjugal focus of families serves to divert attention from the care of parents.

Of course, changes in living arrangements need not signal an end to family responsibility for the elderly. Intergenerational transfers can occur across as well as within households. In-kind transfers of goods and labor, remittances, and child-care services can flow across generations. The question is whether these mechanisms fully substitute for the traditional within-household transfers. Davis-Friedmann (1991) expresses concern that weakened family ties, in a situation of market-oriented growth and a decline in government-provided social services, will isolate the elderly. Selden (1993: 147) echoes this concern, noting that "it is difficult to escape the conclusion that in rural China as elsewhere the transition to the nuclear family imposes a heavy price on the rural elderly."

Our objective is to provide an overview of the factual background to these issues. We begin with the current living arrangements of the elderly, since these arrangements underlie many current assumptions about elder care in the countryside. To do so, we draw on a household survey conducted in northern China in 1995. To provide a context for our results, we make two types of comparisons. First, using a historical survey of the same region in the mid-1930s, we compare the present with the past, when extended households are believed to have been a more common form of living arrangement. Second, using data for 1989 obtained from the China Health and Nutrition Survey of 1990, we compare urban and rural households. We then examine the economic circumstances of the elderly, beginning with their ability to work. We consider whether retirement is a meaningful concept in rural China. Most important, we look at the relative economic standing of the elderly as indicated by their income and consumption levels. To anticipate, our results strongly suggest that the current policy emphasis on the urban elderly is misplaced. By almost any criterion, the marginal social value of a yuan transferred to the elderly in rural areas exceeds that of one transferred to the elderly in urban areas. Furthermore, the current level of assets owned by the rural elderly suggests that their economic status may worsen with economic reform. In short, the concerns of Davis-Friedmann and Selden seem well founded.

The data

As just mentioned, we make use of three surveys. The first was conducted by Chinese colleagues and ourselves in 1995. The second, used for historical comparison, was conducted by Japanese investigators in 1936 and covers 1935. The third, containing 1989 data, is the China Health and Nutrition Survey (CHNS), carried out in 1990.

The 1995 survey covered 780 households in six counties and 30 villages in Hebei and Liaoning provinces (north-northeastern China). It provided detailed household-level information on income, expenditure, labor supply, and farm management. The six counties were chosen to correspond to the site of the intensive household-level study carried out by Japanese investigators in 1936. We selected five villages in each of the six counties, one of which had been fully enumerated in the 1930s. The other four villages in each county included one village located in the same township as the administrative capital of the county; another located in the same township as the village surveyed in the 1930s; and two villages drawn from a third township. Altogether, 130 households were surveyed in each county—50 from the village surveyed in the 1930s, and 20 from each of the remaining four villages. Households were chosen by random sampling using the most recent village registry.

The 1936 Japanese survey gathered household data from some of the same villages as those we surveyed in 1995. A detailed description of these data, including a comparison with John Lossing Buck's widely cited survey (Buck 1937), is contained in Benjamin and Brandt (1995). The Japanese survey included 1,095 households in 22 villages of the provinces of Liaoning, Jilin, and Heilongjiang.

Our urban and rural comparisons are made with 1989 data from the CHNS of 1990. A description of these data (as well as the data themselves) can be obtained at the CHNS web site.[3] The CHNS covers eight provinces—Liaoning, Shandong, Jiangsu, Henan, Hubei, Hunan, Guangxi, and Guizhou—only two of which, Liaoning and Shandong, can reasonably be considered as being in northern China. However, to maximize sample size, we use all provinces in this study. We have replicated our results using the northern Chinese provinces only, obtaining virtually identical results.

Living arrangements

Our primary question is whether extended families remain an important means by which the young, primarily the adult sons, care for their elderly parents. One sign of the possible erosion of transfers to the elderly would be a decline in the percentage of the elderly living with adult children.

We begin with a brief description of the age structure of the population. It had significantly fewer children aged 0–10 in 1995 than in 1935 (16.0 percent versus 28.2 percent), more adults in the prime ages of 20–50 (51.5 percent versus 39.3 percent), and slightly more elderly aged 61 and older (8.7 percent versus 6.7 percent). Although the fraction of elderly in 1935 was smaller, the dependency ratio was actually greater because there were proportionately many more children. Moreover, from contemporary data (the CHNS) we find more children living in rural than in urban areas

(20.1 percent versus 14.7 percent), but many more elderly as a share in urban areas: 12.3 percent versus 6.6 percent in rural areas. The basic pattern is also seen in the 1995 census, which recorded 10.6 percent of the urban population as over age 60, as compared with only 5.0 percent of the rural population (State Statistical Bureau 1996). The fraction of the population in the prime ages is approximately the same. This suggests a higher elder dependency ratio in urban areas, but fewer children to support. Seventy percent of elderly Chinese still live in the rural sector.

Using household registries for nineteenth-century Liaoning, Lee and Campbell (1997) provide a useful historical baseline on household structure and living. They use the classification system for household types developed by the Cambridge Group for the History of Population and Social Structure. The key defining feature in the system is the number of conjugal pairs (married couples) in the household. Households are divided into four basic types: fragmentary (no conjugal unit), simple (one conjugal unit), extended (one pair with other co-resident adult kin), and multiple (two or more conjugal units). Lee and Campbell's data show that a majority of individuals lived in multiple-family units. Almost half (47.2 percent) of all households were multiple, and three-quarters of individuals lived in such households.[4] A further 15 percent of households were extended and accounted for 10 percent of the population. The remaining 15 percent of individuals lived in simple or fragmentary households. As for the elderly themselves, a majority (75 percent) lived in extended or multiple households, whereas only 25 percent lived on their own.

The 1995 and 1935 data allow estimates of household size, household type, and living arrangements for the elderly that can be compared directly with the findings of Lee and Campbell. Average household size in rural Hebei and Liaoning in 1995 was only 3.7 persons. By comparison, it was 6.3 in the 1930s, a figure similar to that (6.0) implied by Lee and Campbell's data for the 1800s in Liaoning. However, a decline in household size alone may not tell us much about living arrangements, since fertility also fell sharply over that time period.

Figure 1 compares the percentages of households by type in 1935 and 1995. The 1935 data lack information on the types of relationship between household members. Using the information on the age and sex distribution of members, however, we estimate the number of conjugal pairs in the household, and thus household type. We report two sets of figures for 1995. The first is our "best" estimate of household type, based on extensive information on the relationship of household members to the household head. In the second set (D), we degrade the 1995 data set by ignoring information unavailable in the 1935 survey. This allows us to compare the 1990s and 1930s on a common basis, with the same data restrictions. To minimize detail, we also pool extended and multiple households, distinguishing

FIGURE 1 Distribution of households by type and elderly individuals by household type: Northern China, 1935 and 1995

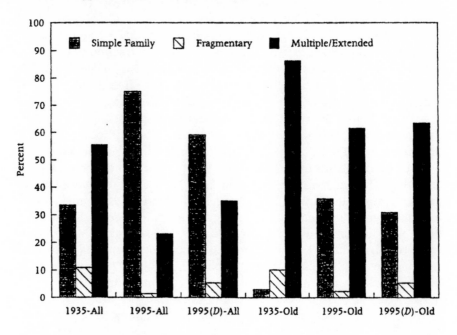

D = Degraded data set. See the text for explanation.

primarily between simple and more broadly defined "extended" households. We can still see whether the elderly are living with relatives other than a spouse.

Figure 1 shows that, by far, most households in 1995 were simple family households. Our "best" estimate identifies 73 percent of all households as simple, with the remainder evenly divided between extended and multiple, which combined represent slightly less than a quarter of all households. The estimates for the 1930s, in contrast, show that one-third of the households were simple, implying a radical shift in household structure. Unfortunately, these two snapshots do not allow us to pinpoint the timing of the decline of the multiple-family household and thus isolate the role of collectivization in shaping family structure. Selden (1993) and others argue that collectivization in the 1950s contributed to the demise of the extended and multiple household. Our own results do not preclude an earlier decline, preceding the establishment of the People's Republic of China and the reorganization of agriculture into collectives. (See Davis and Harrell 1993, Goode 1963, and Whyte 1995 for more discussion of this issue.)

Is the rapidly growing prominence of single-family households paralleled by an equally radical shift in living arrangements among the elderly? Actually not. Both our series for 1995 show that more than 60 percent of the elderly were living in extended or multiple households, while about 30 percent were living on their own (with a spouse). Compared with the rest of the population, the elderly are more likely to live in extended or multiple households. In the 1930s, by contrast, almost none of the elderly lived in simple households, and in comparison with 1995 an even higher share (86 percent) lived in extended or multiple households.

The Cambridge Group's classification is not the only possible way to summarize living arrangements, but it does capture the key features. An alternative would be to look directly at those with whom the elderly live. As it turns out, of the households containing an elderly member, 26 percent are composed of an elderly couple only, and such households comprise three-quarters of the simple-family category. The rest are almost evenly divided between an elderly person living with children but without a spouse (38 percent of elderly households and most of the extended-family category), and an elderly couple living with children (32 percent and most of the multiple-family category). Unfortunately, data limitations do not permit us to show a comparable breakdown for the other data sets.

Our definition of "household" is based on the survey definition, which requires that household members eat together. It may be that some elderly live next door to their children but are not officially part of the same household. In such cases we would understate the economic links between households that came from shared living arrangements. In fact, 77 percent of the elderly who do not live with their children have either a son or daughter living in the same village (75 percent have a son, 31 percent a daughter). The survey, however, was designed to measure interhousehold transfers and should capture these linkages, a point to which we shall return later.

Using the 1989 CHNS data, we find that household size is only slightly larger in rural than in urban areas (4.2 versus 3.8 persons). Part of this difference reflects the earlier and stricter enforcement, in urban areas, of state policy limiting the number of children per household. There is little difference between the urban and rural distributions of household types (Figure 2). In fact, urban areas actually have a slightly higher percentage of extended or multiple households. In both urban and rural areas, almost two-thirds of the elderly live in extended or multiple households, as in the 1995 data. This does not necessarily mean that traditional family values remain as strong in the cities as in the countryside. The price of housing is much higher in the cities, and shared living arrangements may simply reflect an economizing activity of families. As incomes increase, one may expect a rapid shift from shared living arrangements in the city. Neverthe-

FIGURE 2 Distribution of households by type and elderly individuals by
household type: Urban versus rural area, northern China, 1989

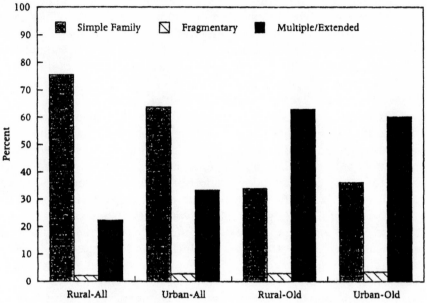

less, these data do not allow us to conclude that there is any observable
difference in the living arrangements of the urban and rural elderly. Indeed, the similarity is impressive.

Work and the elderly

The economic welfare of the elderly depends on the resources they command, whether from their own earnings or from transfers from children
or the state. Documenting the associations between age and work provides
evidence of the elderly's capacity for independence.

We begin by looking at the work patterns of the elderly in 1995, in
particular looking for evidence of "retirement." It is withdrawal (voluntary
or involuntary) from earning activities that usually explains the loss of income in old age and necessitates some form of provision for the elderly. A
simple measure of work activity is an indicator of whether an individual
worked during the previous year. Figure 3 shows such a profile of labor
force participation for both men and women by age group. The employment indicator refers to work on or off the farm, including family businesses. It excludes housework, however, which may be an important way
in which the elderly, especially women, contribute to their families. A fur-

FIGURE 3 Proportion of men and women who worked during the previous year by age: Northern China, 1995

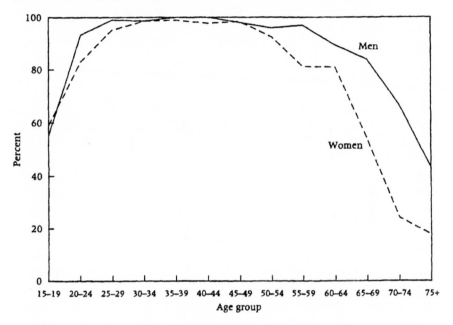

ther word of caution: Although we would like to interpret the differences between age groups as the pure effect of aging, they may be due in part to cohort effects, especially at younger ages. The young, especially girls, are growing up in a different economy from that experienced by their parents at comparable ages. Young women may be more likely to participate in the labor force than their mothers, in which case the age profile would appear to be flatter than it really is.

The most important point is the high labor force participation rate for men and women at all ages, a statistical reflection of the "ceaseless toil" described by Davis-Friedmann (1983: 18). To the extent that withdrawal from employment occurs at all, it begins earlier for women than for men, beginning with the 50–54 age group, versus the 60–64 age group for men. Even so, at ages 60–64 almost 80 percent of men and women are still working. There is no sense in which early retirement occurs in rural China, at least in the ways we think of it in industrialized countries. Women's participation drops off sharply by age 65, whereas men's declines more gradually. If they are still alive, most rural Chinese men can anticipate working into their 70s. A slightly sharper age profile emerges if we consider days worked per year (not shown), instead of the coarser measure of participation reported in Figure 3. If income is proportional to the number of days worked, we would expect that earned income begins to decline at age 45 for men and at age 35 for women.

In urban areas, employees of state enterprises are subject to mandatory retirement at age 55 for women and age 60 for men. By contrast, rural residents have farms from which they need not retire until they are physically incapable of working. Furthermore, most urban workers have state-provided pensions, which reduce the need to work.

Figure 4 shows employment-age profiles based on the 1989 CHNS data. The measure of employment in the CHNS is whether an individual is currently working. We might therefore expect the mean participation rates to be lower in the CHNS than in the 1995 data. The rural pattern for men resembles the 1995 figure, with the steepest age-related drop at ages 60–64 and a large fraction of men working into their 70s. The urban numbers for men reflect the mandatory retirement age at 60, but also show a large drop in participation for those aged 55–59. Urban men are less than half as likely as rural men to work beyond age 60, and urban employment rates are less than 20 percent for men over age 65.

The obviously interesting questions pertain to retirement decisions in the countryside and the city. Do urban men stop working because of mandatory retirement, or do more generous state pensions facilitate earlier retirement in urban areas? In rural areas the main transfer to elderly house-

FIGURE 4 Proportion of men and women currently working, urban versus rural areas: Northern China, 1989

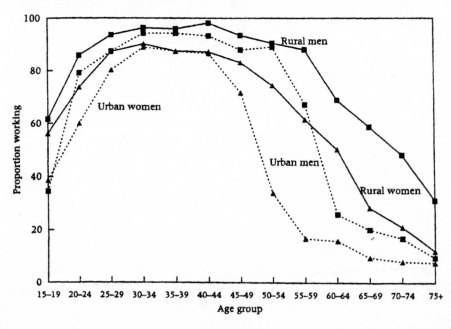

holds is land. Although land remains collectively owned in rural China, households are allocated use rights, usually on the basis of the size of the household or the farm labor force. Transferred land yields income only if it is worked. If land and labor markets are thin, the rural elderly may have a greater need to work than those in the city. Of course, the rural elderly may work more either because the returns to farming are higher than those to participation in state enterprises, or because they have a greater preference for work. Neither explanation seems likely.

As for women, the rural patterns in the CHNS are similar to those in the 1995 data, with gradual withdrawal from employment beginning at age 50. As with the men, the urban-rural comparison reflects the salience of mandatory retirement. Urban women's participation drops sharply beginning at age 50, by which time urban women are less than half as likely as rural women to work.

Have retirement patterns changed since the 1930s? Unfortunately, the data for the 1930s are available only at the household level, so that it is not possible to draw direct comparisons of individual behavior across data sets. We can conduct an indirect exercise, however, comparing aggregate household labor supply in the 1935 and 1995 samples, testing for changes in the correlation between household demographic structure and family labor supply. For example, we can compare the total labor supply of one household with another, one of which differs only by having an elderly male present. If household members do not adjust their labor supply to the presence of other members, then the estimated effect of adding an elderly male to the total household labor supply would be the amount of labor supply he provides. Of course, there are likely to be indirect effects as the labor supply of one household member substitutes or complements others. (See Benjamin and Brandt 1995 for a detailed discussion.)

Our measure of household labor supply is the number of men and women (separately) engaged in farming. The results are presented in Table 1, which shows the effect of adding members to the household. Column 1 suggests an age profile for men in the 1930s. The profile has the expected shape: a young boy adds the equivalent of 0.08 adult males to the farm labor force, a teen adds 0.34 men, a prime-age male adds 0.55, and a man aged 61 or older adds 0.30. The results for 1995 are shown in the next column, and columns 3 and 4 compare the profiles for females. (An asterisk or double asterisk in the 1995 columns indicates coefficients that are significantly different from those for the 1930s.) Overall, for males the 1995 coefficients are larger than those for 1935, except for teens. This could reflect differences in the measure of participation, though such differences should be absorbed by the constant (and 1935 dummy). Alternatively, it could reflect higher participation in agriculture in the 1990s, possibly due to the more even distribution of land. As we would expect, in 1995 younger men were less likely to be working on the farm, and were instead working off the farm or attending school. Nevertheless, we cannot reject the hypothesis that the coefficients in 1995 and 1935 are the same. This is consistent with (though it does not imply) the hypothesis that the relationship between age and participation in agriculture was the same in 1995 as in the 1930s.

TABLE 1 Regression estimates of the effect of the number of household members on male and female labor supply to the family farm: Northern China, 1935 and 1995

Type of labor	Males		Females	
	1935	1995	1935	1995
Children (ages 0–10)				
Males	0.080	0.027	–0.139	0.015**
	(0.033)	(0.037)	(0.038)	(0.035)
Females	0.065	–0.005	–0.024	–0.043
	(0.033)	(0.037)	(0.038)	(0.035)
Teens (ages 11–19)				
Males	0.340	0.313	–0.046	0.036
	(0.040)	(0.039)	(0.045)	(0.037)
Females	–0.002	0.022	0.137	0.310**
	(0.034)	(0.035)	(0.039)	(0.033)
Prime ages (20–50)				
Males	0.552	0.690	–0.072	0.007
	(0.041)	(0.037)	(0.047)	(0.035)
Females	0.088	–0.028	0.509	0.607
	(0.046)	(0.041)	(0.052)	(0.039)
Middle ages (51–60)				
Males	0.595	0.641	–0.264	–0.039*
	(0.069)	(0.060)	(0.079)	(0.056)
Females	0.165	0.078	0.711	0.501
	(0.081)	(0.067)	(0.092)	(0.063)
Elderly (61+)				
Males	0.301	0.449	–0.229	0.172**
	(0.069)	(0.062)	(0.079)	(0.058)
Females	–0.172	0.037*	0.126	0.066
	(0.080)	(0.059)	(0.091)	(0.056)
Intercept	0.286	0.265	0.225	0.311**
	(0.060)	(0.064)	(0.068)	(0.060)

NOTES: The dependent variable is the number of males or females (per household) engaged in agriculture over the previous year. Standard errors are shown in parentheses. Sample size for 1935 is 836; for 1995 it is 734. Each demographic variable is the number of household members in the designated age-sex group.
* Significant at p = 0.10.
** Significant at p = 0.05.

The corresponding results for women indicate that females in the 1990s were more likely, at any age, to be working on the farm than was the case in the 1930s. The implied age pattern for women is similar to that observed in Figure 3. More interestingly, as with the men, the age profiles are similar in the two samples. The most important differences are that in 1995 teenage females were much more likely to work on the farm than was the case in the 1930s, and the effects of men in the household are different in the two samples. In the 1930s, having additional older men was associated with a decline in the number of women working (all else being equal), whereas this indirect effect is not present in the 1995 data. The 1935 results may reflect the need for care of older men by their wives, or the substitution of older men for older women on the farm. Whatever the case, these data do not provide evidence that work participation of elderly men or women has declined since the 1930s.

Next we consider work patterns and living arrangements. Does the labor supply of the elderly living on their own differ from that of elders living with their children? We can document the interaction between work and family structure, but it is impossible to determine the direction of causality. Perhaps only the "independent" (economically capable) elderly can live on their own, in which case only selected elderly will be able to live apart from their children. Alternatively, the extra resources associated with living in an extended household may permit older individuals to work less, in which case the causality runs from family structure to work. For the remainder of this study we use the terms "extended" and "multiple" households interchangeably when referring to households with more than a single conjugal unit. Essentially, either term is equivalent to "living with children."

Table 2 reports regression estimates of participation and days worked for men and women. In a regression context we can more formally estimate the age profiles, controlling for other individual-level variables, namely measures of education, that might be correlated with the birth-cohort effects we have previously noted. For clarity of presentation we report only the age coefficients for older individuals (ages 50 and over). For each measure of labor supply we show the coefficients for the whole sample, as well as the coefficients interacted with an indicator that the individual lives in an extended or multiple household.

Column 1 confirms the pattern that we have already seen in Figure 3, that participation begins to decline for men over age 60. Column 2 shows that the participation rate for older men in simple family households is much higher (0.94) than for men living in multiple households (0.61). Furthermore, the decline in employment with age occurs only for those men living in multiple households. This result suggests that the elderly who live on their own work as much as they did when they were younger. Again

TABLE 2 Regression estimates of labor participation and days worked per year, by individual age, sex, and household type: Northern China, 1995

	Men				Women			
	Participation		Days per year		Participation		Days per year	
Means and coefficients	(1)	(2)	(3)	(4)	(5)	(6)	(7)	(8)
Means								
All adults	0.91		159.8		0.84		99.01	
Elderly in simple household		0.94		109.4		0.70		43.46
Elderly in multiple household		0.61		60.6		0.34		17.65
Coefficients by age group								
50–54	–.038	–.038	–37.04*	–19.86	0.059	–0.039	–51.21*	–57.05*
	(.025)	(.029)	(16.57)	(19.62)	(0.039)	(0.042)	(13.05)	(15.46)
55–59	–.024	–.026	–58.84*	–61.08*	–0.174*	–0.171*	–61.35*	–64.38*
	(.024)	(.030)	(16.35)	(20.64)	(0.049)	(0.068)	(12.98)	(16.75)
60–64	–.100*	–.070	–75.86*	–69.99*	–0.168*	–0.110	–59.25*	–57.05*
	(.042)	(.048)	(18.35)	(21.94)	(0.065)	(0.079)	(15.34)	(17.24)
65–69	–.146*	.014	–94.40*	–56.89*	–0.431*	–0.281*	–91.70*	–84.19*
	(.067)	(.014)	(18.75)	(25.12)	(0.088)	(0.131)	(12.69)	(16.40)
70–74	–.322*	.016	–112.02*	–53.75*	–0.732*	–0.371*	–105.83*	–91.24*
	(.092)	(.018)	(21.04)	(30.17)	(0.083)	(0.159)	(11.82)	(17.04)
75+	–.553*	–.198	–163.36*	–173.91*	–0.796*	–0.773*	–114.72*	–117.54*
	(.105)	(.177)	(14.55)	(21.68)	(0.070)	(0.183)	(10.80)	(12.77)

266

Multiple household	.001	9.86	.019	–11.88
	(.006)	(27.67)	(.014)	(22.44)
Multiple household				
x age 50–54	–.004	–60.11	–0.069	22.91
	(.054)	(36.66)	(0.087)	(28.45)
x age 55–59	–.000	–1.10	–0.020	13.88
	(.045)	(36.35)	(0.097)	(27.75)
x age 60–64	–.094	–23.61	–0.138	2.56
	(.096)	(38.87)	(0.124)	(32.17)
x age 65–69	–.265*	–69.36	–0.255	–3.69
	(.102)	(39.26)	(0.169)	(26.52)
x age 70–74	–.484*	–91.50*	–0.568*	–13.88
	(.114)	(42.09)	(0.166)	(25.45)
x age 75+	–.459*	4.46	–0.045	12.50
	(.211)	(33.46)	(0.196)	(22.78)
F-test for multiple family	7.57	2.53	3.77	1.32
	(.000)	(0.39)	(.005)	(.263)

NOTES: Standard errors are shown in parentheses. The means panel shows sample means for each dependent variable for the whole sample, as well as the separate means for the elderly in simple households (one conjugal unit) and multiple households (more than one conjugal unit). For each dependent variable the coefficients represent the difference of the specified age indicator from individuals aged 35–39. For each dependent variable there are two specifications: without interactions (odd-numbered columns) and with interactions of the age profile with an indicator for multiple households (even-numbered columns). Sample size is 1,072 for men, 1,075 for women. The F-test for differences in age profiles for multiple households is reported in the last row. Regressions also include controls for years of education and technical training.
* Significant at p = 0.05.

we cannot tell whether the elderly living in multiple households are working less because they cannot, or because they do not have to. The elderly living in simple households could be the independent, self-selected elderly who prefer to farm until they die, in which case we cannot conclude that extended households facilitate retirement. However, the numbers do suggest a positive association between living in extended households and the *possibility* of retirement.

The next two columns show the profiles for days worked. The relationship between age and days is stronger than that between age and participation. The average number of days worked for all men is 159.8 per year. Beginning at age 50, men work fewer days. As with employment rates, men in simple households reduce their labor supply less as they age than do those living in multiple households. Older men living alone with their wives work as much as younger men.

The next four columns show the corresponding results for women. Again there are sharp differences in labor force attachment between women living in multiple households and those living on their own. However, despite the overall difference in participation and days worked, the age profiles for employment are similar for women in extended and simple households. This suggests that the economic role of women changes as they age, in a way that is common to the two types of households. It also suggests that need does not drive women in simple households to work any more than those in the multiple households. (See Davis-Friedmann 1991 for a more extensive description of the role of women as they age.)

Living standards of the elderly

How do living standards of the elderly compare with those of the young, and has the relative position of the elderly changed over time? Are living arrangements related to living standards? In addressing these questions we confront several empirical difficulties, particularly because income and consumption are measured at the household, not individual, level. An elderly woman's living standards will depend on both the income of the household in which she lives and the distribution of resources within the household, yet we do not observe her individual share. Instead, we can estimate her access to household resources by attributing to her an equal piece of the household pie—that is, by imputing per capita household income to each household member. Obviously, doing so will be misleading if resources are not shared equally. There is another potential problem. If children require fewer resources than adults, then adults in households with children will actually have higher living standards than adults in households without children and the same per capita income. Essentially, we may overcompensate for household size by counting children and adults as equal.

These issues are discussed in detail by Deaton and Paxson (1992 and 1998). One correction is to calculate the "per adult-equivalent" level of consumption. Following Deaton and Paxson, we assume that children under age 5 are equivalent to 0.25 adults, and that those between ages 5 and 14 are equivalent to 0.45 adults. We have chosen these numbers not because they are necessarily accurate, but because they allow us to explore the sensitivity of our conclusions to the possibility that children need fewer resources.

We begin by assuming that each household member receives an equal share of family resources; that is, we attribute household per capita income to each individual and pretend that it represents the individual's living standard. Table 3 shows estimated age profiles from the 1995 sample (ages 31–50 being the omitted category). The ideal measure of access to resources would be based on consumption, rather than income, especially for the elderly. Column 1 shows that children have lower per capita consumption levels than do prime-age adults, but that per capita consumption is lowest for the elderly. Adults of ages 51–60, however, have consumption levels no different from those of prime-age adults. Column 2 indicates that the age profile for per capita income is virtually identical to that for

TABLE 3 Regression estimates of differences in annual per capita household income and consumption between prime ages (31–50) and other ages: Northern China, 1995

Age category	Per capita consumption	Per capita income (PCY)	Per adult equivalent income	PCY (base: simple household)	PCY (interaction multiple household)
Children (0–10)	–247.97*	–216.53*	73.99	–209.50	156.99
	(52.03)	(108.63)	(129.15)	(144.21)	(187.37)
Teens (11–19)	–30.17	–82.63	–137.44	–128.32	34.13
	(42.54)	(97.39)	(111.55)	(111.51)	(188.79)
Prime ages 1 (20–30)	–21.23	–120.16	–181.93	177.00	421.55
	(71.41)	(136.44)	(167.66)	(188.51)	(239.61)
Middle ages (51–60)	85.58	–108.89	–459.94*	–188.48	463.32
	(106.17)	(153.00)	(175.09)	(208.07)	(289.67)
Elderly (61+)	–449.50*	–726.22*	–1,038.58*	–927.85*	732.75*
	(79.41)	(171.26)	(189.05)	(336.95)	(351.87)
Multiple-family indicator					–675.53*
					(188.10)
Mean income (yuan)	2,314.45	2,691.13	2,840.06		

NOTES: Coefficients are estimates of individual age indicators from OLS regressions of household per capita income, defined as the head of each column. All specifications include village fixed effects. Standard errors are shown in parentheses. Sample size is 2,881. The omitted category is prime ages 31–50. The F-test for differences between age coefficients in multiple and simple families is 2.73 (p = 0.000). The F-test for whether multiple- and simple-family coefficients for elderly sum to zero is 3.07 (p = 0.082), and the F-test for whether elderly have the same income in multiple and simple households is 0.03 (p = 0.8648). In 1994, 1 RMB (yuan) = US$0.12.
* Significant at p = 0.05.

consumption. (Note that there is virtually no overlap in the measurement of these two variables.) Income does decline more steeply for the elderly than does consumption, a pattern that is consistent with a life cycle model, wherein individuals smooth consumption between their working years and old age. The implied degree of consumption smoothing is quite small, however; income and consumption essentially track each other. As in the employment regressions, it is important to beware of cohort effects when interpreting the age profile. In this case, declines in income and consumption for the current elderly may reflect their permanently poorer economic position in relation to those born more recently. Nevertheless, the interpretation of a purely aging effect is bolstered by the decline between "middle" and "old" age, age spans in which we do not expect the cohort effects to be as strong. Rather than repeat this caution again, we shall treat the estimated age coefficients as age effects throughout the remainder of the discussion. In column 3 we adjust income for adult equivalents. This has the effect of steepening the age profile: the elderly appear much worse off because they tend to live with other adults, rather than with young children. Thus any adjustment in living standards for family composition would probably lead to a downward revision of the relative position of the elderly.

In the last two columns we compare the income levels of individuals in simple and multiple households. As before, the possible endogeneity of household structure contaminates causal interpretations between household structure and income. Our more limited interest is in measuring the differences in living standards between the elderly in the two types of households. In particular we wish to know whether the elderly who live on their own are worse off than those living with their children. If the elderly who live on their own are positively selected (i.e., are the most productive), then we exaggerate their relative position. On the other hand, if living alone reflects neglect and is not a matter of choice, then they may be genuinely worse off.

Column 4 shows the age-income profile for simple households. The profile is slightly steeper than the comparable (pooled) profile in column 2. Column 5 shows the difference in age profiles between persons in extended and simple households, so that the net effect of being in any age group in an extended household is the sum of the relevant coefficient in columns 4 and 5. The elderly in extended households are associated with an age "penalty" that is 732.75 yuan lower than the income of those in simple families. The net effect is that they earn 195.10 (927.85 − 732.75) yuan less than prime-age adults in extended households, although the difference is statistically insignificant. This should not be surprising, since we have assumed that all members of extended households receive the same per capita income; but it also suggests that these households suffer no penalty for having elderly members. Nevertheless, the per capita income of extended households is lower for all ages than that of simple households (by 675.53 yuan).

Given a choice, though, an elderly person would still come out slightly ahead in an extended household, by 57.22 yuan (732.75 − 675.53), though this difference is insignificantly different from zero. If there is any positive selection into simple households, this result suggests that the average elderly person is slightly better off in an extended household, and that the extended household plays some social security role. This implication is even stronger once we recognize that the elderly in simple households also work more.

Table 4 shows comparable results from our other data sets. The first two columns report estimates from the 1935 data. The most striking feature of the 1935 profile, and a key result of this study, is the absence of any effects of old age. The elderly live in as well-off households as the young, unlike the situation observed in 1995. This remains true even when we adjust for adult equivalents. In the last four columns we use the CHNS data to compare the urban and rural age profiles in 1989. The main conclusion here, as we have seen before, is that the profiles are similar. With respect to mean incomes, the elderly fare slightly worse in the rural areas, whereas children fare worse in cities. Mean incomes, however, are significantly higher in urban areas. Furthermore, urban families have access to better public services. If we also take account of the fact that the elderly

TABLE 4 Regression estimates of differences in annual per capita household income between prime ages (31–50) and other ages, three data sets compared: Northern China, 1935 and 1989

	Rural, 1935		Rural, 1989 CHNS		Urban, 1989 CHNS	
Age category	Per capita income	Per adult equivalent income	Per capita income	Per adult equivalent income	Per capita income	Per adult equivalent income
Children (0–10)	−2.50*	−0.33	−33.30	40.96	−110.44*	−59.04
	(1.00)	(1.29)	(19.94)	(24.32)	(35.57)	(39.44)
Teens (11–19)	−1.75	−2.59	−20.85	−65.79*	18.60	−33.01
	(1.11)	(1.42)	(20.72)	(25.27)	(37.64)	(41.72)
Prime ages 1 (20–30)	0.24	−1.10	48.22*	25.11	18.87	−63.64
	(1.14)	(1.46)	(20.92)	(25.52)	(33.71)	(37.37)
Middle ages (51–60)	−0.04	−2.58	80.14*	−20.00	95.89*	−33.25
	(1.54)	(1.98)	(29.24)	(35.67)	(39.69)	(44.00)
Elderly (61+)	0.13	−1.90	−63.04*	−152.42*	−62.85	−171.09*
	(1.56)	(2.00)	(30.13)	(36.74)	(39.77)	(44.09)
Mean income (yuan)	34.72	45.41	703.83	853.51	1,196.60	1,364.73
Sample size	6,719	6,719	10,356	10,356	4,802	4,802

NOTES: Coefficients are estimates of individual age indicators from OLS regressions of household per capita income, defined at the head of each column. All specifications include village fixed effects. Standard errors are in parentheses. The omitted category is prime ages 31–50. In 1935, 1 yuan = US$0.48; in 1989, 1 RMB (yuan) = US$0.27.
* Significant at p = 0.05.

work much harder in rural areas, and if we place a positive weight on nonmarket time, then this further widens the welfare gap in favor of the urban elderly.

We next explore the relative position of the elderly in other parts of the income distribution. (See Chu and Jiang 1997 for a related attempt to explore the links between the age composition of household members and individual-based measures of income distribution—in their case, indicators of income inequality.) We begin by calculating the cumulative distribution functions of per capita income. With these results, one can (for example) choose any poverty line, z, and then compare the proportion of individuals living in households with per capita incomes below z. Figure 5 shows the cumulative distribution functions for the elderly and non-elderly in 1995. As suggested by the regressions, this figure indicates that the elderly have lower mean income than younger household members. However, it also suggests that for whatever poverty line one might choose, the elderly would have a significantly higher cumulative distribution function, or poverty rate, than the non-elderly. For example, at a poverty line of 1,000 yuan, the poverty rate is almost twice as high for the elderly.

Figure 6, based on the 1935 data, provides a striking contrast. Here, the cumulative distribution functions for the two groups are virtually coincident. Thus for any poverty line, the poverty rates of the elderly and the non-elderly are the same. This finding reinforces the case that the elderly were significantly better off in relation to the non-elderly during the 1930s than in the 1990s.

FIGURE 5 Cumulative distribution function of per capita income, elderly versus non-elderly: Northern China, 1995

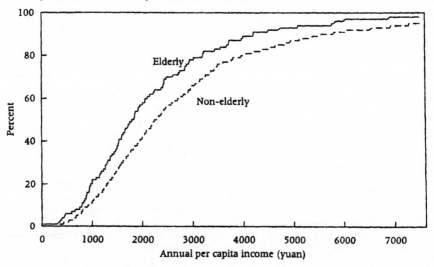

FIGURE 6 Cumulative distribution function of per capita income, elderly versus non-elderly: Northern China, 1935

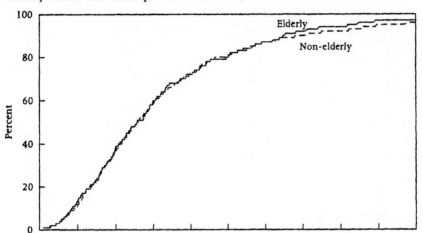

Our final comparison is between the rural and urban CHNS samples. The results (not shown) reinforce the earlier observation that there is no difference between the urban and rural areas besides mean incomes.

As a final exercise, we repackage the individual-level data and examine the overall correlation between household demographic structure and household income. Again we must be careful to avoid placing a causal interpretation on the coefficients. If family structure were exogenous, we could interpret the coefficient on the number of elderly people as the effect on family income of adding an elderly person to the household. But richer households can support more members, and a positive coefficient may only reflect this fact (see Benjamin and Brandt 1995). Nevertheless, the coefficients indicate the level of household resources associated with an increase in the number of individuals of a given type. The results are shown in Table 5. We report results for a logarithmic specification, since it has the advantage of permitting the coefficients to be interpreted (approximately) as percentage increases in household income associated with additional members, and it allows easy comparison among data sets.

Column 1 shows the results for rural households in 1995. Here we see that the elderly are associated with the smallest increases in household income, smaller even than those associated with children. The elderly are the only group with an insignificant coefficient, suggesting that adding an elderly person to a rural household is associated with an increase in household income of only 1 percent, certainly less than enough to cover the cost of caring for an elderly person. These low numbers for the elderly are also

TABLE 5   Regression estimates of log household income and demographic structure: Northern China, 1995, 1989, and 1935

Age category	Rural, 1995	Rural, 1989	Urban, 1989	Rural, 1935
Children (0–10)	0.10*	0.06*	0.02	0.07*
	(0.04)	(0.02)	(0.03)	(0.02)
Teens (11–19)	0.15*	0.13*	0.16*	0.15*
	(0.05)	(0.02)	(0.03)	(0.02)
Prime ages 1 (20–30)	0.27*	0.20*	0.29*	0.20*
	(0.04)	(0.02)	(0.02)	(0.02)
Prime ages 2 (31–50)	0.30*	0.25*	0.37*	0.24*
	(0.04)	(0.03)	(0.03)	(0.03)
Middle ages (51–60)	0.22*	0.23*	0.29*	(0.03)
	(0.05)	(0.03)	0.24*	(0.04)
Elderly (61+)	0.01	0.06	0.16*	0.22*
	(0.04)	(0.03)	(0.03)	(0.04)
Sample size	769	2,448	1,251	1,075

NOTES: Coefficients are estimates of OLS regressions of log household income on the number of people in each age category. All specifications include village fixed effects. Standard errors are shown in parentheses.
* Significant at $p = 0.05$.

reflected in the next column, which presents estimates for the rural CHNS. Here the elderly are also associated with a small (6 percent) and insignificant increase in household income. The urban coefficients (column 3) are slightly different. Here the elderly have lower coefficients than prime-age adults, but the number is higher than for their rural counterparts (16 percent) and significant. The most striking results are for rural households in 1935, shown in the last column. Household income increases as much with the number of elderly as it does with prime-age adults. However it is accomplished, whether by income directly associated with the elderly, or through harder work on the part of the non-elderly, it appears that the elderly lived in more fortunate circumstances in the 1930s (compared with the young) than in the 1990s.

Beyond working, how do the elderly support themselves, especially with the declining prevalence of extended-household living arrangements? Extended *families*, versus households, may yet be important as long as children are supporting their parents through interhousehold transfers. Furthermore, individuals who worked for state-owned enterprises (mostly in urban areas) have state-financed pensions. Finally, local governments may provide direct relief to the poorest elderly.

Tables 6 and 7 document the magnitudes of these types of income transfer: private (family) remittances, pensions, and government transfers. They compare households with and without elderly members, both for simple and extended households. In Table 6 we focus on the 1995 rural

TABLE 6   Mean transfers to households with elderly members, by
household type: Rural northern China, 1995

Indicators of transfer income (per year)	All household types		Only-elderly households	
	Elderly	Non-elderly	Simple family	Multiple family
Mean annual household income (yuan)	10,294.1	11,422.8	3,981.4	13,717.9
Percentage with pensions	7.1	0.1	7.8	6.8
Mean pension income (yuan)	95.4	23.0	75.5	106.3
Percentage with government transfers	8.8	5.0	10.9	7.6
Mean government transfer income (yuan)	25.5	29.8	33.4	21.3
Percentage with remittances	44.0	23.9	70.3	30.0
Mean remittance income (yuan)	516.4	201.9	631.7	453.9
Sample size	182	603	64	118

NOTES: The table shows the percentage of households that received each type of transfer income, as well as the sample average level of that type of income, calculated over all households. Elderly households are defined as those households with members over 60 years of age. In 1994, 1 RMB (yuan) = US$0.12.

sample. To begin, very few rural elderly households have pension income, and it represents a tiny fraction of their income. Similarly, government transfers are irrelevant to elderly and non-elderly households alike. This finding reflects the limits of village financial resources and indicates that access to land is the primary form of social relief. Private transfers (remittances), however, are very important. Forty-four percent of elderly households, versus 24 percent of non-elderly households, receive remittances. Moreover, the level of remittance income is also more than twice as high in the elderly households (accounting for about 5 percent of total income) as in non-elderly households. Remittance activity appears to be highly age-motivated. In the last two columns we compare transfers to simple and extended elderly households. The most striking feature is that 70 percent of simple families receive remittances, compared with 30 percent of extended households. In levels, the elderly in simple households receive slightly higher remittances. Although remittances are more important to those elderly living outside extended families (remittances accounting for almost one-sixth of their household income), remittances are still large for the elderly in extended households. On the basis of these levels, it is difficult to argue that the elderly living on their own receive enough remittances to offset the implicit intrahousehold transfers they would receive in an extended household.

Table 7 draws an urban-rural comparison. Two features stand out. First, the elderly in urban areas have significantly higher pension income than do the rural elderly. More surprisingly, they are also more likely to receive remittances, though this receipt is less age-related than in rural

275

TABLE 7   Mean transfers to households with elderly members, by household type: Rural and urban northern China, 1989

Indicators of transfer income (per year)	Rural		Urban	
	Elderly	Non-elderly	Simple family	Multiple family
Mean annual household income (yuan)	3,044.6	2,929.2	4,517.1	4,616.9
Percentage with pensions	11.9	1.7	49.3	14.1
Mean pension income (yuan)	120.9	14.2	670.4	14.1
Percentage with gov. transfers	3.3	0.1	1.6	1.1
Mean gov. transfer income (yuan)	5.0	1.8	4.1	2.2
Percentage with remittances	31.0	20.3	36.5	29.1
Mean remittance income (yuan)	100.4	41.5	122.1	91.9
Sample size	521	1,943	436	818

NOTES: The table shows the percentage of households that received each type of transfer income, as well as the sample average level of that type of income, calculated over all households. Elderly households are defined as those households with members over 60 years of age. In 1989, 1 RMB (yuan) = US$0.27.

areas. In their broader implications for social security, these results, combined with the evidence on living arrangements, suggest that there is little difference between urban and rural areas with respect to private support for the elderly. Families are as important in urban as in rural areas, but they have the bonus of state-financed pensions. An interesting question at this point is how much the state pensions crowd out some of the private urban transfers. If there is any crowding out, it is nevertheless the urban, not the rural, elderly who have the more developed private social security system. (See Case and Deaton 1998 for a discussion of the difficulties in addressing this question, and Jensen 1998 for an attempt to answer the question in a South African context.)

A common theme in the study of Chinese families is that the elderly have lost control over resources as the balance of power has shifted away from them, especially with collectivization (Davis-Friedmann 1991; Goode 1963; Selden 1993; Whyte 1995; Yan 1997). This helps explain the worsening economic standing of the elderly both inside and outside extended households. Prior to collectivization the elderly did not need to rely on the goodwill of their children, since "the heart of the family compact was the exchange of the care of aged parents by male offspring and the eventual transfer of land" (Selden 1993: 148). Parents could disinherit negligent sons. The elderly also embodied considerable human capital. As Goode (1963) notes, there was a high return to the accumulated farming experience. Neither of these advantages of age is present now. According to Whyte (1995: 1012), "the elimination for a generation of meaningful family property, combined with the rising education of the young and other trends, significantly softened the power of the senior generation in Chinese families."

Compounding the loss of bargaining power, the inability to accumulate land reduces the ability of the elderly to save, and their relative decline in human capital reduces their current earning power. Thin land and labor markets may further constrain the ability of the elderly to convert even their allocated land into income. This shows how a seemingly egalitarian institution, such as a property rights regime that prohibits land ownership, can have unintended adverse consequences on income distribution, and it provides another example of the need to evaluate the distribution of land in the context of the development of factor markets. (See Benjamin and Brandt 1997 for a more extensive discussion of these issues, focusing on the 1930s.) As emphasized by Davis-Friedmann (1991), the reduction in the bargaining position of the elderly was not a problem when the state was committed to care for the elderly; but with the demise of social programs the elderly have been left to fend for themselves, and the current elderly are particularly at a disadvantage.

This decline in asset holdings of the elderly is apparent in our data. In Table 8 we show estimates of household per capita land and its relationship to household demographic structure. In the 1990s land was distributed on an egalitarian, essentially per capita, basis. Not surprisingly, then, column 1 shows that household per capita land is virtually orthogonal to

TABLE 8   Regression estimates of per capita controlled land and household demographic structure: Northern China, 1995 and 1935

Age category	Additional household land per capita (in *mu*)	
	1995	1935
Children (ages 0–10)	–0.31	–0.24
	(0.17)	(0.33)
Teens (11–19)	–0.17	–0.18
	(0.19)	(0.35)
Primes ages 1 (20–30)	–0.11	–0.28
	(0.14)	(0.36)
Prime ages 2 (31–50)	0.24	2.13*
	(0.17)	(0.45)
Middle ages (51–60)	–0.01	2.39*
	(0.19)	(0.62)
Elderly (61+)	–0.11	2.41*
	(0.17)	(0.66)
Sample size	787	1,095

NOTES: Coefficients are estimates from OLS regressions of household-controlled land per capita (owned in 1935 and allocated in 1995) on the number of household members in each age category. All specifications include village fixed effects. 1 *mu* = 0.067 hectares.
* Significant at p = 0.05.

household age structure: the old command no more land than the young. In the 1930s, in contrast, the age of household members was highly correlated with per capita land. Column 2 reveals that those households with the most elderly had the most per capita owned land, reflecting the accumulation of land over the lives of the elderly. These two regressions show the most striking difference in the relative economic position of the elderly in rural China before and after collectivization. There is no way to confirm this view, but we doubt that it is pure coincidence that the elderly controlled more land and enjoyed relatively higher living standards before collectivization.

Finally, in the 1995 survey we find large differences in educational attainment by birth cohort, on the order of one year's education for each ten years of age (not shown). The gap between young and old is especially pronounced for women. Given the increased value of education, especially in gaining off-farm income, the elderly will continue to be at a disadvantage for decades to come. (See Benjamin et al. 2000 for more discussion of this point.)

Conclusion

The living conditions of the Chinese rural elderly documented here indicate that an urban bias, reflected in other aspects of public policy, extends to the provision of social security. There is no foundation for the notion that the rural elderly are well taken care of, at least in comparison with the urban elderly. Most evidence instead points to a relative deterioration of the economic position of the elderly in rural areas, and a weakening of the family as a social security institution. It is difficult to build a case that urban elderly are at a particular disadvantage and merit additional pension resources. To design alternative social security schemes will undoubtedly be complicated, but the evidence reviewed here suggests that the rural elderly warrant more attention than they have received.

Notes

We appreciate the comments of seminar participants at the University of Melbourne, Australian National University, and the University of New South Wales. Benjamin and Brandt thank the Social Sciences and Humanities Research Council of Canada for financial support.

1 One telling sign of this inattention is that the World Bank's (1997) volume in the China 2020 series devotes only a one-page sidebar to the rural elderly, essentially suggesting that old-age security in rural areas is not a matter of concern.

2 Excellent discussions of the evolution of families under collectivization, and the implied position of the elderly, can be found in Davis and Harrell (1993), Davis-Friedmann (1983 and 1991), Goode (1963), Selden (1993), and Whyte (1992 and 1995).

3 http://www.cpc.unc.edu/china/home.html.

4 A referee correctly points out that care must be taken in drawing inferences from the Liaoning data because they are drawn from a regimented population administered directly

by central authorities (the banner system). Under the banner system, households were organized into groups called *zu* that were modeled after organizational units (*mukun*) originating in the Manchu Dynasty. *Zu* were not lineage groups based on descent from a common male ancestor; rather, they functioned as basic units of state civil, fiscal, judicial, and military administration. A group typically consisted of two or three households. Leaders of each group, who occupied the lowest rung in the banner system's formal organizational hierarchy, were charged with carrying out the ad-

ministrative work associated with the official functions of the group. They had other duties as well, including authorizing marriages, ruling on inheritance disputes, and ratifying family divisions. Lee and Campbell (1997) argue that the impediments to household division under the banner system may have contributed to the high percentage of nonsimple households. Despite these caveats, their data, along with those of Wolf (1984 and 1985) for Taiwan, suggest that a majority of individuals lived in multiple or extended households, as do our data for the 1930s.

References

Benjamin, Dwayne and Loren Brandt. 1995. "Markets, discrimination, and the economic contribution of women in China: Historical evidence," *Economic Development and Cultural Change* 44(1): 63–104.

———. 1997. "Land, factor markets, and inequality in rural China: Historical evidence," *Explorations in Economic History* 34(4): 460–494.

Benjamin, Dwayne et al. 2000. "Markets, human capital, and inequality: Evidence from rural China." W. Davidson Institute Working Paper No. 298 (March), University of Toronto.

Buck, John Lossing. 1937. *Land Utilization in China*. New York: Paragon Press.

Case, Anne and Angus Deaton. 1998. "Large cash transfers to the elderly in South Africa," *Economic Journal* 108(450): 1330–1361.

Chu, C. Y. Cyrus and Lily Jiang. 1997. "Demographic transition, family structure, and income inequality," *Review of Economics and Statistics* 79(4): 665–669.

Davis, Deborah and Stevan Harrell (eds.). 1993. *Chinese Families in the Post-Mao Era*. Berkeley: University of California Press.

Davis-Friedmann, Deborah. 1983. *Long Lives: Chinese Elderly and the Communist Revolution*. Cambridge, MA: Harvard University Press.

———. 1991. *Long Lives: Chinese Elderly and the Communist Revolution*. Expanded ed. Stanford, CA: Stanford University Press.

Deaton, Angus and Christina Paxson. 1992. "Patterns of aging in Thailand and Côte d'Ivoire," in *Topics in the Economics of Aging*, ed. David A. Wise. Chicago: University of Chicago Press, pp. 163–202.

———. 1998. "Measuring poverty among the elderly," in *Inquiries in the Economics of Aging*, ed. David A. Wise. Chicago: University of Chicago Press, pp. 169–200.

Fang, Yuan, Wang Chuanbin, and Song Yuhua. 1992. "Support of the elderly in China," in *Family Support for the Elderly: The International Experience*, eds. Hal L. Kendig, Akiko Hashimoto, and Larry C. Coppard. New York: Oxford University Press, pp. 250–259.

Goode, William J. 1963. *World Revolution and Family Patterns*. London: Free Press of Glencoe.

Jensen, Robert. 1998. "Public transfers, private transfers, and the 'crowding out' hypothesis: Evidence from South Africa." Unpublished manuscript, John F. Kennedy School of Government, Harvard University, Cambridge, MA.

Lee, James Z. and Cameron D. Campbell. 1997. *Fate and Fortune in Rural China: Social Organization and Population Behavior in Liaoning, 1774–1873*. Cambridge: Cambridge University Press.

Selden, Mark. 1993. "Family strategies and structures in rural North China," in *Chinese Families in the Post-Mao Era*, eds. Deborah Davis and Stevan Harrell. Berkeley: University of California Press, pp. 139–164.

State Statistical Bureau. 1996. *Quanguo 1% Renkou Chouyang Tiaocha Ziliao* [1995 1% National Sample Population Survey]. Beijing.

———. Various years. *Provincial Statistical Yearbook.* Beijing.

———. Various years. *Zhongguo Tongji Nianjian* [Statistical Yearbook of China]. Beijing.

Tuan, Chi-hsien. 1992. "The process of population ageing and the status of old people in China," in *The Elderly Population in Developed and Developing World,* eds. P. Krishnan and K. Mahadevan. Delhi: B. R. Publishing Corporation, pp. 218–260.

Whyte, Martin King. 1992. "Introduction: Rural economic reforms and Chinese family patterns," *China Quarterly,* No. 130: 317–322.

———. 1995. "The social roots of China's economic development," *China Quarterly,* No. 144: 999–1019.

Wolf, Arthur. 1984. "Family and the life cycle in rural China," in *Households: Comparative and Historical Studies of the Domestic Group,* eds. Robert McC. Netting, Richard Wilk, and Eric Arnould. Berkeley: University of California Press, pp. 279–298.

———. 1985. "Chinese family size: A myth revitalized," in *The Chinese Family and Its Ritual Behavior,* eds. Hsieh Jih-chang and Chuang Yinghang. Taipei: Institute of Ethnology, Academia Sinica, pp. 30–49.

World Bank. 1994. *Averting the Old Age Crisis.* New York: Oxford University Press for the World Bank.

———. 1997. *Old Age Security: Pension Reform in China.* China 2020 Series. Washington, DC: World Bank.

Yan, Yunxiang. 1997. "The triumph of conjugality: Structural transformation of family relations in a Chinese village," *Ethnology* 36(3): 191–212.

RETIREMENT TRENDS AND POLICIES TO ENCOURAGE WORK AMONG OLDER AMERICANS

by

GARY BURTLESS AND JOSEPH F. QUINN*

January 2000

Abstract

The trend toward earlier and earlier retirement was one of the most important labor market developments of the twentieth century. It was evident in all the major industrialized countries. In the United States, however, the trend toward earlier retirement came to at least a temporary halt in the mid-1980s. Male participation rates at older ages have stabilized or even increased slightly. Older women's participation rates are clearly rising. This paper examines the environmental and policy changes contributing to the long-term decline in the U.S. retirement age as well as developments that contributed to the recent reversal.

The dominant source of earlier retirement was the long-term increase in Americans' wealth, which permitted workers to enjoy rising living standards even as they spent a growing percentage of their lives outside the paid work force. The expansion of Social Security pensions and of employer-sponsored pension plans and the introduction of mandatory retirement rules also encouraged earlier retirement over much of the last century.

Many public policies and private institutions that encouraged early retirement have been modified in recent years. Mandatory retirement has been outlawed in most jobs. Social Security is no longer growing more generous, and worker coverage under company pension plans is no longer rising. Both Social Security and many private pensions have become more "age neutral" with respect to retirement. Public and private pension programs now provide weaker financial incentives for workers to retire at particular ages, such as age 62 or age 65, and offer stronger incentives for aging workers to remain in the labor force. The paper outlines additional policies that could encourage later retirement. An open question is whether such policies are needed. Rising labor productivity and increased work effort during the pre-retirement years mean that Americans can continue to enjoy higher living standards, even as improved longevity adds to the number of years that workers spend in retirement. If opinion polls are to be believed, most workers favor preserving the institutions that allow early retirement even if it means these institutions will require heavier contributions from active workers.

---

* Copyright © Gary Burtless and Joseph F. Quinn. The authors are Senior Fellow, The Brookings Institution, Washington, DC 20036; and Dean, College of Arts and Sciences, Boston College, Gasson Hall 103, Chestnut Hill, MA 02467, respectively. Both authors are affiliates of the Center for Retirement Research at Boston College. We gratefully acknowledge the research assistance of Claudia Sahm of Brookings. This paper was prepared for the annual conference of the National Academy of Social Insurance, Washington, DC, January 26-27, 2000. The views are solely those of the authors and should not be ascribed to Brookings, the Boston College Center for Retirement Research, or the National Academy of Social Insurance.

RETIREMENT TRENDS AND
POLICIES TO ENCOURAGE WORK AMONG OLDER AMERICANS

by

Gary Burtless and Joseph F. Quinn

THE UNITED STATES and other industrial nations face key challenges associated with a graying population. Depressed birth rates and rising longevity have increased the dependency ratio throughout the industrialized world. Population projections of the Social Security Trustees suggest the U.S. aged-dependency ratio -- the ratio of Americans older than 64 to Americans aged 20 to 64 -- will increase almost 70 percent between 2000 and 2030. The increase will be even larger in some other rich countries. As the U.S. population grows older, the cost of paying for pension and health benefits must rise, boosting tax burdens and impairing the nation's ability to pay for other government obligations. The burden imposed by an aging population would rise more gradually if workers could be persuaded to delay their retirements and continue contributing to the health and pension systems.

In this paper we consider long-term trends in retirement as well as recent trends that signal at least a pause in the historical pattern of earlier withdrawal from the work force. We also discuss public policies that might reinforce the very recent trend toward greater labor force participation among older workers.

Retirement trends

At the beginning of the last century, retirement was relatively uncommon but not unknown. Two out of three American men past age 65 were employed, but one-third were not (U.S. Department of Commerce 1975, pp. 132).[1] By middle of the twentieth century retirement was far more common. Fewer than half of men 65 and older held a job in 1950. By 1985 the proportion at work fell still further. Just 16 percent of men over 65 were employed or actively seeking a job. Eighty-four percent were outside the active labor force. The percentage of women past 65 who were employed or looking for work also shrank during the first four decades after World War II, though this was mainly because the average age of women past 65 was rising. The reduction in women's employment was far smaller than among men because the percentage of older women who worked outside the home had never been high.

The decline in labor force participation at older ages has not been confined to the United States. It is characteristic of all rich industrialized countries. In most European countries employment rates among the elderly are now significantly below those in the United States Quinn and Burkhauser 1994). Along with a shrinking work week and rising paid employment among married women, earlier retirement among men has been a distinctive feature of economic progress in all the developed countries.

Trends in the United States. The pattern of declining work among older men is clearly evident in Figure 1. Each line in the figure traces the labor force participation rate of older American men, by age, in a different year of the past century.[2] (A person is considered to be a labor force participant if he or she holds a job or is actively seeking work.) The top line shows age-specific participation rates of older men in 1910. Note that there is a clear pattern of labor market withdrawal with advancing age. Even at age 72, however, the male participation rate in 1910 was over 50 percent. Participation rates in 1940, 1970, 1984-85, and 1998-99 are displayed in the lower four lines. Each of these lines shows a characteristic pattern of labor market withdrawal as men grow older. The crucial difference between 1910 and later years is that the fall-off in labor force participation begins at an earlier age and proceeds at a faster pace.

The decline in male participation was neither smooth nor uniform over the century. By far the largest proportionate declines in participation occurred among men past the age of 65. In 1998-99, for example, the participation rate among 72-year-olds was only one-quarter the equivalent rate in 1910. The fall-off in participation was smaller at younger ages. In general, large declines in participation occurred in the early and middle parts of the century for the oldest age groups; major declines occurred after 1960 among younger men. The largest percentage declines among men older than 70 occurred between 1910 and 1940. The fastest declines among 65-to-69 year-olds took place between 1940 and 1970. The biggest declines among men under 65 did not occur until after 1960, after the earliest age of eligibility for Social Security benefits was reduced to 62. A striking feature of Figure 1 is that there has been *no* decline in older men's participation rates since the mid-1980s. After a long period of decline, the participation rates of older men stabilized or even increased slightly after 1985.

284

The story for older American women is different. Older women's participation rates in the post-World-War-II era have reflected two partially offsetting phenomena – the early retirement trend of older workers in general and the increasing labor force participation of married women. As a result of the latter, the participation rates of older women did not exhibit the dramatic post-war declines seen among men. Instead, as shown in lower panel of Table 1, age-specific labor force participation rates generally increased among women. Between 1950 and 1998-99, the female participation rate rose 39 percentage points at age 55, 26 points at age 60, 8 points at age 65, and 7 points at age 70.

What is similar to the male experience is the shift in trends after 1985. As with men, there is a noticeable break from the earlier trend in older women's labor force participation. Between 1970 and 1985 older women's labor force participation rate barely increased at all and even declined among people past age 62. In contrast, female participation rates surged in the 15 years after 1985. Figure 2 shows the annual percentage-point change in participation at selected ages in the two different periods. The lighter bars show changes between 1970 and 1985; the darker bars show changes between 1985 and 1999. The top panel shows trends in the participation rate of older men, and the lower panel shows trends at the same five ages for women. At age 62, the male participation rate fell 1.5 percentage points a year from 1970 to 1985. The rate among 62-year-old women declined 0.2 points a year over the same period. Between 1985 and 1999, the male participation rate at age 62 rose 0.3 percentage points a year; the female rate increased 0.7 points a year. At each age the rate of increase in participation rates accelerated, the rate of decline in participation rates shrank, or a decline in participation rates was reversed. The similarity of the break points in the male and female time series is striking (Quinn 1999b). Women's participation rates at older ages have risen strongly over the past 15 years, while among older men the long-term decline in participation rates has ended and may even have reversed.

Historical information about participation rates can be used to trace out the long-term trend in retirement. Figure 3 shows the trend in the "average" male retirement age if we define that age as the youngest age at which fewer than half the men in the age group remain in the work force. Under this definition, the average male retirement age fell from 74 years in 1910 to 63 years in 1998-99, a drop of about 1.2 years per decade. The tabulations in Figure 3 also indicate, however, that the trend toward earlier male retirement has recently slowed and may even have ceased.

The decline in the average retirement age has occurred in an environment of rising life expectancy among older Americans, especially in the period since 1940. Falling mortality rates among the elderly added almost four years to the expected life span of a 65-year-old man and more than 5½ years to the life expectancy of a 65-year-old woman after 1940. Since expected male life spans increased about 0.8 years per decade during a period in which the retirement age dropped 1.2 years per decade, the amount of the male life span devoted to retirement climbed about 2 years per decade, adding almost 12 years to the amount of time men spend in retirement. Retirement now represents a substantial fraction of a typical worker's life. For many workers, retirement will last longer than the period from birth until full-time entry into the job market.

Trends in other rich countries. The long-term trend toward earlier retirement in the United States has been matched – and usually surpassed – by equivalent trends in other rich countries. In a recent survey of the determinants of retirement in rich countries, OECD economists produced estimates of the average retirement age in 24 high-income nations (Blöndal and Scarpetta 1998). They estimated the average age at which men and women withdrew from the active workforce for selected years between 1950 and 1995. Their estimates show that the average retirement age has declined in nearly all of the countries since 1950. In 1950 the average retirement age for men was 65 or higher in almost all the 24 countries. By 1995 the male retirement age had fallen everywhere except Iceland. In most countries the drop in the average retirement age was at least three years. In a quarter of the countries, an average male now leaves the work force before attaining age 60. The drop in the average retirement age of women has been even faster.

As one of the richest OECD countries, the United States might be expected to have one of the lowest retirement ages. Instead, it has one of the highest. In 1950 its average retirement age placed the United States in the middle of the 24 countries surveyed by the OECD. By 1995 it had one of the oldest retirement ages. Only four out of the 24 countries had a higher male retirement age (Iceland, Japan, Norway, and Switzerland), and only five had a higher female retirement age (Iceland, Japan, Norway, Sweden, and Turkey). Figure 4 shows the 1960-1995 trend in average retirement ages in the seven largest OECD economies, separately for men and women. In all seven countries women retire at a younger age than men. (The male-female gap in retirement ages averaged 2½ years in 1995.) And in all seven countries the average retirement age of both men and women has fallen over time. But the decline has been smaller in the United States and especially in Japan than in the other five countries.

Some of the recent divergence in retirement trends is due to differences in the state of the overall job market. The United States and Japan maintained much lower unemployment rates than the other five countries through most of the 1990s. The tighter labor markets in those two countries probably encouraged older workers to remain employed longer than they would have if the unemployment rate approached European levels. It is also likely, however, that cross-country differences in old-age and disability pensions, unemployment benefits, and health insurance coverage played important roles in keeping older American and Japanese workers in the labor force (Gruber and Wise 1999).

The retirement-age trends displayed in Figure 4 obviously have different implications for a nation depending on whether its working-age population is growing or shrinking. The extra burden implied by an earlier retirement age is easier to bear if the working-age population is expanding rapidly, either as a result of natural population increase or immigration. In this respect Canada and the United States enjoy a significant advantage over the other five countries. High immigration and moderate fertility rates ensure substantial labor force growth in North America over the next few decades, even if U.S. and Canadian retirement ages should continue to fall. Germany, Italy, and Japan face much less favorable prospects. Fertility in all three countries is extremely low, and immigration into Japan is negligible. The three countries face a future in which their active working populations will decline, even if the average retirement age remains unchanged (Bosworth and Burtless 1998). If the average age at retirement continues to decline, these countries will face even heavier burdens in supporting their growing elderly populations.

Explaining the trends

Research by economists and others has shed valuable light on the evolution of retirement in the United States. Most of the early research on American retirement trends was conducted by analysts in the Social Security Administration using survey information from retired workers receiving Social Security benefits or workers who had recently retired (Quinn et al. 1990, pp. 43-53; Quinn 1991, pp. 119-23). In the earliest surveys of new retirees an overwhelming majority of male respondents said they retired because they were laid off by their last employer or were in such poor health that further work was unappealing or impossible. In the 1940s and early 1950s, fewer than 5 percent of new retirees reported leaving work because of a wish to retire or enjoy more leisure. About 90 percent left because of poor health or a layoff. These explanations for retirement dominated survey responses and the research literature from the 1940s through the early 1970s. Only a very small percentage of retired men reported leaving work because they wanted to retire. An early analyst suggested that "most old people work as long as they can and retire only because they are forced to do so... [O]nly a small proportion of old people leave the labor market for good unless they have to" (Quinn 1991, pp.120).

In recent surveys of new Social Security beneficiaries, a larger percentage of pensioners reports leaving work because of a desire to enjoy additional leisure or to retire. By the early 1980s, the desire to leave work explained nearly half of all retirements among men 65 or older, while poor health accounted for only a little over a fifth and involuntary layoff about 15 percent of retirements. The proportion of workers who say they have retired for purely voluntary reasons is plainly on the increase.

Many people will accept these responses at face value, but there are reasons to be skeptical of the story they tell. From 1940 through the early 1970s, well over a third of respondents explained their entry into retirement as the result of involuntary job loss. While this explanation might seem plausible, labor economists recognize that millions of workers lose their jobs each year without choosing to retire. The overwhelming majority of workers who state that job loss was the reason for their retirement lost several jobs earlier in their careers, but on no previous occasion did their layoffs cause them to permanently exit the labor force. When forced into unemployment at younger ages, these same workers looked for another job and eventually found one. It is natural to ask why job loss pushed them into retirement on this one occasion but not on the others.

Even the explanation of "poor health" should be treated with caution. Social Security beneficiaries may account for their retirement with the explanation that bad health left them no alternative, but it seems reasonable to ask whether their decision to retire would have been different if Social Security or other pensions were unavailable. In the early post-war era some retirees may have explained their employment status in terms of job loss or bad health because the desire for more leisure was not yet considered an acceptable reason to be without a job. As retirement has come to be considered a normal and even desirable part of life, workers may feel less reason to describe their joblessness as involuntary.

Wealth, health, and the physical demands of work. However we interpret the survey responses of people who collect pensions, it should be plain the long-term trend toward earlier male retirement has had an important *voluntary* component. The trend in survey responses suggests this is true, and a growing body of research evidence also supports the conclusion. The simplest and probably most powerful explanation for earlier retirement is rising wealth. The United States and other industrialized countries have grown richer over time. Real per capita GDP in the United States has more than doubled since 1960, increasing about 2 percent a year. Some of this increased wealth has been used to purchase more leisure. Americans stay in school longer than they once did, enter the workforce later, work fewer hours per year, and leave the labor force earlier.

For many of today's retired workers, the increases in wealth flowing from greater national prosperity have been augmented by windfall gains from two sources – higher prices for the houses they own and generous benefits from Social Security and Medicare. Because the Social Security system has historically been very generous, most generations retiring up to the present have received larger pensions than their contributions alone could have paid for if the contributions had been invested in safe assets. Workers who retired under Social Security before the mid-1980s received pensions well in excess of the benefits they would have received if Social Security offered normal returns on their contributions (Leimer 1994; Geanakopolos et al. 1998). Retired Americans continue to receive Medicare benefits that are vastly larger than those that could be financed solely out of their contributions and the interest earnings on those contributions. This fact is well known to students of social insurance, who recognize that most early contributors to a pay-as-you-go retirement system obtain exceptional returns on their contributions. The exceptional returns on Social Security and Medicare taxes, like those on owner-occupied homes, have increased the amount of consumption that older Americans can afford. One way workers have used these windfall gains is to retire at a younger age.

While some researchers have attributed most of the post-war decline in male labor force participation to the introduction and liberalization of Social Security, most specialists think the impact on retirement has been considerably smaller. Because of the long-term rise in productivity, workers are much wealthier today than they were at the beginning of the twentieth century. This would have led workers to retire earlier than previous generations, even in the absence of Social Security and Medicare. Social Security, Medicare, and employer-sponsored retirement plans were established and expanded in part to help workers achieve the goal of living comfortably without work in old age. If these programs had not be developed, it is likely that workers and employers would have found other ways to achieve the same goal.

Of all the explanations advanced for earlier retirement, two of the least persuasive are declining health and the changing physical requirements of work. While nearly all good retirement studies find that health plays an important role in the timing of retirement, there is no convincing evidence that the health of 60-year-olds or 65-year-olds was declining over the period in which older Americans' labor force participation rates were falling. Declining mortality rates as well as recent evidence about the trend in the physical disabilities of the aged suggest instead that the health of Americans is improving, at least in early old age. Moreover, analyses of the growth of different kinds of occupations and in their physical requirements imply that the physical demands of work are now easier to meet than they were in the past. A much smaller proportion of jobs requires strenuous physical effort; a larger percentage requires only moderate or light physical exertion (Manton and Stollard 1994; Baily 1987). Of course, within every generation there will be workers who are in poor health and who work in physically demanding jobs. These workers will be among the first to retire. But it seems unlikely that general health deterioration or widespread increases in the physical demands of employment can explain the general tendency for recent generations to retire earlier than workers in the past.

Financial incentives. Besides increasing most current retirees' lifetime wealth, the Social Security system also affects the financial attractiveness of remaining at work. Most workers can choose to collect Social Security starting at age 62, and many do. The effect of Social Security on retirement behavior before age 62 depends on the Social Security tax and on the benefit formula that links eventual monthly pensions to a worker's past covered earnings. Employers and workers pay a combined tax equal to 12.4 percent of wages into the system. The tax thus reduces workers' wages by about 12 percent in comparison with the wages they would earn if the program did not exist. On the other hand, contributions allow a worker to earn credits toward a Social Security pension. The pension entitlement goes up as the worker's covered lifetime wages increase. Whether the increase in the pension entitlement is large enough to compensate a worker for his extra contributions is an empirical question. Low-wage workers typically receive favorable treatment under the Social Security benefit formula, so they often receive a generous return on their extra contributions. High-wage workers usually receive lower returns. For any worker who is less than 62 years old, Social Security affects the marginal return from working by reducing net current pay by about 12 percent and increasing the present value of future Social Security pensions. Whether this increases or reduces the willingness of a worker to continue working depends on the exact amount of the future pension increase (which depends on the worker's expected longevity) and on the worker's feelings about the relative value of current versus future income and the attractiveness of immediate retirement.

Starting at age 62 Social Security has a different kind of effect on the retirement decision. When a worker delays receipt of retirement benefits by working another year after the earliest age of eligibility, two things happen, one good and one bad. The bad news is that the worker passes up the chance to collect a Social Security check. The good news is that future retirement benefits will be higher because average lifetime earnings are recalculated and because the monthly pension check is increased for every month of delay in asking for benefits. If a worker is entitled to a $500-per-month pension, for example, she sacrifices $500 in retirement income every month she postpones retirement past age 62. If her regular monthly pay is $10,000, this represents a small sacrifice. But if her usual pay is $1,000, the sacrifice amounts to half her wage. Between the ages of 62 and 64 the Social Security formula offers average workers a fair compensation for giving up a year's benefits. Monthly benefits are adjusted upwards about 8 percent for each year's delay in claiming them. For workers with average life expectancy and a moderate rate of time preference, this adjustment is just large enough so that the sacrifice of a year's benefits is compensated by eligibility for a higher pension in the future. After age 65, however, the benefit formula has historically been less generous toward delayed retirement. Postponement of retirement after that age was not fairly compensated by increases in the monthly pension. For most workers this is true even taking account of the fact that the basic pension calculation gives them extra credit for their most recent wages.[3] In essence, the Social Security formula forces workers who delay retirement after 65 to accept a cut in the lifetime value of their Social Security payments. This is a clear inducement to retire no later than age 65.

It is worth noting that almost no workers are "average." A benefit calculation rule that is age-neutral or actuarially fair on average can still provide strong financial incentives to retire for a worker who has below-average life expectancy. This worker may not expect to live long enough for the future benefit increase to make up for the benefits he gives up by delaying retirement for one more year. Similarly, a worker who applies a high discount rate when evaluating future benefits may not be impressed that the pension adjustment is "fair" for an average worker. For workers who are impatient to consume, an 8-percent hike in benefits starting one year from today may not be enough to compensate for the loss of twelve monthly benefit checks over the next year. Even an actuarially fair pension adjustment might be insufficient to persuade workers who are tired of their jobs to delay retirement.

One reason that many people must retire in order to collect a Social Security check is that the program imposes an earnings test in calculating the annual pension. Workers who are between 62 and 64 and who earn more than $10,800 a year lose $1 in annual benefits for every $2 in earnings they receive in excess of $10,800. Workers between 65 and 69 lose $1 in benefits for every $3 in annual earnings in excess of $17,000. (Pensioners age 70 and older do not face an earnings test.) At one time the earnings limits were much lower, discouraging pensioners from work and possibly encouraging them to postpone claiming a pension until they were confident their earnings would remain low.

Many employer-sponsored pension plans are structured similarly to Social Security pensions. Workers who are covered under an old-fashioned defined-benefit plan earn pension credits for as long as they work for the employer that sponsors the plan (sometimes up to a maximum number of years). The longer they work under the plan, the higher their monthly pension. Most defined-benefit plans are structured to encourage workers to remain with the employer for a minimal period – say, 10 years – or until a critical age – say, age 55. Workers who stay for shorter periods may receive very little under the plan. On the other hand, workers who stay in the job too long may see the value of their pension accumulation shrink. This would happen if the plan offered benefits to workers starting at age 55 but then failed to significantly increase the monthly benefit for workers who delayed retirement after age 55. If a 55-year-old worker can collect a monthly pension of $1,000 when he retires immediately and a monthly check of $1,001 if he delays his retirement one year, he will clearly lose a substantial amount of lifetime benefits – nearly $12,000 – for each year he postpones receipt. The worker essentially suffers a pay cut when he reaches age 55, and the cut is equal to the loss in lifetime benefits he suffers by postponing retirement. Such a pay cut might seem illegal under U.S. age discrimination laws, but it is perfectly legal as long as the pay cut is reflected in reduced lifetime pensions rather than reduced money wages. Many employers find this kind of pension formula to be an effective prod in pushing workers into early retirement.

There is one important difference between Social Security and employer-sponsored defined-benefit pensions. Social Security imposes an earnings test on income received from *all* employment, including self-employment. Employer-sponsored pensions may impose an even tougher earnings test, but the test applies only to earnings received from the sponsoring employer or group of employers. Workers who wish to claim a pension may be forced to leave the job on which they earned the pension, but they are not forced to leave work altogether. Nevertheless, the effects of employer-sponsored pensions on retirement may be similar to those of Social Security, because many older workers find it hard to get attractive job offers after they have retired from their career jobs.

This explanation of the financial incentives in Social Security and employer-sponsored pensions sheds some light on the retirement trends discussed earlier. Social Security is now the main source of cash income of households headed by someone 65 or older. The program provides slightly more than 40 percent of the total cash income received by the aged. Among aged households in the bottom 60 percent of the elderly income distribution, Social Security provides over three-quarters of cash income. Until 1941, Social Security provided no income at all to the aged. Today the program replaces about 42 percent of the final wage earned by a full-career single worker who earns the average wage and claims a pension at age 65. If the worker has a non-working dependent spouse, the benefit replaces 63 percent of the worker's final wage. Benefits are clearly large enough so they can be economically significant in influencing the choice of retirement age.

The distributions of male retirement ages in 1940, 1970, and 1998-99 are plotted in Figure 5. The chart shows the percentage of men leaving the labor force at each age from 56 to 72, computed as a fraction of the men in the labor force at age 55.[4] The calculations are based on the data displayed in Figure 1. Not surprisingly, the retirement-age distributions for 1970 and especially for 1998-99 are skewed toward the left. Labor force withdrawal occurred at earlier ages in those years than it did in 1940. Both the 1970 and 1998-99 distributions show evidence of clustering in retirement at particular ages. In 1970 the peak rate of retirement occurred at age 65; by 1998-99 the peak occurred at age 62. There are peaks in the distribution of retirements in

1940 at ages 65 and 70, but these are far lower than the peaks in 1970 and 1998-99 when the timing of retirements was influenced by Social Security.

Our description of the financial incentives in Social Security suggests a simple explanation for the clustering of retirements at ages 62 and 65, at least in years after 1940. Workers who continued to work beyond age 65 give up Social Security benefits for which they were not fairly compensated. This feature of the benefit formula clearly encourages retirement at age 65. The clustering of retirements at age 62 can be explained using similar logic. Starting in 1961, age 62 became the earliest age at which men could claim a Social Security pension. Before 1961 there was no evidence of clustering in retirements at age 62, but by 1970 retirement was more common at 62 than at any other age except 65. By the mid-1990s, age 62 was by a wide margin the most popular age of retirement. In principle, the Social Security formula fairly compensates "average" workers if they delay claiming a pension past age 62. As we have seen, however, a worker with a high rate of time preference or short life expectancy might not regard the compensation as fair. In that case, we should expect many workers to prefer retiring at age 62 rather than a later age.

Of course, the clustering of retirements at ages 62 and 65 may be due to factors other than Social Security. It is hard to believe, however, that health or work opportunities decline abruptly at particular ages. Another explanation is that some workers were affected by mandatory retirement rules. This explanation may have been valid in 1940 and 1970, when mandatory retirement rules covered up to one-half of American workers, but it is not persuasive today. Amendments to the Age Discrimination in Employment Act passed in 1986 prohibit employers from dismissing workers solely on account of their age.

The simplest alternative explanation for the clustering of retirement ages is that workers are affected by employer-sponsored pension plans. But many older workers are not covered by an employer plan. The Current Population Surveys suggest that employer-sponsored pensions do not provide a large percentage of income to older Americans, except in more affluent households. But for those workers who are covered by a private pension plan, the financial incentives in the plan may provide powerful incentives for workers to leave their career jobs at a particular age.

Health insurance. Unlike most other industrialized countries, the United States does not provide universal health insurance to its citizens. Instead, most working-age Americans receive health insurance coverage as part of an employer's compensation package. In 1995, 72 percent of American workers between 18 and 64 had health insurance coverage under an employer-based plan, either through their own employer or through the employer of another family member. Some workers obtain insurance through publicly provided Medicaid or privately purchased health plans, but 18 percent of American workers were left uninsured. Some employers offer continuing health insurance to their workers, even after they leave the firm. In 1995, of those full-time employees in medium and large firms who had health insurance on their jobs, 46 percent also had retiree health coverage before age 65, and 41 percent had retiree coverage at ages 65 and older. The percentage of the labor force employed by firms offering such protection is shrinking, and many employers now require their retired workers to pay for more of the cost of the plans (EBRI 1997a).

The nation's peculiar health insurance system provides a complicated set of incentives for retirement. Health insurance is particularly important for workers who are past middle age but not yet eligible for Medicare, because many of them face high risk of incurring heavy medical expenses. Workers with health insurance on the job who would lose it if they retire have an obvious incentive to remain on the job, at least until age 65 when they become eligible for Medicare. Those with post-retirement health benefits have less incentive to remain employed, although how much less depends on how the insurance costs after retirement are shared between the employee and employer.

As with Social Security and private pensions, there is considerable evidence that health insurance coverage before and after retirement has an important influence on individual retirement decisions. Alan Gustman and Thomas Steinmeier find, for example, that the effects of insurance plans are similar in nature to those of employer-sponsored pension plans (Gustman and Steinmeier 1994). If workers can become eligible for retiree health benefits only after a delay, the availability of the plan tends to delay workers' retirements until they gain eligibility. After eligibility has been achieved, the availability of retiree health benefits encourages earlier retirement than would occur if no benefits were offered. Quinn estimates that men and women in career jobs in 1992 were 8 to 10 percentage points less likely to leave their jobs over the next four years if they would lose health insurance coverage by doing so (Quinn 1999b). Inferring the overall effect of health insurance incentives on retirement patterns is tricky, however. A number of components of employee compensation, including wage rates, pension coverage, health insurance, and retiree health benefits, tend to be highly correlated with one another. This makes it difficult to distinguish statistically between the separate effects of each component of compensation. Nonetheless, the rising importance of health insurance coverage to older Americans suggests that the evolution of the public and private health insurance system may have had a sizable impact on retirement patterns.

The change in retirement trends after 1985. There are two types of explanation for the slowdown or reversal of retirement trends in recent years. One hypothesis is that permanent changes in the retirement environment have encouraged additional work by older Americans. Under this conjecture, the long-term trend toward earlier retirement is over. Another view is that temporary cyclical factors are responsible for a pause in the historical retirement trend. When these cyclical factors are behind us, the historical trend toward earlier retirement will resume. Although it will be many years before we can be sure of the relative importance of these explanations, it is possible to assess some of the permanent and temporary factors that have influenced recent retirement trends.

The most important cyclical factor affecting retirement is the state of the economy. The American economy is currently growing strongly, and the unemployment rate is near a 30-year low. The second half of the 1980s and the 1990s saw lengthy economic expansions and strong employment growth. There was only one recession after 1985. These factors made it easier for workers to find jobs when they were dismissed and more likely to find the terms and conditions of employment that they desire. In contrast, economic growth was much less even in the 15 years after 1970. The period saw three recessions. Two of the recessions – in 1974-75 and 1981-82 – were the worst of the post-war era. Weak labor demand discourages jobless workers from persisting in their job search. Strong demand creates employment options for older workers who want to keep working.

Although we think a strong economy has contributed to the recent rise in older Americans' participation rates, it is probably not a big part of the story. The economy also grew strongly and unemployment reached very low levels in the 1960s, yet older men's labor force participation rates fell in the decade and older women's participation rates changed very little (see Table 1). In earlier work, Quinn estimated the impact of the business cycle on older workers' participation rates, and found that changes in the overall unemployment rate account for a relatively small proportion of the change in participation trends since 1985 (Quinn 1999b).

Most of the change in participation trends since 1985 is probably due to factors other than the cyclical movement in economy-wide unemployment.

It is easier to point to factors in the retirement environment that have permanently changed in a way that encourages later withdrawal from the job market. One important change is that the nation's main pension program, Social Security, is no longer growing more generous. Workers who retired between 1950 and 1980 retired in an environment in which Social Security benefits were rising, both absolutely and in relation to the average earnings of typical American workers. Most workers received pensions that were higher than those they would have obtained if their Social Security contributions had been invested in safe assets. The maturation of the Social Security program meant that fewer workers who retired after 1985 received windfalls from the program. The Social Security amendments of 1977 and 1983 brought an end to a four-decade expansion and liberalization of benefits. In fact, the amendments trimmed retirement benefits modestly in order to keep the program solvent.

Congress has changed Social Security rules and the pension formula to make work late in life more attractive. The amount of income a recipient can earn without losing any Social Security benefits has been increased, and the benefit loss for each dollar earned over the exempt amount has been reduced (from 50 to 33 cents) for pensioners between 65 and 69. In the 1977 and 1983 Social Security amendments, Congress also increased the reward that workers receive for delaying initial benefit receipt past the normal retirement age (NRA). Instead of penalizing work after the NRA, Social Security is becoming more age-neutral. When this formula change is fully implemented, for workers attaining age 62 after 2004, the adjustment for delayed benefit receipt will be approximately fair for retirements up through age 70. It is nearly so today. (At age 70 workers receive full pensions regardless of the amount they earn.) There will be no retirement penalty for delaying retirement beyond the normal retirement age.

Important changes have also occurred in the private sector. There has been a sharp increase in the relative importance of defined-contribution pension plans and a continuing decline in the importance of old-fashioned defined-benefit plans. Defined-contribution plans are age-neutral by design, and therefore they have none of the age-specific work disincentives that are common in traditional defined-benefit plans. As a growing percentage of workers reaches retirement age under defined-contribution plans, there will be less reason for workers to leave their jobs to avoid a loss in lifetime retirement benefits.

Some changes in the environment are the result of policy initiatives aimed specifically at encouraging more work at older ages. For example, mandatory retirement has been nearly eliminated in the United States. In the early 1970s about half of all American workers were covered by mandatory retirement provisions that required them to leave their jobs no later than a particular age, usually age 65. In 1978 the earliest legal age of mandatory retirement was raised from 65 to 70, and in 1986 mandatory retirement provisions were outlawed altogether for the vast majority of workers. The increase and eventual elimination of mandatory retirement ages not only increased the options open to older employees who wanted to remain on their jobs, but also sent an important message to Americans about the appropriate age to retire.

This message was reinforced by a provision of the 1983 Social Security amendments that is gradually raising the normal retirement age in Social Security from 65 to 67. The higher NRA will become fully effective for workers who reach age 62 in 2022. So far as we know, the United States was the first industrial nation to pass a law lifting the retirement age under its main public pension program. Although few workers may be aware of the higher retirement age, many are affected by it already. Workers reaching age 62 in 2000 face a normal retirement age of 65 years and 2 months, which means that they will qualify for age-62 pensions that are 1 percent smaller than age-62 benefits under the traditional NRA. The delay in the eligibility age for unreduced pensions has an effect on benefit levels that is almost identical to across-the-board benefit cuts.

These changes in the retirement environment suggest that the future will not look like the past. The relative attractiveness of work and retirement at older ages has been altered in favor of work, though the changes may have produced only modest effects so far. The break in the early retirement trend that occurred in the mid-1980s suggests that changes in the retirement environment are having an impact in the expected direction.

Should we encourage later retirement?

Even if the trend toward earlier retirement has stopped, it is natural to ask whether the nation should take additional steps to encourage later retirement. One reason often mentioned to induce later retirement is concern over public finances. Social Security is the largest item in the federal budget. In 1995 Social Security outlays represented 4.6 percent of GDP and a little less than 22 percent of overall federal spending. After the income tax, the program is the most

298

important source of federal tax revenues. Over the next 10 to 15 years the financial outlook for Social Security is relatively secure, even under pessimistic assumptions about the state of the economy. When the baby boom generation reaches retirement age in the second decade of the next century, however, benefit payments will begin to climb much faster than tax revenue. Outlays will exceed taxes and will eventually exceed tax revenues plus interest payments earned by the Trust Funds. Under the intermediate assumptions of the Social Security Trustees, the Trust Funds will begin to shrink. Unless benefits are trimmed or tax rates increased, the Trust Funds will eventually fall to zero, making it impossible under current law to make timely benefit payments. The financial condition of the Medicare program is more perilous than that of Social Security. The reserves of the system are smaller, and they will be depleted much sooner than the OASDI Trust Funds.

Restoring both Medicare and Social Security to long-term solvency will be costly. The federal budgetary cost of achieving solvency would obviously be smaller if workers' eligibility for benefits under the two programs were delayed. In the remainder of this paper we focus on options to encourage later retirement under the Social Security program.

The solvency of Social Security, like that of any pension program, depends on four crucial elements: (1) the contribution rate imposed on workers and their employers; (2) the pension fund's rate of return on its investments; (3) the age of eligibility for pensions; and (4) the average monthly pension paid to retirees. The first two elements determine the annual amount of funds flowing into the system; the last two determine the annual amount flowing *out* of the system. Each of the four elements must be carefully calibrated to ensure that benefit promises are matched by expected future revenues. If a pension program is exactly solvent and one of the four elements changes, some adjustment in the other three elements may be necessary to restore the solvency of the program. For example, if the rate of return on pension fund investments falls, it will be necessary to increase the contribution rate, delay the age of eligibility for pensions, or lower monthly pensions in order to restore the pension program to solvency.

Improvements in life expectancy increase the funding requirements of a pension plan. If contributors live one additional year in retirement, the plan must find enough extra resources to finance the added benefit payments. To keep the pension system solvent, this requires higher contributions to the program, a higher rate of return on investments, a delay in the retirement age, or a reduction in monthly benefits. It is worth emphasizing that this is true for every type of pension plan whether public or private. If Social Security had never been established, increases in American life spans over the past half century would have required private pension plans to increase their contribution rates, find investments that yield higher rates of return, delay the age of eligibility for pensions, or reduce monthly pension payments.

A large part of Social Security's long-term funding problem arises because of good news about longevity.[5] Americans now live longer than their parents and grandparents did. Their children and grandchildren can be expected to live longer than we do. The improvements in longevity mean that living Americans will survive much longer past age 65 than was true when Social Security was established in the Great Depression. The longevity increases provide the equivalent of a benefit increase to Social Security recipients. The benefit increase must be paid for if the system is to remain solvent.

Political unpopularity. While it might seem logical to raise the retirement age in Social Security to reflect improvements in longevity, that logic has so far escaped the general public. American voters and workers routinely reject the idea of a higher retirement age when it is suggested as a solution to Social Security's problems. Lawrence Jacobs and Robert Shapiro recently summarized the findings of 18 polls that asked Americans about their attitudes toward an increase in the retirement age (Jacobs and Shapiro 1998, pp. 381-384). The polls were conducted over a twenty-year period ending in 1997, and each poll was administered to at least 750 respondents. With rare exceptions, solid majorities of respondents reject any proposed hike in the retirement age. The size of the majority opposing a higher retirement age was higher in the 1990s than it was in the 1980s. Political leaders apparently take their cue from the polling numbers. Nearly all of the presidential candidates in both political parties have expressed strong opposition to the idea of a higher Social Security retirement age.[6]

Americans' hostility to a higher retirement age does not provide much guidance to policymakers, however. Solid majorities also oppose other basic steps that would solve Social Security's long-term funding problem. Most poll respondents are against higher payroll taxes, lower monthly benefits, and investment of Social Security reserves in stocks, where they would earn a higher return (Jacobs and Shapiro 1998; EBRI 1997c, pp. 11). Many workers' may oppose a higher retirement age in Social Security because they intend or at least hope to retire several years before attaining the *early* eligibility age for Social Security benefits. When asked in an EBRI poll when they hope to start retirement, one-third of active workers answered "age 55 or younger." When asked when they actually *expect* to retire, however, only 15 percent thought their retirements would occur before age 56 (EBRI 1997b, Chart 1). If the Social Security retirement age were increased, early retirement would become a less affordable dream.

Other options. There is no compelling reason to raise either the Social Security retirement age or the average retirement age, of course. If Americans' incomes continue to grow 1 or 2 percent a year, some fraction of the increase can be used to finance comfortable incomes during longer spells of retirement. This means, however, that more of the income earned by active workers must be set aside to pay for longer retirements. This could take the form of higher payroll or income taxes to pay for Social Security benefits to the currently retired or higher personal saving to make up for the loss of monthly Social Security benefits if Social Security pensions are trimmed to preserve solvency. There is some evidence that workers understand this trade-off. When forced to choose between the option of making larger contributions to pay for retirement or accepting smaller pensions after they retire, most workers opt to make larger contributions. By a 2-to-1 majority, workers favor higher payroll taxes over reduced Social Security pensions (EBRI 1997b, Chart 6). This suggests a simple conclusion: Americans would rather set aside more of their wages for retirement than postpone their retirement.

Workers can offset the effect of higher retirement contributions by working longer hours during their prime working years. There is some evidence this is occurring. American work patterns have changed slowly but significantly over the past generation. Since the 1960s three major trends have affected adults' use of time. Women have joined the paid work force in record numbers; men have retired from their jobs at younger ages; and both men and women have devoted more years to formal schooling. The effects of these trends on average work effort can be seen in Figure 6, which shows changes in weekly hours of paid work between 1968 and 1998. The darker bars show average hours on a job during the second week of March 1968; the lighter bars, average hours exactly 30 years later in March 1998. The weekly average is calculated as the total hours of work during the survey week divided by the total number of men and women in the indicated age group. People who do not work are included in these estimates. (The estimates would show higher average hours if they reflected the work effort only of people who held jobs.)

In spite of the trend toward earlier male retirement since 1968, the figure shows a sizable jump in the total amount of time that Americans spend at work. The increase in hours was driven almost entirely by the surge in women's employment. The CPS interviews show only a small change in average weekly hours among men and women who actually hold a job. Averaging across all ages, women worked 49 percent more hours in March 1998 than they did in March 1968 (20.3 hours a week in 1968 versus 13.6 hours in 1968). The rise was due to a 45 percent jump in the fraction of women holding jobs. Partly offsetting the rise in women's employment was the dip in men's paid work. Most of the drop occurred as a result of sinking employment among men past age 54. Across all age groups, the male employment rate slid 6 percentage points (or 8 percent) between 1968 and 1998, but it fell 15 percentage points among men between 55 and 64 and 9 points among men past 64.

The combined effects of the shifts in male and female work patterns are displayed Figure 6. Averaging the trends of both men and women, we see that hours spent on the job increased for people 18 to 54 years old and declined for people past age 54. Older Americans clearly enjoyed more free time in 1998 than their counterparts in 1968, mainly because of earlier male retirement. For adults between 25 and 54, however, the estimates imply that paid employment consumes a much bigger percentage of available time. The employment rate of people in their prime working years jumped 11 percentage points – almost 17 percent – between March 1968 and March 1998, boosting the average amount of time spent in jobs from 28 hours to 32 hours a week. This increase is equivalent to five extra 40-hour work weeks a year for adults between 25 and 54. In short, Americans are working longer hours between 25 and 54. The increase in hours should help them pay for shorter hours and longer retirements when they are older than 55.

How could we encourage later retirement?

Assuming that it is desirable to do so, how might we encourage American workers to delay their retirements further? In this section we consider some alternatives and discuss their likely impact on future trends in the average retirement age.

Changing the incentives in Social Security. Since the eligibility age for pensions is one of the main features of Social Security affecting its solvency, it is sensible to consider adjustments in the eligibility age to help restore the system's financing. One possibility is to accelerate the increase in the NRA already scheduled under present law. Instead of phasing in the increase over 23 years (with a 12-year hiatus between the change from 65 to 66 and the change from 66 to 67), Congress could phase in the NRA change over just 12 years. This would mean that the higher NRA will be fully implemented for workers reaching age 62 in 2011, rather than 2022.

A second possibility is to increase the NRA automatically in line with increases in life expectancy after 65. A majority of members of the 1994-96 Social Security Advisory Council proposed increasing the NRA as necessary after 2011 to maintain a constant ratio of retirement years to potential years of work. "Retirement years" is defined as life expectancy at the NRA, and "potential years of work" as the number of years from age 20 to the NRA. Under the Social Security Trustees' intermediate assumptions, this proposal would push up the NRA to age 70 by about 2080. The Social Security Actuary estimates that the combination of accelerating the NRA increase and then increasing the NRA in line with longevity improvements eliminates nearly one-quarter of Social Security's long-term funding gap.

Lifting the NRA while leaving the early eligibility age (EEA) unchanged produces almost exactly the same effect on retired workers' Social Security benefits as a proportional reduction in the full pension (usually referred to as the "primary insurance amount" or PIA). Even though most people describe an increase in the normal retirement age as a "delay" in the retirement age, it is in fact closer to a reduction in the monthly benefit amount. Workers can still obtain pensions at the same age as before, but their monthly pensions are smaller, no matter what age they choose.

There are some important *noneconomic* differences between raising the NRA and cutting the full Social Security pension, however. First, increasing the NRA signals to workers that the same monthly benefit can be obtained by postponing retirement, which may encourage some workers to delay retirement rather than accept a lower pension. Sponsors of employer pension plans might also be induced to modify their plans to encourage delayed pension acceptance if the Social Security NRA were increased. Second, in light of the well-known improvements in life expectancy, American workers might find increases in the retirement age to be more understandable and fairer than equivalent reductions in full pensions. By increasing the retirement age rather than reducing full pensions, Congress conveys the message that the benefit level is appropriate, but the timing is not – workers ought to postpone their retirements.

Congress might increase the early eligibility age (EEA) at the same time and at the same pace as it increases the NRA. An increase in the EEA is fundamentally different from an increase in the NRA. If the EEA is increased above age 62, 62-year-old workers will be prevented from obtaining old-age pensions. Under current law they can collect reduced old-age pensions or they can apply for Disability Insurance (DI) pensions. When the possibility of obtaining old-age pensions is eliminated, some 62-year-olds who otherwise would have received old-age pensions will apply for DI. This will increase Social Security administrative costs, because eligibility is much more expensive to determine in the DI program. It may also impose serious hardship on workers whose DI applications are denied.

These consequences of increasing the early eligibility age make many people reluctant to tamper with it. Many policymakers are more uneasy about a reform that denies benefits completely to an identifiable class of people than they are about one that reduces benefits modestly to a much wider population. It is important to recognize why Social Security has an early eligibility age, however. If workers could apply for benefits as soon as they accumulated enough earnings credits, some low-income workers would be tempted to apply for benefits in their late 50s or even their late 40s. But their monthly benefits would be very low, because early pensions are reduced below the full pension in proportion to the number of months between the age a worker claims benefits and the NRA. The low level of the initial pension might not represent a problem for a worker who is 50 or 60 years old and can supplement monthly pensions with modest wages or an employer-sponsored pension. But it could cause serious hardship when a worker reaches age 68 or 70 and finds she is no longer able to work and the company pension no longer covers the cost of groceries and the monthly rent. The existence of the early entitlement age prevents short-sighted workers from applying for pensions that will be too small to support them throughout a long retirement.

When the NRA eventually reaches 67, workers claiming early pensions at age 62 will receive 70 percent of a full pension – a 30 percent reduction below the full pension rather than the current 20 percent reduction. If the NRA were eventually increased to 70 and the early eligibility age remained unchanged, workers claiming pensions at age 62 would receive monthly benefits as low as 52 percent of a full pension – probably too little to live on for a low-wage worker with few other sources of income. If the NRA is increased above 67, it seems sensible to increase the early eligibility age as well. Since Social Security is intended to assure a basic floor of support for retired Americans, it seems perverse to allow full-career workers to claim benefits so early that their monthly benefit will be too low to live on. This implies that the early eligibility age must eventually be raised above 62 if the NRA rises much above age 67. In order to implement this reform in a humane way, Congress might consider liberalizing eligibility requirements for Disability Insurance benefits starting at age 62. People who have worked in physically demanding occupations and are in impaired health could be given access to benefits that permit them to retire with a decent standard of living, even if they do not meet the strict standard for health impairment that is used to evaluate DI applications today.

Effects of changing the NRA and EEA on actual retirement ages. It is natural to ask whether increasing the early and normal retirement ages would have much effect on when workers actually retire. Almost all researchers who have examined this question agree that such reforms would tend to increase the average age at retirement, though the effect may not be large. This conclusion was reached in a great majority of economists' studies conducted in the 1980s and early 1990s. Most studies found that even big changes in Social Security would cause only small changes in the average retirement age. Burtless and Robert Moffitt estimate, for example, that increasing the normal retirement age in Social Security from 65 to 68 would add only a little more than 4 months to the full-time working careers of men who have no disabilities (Burtless and Moffitt 1985).[7]

One way to assess the impact of Social Security reforms is to examine differences in retirement patterns among people who face different incentives because the program has been changed in an unanticipated way. In 1969 and again in 1972 Social Security benefits were increased much faster relative to wages than at any time in the recent past. By 1973 benefits were 20 percent higher than would have been the case if pensions had grown with wages as they did during the 1950s and 1960s. In 1977 Congress passed amendments to the Social Security Act sharply reducing benefits to workers born in 1917 and later years (the "notch" generation) in comparison with benefits available to workers born before 1917. Burtless examined the first episode, and Alan Krueger and J.S. Pishke examined the second (Burtless 1992; Kreuger and Pischke 1992).

Both studies reached an identical conclusion: Major changes in Social Security generosity produced small initial effects on the retirement behavior and labor force participation of older men. Burtless found, for example, that the 20-percent benefit hike between 1969 and 1973 caused only a 2-month reduction in average retirement age of men who were fully covered by the more generous formula. This is equivalent to a reduction in the labor force participation rates of 62-year-old and 65-year-old men of less than 2 percentage points. The effects of the 1977 amendments found by Krueger and Pischke were even smaller.

These findings suggest that an increase in the normal retirement age will probably have only a small effect on the age that male workers withdraw from the work force. It is harder to predict the effects of an increase in the early retirement age because we do not have good enough historical evidence to evaluate the impact of this kind of change. When the earliest age of eligibility for Social Security retirement benefits was decreased from 65 to 62 (in 1956 for women and in 1961 for men), labor force participation rates fell significantly, and much faster than they had previously. The reversal of this policy would likely have a larger impact than the change in the normal retirement age, especially for low wage workers who have no other sources of retirement income except Social Security. The magnitude of the increased labor force participation would depend, in part, on how employer pensions responded to the change in Social Security rules and the extent to which eligibility criteria for DI benefits were loosened.

Employer responses. Some people wonder how employers would respond to changes in the early and normal retirement ages in Social Security. Would firms with defined-benefit pension plans increase their early retirement incentives, to offset the loss of the Social Security incentives, or make their plans more age-neutral? If workers wanted to delay their retirements to become eligible for more generous Social Security pensions, could the economy create enough extra jobs to employ them? Would employers discriminate against older job seekers, making it hard for them to find and keep jobs?

Historical evidence about the job creating capacity of the U.S. market is reassuring. Over the long run, the U.S. labor market seems capable of absorbing large numbers of extra workers without a significant rise in joblessness. From 1964 through 1989, when the baby boom generation reached adulthood and entered the job market, the labor force grew by 50.4 million persons, or slightly more than 2 million new entrants a year. Most of this surge was driven by the jump in U.S. fertility between 1946 and 1964, but part was also due to a growing demand for employment by women, who entered the workforce in record numbers. From 1964 to 1989 the number of Americans holding jobs climbed by 47.7 million, or slightly more than 1.9 million workers a year. In other words, about 95 percent of new job seekers in the period were able to find jobs, though the number of people available for work swelled by two-thirds. The unemployment rate rose only slightly, increasing from 5.0 percent to 5.2 percent.

Many people find it surprising that so many extra job seekers can be absorbed by the labor market. They overlook a basic reality of flexible labor markets like those in the United States. In the long run employers are free to change their product lines and production methods to exploit the availability of a newly abundant type of labor, and they can adjust relative wages in response to the entry and exit of different classes of workers.

In the 1970s, for example, the wages received by younger workers fell in comparison with those earned by older workers, in large measure because younger workers became much more abundant. Faced with a huge increase in the availability of workers who had limited job experience, employers adopted production methods that took advantage of less experienced workers. Restaurant meals were prepared and served by eleventh grade students and high school dropouts rather than by experienced cooks or waiters. Gardening and domestic cleaning were performed by unskilled and semi-skilled employees rather than by homeowners themselves. In the end, 95 percent of new job seekers were successful in finding jobs. Of course, many of the new jobs were not particularly well paid. The huge increase in the abundance of less experienced workers is one reason that pay in many jobs fell.

If older workers were forced to wait for two or three extra years for full Social Security retirement benefits to begin, many would choose to remain in their career jobs for a few months or years longer than workers presently do. Older workers who lose their jobs would try harder and more persistently to find new jobs. The jobs that many find would pay lower wages than the jobs they previously held, as is the case for most workers who leave career jobs today. The availability of increased numbers of older workers would almost certainly depress the relative wages of aged job seekers. But low U.S. fertility means the future labor force will grow slowly, placing some pressure on employers to retain older workers and make jobs attractive to older job seekers.

Although some observers are pessimistic about the willingness of employers to accommodate the special needs of an aged workforce, such pessimism may be misplaced. Employers have created millions of part-time jobs to accommodate the needs of students and mothers who are only available to work short weekly hours. People who work on part-time schedules pay a price for short hours in terms of low weekly earnings and lost fringe benefits, but they accept these jobs nonetheless. Comparable accommodations could be made for the special needs of older workers. Many older workers who want jobs to tide them over between the time their career jobs end and eligibility for full Social Security pensions will be able to find suitable employment.

Other policies. As noted above, Social Security rules are moving toward age-neutrality. Employer pension coverage is shifting toward defined-contribution plans, which have none of the age-specific retirement incentives present in traditional defined-benefit plans. Mandatory retirement has been eliminated for the vast majority of American workers, and equal employment opportunity laws forbid employment discrimination based on age. Federal policies have been enlightened in these areas and are partly responsible for the changes in men's and women's retirement patterns over the past 15 years. Are there other policies that would improve the employment prospects of older Americans? Several come to mind:

♦ Permit workers aged 65 or older to opt out of additional Social Security contributions. If this option were chosen, workers would also forego the increases in future benefits that these earnings would have caused. A variant of the same idea would be to exempt earnings up to some dollar limit from F.I.C.A contributions as well as Social Security benefit recalculation. This would lower employers' cost of hiring older workers, because their payroll tax liabilities would fall, and it would make older workers relatively more attractive to hire and retain. It would also require Congress to find a source of revenue to make up for payroll taxes lost as a result of the reform.

♦ Allow employers to offer pro-rated fringe benefits for employees working less than full-time hours rather than requiring them to provide the same fringe benefits to all employees working more than 1,000 hours per year (as the Employee Retirement Income Security Act, or ERISA, currently mandates). The present law encourages employers to restrict the hours worked by part-time employees to fewer than 1,000 per year. Giving employers more flexibility would allow older employees and employers to work out mutually agreeable fringe benefit packages that might keep more older workers employed.

♦ Make Medicare the first source of health insurance coverage for workers over age 65. Current law requires that the employer's health plan serve as "first payer" for a worker who has dual insurance coverage. Employers could provide additional insurance coverage if they chose. The reform would lower employers' cost of hiring or retaining older workers. Of course, it would also increase Medicare outlays, which in turn would require lawmakers to find additional sources of revenue for that program.

♦ Expand the Earned Income Tax Credit to include workers aged 65 and older who have no dependent children. This would provide a federal earnings subsidy to aged low-wage workers who are currently ineligible for the credit, and it could boost the available supply of older workers.

♦ Repeal the earnings test to eliminate the perception that pensioners who continue to work after age 62 lose Social Security benefits by doing so. It is true that workers do lose benefits during any year in which their earnings exceed the exempt amount. But for the average worker, the actuarial adjustment before age 65 and the delayed retirement credit between 65 and 69 return all or most of the foregone pensions through higher future benefits. Of course, most workers are not average, and those who anticipate shorter than average life expectancies or who have high discount rates will still find the earnings test a disincentive to work   Even for average workers the existing test can act as a work disincentive. Most Social Security recipients seem unaware of the benefit adjustment, so the current earnings test discourages them from earning more than the exempt amount. The repeal of the earnings test would probably increase recipients' earnings modestly, and the long-term budgetary cost would be negligible.

In an economy as strong as the one we have enjoyed over the past five years, none of these reforms may be needed to encourage higher employment among the aged. But if voters and policymakers want to provide incentives that will delay workers' exit from the labor force or change employers' attitudes toward older job applicants, some or all the reforms could be helpful.

Conclusion

After a long period of decline, the trend toward earlier retirement came to at least a temporary halt in the mid-1980s. Labor force participation rates of American men past age 60 leveled off, and in the past few years they have actually increased slightly. Participation rates among older women have risen significantly since 1985, though this trend may be the result of the historic shift in women's attitudes toward career employment rather than to a change in their retirement behavior *per se*.   Along with workers in Japan and Scandinavia, Americans now leave the paid work force later than workers almost anywhere else in the industrialized world.

The question is, do Americans retire at an age that will ultimately prove unaffordable? As life spans increase, the fraction of life spent in retirement will rise unless we delay our exit from paid work. Improved longevity places heavier burdens on active workers if retirees are supported by contributions from current payrolls. Even without any further improvement in longevity, the long-term decline in birth rates has slowed labor force growth and will eventually increase the ratio of retired to active workers. This will place extra pressure on retirement programs like Social Security and Medicare that depend on payroll taxes for most of their funding. To reduce this pressure, the country could adjust the age of eligibility for early and/or normal retirement benefits and take other measures to encourage workers to postpone their exit from the labor market. These steps would directly improve the finances of Social Security and Medicare. They would encourage some workers to delay their departure from career jobs and induce others to find bridge jobs to tide them over until full retirement benefits begin. The United States has already taken several steps in this direction, and these steps have contributed to the recent growth of employment among older Americans.

Although most workers today claim that they expect to keep working after age 65, or "retirement," most oppose additional changes in the retirement system that would push them to retire at a later age. A majority resists the idea that a higher retirement age is needed to protect Social Security. The United States is a rich country and will become wealthier in the future. It can certainly afford to maintain current retirement patterns if its citizens choose to spend their additional wealth in this way. The important public policy issue is the importance of this goal in comparison with other legitimate uses of the rise in wealth.

Proponents of a higher retirement age often focus on the long-term trend in older people's employment rates without considering what has happened to work effort and productivity among people before they reach the retirement age. They worry about the budget cost of retirement at age 62 without reflecting on the fact that younger workers may be paying for their longer and healthier retirements by working harder and more productively in their pre-retirement careers. As long as productivity continues to improve, American society and individual workers can choose how they want to allocate the income gains that flow from higher productivity. The evidence of the twentieth century suggests they will use at least part of it to pay for a longer retirement.

Endnotes

[1] Retirement patterns were much more difficult to measure among women because most worked primarily within the home (and without pay) during most of their adult lives.

[2] Labor force participation rates for 1910, 1940, and 1970 are based on responses to employment questions in the decennial censuses. See Ransom et al. (1991), especially pages 45-46, and Munnell (1977), page 70. Rates for 1984-85 and 1998-99 are the arithmetic average participation rates on the March Current Population Survey (CPS) files for 1984, 1985, 1998, and 1999. Participation rates measured on the Census differ somewhat from those measured by the CPS, partly because the main goal of the CPS is to obtain reliable labor force statistics. Adjusting the decennial Census statistics to make them strictly comparable to the CPS estimates would have only a slight effect on the patterns displayed in Figure 1, however.

[3] Before their 62nd birthdays, workers who contribute to Social Security for an additional year obtain better future pensions because the basic pension formula is based on workers' average lifetime wages. Between ages 62 and 64 workers who contribute to Social Security obtain that benefit enhancement *plus* an actuarial increase equal to about 8 percent of the basic pension to compensate them for giving up one year's benefit payments.

[4] If the labor force participation rate at age 63 is designated $LFPR_{63}$, the retirement rate at age 63 is calculated as $(LFPR_{62} - LFPR_{63}) / LFPR_{55}$. This calculation ignores the complications involved in computing true cohort distributions and the effects of mortality rates, immigration, and temporary withdrawal from the labor force. It offers a picture of the timing of labor market withdrawal based on the participation choices of men aged 55 through 72 in a particular year.

[5] Much of the future funding problem is due to the maturation of the program (most future retirees will reach the retirement age with enough earnings credits to receive a full pension), slow growth in the future working population, and a long-term slowdown in the rate of real wage growth (which has deprived the system of anticipated revenues). Increased longevity explains only part of the system's funding shortfall.

[6] In the GOP presidential candidates' debate in Manchester, NH, on December 5, 1999, Steve Forbes, Senator John McCain, and Governor George W. Bush all expressed views on increasing the retirement age. Forbes described the idea as a "betrayal": "That's not fair to the people. They were made a promise and it should be kept." McCain said that a retirement age increase was unnecessary. Governor Bush flatly ruled out the possibility he would ask for a retirement-age increase for people already near retirement, and he expressed "hope" such a step would not be needed for younger workers. The Democratic presidential candidates have been equally vehement in their opposition. When asked by Tim Russert whether he supported or opposed hiking the retirement age, Vice President Gore responded "Tim, I strongly oppose raising the retirement age." When Gore posed the same question to Bill Bradley, Bradley responded "We said no. We said no. ... OK?" (*Meet the Press*, December 19, 1999).

[7] Other economists' predictions are discussed in Joseph Quinn et al. (1990).

311

References

Baily, Martin N. 1987. ⬚Aging and the Ability to Work: Policy Issues and Recent Trends.⬚ In *Work, Health, and Income among the Elderly*, Gary Burtless, ed. Washington, D.C.: Brookings, pp. 59-96.

Bl⬚ndal, Sveinbj⬚rn, and Stefano Scarpetta. 1998. "The Retirement Decision in OECD Countries." Economics Department Working Paper no. 202, OECD, Paris.

Bosworth, Barry P., and Gary Burtless, eds. 1998. *Aging Societies: The Global Dimension.* Washington, D.C.: The Brookings Institution.

Burtless, Gary, and Robert A. Moffitt. 1985. "The Joint Choice of Retirement Age and Postretirement Hours of Work." *Journal of Labor Economics* 3(2): 209-236.

Burtless, Gary. 1986. "Social Security, Unanticipated Benefit Increases, and the Timing of Retirement." *Review of Economic Studies* 53(5): 781-805.

Employee Benefit Research Institute. 1997a. *EBRI Databook on Employee Benefits.* Fourth ed. Washington, DC: Employee Benefit Research Institute.

Employee Benefit Research Institute. 1997b. "The 1997 Retirement Confidence Survey: Summary of Findings." Washington, D.C.: EBRI.

Employee Benefit Research Institute. 1997c. *The Reality of Retirement Today: Lessons in Planning for Tomorrow.* EBRI Policy Brief no. 181, EBRI, Washington, D.C.

Geanakopolos, John, Olivia Mitchell, and Steve Zeldes. 1998. "Would a Privatized Social Security System Really Pay a Higher Rate of Return?" In *Framing the Social Security Debate: Values, Politics, and Economics,* R.D. Arnold, M.J. Graetz, and A.H. Munnell, eds. Washington, DC: National Academy of Social Insurance, pp. 137-156 .

Gustman, Alan A., and Thomas L. Steinmeier. 1994. "Employer Provided Health Insurance and Retirement Behavior." *Industrial and Labor Relations Review* 48(1): 124-140.

Gruber, Jonathan, and David A. Wise. 1999. "Introduction and Summary." In *Social Security and Retirement around the World,* Jonathan Gruber, and David A. Wise, eds. Chicago: University of Chicago Press.

Jacobs, Lawrence R., and Robert Y. Shapiro. 1998. "Myths and Misunderstandings about Public Opinion toward Social Security." In *Framing the Social Security Debate: Values, Politics, and Economics*, R. Douglas Arnold, Michael J. Graetz, and Alicia H. Munnell, eds. Washington, DC: National Academy of Social Insurance, pp. 355-388.

Krueger, Alan, and Jörn-Steffen Pischke. 1992. "The Effect of Social Security on Labor Supply: A Cohort Analysis of the Notch Generation." *Journal of Labor Economics* 10(4): 412-437.

Leimer, Dean. 1994. "Cohort Specific Measures of Lifetime Net Social Security Transfers." ORS Working Paper no. 59, February, Office of Research and Statistics, Social Security Administration, Washington, D.C..

Manton, Kenneth G., and Eric Stollard. 1994. "Medical Demography: Interaction of Disability Dynamics and Mortality." In *Demography of Aging,* Linda G. Martin, and Samuel H. Preston, eds. Washington, D.C.: National Academy Press, pp. 217-79

Munnell, Alicia H. 1977. *The Future of Social Security.* Washington, D.C.: Brookings.

Quinn, Joseph F., Richard V. Burkhauser, and Daniel A. Myers. 1990. *Passing the Torch: The Influence of Economic Incentives on Work and Retirement.* Kalamazoo, Michigan: Upjohn.

Quinn, Joseph F. 1991. "The Nature of Retirement: Survey and Econometric Evidence." In *Retirement and Public Policy,* Alicia H. Munnell, ed. Dubuque, Iowa: Kendall/Hunt, pp. 119-23.

Quinn, Joseph F., and Richard V. Burkhauser. 1994. "Retirement and Labor Force Behavior of the Elderly." In *Demography of Aging,* Linda G. Martin, and Samuel H. Preston, eds. Washington, D.C.: National Academy Press, pp. 56-61.

Quinn, Joseph F. 1999a. *Retirement Patterns and Bridge Jobs in the 1990s.* EBRI Issue Brief no. 206, February, Employee Benefit Research Institute, Washington, D.C.

Quinn, Joseph F. 1999b. "Has the Early Retirement Trend Reversed?" Chestnut Hill, Massachusetts: Retirement Research Consortium and Boston College.

Ransom, Roger L., Richard Sutch, and Samuel H. Williamson. 1991. "Retirement: Past and Present." In *Retirement and Public Policy,* Alicia H. Munnell, ed. Dubuque, Iowa: Kendall/Hunt, pp. 23-50.

U.S. Department of Commerce, Bureau of the Census. 1975. *Historical Statistics of the United States: Colonial Times to 1970.* Washington D.C.: Government Printing Office.

313

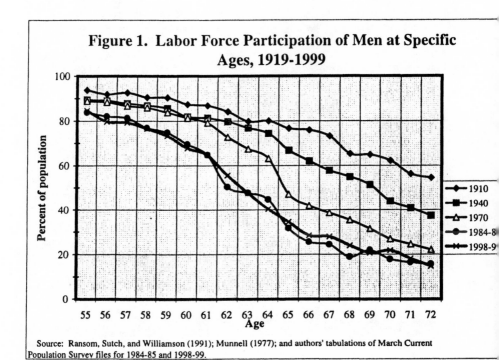

Figure 1. Labor Force Participation of Men at Specific Ages, 1919-1999

Source: Ransom, Sutch, and Williamson (1991); Munnell (1977); and authors' tabulations of March Current Population Survey files for 1984-85 and 1998-99.

Figure 2. Annual Change in Labor Force Participation Rate at Selected Ages, 1970-1985 and 1985-1999

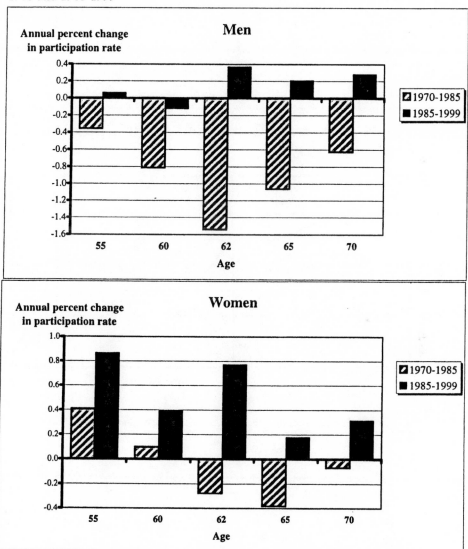

Source: Authors' tabulations based on Munnell (1977), p. 70, and March CPS files for 1984, 1985, 1998, and 1999.

Figure 3. Average Retirement Age of American Men, 1910-1999

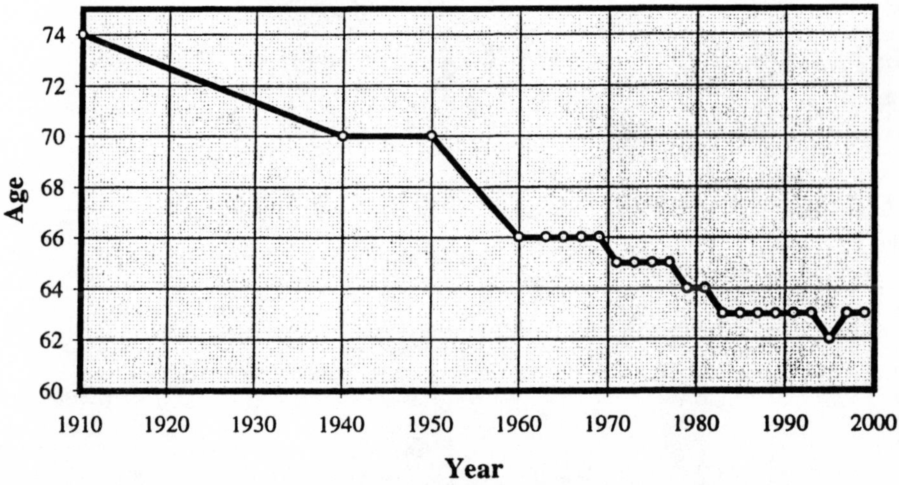

Note: The average retirement age is the youngest age at which at least half of men have left the labor force.

Figure 4. Estimates of the Average Age of Transition out of Active Workforce in the G-7 Countries, 1995

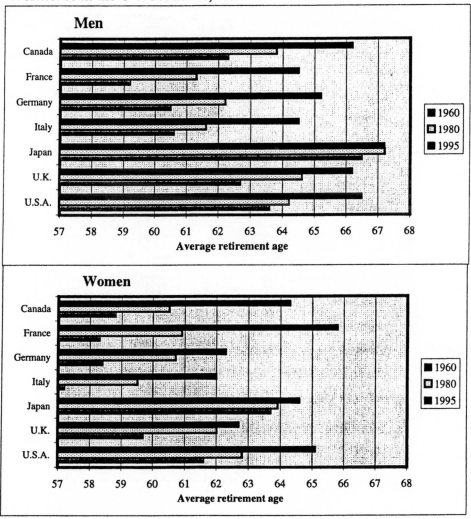

Source: Blondal and Scarpetta (1998), Table II.1.

Figure 5. Male Retirement Rate bs Age, 1940 - 1999

1940

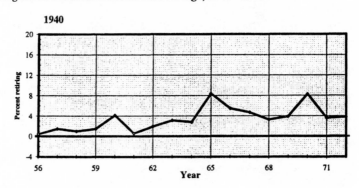

1970

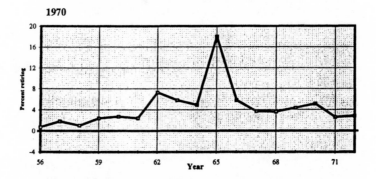

1998-1999

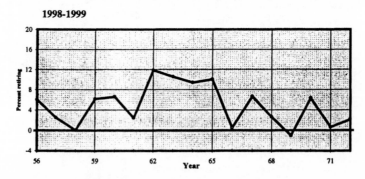

Note: Percent retiring each year is a constructed number reflecting the fraction of men leaving the workforce at the designated age, measured as a percent of men in the labor force at age 55.

Source: Authors' tabulations of participation rates in Munnell (1977), p. 70, and estimates from the March 1998 and March 1999 CPS files.

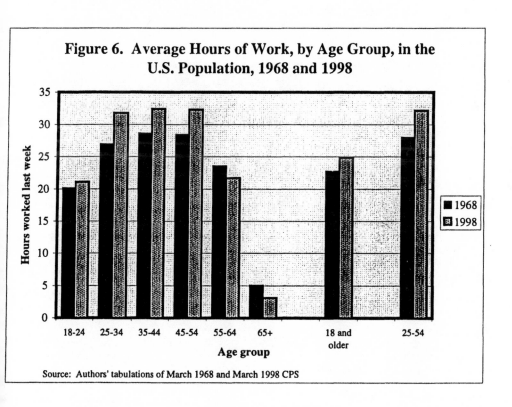

Figure 6. Average Hours of Work, by Age Group, in the U.S. Population, 1968 and 1998

Source: Authors' tabulations of March 1968 and March 1998 CPS

Table 1. Labor Force Participation Rates at Selected Ages by Sex, 1940-1999

Percent of population

Year	Age				
	55	60	62	65	70
Men --					
1940	90	82	80	67	44
1950	88	82	80	68	45
1960	90	83	79	54	33
1970	89	81	73	47	27
1984-85	84	70	50	32	18
1998-99	85	68	55	35	22
Women --					
1940	20	17	15	12	6
1950	28	23	21	16	8
1960	43	35	29	20	12
1970	50	43	36	22	11
1984-85	55	44	32	16	10
1998-99	68	49	43	19	12

Source: Munnell (1977), p. 70, and authors' tabulations of March CPS files for 1984, 1985, 1998, and 1999.

Population Research and Policy Review **18**: 411–432, 1999.
© 1999 *Kluwer Academic Publishers. Printed in the Netherlands.*

Economic development and labor force participation of older persons

ROBERT L. CLARK[1], E. ANNE YORK[2] & RICHARD ANKER[3]
[1]*College of Management, North Carolina State University, USA;* [2]*Department of Business and Economics, Meridith College, USA;* [3] *Employment Department, International Labour Office, Geneva, Switzerland*

Abstract. The effect of economic development on labor force participation rates of older men and women is examined using national data for 134 countries. The analysis provides new insights into the evolution of retirement patterns with rising personal income, slowing population growth, the aging of the population, and shifts in the composition of employment. The analysis indicates a negative relationship between per capita income and labor force participation rates. This relationship is stronger for older men than for older women and is most apparent among middle income countries. An older population is associated with lower participation rates for older men and higher widow rates produce higher participation rates among older women. Industrial changes such as a decline in the proportion of the labor force employed in agriculture lower the proportion of older persons in the labor force. Finally, national social security policies are shown to impact the proportion of older persons that remains in the labor force.

Keywords: Economic development, Population aging, Retirement, Social security

Introduction

Economic development produces a series of changes in a country's economic environment. These changes typically produce increases in real income per capita, declines in the rate of population growth and the aging of the population, changes in the industrial structure of the economy, and the development of national retirement programs. In response to rising income and other socioeconomic changes, the proportion of older persons who remain in the labor force tends to decline. Due to data limitations, relatively few studies have investigated the aggregate labor supply response to economic development over time in a single country or across a large sample of the countries of the world.

Detailed studies of historical patterns of labor force participation among older persons in the USA (Long 1958; Costa 1998) suggest that increases in income per capita over long periods played a significant role in the decline in the proportion of older men that remain in the labor force. In addition to these time series studies, several cross-sectional studies have examined differences in national participation rates. However, almost all of these studies are limited to high income, industrial countries[1] and most are limited to men.[2] These studies conclude that increases in national income per capita, increases in the relative size of the older population, and increases in the generosity of social security programs reduce the proportion of older men in the labor force. In contrast to these limited studies, Clark & Anker (1990, 1993) estimated the effect of various indicators of economic development including income per capita on the participation rates of older men and women for 102 countries in 1980. Their studies confirmed that there is a negative relationship between national income and labor force participation rates of older persons.

The present study uses data from 134 countries to estimate how labor force participation rates of older men and women vary with economic development. The findings confirm the existence of a nonlinear relationship between income and participation rates and document the importance of social security programs, industrial structure, and population aging on labor supply decisions.

Data description and model specification

The primary objective of this analysis is to examine how labor force participation rates vary across countries that are in various stages of economic development, as reflected by differences in national economic conditions, retirement programs, and demographic structures. No single data source provides sufficient information to investigate these relationships. Thus, key indicators of economic development are obtained from several international agencies and are merged into a single data file for statistical analysis. Age and gender specific labor force participation rates, as well as the industrial structure of the labor force, are provided by the International Labour Office (ILO 1999). Per capita income was obtained from the World Bank and Penn World Tables and the population age structure information from the United Nations. Finally, published material from the United States Social Security Administration was reviewed to determine various characteristics of the national social security programs.

The ILO collects information concerning the composition and size of the national labor force.[3] The participation rates used in this analysis are for 1990 the most recent year of actual data. Male and female labor force participation rates for each country are grouped by 5 year age intervals, starting with ages 10 to 14, and concluding with the open-ended age category for individuals aged 65 and over. This study examines the labor force participation rates for persons aged 55 to 59, those aged 60 to 64, and individuals aged 65 and over.

Labor force participation rates are available from the ILO for 176 countries and territories.

Economic and demographic variables hypothesized to influence labor force participation of older persons are per capita income (INCOME), the percentage of elderly relative to younger persons (ELDERLY), the ratio of older women to older men (WIDOWRATE), and the percentage of labor force involved in the agricultural sector (AGRICULTURE). In addition, a series of variables reflecting the basic characteristics of a country's social security program are included in the regression equation.

Per capita income is an indicator of the level of national economic well being. Economic theory suggests that higher annual income would be associated with a lower probability of older individuals remaining in the labor force. The natural log of INCOME is included in the analysis to capture the expected nonlinear relationship between income and work.[4] Per capita income for 1990 is obtained from two sources. The primary income variable used throughout the analysis is per capita GNP, obtained from the World Bank's *World Tables of Economic and Social Indicators, 1950–1992*. INCOME is available for 134 of the 176 countries for which the ILO reports labor force participation data. A majority of the countries with missing GNP data are from former communist countries, and to a lesser extent, small island economies.

In order to measure better differences in real economic well being, a second income variable based on the concept of purchasing power parity across countries is employed. This variable is a chain-weighted measure of per capita real GDP from the Penn World Table (see Summers & Heston 1991; Heston & Summers 1996).[5] These data are available for only 102 of the 176 countries with LFP data. Because of this further reduction in sample size, the Penn World Table (PWT) data were used only as a comparative tool for the analysis based on the World Bank income data.

Data for the ELDERLY and WIDOWRATE variables for 1990 are from the 1994 revision of the United Nation's *Sex and Age Quinquennial, 1950–2050*. ELDERLY is calculated as the ratio of the number of men (women) aged 65 and older to the number of men (women) who are aged 15 to 64 years old times 100. This variable is calculated separately for men and women in order to take account of labor market segmentation by sex and serves as an indication of the relative sex-specific supply of older persons in a country who might compete for available jobs. An increase in the number of older men or women would tend to depress their wage rates and decrease their economic opportunities.[6]

The WIDOWRATE variable measures the excess of women aged 55 and over in 4 country relative to the number of men aged 55 and over. This variable is calculated as the number of women aged 55 and over divided by the number of men aged 55 and over minus one times 100.[7] In most countries, widowhood is associated with lower economic well being. Thus, countries with higher rates of widowhood are expected to have higher participation rates among older women. The percent of the labor force that is employed in the agricultural sector is available in ILO (1999). A larger agricultural sector is expected to be associated with increased opportunities for older workers to continue working. Agricultural employment may provide more flexibility in the number of hours worked and the timing of these hours. The ability to gradually retire tends to be less prevalent in other sectors of the economy.[8]

It would be desirable to have direct measures of the proportion of the labor force covered by social security, the average benefit at the normal retirement age, and how the value of the benefit changes when retirement is postponed. Unfortunately, such data are not available for most countries. Instead, available provisions of the national social security programs are used as proxies for these effects. These data are obtained from US Social Security Administration (1990, 1994).[9] A variable, SSLAW, was created to measure the maturity of the national social security program. This variable is constructed by subtracting the year in which a country's social security program was first established from 1990. Typically, more mature social security programs will be more generous and cover a larger proportion of the national labor force. Therefore, SSLAW is used as a proxy for these generosity and coverage characteristics.[10]

A dichotomous variable was created to indicate whether the national social security system is a provident fund (PROVIDENT). Provident funds are retirement savings plans based on contributions from workers and employers.[11] The existence of provident funds instead of annuity-type social security benefits may alter the decision to remain in the labor force. For women in low-income countries who have relatively short working careers, provident funds would provide a very low lump-sum payment. Compared to women covered by annuity social security benefits, which often provide relatively larger benefits compared to career earnings for low paid workers, women covered by provident funds would tend to be more likely to remain in the labor force.

The age at which one is eligible to receive social security retirement benefits is an important factor determining the proportion of older persons who remain in the labor force (SSAGE). An older age of eligibility is expected to have a positive effect on the participation rates of persons who have not yet reached that eligibility age threshold. Thus, the regressions for person's aged 55 to 59 years old use a dichotomous variable to indicate whether or not their country has a social security eligibility age of 60 or greater. The social security age variable used in regressions for those who are aged 60 to 64 years old indicates whether or not their country has an eligibility age of 65 years old and up. For persons aged 60 to 64, being eligible to start social security benefits should significantly lower the national labor force participation rate. On the basis of the theory of labor supply and the available national data, the following regression equation was specified:

$$LFPRATE = a + b\text{INCOME} + c\text{ELDERLY}$$
$$+ d\text{AGRICULTURE} + e\text{WIDOWRATE}$$
$$+ f\text{SSLAW} + g\text{PROVIDENT} + h\text{SSAGE}$$

SSAGE is used only in the regressions for the two youngest age groups.

Table 1. Means for sample data[a]

	Men	Women		Men	Women
LFP 55–59 (%)	85.5	44.5	SSLAW (years)	43.6	43.6
LFP 60–64 (%)	69.7	33.4	PROVIDENT[b] (%)	12.7	12.7
LFP 65+ (%)	43.6	18.4	SSAGE60 (%)	59.0	40.3
ELDERLY (%)	8.5	11.2	SSAGE65 (%)	23.1	12.7
AGRICULTURE (%)	39.3	39.3	GNP per capita	$5061.94	$5061.94
WIDOWRATE (%)	16.7	16.7			

[a] There are 134 countries in the GNP sample.

[b] The means for the binary variables represent the percent of countries with that characteristic.

Sources: Labor force participation by age category and for agriculture are obtained from the International Labour Office. ELDERLY and WIDOWRATE are derived from the United Nations, and social security information comes from the US Social Security Administration.

Table 1 presents the means of the variables for the 134 countries for which per capita GNP data is available. These means are calculated as an average across all countries and are not weighted for population size. As expected, labor force participation rates decline with age for both men and women. For women, the labor force participation rate declines from 44.5 percent for women aged 55 to 59, to 33.4 percent for women aged 60 to 64, and further to 18.4 percent for women aged 65 and older. Male labor force participation is higher than female labor force participation for each age category. The male labor force participation rate falls from 85.5 percent for men aged 55 to 59, to 69.7 percent for men aged 60 to 64, and further to 43.6 percent for men aged 65 older.

The social security age variables indicate that about three-fifths of the countries have eligibility ages of 60 years old or older for men, but only two-fifths of the systems have eligibility ages of 60 and up for women. Twenty-three percent of countries have eligibility ages of 65 or older for men, while only thirteen percent have eligibility ages of 65 or older for women. Greater life expectancy of women throughout the world is reflected in the

ELDERLY and WIDOWRATE variables. For women, the ratio of persons aged 65 and older to those aged 15 to 64 is 11 percent while for men this ratio is only 8.5 percent. There is an average of 17 percent more women age 55 and over than men in these countries. The mean proportion of the labor force working in the agricultural sector is almost 40 percent. The high proportion of the national labor force employed in the agricultural sector is due to the large number of low-income countries in the early stages of economic development.

Income and differences in LFP rates

There is substantial variation in the participation rates for older persons across the countries. For men aged 65 and over, there are 16 countries with participation rates of less than 10 percent, 15 of which are in Europe. At the other extreme, 27 countries have participation rates for men aged 65 and older in excess of 70 percent. Most of these countries with very high participation rates for older men are in Africa and have very low per capita income. In contrast, there are 36 countries with participation rates for women aged 65 and older of less than 5 percent and only 13 countries with participation rates in excess of 40 percent.

Table 2 reports average labor force participation rates for workers in each of the three age categories by level of per capita GNP. The income categories are those used by the World Bank to indicate low, middle, and high income countries. Within each income category, labor force participation declines with age. Countries with higher levels of average income have lower rates of labor force participation of older men and women for each age group, except for women aged 55 to 59. There is a large drop in the labor force participation rate for these women from the low to the middle income countries, but an increase in their labor force participation rates from the middle to the high-income countries. This finding reflects the increased labor force participation of women over the past few decades in more developed countries.

In general, these data support the hypothesis that there is a negative relationship between income and labor force participation. Comparing per capita GNP with participation rates for individual countries strengthens this conclusion. All of the countries with participation rates in excess of 70 percent for men aged 65 and over had per capita income of less than $1,000 in 1990. In contrast, the lowest income among those countries with participation rates less than 10 percent was Romania with per capita income of $1,670 and 13 of these countries had incomes in excess of $11,000.

Sorting the individual countries into regions and subregions provides further evidence on the relationship between income and labor force particip-

Table 2. Average labor force participation rates by per capita gross national product[a]

| | | Men | | | Women | | |
Income[b]	N	55–59	60–64	65 +	55–59	60–64	65 +
$0–$610	43	93.0	85.4	66.5	62.5	52.1	33.9
$611–$7620	63	83.7	66.8	40.5	34.2	25.6	13.9
$7621 and up	28	78.1	52.1	15.4	40.0	22.1	4.7

[a] Table entries indicate the average LFP rate for all countries within the range for per capita GNP for that row.
[b] The ranges for per capita GNP, in 1990 dollars, come from the World Bank data categories for low, middle, and high income countries.

ation. The observed variation in the proportion of older workers remaining in the labor force across regions also reflects cultural, ethnic, and religious differences. The regions included in the analysis are Asia, Africa, Europe, Latin America and the Caribbean, Oceania, and North America. Countries are sorted into these regions based on classifications used by the United Nations. Table 3 contains a listing of labor force participation rates for workers aged 65 and older by geographic region and subregion. Examination of these data generally supports the finding that regions composed of countries with low average income tend to have higher rates of labor force participation. For men, the inverse relationship of income and LFP rates holds, except for Europe having slightly lower LFP rates than North America. For women, Africa has the highest average LFP rate and the lowest average income.

When comparing subregions, exceptions to the hypothesis of the inverse relationship between income and LFP rates are evident. For example, Northern Africa has lower average income than Southern Africa, but Southern Africa has much higher average LFP rates for men and for women. Southeast Asia and Eastern/Central Europe have similar average income levels, but Eastern/Central Europe has LFP rates that are about a third of those in Southeast Asia. In fact, the LFP rates for Eastern Europe are much lower than the LFP rates for many of the subregions that have higher average income levels. These anomalies may reflect religious and cultural norms, differences in the importance of agriculture, the high oil-based income for some countries in Northern and Southern Africa, and the vestiges of social welfare systems left over from the days of central planning in Eastern/Central Europe.[12]

Table 3. Labor force participation rates for age 65 and older and per capita income by region

Region[a]	N	Income[b]	Men	Women
Africa	45	$705	64.6	33.8
East	14	419	71.8	44.0
Middle	7	949	67.6	38.5
North	4	1,342	29.2	8.6
South	5	1,524	49.7	17.3
West	15	415	70.8	34.3
Asia	29	$4,994	42.9	14.1
East	4	10,885	32.9	12.1
Southcentral	7	614	57.4	20.4
Southeast	7	2,548	45.2	21.7
West	11	7,196	35.9	5.8
Europe	26	$14,004	11.0	4.7
Eastern/Central	7	2,527	14.9	7.9
North	7	20,369	14.9	5.9
South	5	9,162	10.1	3.4
West	7	22,576	3.8	1.3
Latin America & Caribbean	27	$2,319	44.3	10.9
Caribbean	7	4,326	40.8	14.0
Central America	8	1,405	52.6	10.6
South America	12	1,758	40.7	9.4
North America	2	$21,060	13.5	6.2
Oceania	5	$6,578	36.7	21.2

[a] Countries are grouped by geographical region as specified by the United Nations, except for Eastern/Central Europe. See endnote 14.
[b] Table entries for income and LFP rates are averages for all countries in that region.

Estimates of income effects

Analysis of the mean participation rates indicated that labor force participation rates tend to be lower in the presence of higher per capita income. We now estimate the response of national participation rates to higher levels of national income in the presence of other economic and demographic differences. The empirical analysis is divided into three parts. First, participation rates are estimated as a function of GNP per capita, variables that are proxies for the labor market opportunities of older persons, and a series of social security variables. Second, separate participation equations are estimated for the three income levels identified by the World Bank. Finally, the model is reestimated using the purchasing power parity variable for INCOME based on Penn World Tables and the results are compared to a regression of the same countries with the INCOME variable from World Bank.

Labor force participation equations: older men and women

Participation rates of older persons are estimated for each of the six age-gender groups using a specification that includes log income (GNP per capita) as the only explanatory variable (see Table 4). The predicted negative relationship between log income and labor force participation is found in all cases. For men, the estimated coefficients increase from −3.9 for those aged 55 to 59, to −8.8 for men aged 60 to 64, to −13.0 for those aged 65 and over. All coefficients are statistically significant and imply substantial declines in the proportion of older men who remain in the labor force with an increase in per capita income.

Table 4. Income only regressions

	Men			Women		
	55–59	60–64	65 +	55–59	60–64	65+
Intercept	114.13*	134.48*	140.06*	92.75*	93.53*	75.54*
	(3.41)	(6.48)	(6.16)	(8.37)	(7.27)	(5.30)
ln INCOME	−3.87*	−8.77*	−13.04*	−6.53*	−8.13*	−7.73*
	(0.45)	(0.86)	(0.81)	(1.11)	(0.96)	(0.70)
Adjusted R^2	0.35	0.44	0.66	0.20	0.35	0.48

Standard errors are in parentheses. Number of countries is 134.
* Coefficient is significantly different from zero at the 0.01 confidence level.
** Coefficient is significantly different from zero at the 0.10 confidence level.

For men aged 65 and older, the coefficient indicates a 1.3 percentage point reduction in the participation rate in response to each 10 percent increase in per capita income. For these men, this income-only equation explains two-thirds of the variation in participation rates across the countries. A smaller proportion of the total variation is explained for the younger men. For women, the estimated coefficients also show statistically significant declines in participation rates in response to a 10 percent increase in per capita income, ranging from 0.65 percentage points for those aged 55 to 59 to 0.8 percentage points for the older two age groups. The income-only equation explains almost half of the variation in participation rates for the oldest women, but the equations for younger women explain only one-fifth to one third of the variation in participation rates.

Table 5. Full regression model

	Men			Women		
	55–59	60–64	65 +	55–59	60–64	65 +
Intercept	98.3*	99.50*	63.98*	−22.92	−7.86	−4.46
	(9.02)	(14.80)	(13.90)	(17.74)	(16.46)	(12.51)
In INCOME	−1.07	−2.98**	−2.70**	3.88**	1.76	0.94
	(0.99)	(1.66)	(1.56)	(2.06)	(1.90)	(1.44)
ELDERLY	−0.53**	−1.82*	−1.77*	0.70**	−0.01	−0.12
	(0.25)	(0.43)	(0.39)	(0.34)	(0.31)	(0.24)
AGRICULTURE	0.09*	0.25*	0.41*	0.79*	0.67*	0.47*
	(0.05)	(0.08)	(0.08)	(0.10)	(0.09)	(0.07)
WIDOWRATE	−0.04	−0.20*	−0.04	0.29*	0.22*	0.14*
	(0.05)	(0.08)	(0.07)	(0.10)	(0.09)	(0.07)
In SSLAW	−1.21**	−0.74	−0.21	−2.57**	−1.22	−1.30
	(0.70)	(1.06)	(1.01)	(1.23)	(1.08)	(0.84)
PROVIDENT	−2.25	−4.10	−2.33	8.82**	5.25	7.01**
	(2.46)	(3.63)	(3.45)	(4.27)	(3.75)	(2.94)
SSAGE 60+	1.00			5.72**		
	(2.32)			(3.31)		
SSAGE 65+		16.17*			13.21*	
		(3.43)			(4.14)	
Adjusted R^2	0.43	0.62	0.77	0.57	0.62	0.65

Standard errors are in parentheses. Number of countries is 134.
* Coefficient is significantly different from zero at the 0.01 confidence level.
** Coefficient is significantly different from zero at the 0.10 confidence level.

Along with increases in income, economic development also is associated with changes in the industrial composition of the economy, age structure of the population, and the characteristics of national retirement programs. To assess the effects of these changes along with increases in income, the participation equations are expanded to include the following variables described in the preceding section: ELDERLY, WIDOWRATE, AGRICUL-TURE, SSLAW, PROVIDENT, and SSAGE. The estimated coefficients are reported in Table 5 for each of the six age-sex groups and the results are discussed in the next two sections.

Analysis of men's labor force participation rates

The inclusion of the socioeconomic variables reduces the absolute size and statistical significance of the coefficient on INCOME for men. The estimates now indicate that each 10 percent increase in national income is associated with a statistically significant reduction in the age-specific participation rate of only 0.3 percentage points for the two oldest age groups. The estimated income effect for men aged 65 and older is only about one-fifth its estimated size in the income-only regression, while for men aged 60 to 64, the estimated effect of income is about one-third of its size in the income-only regression. For men aged 55 to 59, the estimated coefficient is no longer statistically significant. In general, these results provide further confirmation that labor force participation declines with increases in income.

Increases in the two demographic variables are associated with reductions in the proportion of older men who remain in the labor force. The estimated relationships for men indicate that increases in the relative size of the older population of men (ELDERLY) results in statistically significant reductions in the proportion of these men who remain in the labor force. For example, a one percentage point increase in the ratio of men aged 65 and older to men aged 18 to 64 is associated with a reduction in the labor force participation rate of men aged 65 and over of 1.8 percentage points. Significant results are also estimated for the other two age groups. In evaluating these results, one should remember that the mean value for ELDERLY for men is only 8.5 percent so that a one-percentage point change is a rather large shift in the population age structure. Although all of the estimated coefficients for WIDOWRATE are negative, they are rather small and only the coefficient for men aged 60 to 64 is statistically significant. As expected, increases in the national widow rate have only minor effects on the proportion of older men who remain in the labor force.

An increase in the proportion of the labor force working in agriculture is associated with a larger proportion of older men who remain in the labor force. The estimated coefficients are statistically significant for all three age groups. For men aged 65 and older, the coefficient indicates that a one percentage point increase in the proportion of all workers employed in agriculture is associated with a 0.4 percentage point increase in the proportion of older men who remain in the labor force. The estimated effect of agriculture on the labor force participation rates for the two younger age groups of men is also statistically significant, but smaller in magnitude.

After accounting for these other factors associated with economic development, the existence of a national social security system and the key characteristics of this system do not significantly affect the labor force participation rates of men aged 65 and older. However, for men aged 60 to 64, the participation rate is 16 percentage points higher if the social security system has an age of eligibility for benefits of 65 or higher. For men aged 55 to 59, the maturity of the national social security system significantly reduces the participation rate. For all age groups, the estimated effects of having a provident fund are negative but are not statistically significant. Together these results suggest that social security programs have their greatest impact on the participation rates of older men prior to the age of 65.

Analysis of women's labor force participation rates

In the presence of the additional variables associated with economic development, the estimated coefficients on the income variable for all three age groups of women become positive. However, this effect is statistically significant only for the youngest age group of women in the analysis. For women aged 55 to 59, a 10 percent increase in income is associated with 0.4 percentage point increase in the participation rate. The coefficients for the other two age groups are less than half this size. The implication is that holding constant other economic and demographic changes associated with economic development, increases in income are associated with higher levels of labor force participation among older women.

Increases in the proportion of the labor force employed in the agricultural sector have a very large effect on the labor force participation among older women. These estimated effects are highly significant for all age groups and are larger than those estimated for men. Given the lower level of participation rates for older women, this finding illustrates the greater importance of employment opportunities in the agricultural sector for older women compared to men. Also, contrary to the findings for older men, the effect of agriculture on participation decreases with age for older women. As expected, the widow rate is also much more important in the labor supply decisions of older women. The estimated coefficients of WIDOWRATE indicate that a one-percentage point increase in this demographic variable increases the participation rate of older women by 0.1 to 0.3 percentage points.

Estimated effects of the maturity of the national social security system are similar for men and women. The estimated coefficients of SSLAW are negative for all age groups but statistically significant only for those aged 55 to 59. For women in the 55 to 59 age group, the participation rate is 6 percentage points higher when the social security system has an eligibility age of 60 or higher. For women aged 60 to 64, a social security eligibility age of 65 or higher is associated with a 13 percentage point higher participation rate. Provident funds have a relatively large, positive, and statistically significant effect for women compared to the smaller, negative, and insignificant effect found for men.

Residual analysis

While the regression model explains approximately one-half to three-quarters of the variation in participation rates in all six age/gender regressions, certain countries and groups of countries have relatively large residuals. The residuals indicate the actual participation rate minus the predicted rate. Table 6 contains a listing of the average residual by region and subregion for each age/gender group. For men, several of the Eastern/Central European countries have some of the largest negative residuals in the sample. For example, the average residual for men aged 60 to 64 in these countries was −16.2 percentage points and for men aged 65 and over the average residual was −9.8 percentage points. All of the countries in Western and Southern Europe with the exception of Switzerland and Portugal also have negative residuals for men aged 65 and older. However, these negative residuals tend to be much smaller than those of the Eastern European countries, averaging −3.9 percentage points for the countries in Southern Europe for men aged 65 and older and −5.4 percentage points for these older men in the countries in Western Europe.

In sharp contrast, all of the countries of Northern Europe have positive residuals for men in all three age groups with the exception of Finland, which has a large negative residual in all three age groups. Residuals for the countries in Northern Europe average 8 percentage points for men aged 65 and older and 12.2 percentage points for men aged 60 to 64. Among developed countries, Japan has by far the highest positive residual at 26.4 percentage points for men aged 65 and older. In North America, the United States has a positive residual of 7.0 percentage points for the oldest group of men, while Canada has a negative residual of −1.5 percentage points.

Africa presents another interesting contrast in residuals across the continent. For men aged 65 and older, four of the five regions have average positive residuals while North Africa has the largest mean negative residual of all the subregions, −17.3 percentage points. The four countries in this subregion are Egypt (−22.2 percentage points), Algeria (−19.8 percentage points), Morocco (−17.3 percentage points), and Tunisia (−10.0 percentage points). The residuals of Egypt, Algeria, and Morocco are among the twelve largest negative residuals found for the 134 countries. Several final points are notable from the residual analysis of older men. First, all of the subregions for Asia have small negative average residuals and second, all of the subregions in Latin America have positive mean residuals, with the largest for those countries in the Caribbean and in Central America.

For older women, the average residuals across the regions tend to be similar to, although somewhat smaller than, those reported for men. Among the European subregions, the pattern of residuals for women aged 65 and

Table 6. Residual analysis by region

Region[a]		Men[b]			Women		
	N	55–59	60–64	65 +	55–59	60–64	65 +
Africa	45	1.43	1.74	2.03	2.60	3.57	2.80
East	14	0.98	−0.69	2.03	5.10	6.64	6.71
Middle	7	2.12	6.17	6.04	7.15	9.43	8.19
North	4	−0.39	−7.00	−17.32	−9.64	−7.67	−5.18
South	5	2.44	3.69	1.05	−4.28	−2.58	−4.99
West	15	1.66	3.62	5.65	3.70	3.03	1.34
Asia	29	−1.11	−1.73	−4.10	−3.49	−4.30	−3.97
East	4	3.44	4.14	−0.54	6.32	4.54	0.61
Southcentral	7	−1.02	−4.27	−4.35	−12.32	−14.11	−9.97
Southeast	7	−3.54	−4.31	−8.29	2.38	−0.77	−5.14
West	11	−1.28	−0.61	−2.56	−5.17	−3.53	−1.08
Europe	26	−2.92	−4.42	−2.67	−2.75	−1.06	−0.49
East	7	−9.18	−16.23	−9.81	−5.42	−3.18	−0.95
North	7	7.15	12.23	8.00	16.66	9.82	2.74
South	5	−3.04	−1.46	−3.86	−13.63	−3.28	−2.05
West	7	−6.66	−11.38	−5.36	−11.74	−8.25	−2.13
Latin America & Caribbean	27	1.89	4.68	4.53	0.78	−0.38	0.01
Caribbean	7	2.89	3.73	8.18	13.18	7.33	4.97
Central America	8	2.60	6.07	6.63	−9.17	−7.76	−3.15
South America	12	0.83	4.30	1.00	0.19	0.05	−0.77
North America	2	2.87	1.01	2.75	15.1	4.07	4.10
Oceania	5	−2.55	−8.29	−6.18	0.90	−1.24	−1.29
Islamic	27	−1.49	−1.94	−3.10	−3.87	−2.67	−2.62

[a] Countries are grouped by geographical region as specified by the United Nations, except for Eastern/Central Europe. See endnote 14. See endnote 15 for Islamic Countries.
[b] Table entries for are average residuals for all countries in that region.

older is the same as that reported for men, but the magnitudes of the residuals for these older women only range from −2.1 percentage points for Western and Southern Europe to 2.7 percentage points for Northern Europe. Historically, Islamic countries tend to report very low participation rates for women. Therefore, as would be expected, for women aged 65 and over, 20 of the 27 Islamic countries have negative residuals, which means that the estimated equation over predicts the LFP rate for women in Islamic countries.[13] Most Islamic countries also have negative residuals for the two younger age groups of women.

Table 7. Men age 65 and up by income group

	Pooled	Low	Middle	High
Intercept	63.98*	68.90**	86.45*	2.50
	(13.90)	(37.84)	(30.20)	(75.56)
ln INCOME	−2.70**	−0.66	−6.35**	1.79
	(1.56)	(5.32)	(3.33)	(7.15)
ELDERLY	−1.77*	−4.52**	−2.29*	−1.36**
	(0.39)	(2.34)	(0.59)	(0.81)
AGRICULTURE	0.41*	0.37*	0.45*	0.45
	(0.08)	(0.13)	(0.14)	(0.65)
WIDOWRATE	−0.04	0.16	0.004	−0.39
	(0.07)	(0.21)	(0.11)	(0.23)
ln SSLAW	−0.21	−1.38	1.99	5.24
	(1.01)	(1.48)	(2.06)	(5.99)
PROVIDENT	−2.33	4.83	−10.60**	−3.86
	(3.45)	(4.95)	(6.30)	(12.94)
Adjusted R^2	0.77	0.36	0.61	0.37

Standard errors are in parentheses. Number of countries is 134.
* Coefficient is significantly different from zero at the 0.01 confidence level.
** Coefficient is significantly different from zero at the 0.10 confidence level.

Differences by levels of per capita income

To further examine the nonlinear relationship between income and participation, the countries in this study are divided into low (less than $611 per year), middle ($611 to $7,620), and high income ($7,621 and over) countries. The LFP rate equation is then re-estimated for the countries within each income group and the results for persons aged 65 and older are shown in Table 7 for men and Table 8 for women. Substantial differences in the effect of income on labor force participation rates are found across the three income groups. The first column of both tables repeats the estimates for all of the countries reported in Table 5, while columns two to four show the estimates for low, middle, and high income countries respectively.

For older men and women, the relationship between labor force activity and our economic, demographic, and social security variables is much stronger in the middle income group of countries as compared to the lower and higher income groups. Chow tests on the regression model for the 65 and older age group indicate that the null hypothesis that the three equations are the same is rejected at the one-percent significance level for men and at the ten percent significance level for women.

For men, the estimated effect of increases in per capita income for middle income countries is negative, large, and statistically significant, implying that a 10 percent increase in income produces a 0.6 percentage point decline in the labor force participation rate of men aged 65 and older. In contrast, the estimated effects of income for older men for the low and high-income countries are much smaller and statistically insignificant. These results suggests that in the early stages of economic development, increases in per capita income from a very low level do not lead to a greater proportion of older men retiring and leaving the labor force. As per capita income approaches $600 per year and continues to increase up towards $7,500, significant numbers of men 65 and older begin to leave the labor force. After per capita income passes this level, the negative relationship between income and male participation weakens once again. In fact, the estimated coefficient for the high-income countries is actually positive although insignificant.

Changes in the population age structure that increase the relative size of the older population may adversely affect their employment opportunities. This effect is stronger among the low-income countries. The estimated effect of ELDERLY indicates that a one percentage point increase in the ratio of older men to those aged 15 to 64 is associated with a 4.5 percentage decrease in the labor force participation rate of men in low income countries. The effect of a one-percentage point increase in this elderly ratio is only 2.3 percentage points among the middle income countries and 1.4 percentage points for the high-income countries.

The importance of agricultural employment opportunities for older men remains relatively stable with increases in per capita income. This estimated effect indicates that each one-percentage point increase in the proportion of the labor force employed in agriculture raises the participation rate by about 0.4 percentage points among countries in each of the income groups. However, the coefficient for the high-income sample is statistically insignificant. As expected, the widow rate has small and insignificant effects on the participation of older men. Once countries are sorted by their level of economic development, the presence and maturity of social security programs have only insignificant effects on the participation rate of men aged 65 and older. However, the participation rates of countries with provident funds in the middle income levels are much lower than other countries with annuity type social security systems.

Estimating participation equations for older women separately (see Table 8) by levels of income also results in considerable changes in the effect of income on labor force participation rates. The estimated coefficient for income is negative but insignificant for women aged 65 and older in the two lowest income categories but is much larger and positive, although statistically insignificant, for women in the high income countries.

Table 8. Women age 65 and up by income group

	Pooled	Low	Middle	High
Intercept	−4.46	40.58	7.60	−42.26
	(12.51)	(43.01)	(22.08)	(35.81)
ln INCOME	0.94	−3.42	−1.36	5.28
	(1.44)	(6.15)	(2.44)	(3.50)
ELDERLY	−0.12	−2.90	0.04	−0.77*
	(0.24)	(2.14)	(0.32)	(0.25)
AGRICULTURE	0.47*	0.37**	0.52*	0.30
	(0.07)	(0.15)	(0.10)	(0.29)
WIDOWRATE	0.14*	0.31	0.11	0.04
	(0.07)	(0.23)	(0.09)	(0.10)
ln SSLAW	−1.30	−0.93	−0.77	3.44
	(0.84)	(1.72)	(1.48)	(2.38)
PROVIDENT	7.01**	10.52**	1.06	−4.54
	(2.94)	(5.84)	(4.45)	(5.72)
Adjusted R^2	0.65	0.29	0.58	0.15

Standard errors are in parentheses. Number of countries is 134.
* Coefficient is significantly different from zero at the 0.01 confidence level.
** Coefficient is significantly different from zero at the 0.10 confidence level.

Relatively few statistically significant effects are found for the other variables in the women's equations. For example, the only significant effect in the high-income sample is that increases in the proportion of older women reduce their participation rate. Another finding consistent with expectations is that the effect of agricultural employment is primarily evident among countries in the two lowest income levels. Finally, the large positive effect of being in a country with a provident fund is only present among women in the low-income countries.

Purchasing power parity vs GNP as a measure of per capita income

To further investigate the relationship between income and labor force activity among older persons, a second measure of per capita income based on the purchasing power parity is used. This income measure is available for only 102 of the 134 countries in the sample. To examine the effect of using this alternative measure of income, the previous model from Table 5 is re-estimated using only the 102 countries for which the new income variable is available. Results shown in Table 9 include those for men and women aged 65

Table 9. Comparison of regressions with World Bank income variable versus Penn World Table income variable

	Men		Women	
	World Bank	Penn	World Bank	Penn
Intercept	73.23*	127.46*	−3.43	13.99
	(16.14)	(25.71)	(14.55)	(23.99)
In INCOME	−3.77**	−9.65*	1.25	−0.93
	(1.94)	(2.90)	(1.76)	(2.71)
ELDERLY	−1.54*	−1.29*	−0.19	0.01
	(0.51)	(0.47)	(0.30)	(0.29)
AGRICULTURE	0.39*	0.24**	0.47*	0.41*
	(0.09)	(0.10)	(0.08)	(0.09)
WIDOWRATE	0.03	−0.02	0.22**	0.19**
	(0.12)	(0.11)	(0.11)	(0.11)
In SSLAW	−1.13	−1.45	−2.45**	−2.53**
	(1.33)	(1.29)	(1.11)	(1.12)
PROVIDENT	−2.09	−1.12	−6.80**	7.00**
	(3.99)	(3.87)	(3.31)	(3.33)
Adjusted R^2	0.77	0.79	0.65	0.65

Standard errors are in parentheses. Number of countries is 102.
* Coefficient is significantly different from zero at the 0.01 confidence level.
** Coefficient is significantly different from zero at the 0.10 confidence level.

and older using both the per capita GNP variable and the purchasing power parity measure.

For men, the results presented in Column 1, Table 9 on the restricted sample are very similar to those reported for the full sample (Column 3, Table 5), although the estimated coefficient on per capita income is −3.8 compared to −2.7 in Table 5. When the model is re-estimated using the purchasing power parity variable, the income coefficient becomes much larger and indicates that a 10 percent increase in per capita income results in a decline in the labor force participation rate of one percentage point. This effect is more than twice the size of the income effect based on per capita GNP. This model also does a slightly better job of explaining the variation in participation rates across countries ($R^2 = 0.79$ compared to $R^2 = 0.77$).

Similar equations were estimated for the two younger age groups of men (not shown). The estimated income coefficients for men aged 55 to 59 is −1.9 using the per capita income variable and −4.9 using the purchasing power parity variable. For men aged 60 to 64, the income coefficient goes from

−4.0 to −9.8 when the PWT variable is used. In both cases, the explanatory power of the equation is greater with the purchasing power parity variable.

The use of the purchasing power parity income variable has much less impact on the regression equation for women aged 65 and older. Although the income coefficient has different signs in the two equations, it is insignificant in both equations. Rather small changes are noted in the other explanatory variables and there is virtually no change in the explanatory power of the regression equation. A similar pattern holds for women aged 60 to 64 (not shown). For women aged 55 to 59, the estimated income effects using the per capita income variable yields a positive and significant coefficient (not shown). Switching to the purchasing power parity variable reduces the size of the income coefficient, but it is now insignificant.

If the purchasing power parity concept more accurately captures the differences in economic well being across countries, then using per capita GNP underestimates the effect of changes in real income on older men's labor force participation. In general, high-income countries have lower levels of income when measured by the purchasing power parity and low and middle-income countries have much higher incomes. For example, the World Bank reports Switzerland's per capita income as $32,310, while the Penn World Table reports it as $16,505. Mozambique's per capita income is measured as $80 by the World Bank and $760 by the Penn World Table.

Conclusions

In countries with extremely low income per capita, most persons remain in the labor force until very old ages or until they are unable to continue working. With economic development, real income increases; the industrial composition of the economy changes and there is typically a decline in agricultural employment; and national retirement programs are established and gradually made more generous in both coverage and benefits. Economic development also is associated with the onset of the demographic transition and the related increases in the relative size of the older population and increases the ratio of older women to older men.

The relationships between these changes and the proportion of older men and women who remain in the labor force were estimated for 134 countries. In general, increases in real per capita income tend to reduce the labor force participation rates of older men and women. This effect is nonlinear and seems to be concentrated among those countries with incomes between $600 and $7,500 dollars. Income measures that take account of purchasing power parity also tend to show more negative income coefficients. Further analysis of the effect of rising income on retirement rates is needed to determine the true nature of this effect.

One of the most consistent relationships affecting a country's labor force participation rates for older men and women is the degree to which its workers are employed in the agricultural sector. In general, a one percent increase in the proportion of a country's workers that are employed in agriculture results in an average of about one-half of a percentage point increase in the proportion of older workers remaining in the labor force. Labor force participation rates decrease as social security programs mature, and when countries have lower eligibility ages for benefits. Increases in widowhood tend to increase women's labor force participation, and, as expected, have little effect on men's labor force participation rates.

Interestingly, this analysis shows that there are differences in how men and women respond to the other factors that affect labor force participation. While there is a significant and negative relationship between income and labor force participation when income is the only regressor, that relationship is substantially altered when other factors are included. For men in the older age categories, there is usually a significant and negative coefficient on income. But for women, there is usually a positive and significant income coefficient only for the younger age categories. This relationship reflects the increased labor force participation rate of women in countries with higher income. The income coefficient is usually statistically insignificant for the two older groups of women.

The variable indicating the relative supply of older relative to younger persons in a country's population consistently shows a significantly negative relationship with male labor force participation. Only for women aged 65 and older in the high-income sample is the coefficient on this variable also negative and significant, but it is much smaller in magnitude than in the men's regressions. Since the coefficient on this variable is often insignificant in the analysis of women's labor force participation, it does not have as much explanatory power as it does in the men's analysis. Women in countries with provident funds have higher participation rates while men in these countries tend to have lower participation rates. This result suggests that women with shorter working careers and lower wages would be better able to 'afford' retirement under an annuity type of national social security plan that also redistributes income.

In summary, an analysis of the variation in labor force participation rates of older persons in most of the nations of the world supports the hypothesized relationships between economic development and the proportion of persons aged 55 and over who remain in the labor force. For both men and women, the growth in real income, the shift away from agricultural employment, the aging of the population, and the development of national retirement programs tend to result in earlier retirement. These relationships are complex and non-linear and further analysis needs to be conducted in order to understand more completely the labor supply responses to economic development.

Notes

1. Durand (1975) is an important exception to this concentration on retirement patterns only in industrialized nations.
2. Examples of these studies include Gordon (1963) and Peckman, Aaron & Taussig (1968). Johnson & Zimmermann (1993) report that around 1900, approximately three quarters of all men aged 65 and above in France, Germany, and Britain were in the labor force, but by the late 1980s considerably fewer than one in ten men over 65 were in work in these countries. Rein & Jacobs (1993) find that there was a decline in the labor force participation rates of men aged 55 to 64 in most of the OECD countries between 1970 and 1990.
3. More detailed discussion of the development of these estimates can be obtained from Richard Anker, Employment and Training Department, ILO, Geneva.
4. The distribution of national per capita incomes is highly skewed; however, the natural log of per capita income is normally distributed.
5. Purchasing power parity is based on the proposition that national price levels of common goods should be equal when they are converted to a common currency. Rogoff (1996) provides a recent discussion of this concept.
6. Johnson & Zimmermann (1993) discuss the linkages between aging populations and the trend toward earlier retirement in Europe.
7. For example, if there were four women aged 55 and over to every three men aged 55 and over, then the WIDOWRATE would be 33.3 percent [(4/3-1) × 100] which implies that a country has one-third more older women than older men.
8. Gordon (1988) states that "historically, industrialization and urbanization have tended to be accompanied by a reduction in the usual age of retirement. Aging farmers, especially those who are self-employed, can gradually turn the responsibility for managing the farm over to adult children without leaving the labor force completely. Thus, the percentage of elderly men in the labor force tends to be relatively high in countries with a large proportion of the labor force in agriculture".
9. The US Social Security Administration publishes a bulletin entitled *Social Security Programs Throughout the World* every two years. The authors decided to employ information contained in the 1989 volume instead of the 1991 volume. This eliminates the chance that changes made after 1990 would be incorporated into our data. Some of the newly created countries formed after the break up of the USSR, Czechoslovakia, and Yugoslavia were not included in either the 1989 or the 1991 volumes. Most of these countries were included in the 1993 volume. For these countries, data included in the 1993 volume were used to create the social security variables.
10. The natural log of this variable is used in regressions since the effect of an additional year of existence of a social security program on labor force participation is expected to decrease with maturity of the system. Several countries in this study do not have a national social security program and are therefore assigned a value of zero of SSLAW.

11. Detailed discussion of national social security systems and the use of provident funds are reported in World Bank (1994) and Kinsella & Gist (1995).

12. The Eastern/Central European countries for which the World Bank provides income per capita include Bulgaria, the Czech Republic, Hungary, Poland, and Romania. We have included Lithuania and Yugoslavia in this group of formerly planned economies.

13. In this analysis, Islamic countries are those that have Islam as the official religion or more than half of the population is Muslim as identified by the Foundation Culturelle Islamic.

References

Clark, R. & Anker, R. (1990). Labour force participation rates of older persons: an international comparison, *International Labour Review* 129(2): 255–271.

Clark, R. & Anker, R. (1993). Cross-national analysis of labor force participation of older men and women, *Economic Development and Cultural Change* 41(3): 489–512.

Costa, D. (1998). *The evolution of retirement*. Chicago: University of Chicago Press.

Durand, J. (1975). *The labor force in economic development*. Princeton, NJ: Princeton University Press.

Gordon, M. (1963). *The economics of welfare policies*. New York: Columbia University Press.

Gordon, M. (1988). *Social security policies in industrial countries*. New York: Cambridge University Press.

Heston, A. & Summers, R. (1996). International price and quantity comparisons: potentials and pitfalls, *American Economic Review* 86(2): 20–24.

International Labour Office (1999). *Labour force estimates and projections: 1950–2010*. Geneva: ILO (forthcoming).

Johnson, P. & Zimmermann, K. (1993). Ageing and the European labour market: public policy issues, pp. 1–25, in P. Johnson & K. Zimmermann (eds.), *Labour markets in an ageing Europe*, Cambridge: Cambridge University Press.

Kinsella, K. & Gist, Y. (1995). *Older workers, retirement, and pensions: a comparative international chartbook*. Washington, DC: US Bureau of Census.

Long, C. (1958). *The labor force under changing income and employment*. Princeton, NJ: Princeton University Press.

Peckman, J., Aaron, H. & Taussig, M. (1968). *Social security: perspectives for reform*. Washington, DC: The Brookings Institution.

Rein, M. & Jacobs, K. (1993). Ageing and employment trends: a comparative analysis for OECD countries, in P. Johnson & K. Zimmermann (eds.), *Labour markets in an ageing Europe*, pp. 53–78, Cambridge: Cambridge University Press.

Rogoff, K. (1996). The purchasing power parity puzzle, *Journal of Economic Literature* 34(2): 647–668.

Summers, R. & Heston, A. (1991). The Penn World Table (Mark 5): An expanded set of international comparisons, 1950–1988, *Quarterly Journal of Economics* 106(2): 327–368.

US Social Security Administration (1990). *Social security programs throughout the world – 1989*. Washington, DC: US Department of Health and Human Services.

US Social Security Administration (1994). *Social security programs throughout the world – 1993*. Washington, DC: US Department of Health and Human Services.

World Bank (1994). *Averting the old age crisis*. Oxford: Oxford University Press.

Address for correspondence: Robert L. Clark, College of Management, Box 7229, North Carolina State University, Raleigh, NC 27695, USA
Phone: (919) 515-4568; Fax: (919) 515-6943; E-mail: robert_clark@ncsu.edu

Population Aging in Canada and Japan: Implications for Labour Force and Career Patterns

Rosemary A. Venne*
University of Saskatchewan

Abstract

The scenario of population aging in developed countries has been discussed mainly in terms of spiralling pension and health care costs. With below-replacement-level fertility rates in most of the developed world, many countries face a stagnant or slow growing labour supply. During the late 1980s in North America, business writers were warning of the coming labour force shortage as the baby bust cohort began to enter the labour force. Despite a slower growing labour force throughout the 1990s, the matter of shortages was a non-issue for Canada during the early 1990s recession with slow growing labour demand during most of the decade. Thus, demand for labour, though difficult to predict, is an important factor that will affect the aging labour force. Another factor is that of career patterns. In North America, career patterns of the immediate three postwar decades (lifelong linear careers) are giving way to more varied career patterns with delayering, rising credentialism, and lifelong learning as issues that are confronting both employers and employees. This paper examines labour force and career pattern issues with respect to Canada and Japan. Comparisons are drawn between demographic patterns and career patterns of the two countries.

Résumé

On a discuté du scénario du vieillissement de la population dans les pays développés principalement par rapport à la montée en fièvre des coûts de pension ainsi que ceux associés aux soins de santé. Avec des taux de fécondité inférieurs au seuil de renouvellement des générations dans la plupart des pays en voie de développement, plusieurs pays font face à une croissance ralentie ou stagnante de l'offre de main-d'oeuvre. Vers la fin des années 1980 en Amérique du Nord, les chroniqueurs en affaires nous allertaient à la «penurie de main-d'oeuvre» quand la génération issue de l'effrondrement de la natalité rentrerait sur le marché du travail. Malgré la croissance ralentie de l'offre de main-d'oeuvre durant les années 1990, la question de penurie ne figurait pas au Canada pendant la recession au début des années 1990 car la demande de main-d'oeuvre était ralentie pendant la plupart de la décennie. Donc, la demande de main-d'oeuvre, bien que difficile à prédire, est un facteur important influant sur une main-d'oeuvre vieillissante. Un autre facteur est celui de l'orientation des carrières. En Amérique du Nord, l'orientation des carrières des trois décennies d'après-guerre (carrières linéaires continues) cèdent le passage à une orientation des carrières plus variée entraînant des questions de déstratification, diplômanie accroissante, et formation permanente affrontant les employés et les employeurs.

Both Canada and Japan have experienced profound demographic changes over the postwar period. This paper will provide a demographic perspective as it relates to career patterns and labour force issues in the postwar period. The scenario of population aging in developed countries has been mainly discussed in terms of spiralling pension and health care costs. With below-

replacement-level fertility rates in most of the developed world, many countries face a stagnant or slow growing labour supply. Despite a slower growing labour force throughout the 1990s, the matter of shortages was a non-issue in Canada during the early 1990s recession. Thus demand for labour, though difficult to predict, is an important factor that will affect the aging labour force. Another factor is that of career patterns. In North America, rigid career patterns of the immediate three postwar decades are giving way to more varied career patterns. Japanese rigidity in career patterns is recently said to be changing as well.

*College of Commerce (IROB), University of Saskatchewan, Campus Drive, Saskatoon, SK, Canada S7N 5A7. E-mail: VENNE@commerce.usask.ca

Canadian Journal of Administrative Sciences
Revue canadienne des sciences de l'administration
18(1), 40-49

© ASAC 2001

344

Table 1
Key Population Statistics—Canada and Japan, 1998

	Canada	Japan
Percent of population <15 years old	20	15
Percent of population 65+ years old	12	16
Percent of population 16-64 years old	68	69
Population (in millions) 1998	30.6	126.4
Projected population 2010	35	127.6
Projected population 2025	40.3	120.9
Natural increase (annual, %)	0.5	0.2
Total fertility rate	1.6	1.4

Source: Population Reference Bureau (1998)

Table 2
Population Distribution by Age and Sex, 1998 (%)

Age Groups	Canada			Japan		
	Total	Male	Female	Total	Male	Female
0-4	6.21	6.44	6	4.72	4.94	4.51
5-9	6.83	7.07	6.6	4.83	5.05	4.61
10-14	6.68	6.92	6.43	5.52	5.78	5.28
15-19	6.76	7.01	6.52	6.17	6.46	5.89
20-24	6.73	6.93	6.53	7.32	7.66	7
25-29	7.03	7.18	6.89	7.69	7.98	7.42
30-34	8.02	8.18	7.86	6.7	6.92	6.49
35-39	8.89	9.03	8.76	6.22	6.41	6.03
40-44	8.33	8.4	8.25	6.31	6.48	6.15
45-49	7.25	7.3	7.19	8.05	8.23	7.87
50-54	6.19	6.22	6.15	7.41	7.53	7.29
55-59	4.75	4.74	4.75	6.75	6.77	6.72
60-64	4	3.97	4.04	6.1	6.02	6.17
65-69	3.77	3.65	3.89	5.42	5.22	5.61
70-74	3.24	2.93	3.55	4.36	3.96	4.75
75 +	5.32	4.01	6.58	6.43	4.58	8.21

Source: Statistics Canada: Canada (1999); Statistics Bureau & Statistics Centre: Japan (1999).

This paper examines labour force and career pattern issues with respect to Canada and Japan and draws comparisons between the demographic profiles and career patterns of the two countries. Conclusions are discussed in terms of labour force shortages and possible policies to deal with this issue.

Canada

Demographic Perspective

In demography, the study of population patterns, there is a saying that "behind most news stories is a pop-

Canadian Journal of Administrative Sciences
Revue canadienne des sciences de l'administration
18(1), 40-49

ulation story" (Haupt & Kane, 1991, p. 2). Population change has an impact on all facets of life. Like most industrialized countries, Canada has a slowly aging population and a below-replacement-level fertility rate (see Table 1). The Canadian fertility rate is currently 1.6, below the level required to replace each generation (the replacement-level fertility rate is usually around 2.1 for an industrialized country; Weeks, 1994). As a country becomes less agrarian and more industrialized, and as women become more educated and enter the labour force, family size becomes smaller (see Novak, 1988; Weeks, 1994). Unlike most other industrialized countries, Canada had a prolonged postwar fertility boom, commonly referred to as the "baby boom", giving a decided middle-age bulge to its current population profile. This population pattern of a prolonged postwar fertility boom period is shared with few other industrialized countries, notably the U.S., Australia, and New Zealand.

The postwar fertility boom, generally defined as a two-decade period from 1947 to 1966, is a central fact of the Canadian population and accounts for approximately one-third of the population (Foot, 1996). The boom is preceded and followed by bust or smaller generations. Prior to the postwar fertility boom, fertility rates (defined as the number of children per woman) declined over the Depression and wartime years. Following the baby boom, fertility rates declined over the late 1960s and 1970s. The latter baby bust period coincided with women entering the labour force in unprecedented numbers. Despite below-replacement-level fertility rates, there was a moderate increase in the number of births over the 1980s and into the mid-1990s as the baby boom women were passing through their prime childbearing years. This is usually referred to as a junior boom or the baby boom echo effect. This echo-boom group is poised to enter the Canadian labour market in the coming decades. Moving from the Depression/wartime era baby bust (mostly in their fifties and sixties), to the postwar baby boom (mostly in their thirties and forties), and then to our most recent baby bust (mostly in their twenties) represents a huge swing in the size of generations in Canada (see Table 2).

Thus Canada's demographic pattern is one with a distinct middle-aged bulge, a slow growing labour force, and an aging population (see Table 1 for population projections in 2010 and 2025). The scenario of population aging with rising pension and health care costs is one that is beginning to be discussed in terms of intergenerational equity issues in North America as greater percentages creep into the elderly dependent group, those aged +65 (see Table 1) (see Corak, 1998; McDaniel, 1997). Of course, North America is aging at a slower pace than most other developed countries as any prolonged increase in fertility will slow down a country's

aging process. Europe and Japan, for instance, are aging at a faster pace as they did not have a significant postwar fertility increase.

In terms of labour force growth, Canada has a slow growing labour force despite new entrants beginning to be drawn from the baby boom echo. In terms of human resource planning, it can be said that the shape of the labour force of the next 20 years is already known as it is already born (except for the factor of immigration). With an aging population in Canada, the factor of immigration can play a more important role in shaping our labour force. Traditionally Canada, as a large immigrant-receiving country, has used immigration to fill in its labour force needs. Foot (1996) points out that Canada is one of the few countries operating an immigration program with numerical targets and selection criteria. He also notes that even if below-replacement fertility continues in Canada (a highly likely scenario), the country needs only a small amount of immigration to maintain a substantial population. Immigration thus remains a tool for controlling population (and labour force) growth in a country such as Canada. Canada's significant international immigration, together with its below-replacement fertility rates and low mortality, yield an annual population increase of 0.5% (Population Reference Bureau, 1998; see Table 1).

Career Patterns

Driver (1985) presents a classification of four career paths commonly found in North America. The first one, found in the immediate postwar period, is the steady state career concept which defines a career as a lifelong commitment to a field with a lifelong career at one firm. The second is the linear career concept, which is associated with upward career movement or climbing the career ladder. During the postwar economic boom in North America, described by Bardwick (1986) as North America's economic heyday of 30 glorious years, linear and steady state career paths held sway as employers grappled with strong economic growth and a small, mainly male labour force. Of course, new labour force entrants over the immediate postwar period consisted of Depression/wartime baby busters. The postwar economic expansion that employers experienced led to disproportionate increases in white collar and managerial positions, lifelong one-company careers, and rapid promotions up tall organizational hierarchies (Bardwick, 1986; Bennett, 1990).

Driver's (1985) third career concept is the spiral career where there is significant change in occupations over a lifetime and career movement consists of mainly horizontal moves as opposed to only promotions. Occupational flexibility is emphasized along with lifelong

Canadian Journal of Administrative Sciences
Revue canadienne des sciences de l'administration
18(1), 40-49

education. There is a great deal of job movement in the transitory career concept. This last career concept is characterized by youth, part-time, and the temporary workforce (e.g., contract work or contingent workforce). These latter two concepts have become more common-place during the 1980s and 1990s in North America as the postwar economic boom ended and a less buoyant economy took its place resulting in more varied career patterns (see Foot & Venne, 1990).

With respect to the large group of postwar boomers, large demographic groups are said to face more within-group competition for jobs. As the baby boom spanned two decades, it is important to realize that different birth years within this boom generation will have different labour force experiences. Early boomers may have faced conditions similar to the Depression/wartime busters immediately preceding them, while middle and later boomers faced more gen-erational crowding and a less favourable economic cli-mate when they entered the labour force. Canada did a good job of absorbing most of the boomers (coupled with rising female labour force participation rates), especially the mid to early boomers, into their labour force (see Foot & Venne, 1990). Generally, baby bust generations do well in their careers and earnings because they face less competition from fellow busters (see Berger, 1989; Weeks, 1994). The caveat for the current busters is that they follow on the heels of a par-ticularly large baby boom generation and they face less favourable economic conditions compared to their Depression/wartime bust counterparts.

The typical employment pattern for the postwar worker, the steady state or linear career path with regu-lar promotions and stable employment (often with life-time employment with one firm), is becoming less com-mon (see Bardwick, 1986; Bennett, 1990; Naisbitt & Aburdene, 1985). The delayering thrust in organizations is said to occur due to technological change, increased global competition, and retrenchment during recessions (Bardwick, 1986). In order to cope with today's fast-paced economy, the old style, rigid organizational hier-archies had to adapt to flatter organizational structures which better suit today's fast-paced environment because they tend to have faster response time. With flat-ter organizational structure come fewer promotions, and fewer linear career patterns. Careers today are more like-ly to have a spiral or transitory pattern with more hori-zontal movement (see Egan, 1994). The increased flexi-bility on the part of many firms (e.g., alternative worktime arrangements, leave programs, flexible benefit plans) reflects the fact that the labour force of today is more diverse than the labour force of the 1950s and

1960s when a one-size-fits-all benefits plan sufficed for the mainly male workforce. The recent attention to issues of work/life balance addresses the fact that the workforce now has a sizable female component and many more dual-earner households (see Duxbury, Hig-gins, Lee, & Mills, 1991; Higgins, Duxbury, & Lee, 1992).

Another factor is slower wage growth during the 1980s and 1990s compared to the immediate three post-war decades (see Rashid, 1993). The postwar decades of the 1950s and 1960s, in particular, saw huge increases in real wages compared to more stagnant wage growth from the mid-1970s to present. Yet another factor affect-ing today's youth, and one reason why they are slower to leave home, is rising skill requirements or escalating credentialism (see Boyd & Norris, 1995; O'Hara, 1993). Compared to just a few decades ago, the so-called school-to-work transition has become a more prolonged and complex process (see Krahn, Mosher, & Johnson, 1993). Fewer jobs require only a high school degree and young people are forced to increase their participation rate in post-secondary education. So this trend to rising skill requirements and the fact of spiral career concepts has turned people into lifelong learners (Naisbitt & Aburdene, 1985).

During the 1960s, 1970s, and part of the 1980s, Canada experienced significant labour growth as the baby boom (coupled with rising female labour force par-ticipation rates) entered the labour force. With the entry of the current busters, the labour force has been slow growing during the mid to late 1980s and into the 1990s (growth of 1.5%, half of what it was during the baby boom entry decades; Foot, 1996). Slowed labour force growth throughout the mid to late 1980s prompted cries of a coming labour shortage in North America (see Nais-bitt & Aburdene, 1985) which were promptly stifled dur-ing the recession of the early 1990s. Economic factors, such as the recession of the early 1990s and its lingering effects, have a powerful effect on labour demand. The subsequent recovery after the recession in Canada was referred to as a jobless one with job demand not picking up until later in the decade. The entrance of the baby boom echo into the labour force in the new millennium will slightly increase the size of the labour force, espe-cially in those parts of the country which have a more significant baby boom echo (Ontario and west; see Foot, 1996). Canadian labour force participation rates are sim-ilar to those of other industrialized countries with high female participation and lessening participation of elder-ly males (due to better pensions and decreasing age of retirement) and lessened participation of youth (due to increased educational attainment) (see Table 3).

Canadian Journal of Administrative Sciences
Revue canadienne des sciences de l'administration
18(1), 40-49

Table 3
Labour Force Participation Rates (%)

Age groups	Canada (1998)		Japan (1996)	
	Male	Female	Male	Female
15-24	63.6	60.4	48.9	47.6
25-44	92.4	78.8	97.7	65.8
45-64	77.3	59.7	84.9	48.8
65 +	10.6	3 4	36.7	15.4

Source: Statistics Canada (1999).

Japan

Demographic Perspective

Japan began its demographic transition from high to low fertility and mortality much later than other developed countries such as Canada, but finished it with record speed (Martin, 1989). Unlike Canada, Japan did not experience a significant postwar baby boom. Japan experienced a precipitous drop in fertility during the immediate postwar period. Romaniuc (1984) notes that the government of Japan, faced with postwar construction, enacted policies that made the easing of population pressure a major national objective. He goes so far as to label these policies "vigorously anti-natalist". Since the early 1960s, Japan has experienced below-replacement-level fertility rates, well ahead of western countries such as Canada. After a slight recovery during the 1970s, Japan's fertility rate slipped to an all-time low of 1.8 in 1979 and is currently hovering around 1.4 (Romaniuc, 1984; PRB, 1998) (see Table 1). Japan's transition has resulted in a rapidly aging population (Martin, 1989). For example, by the year 2025 Japan is projected to have one of the most elderly populations with 23% over age 65. The opposite side of the coin is that while the older sector increases, there is a drastic decline in the number of young people. Seike (1997) points out that there will be a decline of one-third for the 20-29 age group, from approximately 19 million in 1995 to 12.5 million projected in 2015. With no significant international immigration, Japan's low fertility rates and low mortality yield an annual population increase of 0.2% (PRB, 1998, see Table 1).

Japan's age-sex profile or population pyramid reveals mainly bust periods with two brief boom interludes, a brief postwar boom (born 1947-1949, currently entering their fifties) and what is referred to as a junior baby boom, the children of the earlier boom (born 1971-1974, currently in their mid to late twenties) (see Table 2). The Japanese population pyramid continues to collapse at the base due to several decades of declining and below-replacement-level fertility rates. While there was a large segment of women in their prime childbearing years, Japan had population growth momentum and grew (as in the early to mid-1970s). Projections for Japan's population (PRB, 1998) show it declining by six million by 2025 (see Table 1). Japan has the lowest level of mortality in the world and one of the highest life expectancies (PRB, 1998) and, despite low fertility rates, its population is still growing, although very slowly, because of population growth momentum. Put simply, there are still enough women in their main childbearing years that, even at a low fertility rate of 1.4, they produce more babies each year than there are people dying (Weeks, 1994).

Romaniuc (1984) notes that the Japanese government during the 1980s was using measures to encourage natality (e.g., giving child allowances to couples with three or more children). A Japanese policy paper by the Japan Federation of Economic Organizations (Keidanren, 1999) discusses finding answers to the declining birth rate "problem" and the resulting greying of Japan in terms of encouraging pronatalist policies on the part of the government, business, and communities. Specifically, the issues of childcare and other pronatalist policies on the part of government are examined as well as the topic of workplace flexibilities (e.g. more mid-career hiring and part-time work) for the business sector. The policy paper concludes that the decline in fertility rates is attributable to factors in the system which can be reformed through the combined efforts of government, business, communities, and families.

Weeks (1994) points out that Japan has a long history of "demographic consciousness" (p. 147) which is not surprising given its unified history (Thurow, 1992). Confidence in Keidanren's conclusion that fertility may be amendable to change with the right combination of policies may not be warranted based on the experience of other countries' pronatalist policies. The evidence is that various government sponsored pronatalist policies have had little effect on the fertility rate (see Romaniuc, 1984; Weeks, 1994). Weeks (1994) notes that France maintains the policy of providing monthly allowances to couples who have a second or higher-order child despite the lack of evidence that this policy has had any measurable impact on the birth rate. Given that Japan is prevalent in many factors that are associated with low fertility rates (e.g., high education levels of women, women in the paid labour force, easy access to abortion or birth control, and a highly urban society; Weeks 1994), any pronatalist policies may have a negligible effect on current fertility patterns.

Thurow (1992) points out that Japan is underdeveloped in terms of housing, roads, and parks. He describes housing as a critical bottleneck in places like Tokyo where traditions thwart the construction of large-scale housing and infrastructure projects (indeed, fertility rates are lowest in Tokyo). Keidanren's (1999) policy paper acknowledges some of these issues in its policy recommendations. Concerns that future shortages of young workers may thwart Japan's then expanding economy were an issue in trying to increase the fertility rate during the 1980s and continue to be an issue today. Canada and Japan have similar percentages in the main labour force segment of the population, but there are significant differences in the other key segments. Compared to Canada, Japan is an older society with higher percentages in the elderly dependents (65+) and lower percentages in the young dependents (<15) age groups (see Table 1).

Other factors regarding population aging and labour force growth are male/female labour force participation rates. In fact, Japanese female participation rates resemble older Canadian patterns of the immediate postwar decades (see McVey & Kalbach, 1995). There is an untapped source of labour potential in this group of women yet there are constraints in terms of rigidity in both male and female career patterns and male-female roles (see Ogasawara, 1998). Participation rates will be dealt with in the section on careers.

Another factor is that there is little in the way of immigration. Countries with a slow-growing labour force could use immigration to fill in their labour force needs. Unlike Canada, which has traditionally been and continues to be an immigrant-receiving nation, Japan has an extremely restrictive immigration policy, so migrants contribute little to demographic change in Japan (Weeks, 1994). Imano (1997) notes that the flow of mostly skilled foreign workers into Japan has increased, especially since the 1980s. Yet the numbers of these workers are very small relative to population. Not surprisingly, immigration is a non-issue in the Kiedanren (1999) policy paper regarding population aging, whereas in Canada the topic of immigration has been a key part of the population aging discussion (see Foot, 1996; McVey & Kalbach, 1995). Japan has been described as a country that has difficulties integrating outsiders into its labour force and its society, rendering immigration for labour force growth a non-solution (see Thurow, 1992, who refers to Japan as the country "least willing or able to absorb immigrants"; p. 251). He describes the closed Japanese corporate culture as both a strength and a weakness. It is a strength in terms of its powerful cohesive internal culture, unified history, and homogeneity. It is a weakness in terms of integrating foreign managers and professionals as equals into its corporate culture.

Career Patterns

One profound difference between Canada and Japan is the intense and pronounced differences between the genders in career patterns. Educated males employed by large firms seem to follow a combination of the steady state and linear career patterns with lifelong one-company careers. Lu (1987) documents the traditional, white-collar male career path at a large firm. Lifetime employment, a male preserve, begins at the bottom of the hierarchy with slow promotions, job rotation, a great deal of training, and eventual retirement from the same firm where a man started. Intense recruiting and selection procedures are carried out in the spring of the year for these mainly university graduates. Steady state is evident in the lifetime employment security while the linear career path is evidenced by the slow but steady rate of rise up the organizational hierarchy. The steady state career pattern seems to be more prevalent than the linear one (the latter being characterized by power and competition), as the Japanese system seems to place more emphasis on cooperation and security. Also, the lifetime employment system of Japanese firms has the feature of steadily rising seniority-based payments, another feature of the steady state career pattern (Tasker, 1987).

Martin (1989) notes that the lifetime employment system (which applies to less than half or 43% of the labour force) was instituted between the two world wars to ensure company loyalty during labour shortages, especially among the skilled male workers that a company had trained. Those outside of the lifetime employment system (mostly women) seem to have a transitory career path, with more tenuous employment, few benefits, and part-time work (defined as less than 35 hours per week). Thus the two most prevalent career patterns in Japan are the steady state and the transitory.

One of the most important aspects of the career patterns of Japan is the two-track system which is split along gender lines (Ogasawara, 1998). Men and women are recruited immediately after post-secondary education for either the integrated track (who are trained to become managers, almost all males) or the clerical track (all females). Tasker (1987) states that the overwhelming majority of women are stuck in repetitious clerical jobs that offer no prospect of advancement. He goes so far as to refer to these clerical-track office ladies as "decorative", performing simple tasks and making the workplace comfortable.

Ogasawara (1998) discusses female employment patterns and notes that, as with Canadian women, Japan-

Canadian Journal of Administrative Sciences
Revue canadienne des sciences de l'administration
18(1), 40-49

ese women have been entering the workforce since the early 1960s and now constitute about 40% of the labour force (compared with about 45% in Canada). Japan has lower female participation rates compared to Canada and other industrialized countries, with the exception of the 65+ age group (see Table 3). Japanese women's participation rates resemble the traditional M-shaped or double-peaked pattern with two participation rate peaks. First, women enter the workforce after school (twenties), then a significant percentage leave the workforce to raise a family (thirties). The second and lower peak occurs with women returning to the workplace after their children are grown (forties). The M pattern resembles Canadian women's labour force participation rates from the early 1960s (see McVey & Kalbach, 1995). Canadian women's labour force participation increases during the 1970s and beyond have almost obscured the traditional double-peaked pattern. Currently, the patterns are approaching the broad inverted U or high plateau characteristic of the male pattern, which is similar for both Canadian and Japanese males (who enter the workforce after school and stay until retirement; see McVey & Kalbach, 1995).

According to Ogasawara (1998), the two peaks in the pattern of Japanese women's labour force participation rates coincide with different types of jobs. Since the overwhelming majority of large and prominent companies in Japan only recruit female full-time employees directly from school (the first peak), re-entrants (the second peak) usually seek employment either in smaller firms or as part-time workers (Ogasawara, 1998). The secondary treatment of mid-career recruits (those hired at any time other than upon finishing university or high school), and of part-time or temporary employees is tied up in the notion of lifetime employment for those elite, mostly male workers who are lifetime members of the corporate family (Whitehall, 1991). The part-time workers often work as many hours as regular employees, although with lower pay levels and few benefits.

Ogasawara (1998) describes the intense sex discrimination still prevalent in Japan and the male-biased career patterns and sharply delineated sex roles. McMillan (1985) also describes the elite exclusion of women in Japanese firms. Despite increases in educational attainment, they are employed in small and medium-sized firms with limited mobility and concentrated in low-paying sectors. Recruitment of women (referred to as "special employees") is said to be far more casual than the rigorous procedures used for men (referred to as "regular employees") (Whitehall, 1991, p. 141). Differential treatment of these employee groups seems to be an accepted aspect of Japanese society. In Canada, sex segregation in the professions is currently much less pronounced, with women steadily moving into positions of responsibility and previously male-dominated areas during the last few decades, whereas this is rare in Japan. Also, pay differentials between men and women are greater in Japan than in most other highly industrialized countries (Tasker, 1987).

Comparisons Between Canada and Japan

In terms of demographics, Canada starts the aging process from a much younger base than Japan (Foot, 1996). The country's postwar fertility boom slowed its aging compared to either Japan or Europe. With respect to the greying of the population, Foot (1996) proposes that the concept of below-replacement-level fertility and a stabilizing or even slowly declining population is not such a great cause for alarm. He points out that an absence of population growth in a country can result in increased productivity, less unemployment, and reduced pressure on both urban and rural environments. With respect to the latter issue, Alston (1989) refers to environmental quality and industrial pollution as issues of rising concern in Japan. Canada, too, has concerns about industrial pollution but is much less densely populated than Japan. With respect to employment, Rifkin (1995), in his book *The End of Work*, refers to a future with much less regular employment than today, given technological change. Martin (1989) suggests a likely source of labour for Japan will be through the use of increased robotics. Foot (1996) has also noted that Japan has turned to technology in the past to deal with a slow growing workforce. Low fertility rates are common among industrialized, urbanized countries and have been occurring for some decades now, especially in parts of Europe. While some countries institute pronatalist policies (France is the best example; see Romaniuc, 1984) other countries are satisfied or appear unconcerned (see PRB, 1998). Thus, a greying population does not necessarily mean a gloom and doom scenario for an industrialized country.

The topic of future labour force shortages has been much debated in aging, industrialized countries, particularly Japan. Several writers note that pressure to adapt will lead to many changes in the traditional career patterns that Japan has followed. Tasker (1987) notes that changes are coming to job structures in Japan, mainly driven by profound economic changes and not necessarily by ideology. Yet, Sako (1997) points out that the speculation regarding the end of the Japanese employment system has occurred with each economic crisis, but the system has persisted, though with some painful adjustments. The most significant modification is a shift from continuous employment within a single enterprise to that within an extended enterprise grouping (Sako, 1997). Other changes relate to pressure on seniority-based pay.

Canadian Journal of Administrative Sciences
Revue canadienne des sciences de l'administration
18(1), 40-49

Slower growth may force Japanese firms to optimize the use of assets under their control. Japanese women's labour force participation rates, though lower than Canada's, have been rising. Although Johnston (1991) argues that Japan has few women left to add to its labour force, firms may be able to deploy them to more productive jobs. Given that Japanese women are highly educated, according to Tasker (1987), confining them to trivial, routine work represents an immense waste of human resources both for individual firms and the economy as a whole and he predicts that competitive forces will not allow it to continue for long. "The degree of success Japan achieves in the next stage of its development may well depend on the ability of companies to generate a new flow of talent from the women workers they already have" (Tasker, 1987, p. 104). Even in the mid to late 1980s women were already making inroads in new vital areas such as biotechnology and as CEOs in small service-sector entrepreneurial firms.

From a more recent perspective, Ogasawara (1998) documents changes going on in the traditional Japanese workplace, especially with respect to women's jobs. Some firms have introduced merit pay and performance reviews for clerical workers. She documents the reasons for the change in treatment of female employees. Management's recent enthusiasm to utilize their female clerical workers more efficiently may be due to the economic slump that began in the early 1990s, forcing firms to review personnel costs of clerical workers. There are increases in the number of women working for a longer period of time (the gradual smoothing of the M curve in women's labour force participation rates) and the male-female wage gap has narrowed (Wakisaka, 1997). Also there has been a recent increase in the number of women hired as "integrated track" employees, although they tend to be treated as specialists and receive less training than their male counterparts (Ogasawara, 1998).

Another development has been the cost cutting measure on the part of firms to hire temporary workers when replacing retiring clerical employees. Although contingent work is becoming more common in Canada (see Krahn, 1995), it seems a new development in Japan for this particular group of workers. Ogasawara (1998) points out that the overwhelming majority of Japanese firms still refrain from firing regular employees, so this temporary employee measure may be one other way to cut costs without disturbing the traditional system for regular employees. There seems to be great reluctance to disturb the system and rock the boat especially for the so-called regular employees, though this may be changing with more mid-career hiring being called for (Keidanren, 1999).

Alston (1989) also discusses the coming labour shortage in Japan. One short-run solution that he sees being considered is the recruitment of older workers. However, recruiting skilled, older, mid-career workers threatens the Japanese notion of lifetime employment and worker loyalty. He points out that workers are less likely to sacrifice themselves for long-run benefits if mid-career mobility is an option. Another option is the retired worker. Japan has an early retirement age (mostly between 55-60 years) relative to their long life expectancy (Martin, 1989). Extension of the retirement age is one way to increase the size of the labour pool. Seike (1997) expects that large firms will extend the retirement age to 65 in the coming decade. However, Johnston (1991) points out that there is pressure to maintain current retirement ages as older (male) workers typically have higher wages due to the seniority system. Currently the early retirement age allows firms to hire their retired workers back at lower wages for part-time work. Seike (1997) proposes a government wage subsidy to firms that employ older workers. Although increasing the participation rate of the retired worker is an option in Canada, there are several problems with this suggestion in Japan. Labour force participation rates for those 65+ in Japan are already more than three times higher than in Canada (see Table 3). Industrialized countries have declining post-retirement participation rates, earlier average age of retirement, and better pension provisions during the last few decades. Japan has also seen its post-retirement participation rates decline since the 1970s as the government improved public pensions (Seike, 1997).

Most writers on the topic of Japan's greying population, despite their varied suggestions, do agree on one main point: Japan must increase its flexibility in a number of ways. Unlike Kiedanran (1999), they do not suggest trying to increase the fertility rate. One major flexibility is the need for significant changes in career patterns. Martin (1989) predicts that imbalances in the labour supply will get worse unless there are significant changes in attitude toward older workers and female workers. Johnston (1991) predicts that Japan will be compelled to liberalize its strict immigration policies. Thurow (1992) and others argue that these proposed flexibilities may be difficult.

Conclusions

Some of the proposed flexibilities are beginning to occur in Canada as postwar career patterns have changed and become more varied. The concept of contingent work is no longer new. Downsizing, delayering, and rising credentialism are factors that have affected careers during the 1980s and 1990s, resulting in spiral and transitory career patterns becoming more common. Given that Canada is younger than Japan, is dealing with a huge

Canadian Journal of Administrative Sciences
Revue canadienne des sciences de l'administration
18(1), 40-49

351

swing in the size of generations, and is an immigrant-receiving country, concerns about an aging population and a slow growing labour force have been more focussed on rising public pension costs (especially in terms of aging of the large baby boom generation) and health care costs. Also, discussions of labour force shortages (though there are shortages in some areas such as the information technology sector) do not generally occur with high unemployment rates (which were in the double-digit range in Canada until just a few years ago and are much higher than Japan's single digit figures). Thus, though Canada and Japan are both industrialized nations with low fertility rates and slow growing labour forces, some other key demographic differences, as well as social and career pattern differences between the countries, are affecting their response to the issue of slow labour force growth and even whether or not this issue is perceived as a problem.

References

Alston, J.P. (1989). *The American Samurai: Blending American and Japanese managerial practices.* New York: De Gruyter.

Bardwick, J. (1986). *The plateauing trap.* New York: Amacom.

Bennett, A. (1990). *The death of the organization man.* New York: William Morrow.

Berger, M.C. (1989). Demographic cycles, cohort sizing, and earnings. *Demography, 26* (2), 311-322.

Boyd, M. & Norris, D. (1995). The cluttered nest revisited: Young adults at home in the 1990s. Working paper. Florida State University, Centre for Study of Population.

Corak, M. (Ed.) (1998). *Labour markets, social institutions, and the future of Canada's children.* Ottawa: Statistics Canada.

Driver, M.J. (1985). Demographic and societal factors affecting the linear career crisis. *Canadian Journal of Administrative Sciences, 2* (2), 245-263.

Duxbury, L., Higgins, C., Lee, C., & Mills, S. (1991). Balancing work and family: A study of the Canadian federal public sector. Ottawa: Carleton University.

Egan, G. (1994). Hard times contract. *Management Today,* January, 48-50.

Foot, D.K. with Stoffman, D. (1996). *Boom, bust & echo: How to profit from the coming demographic shift.* Toronto: Macfarlane, Walter and Ross.

Foot, D.K. & Venne, R.A. (1990). Population, pyramids and promotional prospects. *Canadian Public Policy, 16* (4), 387-398.

Haupt, A. & Kane, T.T. (1991). *Population handbook: International edition* (3rd ed.). Washington, DC: Population Reference Bureau, Inc.

Higgins, C., Duxbury, L., & Lee, C. (1992). Balancing work and family: A study of Canadian private sector employees. National Centre for Management Research and Development, London, ON: The University of Western Ontario.

Imano, K. (1997). Internalization of the labour market: Foreign workers and trainees. In M. Sako & H. Sato (Eds.), *Japanese labour and management in transition* (pp. 168-183). New York: Routledge.

Johnston, W. (1991). Global work force 2000: The new world labor market. *Harvard Business Review,* Mar-Apr, 115-129.

Keidanren. (1999, March). Finding specific answers to the problem of the declining birth rate. www.keidanren.or.jp/english/policy/pol098.htm

Krahn, H. (1995). Non-standard work on the rise. *Perspectives on Labour and Income, 7* (4), 5-42.

Krahn, H., Mosher, C., & Johnson, L.C. (1993). Panel studies of the transition from school to work: Some methodological considerations. In P. Anisef & P. Axelrod (Eds.), *Transitions: Schooling and employment in Canada.* (pp. 169-187). Toronto: Thompson Educational Publishing.

Lu, D. (1987). *Inside corporate Japan.* Cambridge, MA: Productivity Press.

Martin, L. (1989). The graying of Japan. *Population Bulletin, 44* (2), 2-42.

McDaniel, S. (1997). Intergenerational transfers, social solidarity, and social policy: Unanswered questions and policy challenges. *Canadian Public Policy/Canadian Journal of Aging,* Joint Issue, *23,* 1-21.

McMillan, C. (1985). *The Japanese industrial system.* New York: Walter De Gruyter

McVey, W.W. & Kalbach, W.E. (1995). *Canadian population.* Toronto: Nelson.

Naisbitt, J. & Aburdene, P. (1985). *Re-inventing the corporation.* New York: Warner Books.

Novak, M. (1988). *Aging and society: A Canadian perspective.* Scarborough, ON: Nelson Canada.

Ogasawara, Y. (1998). *Office ladies and salaried men: Power, gender and work in Japanese companies.* Los Angeles: University of California Press.

O'Hara, B. (1993). *Working harder isn't working.* Vancouver, BC: New Star Books.

Population Reference Bureau (PRB). (1998). World Population Data Sheet, Washington, DC.

Rashid, A. (1993). Seven decades of wage changes. *Perspectives on Labour and Income, 5* (2), 9-21.

Rifkin, J. (1995). *The end of work: The decline of the global labor force and the dawn of the post-market era.* New York: Tarcher/Putnam.

Romaniuc, A. (1984). *Current demographic analysis, fertility in Canada, from baby-boom to baby bust.* Catalogue 91-524E. Ottawa: Statistics Canada.

Sako, M. (1997). Introduction: Forces for homogeneity and diversity in the Japanese industrial relations systems. In M. Sako & H. Sato (Eds.), *Japanese labour and management in transition* (pp. 1-24). New York: Routledge.

Seike, A. 1997. Women at work. In M. Sako & H. Sato (Eds.), *Japanese labour and management in transition* (pp. 131-150). New York: Routledge.

Statistics Bureau and Statistics Center: Japan. (1999). Population distribution by age and sex: Japan. http://www.stat.go/jp/english/zuhyou/15k3c-2.xls.

Statistics Canada. (1999). Population distribution by age & sex: Canada. http://www.statcan.ca/english/Pgdb/People/Population/demo10a.htm

Statistics Canada. (1999). Labour force participation rates: Japan. http://www.statcan.ca/english/Pgdb/People/Labour/labor23a.htm

Statistics Canada. (1999). Labour force participation rates: Canada. http://www.statcan.ca/english/Pgdb/People/Labour/labor05.htm

Tasker, P. (1987). *The Japanese: A major exploration of modern Japan.* New York: Truman Talley Books.

Thurow, L. (1992). *Head to head: The coming economic battle among Japan, Europe and North America.* New York: Morrow.

Wakisaka, A. (1997). Aging workers. In M. Sako & H. Sato (Eds.), *Japanese labour and management in transition* (pp. 151-167). New York: Routledge.

Weeks, J. R. (1994). *Population: An introduction to concepts and issues* (5th ed.). Belmont, CA: Wadsworth.

Whitehall, A. (1991). *Japanese management: Tradition and transition.* New York: Routledge.

353

4

Does Medicare Eligibility Affect Retirement?

Brigitte C. Madrian and Nancy Dean Beaulieu

4.1 Introduction

Concern over the lack of portability associated with employer-provided health insurance has precipitated a recent flurry of research activity on the effects of health insurance on labor market outcomes. Several estimates suggest that the costs associated with changing doctors and losing coverage for preexisting conditions are sufficient to deter individuals from changing jobs. These costs may be particularly important for older individuals contemplating retirement because a departure from the labor force may involve not only a change in doctors or lack of coverage for preexisting conditions but a complete loss of access to employer-provided group health insurance.

Although all individuals are eligible for government-provided group health insurance—Medicare—upon reaching age 65, most individuals state a desire to retire before age 65 (Employee Benefit Research Institute 1990). In contrast with social security, however, there is no early retirement age before 65 when individuals qualify for Medicare. For some, this is not an issue because their employers provide postretirement health insurance benefits. The majority of workers, however, are not entitled to such benefits because their employers do not offer them. It is these workers whom we would expect to be most concerned about how early retirement will affect their health insurance coverage.

Understanding the role of health insurance in retirement decisions is important because the government is currently trying to encourage later retirement by increasing the social security normal retirement age to 67 over the next

Brigitte C. Madrian is assistant professor of economics at the University of Chicago and a faculty research fellow of the National Bureau of Economic Research. Nancy Dean Beaulieu is a Ph.D. candidate in health policy at Harvard University.

The authors thank Jonathan Gruber, David Cutler, conference participants, and especially James Stock for helpful comments. Brigitte Madrian acknowledges support from an NBER Health and Aging Fellowship and the Harvard University Milton Fund.

109

several years. There has been some talk about increasing the age of Medicare eligibility correspondingly. Health care reform that makes health insurance more portable from work to retirement may undermine this goal, however, if the potential loss or change in health insurance coverage that currently exists is a significant deterrent to retirement.

While determining the effect of health insurance on retirement is important in its own right, properly accounting for the role of health insurance may also matter in accurately assessing the effects of other factors that have been more extensively studied. For example, previous research by others has concluded that the financial incentives associated with pensions and social security explain a significant fraction of observed retirement behavior; however, these two factors consistently underestimate the retirement that occurs at age 65. One explanation for this "excess" retirement is that individuals wait to retire until they are eligible for Medicare. Separating the effect of social security on retirement at age 65 from that of Medicare is difficult, however, since eligibility for Medicare coincides with the social security normal retirement age of 65. Correctly modeling the role of Medicare may therefore be important in assessing the effects of social security on retirement.

Much of the emerging literature on health insurance and retirement has examined the impact of employer-provided retiree health insurance on retirement, concluding that such health insurance constitutes a significant inducement for early retirement. In contrast, there is little compelling evidence on the effect of Medicare. This paper considers the role of Medicare in the retirement decision and aims to present evidence on whether it, too, impacts this decision.

4.2 The Relationship between Health Insurance and Retirement

4.2.1 Evidence on the Relationship between Health Insurance and Retirement

Table 4.1 summarizes the recent research that considers the relationship between health insurance and retirement. These studies have used several different data sets and a variety of statistical approaches to estimate how health insurance affects retirement. Five of the nine studies listed consider the effect of retiree health insurance on retirement (Madrian 1994; Headen, Clark, and Ghent 1995; Karoly and Rogowski 1994; Gustman and Steinmeier 1994a; Hurd and McGarry 1996). Because such insurance enables individuals to leave the labor force while maintaining the same health insurance coverage available while working, it eliminates the cost associated with giving up one's employer-provided health insurance on retirement. All other things equal, individuals with access to retiree health insurance should thus be expected to retire earlier than individuals without access to such coverage. Indeed, using data from the Current Population Survey (CPS), the National Medical Expenditure Survey (NMES), the Survey of Income and Program Participation (SIPP), the Retire-

Table 4.1   **Estimates of the Effect of Health Insurance (HI) on Retirement**

Study	Data and Sample	Estimation	Results
Rust and Phelan (1997)	Data: RHS Sample: Men 58–63 in 1969 with data through 1979 and no private pension	Structural model of age at retirement *HI variable: 0/1 employer nonretiree HI, 0/1 other HI*	Employer nonretiree HI increases probability of working until 65; Medicare explains spike in retirement hazard at 65 not explained by social security
Gruber and Madrian (1996)	Data: CPS Merged Outgoing Rotation Group 1980–90 Sample: All men 55–64	Probit for being currently retired *HI variable: continuation coverage*	One year of continuation coverage increases probability of being retired by 20 percent
Hurd and McGarry (1996)	Data: HRS Wave I Sample: Men 51–61 and women 46–61, work more than 35 hours/week	Nonlinear regressions for probability of retiring before 62 or 65 *HI variables: 0/1 employer HI and 0/1 retiree HI*	Employer HI increases expected probability of working past 62 or 65; retiree HI decreases these probabilities
Gruber and Madrian (1995)	Data: CPS March 1980–90; SIPP 1984–87 panels Sample: Men 55–64, initial workers	CPS: Probit for retiring during the past year SIPP: Retirement hazard *HI variable: continuation coverage*	One year of continuation coverage increases retirement hazard by 30 percent
Headen, Clark, and Ghent (1995)	Data: CPS August 1988 Sample: All men 55–64 and all women 55–64	Ordered probit for length of time retired *HI variable: 0/1 retiree HI*	Retiree HI increases probability of being retired by 6 percentage points
Madrian (1994)	Data: NMES (1987); SIPP 1984–86 panels Sample: Men 55–84, retired	Truncated regression for age at retirement; probit for retiring before 65 *HI variable: 0/1 retiree HI*	Retiree HI decreases age at retirement by one year; increases probability of retiring before 65 by 7.5 percentage points
Karoly and Rogowski (1994)	Data: SIPP 1984, 1986, and 1988 panels Sample: Men 55–62, initial civilian nongovernmental workers	Probit for retiring during SIPP panel *HI variable: imputed 0/1 retiree HI*	Retiree HI increases retirement hazard by 50 percent
Gustman and Steinmeier (1994a)	Data: RHS Sample: Men 58–63 in 1969 with data through 1979	Structural model of age at retirement *HI variable: imputed value of retiree HI*	Retiree HI delays retirement until age of eligibility, then accelerates it; overall, decreases

(continued)

357

Table 4.1   (continued)

Study	Data and Sample	Estimation	Results
			retirement age by 3.9 months
Lumsdaine, Stock, and Wise (1994a)	Data: Proprietary firm administrative data Sample: Men and women, initial workers	Structural model of age at retirement *HI variable: imputed value of Medicare*	Value of Medicare has little effect on age at retirement

ment History Survey (RHS), and the Health and Retirement Survey (HRS), all five of these studies estimate that retiree health insurance does encourage early retirement.

Two of the studies assess whether continuation of coverage mandates, which allow individuals to maintain their employer-provided health insurance for a limited period of time after retirement, have a similar impact on retirement (Gruber and Madrian 1995, 1996). Using data from the SIPP and the CPS, this research concludes that such mandates also encourage early retirement.

Only two studies focus on the role of Medicare in the retirement decision: Rust and Phelan (1997) and Lumsdaine, Stock, and Wise (1994a). Using data from the RHS on men without pensions, Rust and Phelan find that individuals with employer-provided health insurance that does not continue past retirement are much less likely to retire than those who have other forms of health insurance (including retiree health insurance) or no health insurance; this effect, however, is smaller after age 65, when these individuals become eligible for Medicare, than before. Overall, they conclude that Medicare explains almost all of the excess spike in the retirement hazard at age 65 after the financial incentives associated with social security have been accounted for.

Using administrative data from a single large employer, Lumsdaine et al. reach the opposite conclusion—that Medicare has little effect on retirement. This result is surprising given the consistent results from the previously mentioned studies suggesting that other forms of health insurance are important factors in deciding when to retire. It is difficult, however, to extend the conclusions in Lumsdaine et al. to the population as a whole because the firm that employed all of the individuals in their data set provided postretirement health insurance benefits. With the opportunity to continue their employer-provided health insurance after retirement, it is not surprising that Medicare would not affect the retirement decisions of these particular individuals.

4.2.2   The Role of Medicare in the Retirement Decision

What role should Medicare play in the retirement decision? The answer depends on a variety of factors. While Medicare has several features that distinguish it from the health insurance policies typically provided by employers or in the private market, there are three characteristics that are important in assessing its effect on retirement. The first is eligibility. All individuals, whether retired or not, are eligible for Medicare on reaching age 65. As mentioned earlier, although the age of Medicare eligibility corresponds to the social security normal retirement age, there is no corresponding early accessibility to Medicare if individuals choose to start receiving their social security benefits early, between the ages of 62 and 65 (although some individuals younger than 65 may also receive Medicare coverage if they are eligible for disability benefits).

A second feature distinguishing Medicare from many other insurance plans is that there are no exclusions for preexisting conditions; all medical conditions are covered from the first day of eligibility onward, whether or not individuals have previously sought treatment for these conditions. A third characteristic of Medicare that differentiates it from other forms of health insurance is that coverage is available *only to individuals*. There is no provision allowing for coverage of spouses, children, or other dependents of individuals who are themselves eligible for Medicare coverage.

The interaction between these characteristics of the Medicare program and the availability of employer-provided health insurance for active employees as well as retirees implies that Medicare will have different effects on the retirement decisions of individuals depending on their own health insurance and family situations. For individuals working in jobs that do not provide health insurance, there is no health insurance loss from early retirement. While these individuals may welcome Medicare coverage, it should not affect their retirement decisions; they will receive Medicare on turning 65 regardless of when they retire from their jobs.

Similarly, individuals who work for employers that do provide health insurance for their active employees and who have the option of maintaining this health insurance when they retire should not have their retirement decisions affected by Medicare. Their health insurance situation will be the same whether or not they are retired, both before age 65, when they have access to employer-provided health insurance, and after, when they have access to both Medicare and employer-provided health insurance.

The individuals who should possibly have their retirement decisions affected by Medicare are those who have employer-provided health insurance while employed but who do not have access to employer-provided retiree health insurance on retirement. For these individuals, retiring before age 65 may involve a loss or change in health insurance coverage. To the extent that losing one's employer-provided health insurance is costly, these individuals have an incentive to postpone retirement until age 65. If, however, these individuals have dependents, then retirement, even at age 65, will involve a loss of health insurance coverage for some members of the family. Such individuals

Table 4.2   Health Insurance Coverage of Non–Medicare-Eligible
                   Women (percent)

| | Husband's Age | |
Health Insurance	Below 65	65 or Above
Private	83.5	80.0
Employer		
provided	74.5	52.1
Other group	1.2	5.8
Nongroup	6.0	22.4
Medicare	0.7	4.3
Medicaid	2.0	1.7
CHAMPUS	10.5	11.5
No health insurance	12.0	14.5

Source: Authors' calculations using data from the 1987 National Medical Expenditure Survey.

may thus find it in their interest to further postpone retirement until their family members can be covered by other forms of health insurance.

Table 4.2 illustrates the differences in the sources of health insurance coverage for women not yet categorically eligible for Medicare stratified on the basis of whether their husbands are younger or older than age 65. Although non–Medicare-eligible wives of Medicare-eligible husbands are only slightly more likely to be uninsured than wives of non–Medicare-eligible husbands (14.5 percent vs. 12.0 percent), the sources of their health insurance coverage are very different. They are much *less* likely to be covered by employer-provided group health insurance (52.1 percent vs. 74.5 percent) and much *more* likely to be covered by private nongroup health insurance (22.4 percent vs. 6.0 percent). These numbers suggest that a significant fraction of women lose access to employer-provided group health insurance when their husbands retire. Many are able to substitute nongroup health insurance coverage. However, this may be quite costly (especially if individuals have preexisting conditions), and there are likely many women who would find themselves without health insurance except for the fact that their husbands continue to work after age 65 in order to maintain coverage for their wives.

4.2.3   Identifying the Effect of Medicare on Retirement

The discussion above suggests that one possible identification strategy that could be used to estimate the effect of Medicare on retirement is to compare the retirement behavior of three groups of individuals: (1) those whose employers do not provide health insurance, (2) those whose employers provide health insurance to both active employees and retirees, and (3) those whose employers provide health insurance to active employees but not to retirees. If maintaining health insurance coverage is valuable, then, all other things equal, those in the third group should be least likely to retire before age 65. If Medicare provides coverage that is as valued as employer-provided health insurance, then after age 65 there should be no difference in the likelihood of being retired for these three groups.[1]

There are two problems with empirically implementing this identification strategy. The first is that there are no currently available longitudinal data sets that allow us to observe the type of health insurance available to individuals before they retire and to subsequently track their retirement behavior.[2] While the new HRS will make this type of analysis possible, it will not be feasible until more waves of the data have been released.

The second problem is that all other things are not equal for individuals in the three groups described above. In particular, firms that provide health insurance also tend to provide pensions, and pensions tend to have provisions that encourage retirement at particular ages. Thus, using individuals whose employers provide retiree health insurance as a "control" in assessing the retirement behavior of individuals whose employers provide health insurance but not retiree health insurance will not be valid unless it is possible to adequately account for the differential pension incentives that individuals in these two groups face. Once again, the HRS will allow for this type of analysis when sufficient waves of the data are available, but currently the only data sets with detailed pension information either come from a single firm (as used in several papers by Lumsdaine, Stock, and Wise) or do not also include adequate information on health insurance (as is the case with the Survey of Consumer Finances data used by Samwick, 1993).

Rust and Phelan circumvent this latter problem by restricting their sample to individuals who report having no pension. The earlier discussion on how Medicare should affect retirement suggests another possible identification strategy, however. Because Medicare is provided only to individuals and not to their dependents, there will still be a health insurance cost associated with retiring at age 65 if an individual has dependents who are covered by his or her employer-provided health insurance. Thus, we can determine whether Medicare has an effect on retirement by comparing the retirement behavior of individuals with and without dependents who obtain health insurance from that individual's employment.

Because the majority of individuals who provide health insurance to other

---

1. In fact, Medicare is much less generous than the typical employer-provided health insurance policy. Thus, there may still be some value in maintaining one's employer-provided health insurance even after becoming eligible for Medicare.

2. The RHS does include some information on health insurance coverage. Rust and Phelan (1994) and Gustman and Steinmeier (1994a) have used these data to infer what type of health insurance coverage was available to individuals before they retired. Gustman and Steinmeier, however, have substantially lower health insurance coverage rates than found in data sets typically cited as sources of health insurance coverage such as the NMES or the SIPP. In contrast, Rust and Phelan have coverage rates than are substantially higher for their subset of the population than is found in these other sources. Thus, the health insurance data in the RHS appear to be somewhat unreliable.

family members are men, this paper focuses on the retirement behavior of men. Although some older men nearing the age of retirement still have dependent children at home, most do not. The majority, however, are married. The identification strategy used in this paper will be to compare the retirement behavior of men who have spouses older than age 65 and are thus already eligible for Medicare with the retirement behavior of men whose spouses are not yet eligible for Medicare.

Consider a simple specification for the retirement hazard of an individual covered by employer-provided health insurance that does not continue into retirement:

$$\Pr(\text{Retire}_i | \text{Not retired}_{i-1}) = \alpha \text{ (Demographic characteristics)}$$

(1)
$$+ \beta \text{ (Own financial incentives)}$$

$$+ \gamma \text{ (Spouse's financial incentives)} + \varepsilon$$

The function $\alpha(\cdot)$ may contain such factors as age, health status, marital status, education, and other things that would affect the value of leisure. The function $\beta(\cdot)$ includes financial variables that directly affect one's retirement:

$$(2) \quad \beta_1 \cdot \begin{pmatrix} \text{Social} \\ \text{security} \end{pmatrix} + \beta_2 \cdot \begin{pmatrix} \text{Private} \\ \text{pension} \end{pmatrix} + \beta_3 \cdot \begin{pmatrix} \text{Medicare} \\ \text{eligibility} \end{pmatrix} + \beta_4 \cdot \begin{pmatrix} \text{Other} \\ \text{wealth} \end{pmatrix}.$$

$\beta(\cdot)$ could also include other factors such as an individual's earning capacity. Recent research suggests that both the level of pension and social security wealth and expected future accruals affect retirement. The function $\gamma(\cdot)$ would include a similar vector of variables for the individual's spouse that may also impact the individual's retirement decision: the social security and pension incentives that encourage one spouse to retire at a particular age may also provide liquidity that enables the other spouse to retire as well; similarly, whether a spouse is eligible for Medicare will affect the amount of wealth that can be used to finance nonhealth consumption during retirement in the same way that an individual's own Medicare eligibility does.

Because Medicare eligibility coincides with the social security normal retirement age for most individuals, and with the normal retirement age of many private pension plans, it is difficult to separately identify β_1, β_2, and β_3 in equation (2) above. Similarly, if a spouse has worked and also qualifies for a pension or social security in her own right, it will be difficult to separately identify γ_1, γ_2, and γ_3. There is, however, a nontrivial fraction of older women who have never participated in the labor force. For men married to these women, there are no financial benefits associated with a wife's retirement that would also encourage their own retirement. If a woman has never worked, she can only claim social security benefits based on her husband's earnings, and she can only do so *after* her husband begins to claim benefits himself. In this case, $\gamma_1 = \gamma_2 = 0$ and the effect of a spouse's Medicare eligibility, γ_3, can be identified.

If men value health insurance coverage of themselves and their wives equally, then $\gamma_3 = \beta_3$ and the effect of own Medicare eligibility is identified as well. If men value their own health insurance coverage more than that of their wives, then γ_3 will provide a lower bound on the effect of own Medicare eligibility on retirement.

Note that this identification strategy is essentially based on the spouse's age since, with the exception of those with disabilities, eligibility for Medicare occurs at age 65. Thus, all other things equal, retirement rates should be higher among men with wives who are age 65 or older than among men with wives who are younger than 65.

4.3 Data

We use data from the 5 percent public use samples of the 1980 and 1990 censuses. The primary advantage of census data is that they afford a large sample size. This is particularly important given the identification strategy outlined above based on whether a spouse is eligible for Medicare. Figure 4.1 shows the distribution of the differences between husband's age and wife's age in the census. Over half of the men in figure 4.1 have spouses who are the same age or between one and four years younger than themselves. Because the distribu-

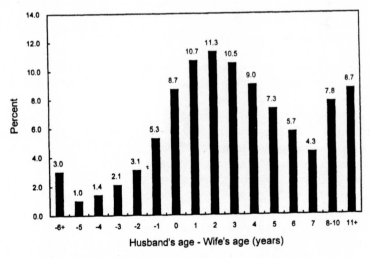

Fig. 4.1   Distribution of spousal age differences: men aged 55–69
Source: Authors' calculations using the 5 percent public use samples from the 1980 and 1990 censuses.

tion of spouse's age relative to own age is so compressed, a big data set like the census allows us to exploit a broader range of variation in spouse's age. The disadvantage of the census is that it includes no information on health insurance coverage. It is therefore impossible to compare the retirement probabilities of those with and without health insurance in order to see whether, as predicted, the effect of Medicare on retirement is confined to those who actually did have employer-provided health insurance before retirement. This, however, should bias us *against* finding an effect of Medicare on retirement since we will essentially be estimating the average of no effect among those without employer-provided health insurance or with retiree health insurance and whatever effect may exist for those with employer-provided health insurance.

The census also does not contain information on pension benefits or expected social security benefits. Rather than impute the values of these variables for individuals, we exclude them from the estimation and assume that spouse's age is uncorrelated with these factors which, by exclusion, become a part of the error term, ε. To us, this does not seem like an unreasonable assumption. We find it unlikely that men who married in their 20s and 30s chose a spouse of a specified age based on their tastes for retirement. It is more likely the case that divorce and later remarriage could be correlated with tastes for retirement or other unobserved factors such as pension benefits. For example, men with extremely generous pension benefits may be more likely to attract "trophy" spouses. We will assume, however, that these effects are small.

Spouse's age may, however, be correlated with who is in the sample. In particular, retirement-aged men who had at one time married women much older than themselves will be more likely to be widowers because their spouses are already deceased. These men will thus be excluded from the sample (divorce will cause a similar type of sample selection problem). This exclusion will be on the basis of spouse's age. As long as the assumption that spouse's age is exogenous is valid, however, this will merely result in a thinning of the sample for men with older wives. The estimates will be less precise, but they will not be biased.

The sample is restricted to married men with a spouse in the data set. We further restrict the sample to men whose wives are no more than 15 years older or 20 years younger than themselves. The restriction is imposed because, beyond this range, the cell sizes are quite small and we do not want the estimation to be driven by a few outliers. Overall, our census sample includes approximately 800,000 individuals. Summary statistics on these individuals are presented in table 4.3.

The definition of retiring in the last year is being currently out of the labor force but having worked one or more weeks in the previous calendar year. In the census, "the last year" represents a 16-month window since the census is conducted in April and the work question is asked about the previous calendar year. Using this definition, 14.4 percent of our sample retired in the last "year."

Table 4.3   **Summary Statistics**

Statistic	Value
Sample size	799,069
Race	
White	91.6%
Nonwhite	8.4
Education	
Less than high school	34.1
High school graduate	29.5
Some college	16.5
College graduate	19.9
Retired in last year (if worked last year)	14.4
Age	60.4
Age of wife	57.1
Spouse never worked	7.5

Source: Authors' tabulations using data from the 5 percent public use samples of the 1980 and 1990 censuses. Sample is all married men aged 55–69 who worked at least one week in the previous calendar year and whose spouses are not more than 15 years older or 20 years younger than themselves.

4.4   Estimating the Effect of Medicare on the Probability of Being Retired

4.4.1   Basic Results

We begin in table 4.4 by simply tabulating the retirement hazards for men whose wives are not Medicare eligible (wife's age < 65) and for those whose wives are Medicare eligible (wife's age ≥ 65). The smallest cell size is 654 for individuals who are age 55 and have a wife older than age 65. These estimates, therefore, are fairly reliable. As would be expected, the retirement hazard is small for men still in their 50s and increases quite substantially at ages 62 and 65. The typical spikes in the retirement hazard at ages 62 and 65 are not as pronounced in the census data because the definition of retirement is one that occurred within the past 16 months and the age in the table is current age rather than age at the start of this 16-month period. Thus, the retirement hazard of individuals initially aged 61 will be spread out over 62- and 63-year-olds in the table.

The retirement hazards in table 4.4 are, as we would predict, higher at all ages for those whose wives are eligible for Medicare. The absolute percentage point differential between these two hazards (the last column) appears roughly constant at about 3 or 4 percentage points. Although these results are suggestive that Medicare eligibility does encourage retirement, one could expect similar results for other reasons. For example, if women face greater financial incentives to retire at older ages and these financial rewards also make it easier for their husbands to retire, then conditional on own age, men with older wives

Table 4.4   Retirement Hazard by Age and Wife's Medicare Eligibility

| | Wife's Age | | |
Age	Below 65 (1)	65 or Older (2)	Difference (1) − (2)
55	0.0468	0.0780	0.0312
56	0.0515	0.0958	0.0443
57	0.0563	0.0880	0.0317
58	0.0625	0.0903	0.0278
59	0.0700	0.0995	0.0295
60	0.0936	0.1390	0.0454
61	0.1075	0.1359	0.0284
62	0.2170	0.2859	0.0689
63	0.2254	0.2737	0.0483
64	0.2139	0.2423	0.0284
65	0.3154	0.3484	0.0330
66	0.3131	0.3425	0.0294
67	0.2915	0.3249	0.0334
68	0.2892	0.3334	0.0442
69	0.3025	0.3419	0.0394

Source: Authors' tabulations using data from the 5 percent public use samples of the 1980 and 1990 censuses. Sample is all married men aged 55–69 who worked at least one week in the previous calendar year and whose spouses are not more than 15 years older or 20 years younger than themselves.

will be more likely to retire. Alternatively, men may value their own leisure time more if their wives are retired, and this too will make husbands more likely to retire if their wives are older and more likely to be retired (for a discussion of joint retirement issues, see Hurd 1990; Gustman and Steinmeier 1994b; Blau 1994, 1995). Or, to the extent that continued work competes with the amount of time that men can spend with their wives before the health problems incumbent with age set in, men with older wives will be more likely to retire than men with younger wives. By stratifying the sample on the basis of whether wife's age is greater or less than 65, one would find a pattern of results similar to those in table 4.4 even if it were not Medicare eligibility per se but one of these other reasons that also implied that having an older spouse leads to earlier retirement.

One way to gauge the importance of these alternative explanations is to look at the pattern of retirement rates associated with spouse's age. Consider the following general specification for a retirement hazard that incorporates all three of the above explanations:

$$(3) \quad \Pr(\text{Retire}_t | \text{Not retired}_{t-1}) = \alpha \left(\frac{\text{PDV}}{\text{assets}} \right) + \beta \left(\begin{array}{c} \text{Spouse not} \\ \text{working} \end{array} \right) + \gamma \left(\begin{array}{c} \text{Age of} \\ \text{spouse} \end{array} \right) + \varepsilon.$$

A spouse's ineligibility for Medicare will operate through the $\alpha(\cdot)$ function above, affecting the retirement hazard by decreasing the present discounted value (PDV) of assets that can be used to finance nonhealth consumption. If the discount rate is positive and the relationship between assets and retirement is linear, then, conditional on own age, the effect of spouse's age on the retirement hazard will be as pictured in figure 4.2A. Before the spouse reaches age 65, the retirement hazard should decline as the spouse is younger and has successively more years before becoming eligible for Medicare. The rate of de-

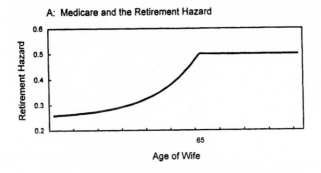

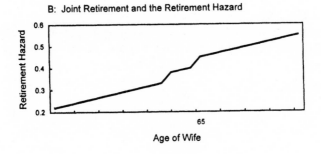

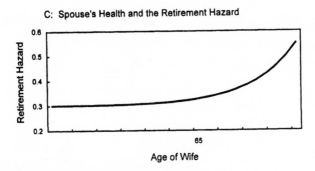

Fig. 4.2   Factors affecting the retirement hazard

cline should slow, however, as expected medical and/or insurance expenditures in the future are discounted. After the spouse is 65, however, there is no further health insurance cost in terms of leaving the spouse without employer-provided health insurance; thus, the hazard rate should not change with spouse's age after the spouse reaches age 65.

Joint retirement considerations will affect the retirement hazard through the $\beta(\cdot)$ function in equation (3). If they are the primary force behind the retirement hazard's increasing with spouse's age, we should see a steady increase in retirement probabilities as the spouse gets older and is herself more likely to retire. We might expect to see especially large increases as the spouse reaches ages 62 and 65 and faces the incentives associated with social security that increase the retirement hazard at these ages (see fig. 4.2B). To the extent that most women have already retired by age 65, the joint retirement hypothesis would not be inconsistent with a constant hazard after the spouse has reached age 65; if there are continued incentives for women to retire after age 65, however, and enough women are still working at this age, then the joint retirement explanation should be associated with increasing retirement hazards with respect to spouse's age even after the spouse is age 65.

Finally, the $\gamma(\cdot)$ function in equation (3) characterizes the effect of spouse's health on retirement. If it is spouse's health that is driving the results in table 4.4, then the retirement hazard should be increasing at an *increasing* rate in spouse's age, as shown in figure 4.2C, as health becomes progressively worse (and mortality more likely) with age.

To examine which of these alternatives appear to be borne out in the data, figure 4.3 graphs the retirement hazards of men at various ages against the

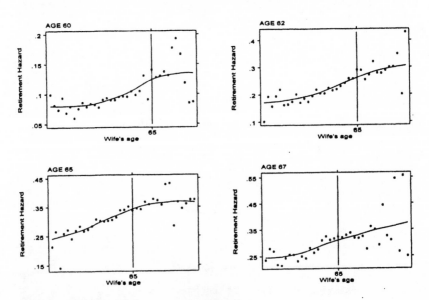

Fig. 4.3   Retirement hazard by wife's age

differences between their ages and their spouses' ages (the ages shown in fig. 4.3 are 60, 62, 65, and 67).[3] The circles in the graph give the actual retirement rates calculated from the 1980 and 1990 censuses for each age difference. The vertical line gives the age at which the wife becomes eligible for Medicare; thus, this line shifts to the right as the age considered in the graph increases. The line drawn through the circles in the graph is a nonparametric weighted smoothed mean (with bandwidth = 0.7). This smoothing was done to decrease the noise in the retirement rates in the tails of the age difference distribution.

The graphs for ages 60, 62, and 65 show a pattern not inconsistent with that in figure 4.2A: roughly constant for spouses older than 65 and decreasing at a decreasing rate with spouse's age less than 65. None of the graphs gives any suggestion of the retirement pattern in figure 4.2C that would prevail if spousal health concerns were a predominant consideration in retirement decisions. None of the graphs is completely inconsistent with the joint retirement hypothesis.

We can parameterize the patterns shown in figure 4.3 with the following regression:

$$
\begin{aligned}
\text{Pr}(\text{Retire} \mid \text{Not retired}_{t-1}) = \; & \beta_1 \cdot \underline{\text{Age}} + \beta_2 \cdot \underline{\text{Age}} \\
& * \left[\ln(65 - \text{Wife's Age}) \mid \text{Wife} < 65 \right] \\
& + \beta_3 \cdot \underline{\text{Age}} * (\text{Wife} \geq 65) + \beta_4 \cdot \underline{\text{Age}} \\
& * (\text{Wife's Age} - 65) .
\end{aligned}
$$

(4)

In this regression, $\underline{\text{Age}}$ is a vector of age dummies and the coefficient vector β_1 will give a baseline retirement hazard for each age. The second term, $[\ln(65 - \text{Wife's Age}) \mid \text{Wife} < 65]$, equals zero if wife's age is 65 or older and equals the log of $(65 - \text{Wife's Age})$ if wife's age is less than 65. This term is meant to capture the decreasing retirement hazard with respect to wife's age for wives younger than 65 shown in figure 4.2A. The third term is a dummy variable for whether or not wife's age is 65 or older. Finally, the fourth term is the preceding dummy variable interacted with the difference between wife's age and age 65 for Medicare-eligible women. The coefficient β_4 will thus measure whether there is any slope in the retirement hazard with respect to wife's age for men with wives older than 65. Note that the last three terms in equation (4) are all interacted with the vector of age dummies so that each variable will be associated with a vector of coefficients for each age between 55 and 69.

Table 4.5 presents the coefficients from estimating equation (4) using ordinary least squares. The regression coefficients tell a story similar to that of figure 4.3. The vector of constant terms, β_1, increases with age and exhibits the familiar spikes at both age 62 and age 65. The β_2 coefficients are all nega-

---

3. Note that these are not mutually exclusive arguments for why men with older wives are more likely to be retired. Indeed, there are men who probably make retirement decisions for all of the reasons suggested.

Table 4.5   **Effect of Spouse's Age and Medicare Eligibility on Retirement**

		Independent Variable		
Age	Constant (β₁)	ln(65 − Wife's Age) if Wife < 65 (β₂)	Wife ≥ 65 (β₃)	Wife's Age − 65 if Wife ≥ 65 (β₄)
55	.0704	−.0094	.0074	.0002
	(.0080)	(.0031)	(.0205)	(.0083)
56	.0775	−.0107	.0074	.0058
	(.0075)	(.0030)	(.0190)	(.0067)
57	.0740	−.0075	.0074	.0032
	(.0069)	(.0029)	(.0157)	(.0049)
58	.0871	−.0110	−.0108	.0063
	(.0063)	(.0027)	(.0142)	(.0041)
59	.0947	−.0115	.0017	.0013
	(.0056)	(.0026)	(.0123)	(.0033)
60	.1210	−.0135	.0161	.0007
	(.0052)	(.0025)	(.0108)	(.0026)
61	.1431	−.0187	−.0164	.0038
	(.0048)	(.0024)	(.0086)	(.0023)
62	.2747	−.0326	.0075	.0016
	(.0042)	(.0023)	(.0082)	(.0020)
63	.2705	−.0278	−.0101	.0057
	(.0040)	(.0029)	(.0074)	(.0017)
64	.2453	−.0211	−.0042	.0006
	(.0038)	(.0023)	(.0065)	(.0016)
65	.3619	−.0337	−.0221	.0044
	(.0039)	(.0024)	(.0059)	(.0014)
66	.3551	−.0321	−.0150	.0012
	(.0044)	(.0028)	(.0061)	(.0013)
67	.3302	−.0305	−.0090	.0016
	(.0050)	(.0033)	(.0065)	(.0013)
68	.3356	−.0372	−.0156	.0052
	(.0060)	(.0038)	(.0071)	(.0012)
69	.3382	−.0287	.0010	.0009
	(.0066)	(.0044)	(.0079)	(.0011)

Source: Authors' calculations using data from the 5 percent public use samples of the 1980 and 1990 censuses. Sample is all married men aged 55–69 who worked at least one week in the previous calendar year and whose spouses are not more than 15 years older or 20 years younger than themselves. The sample size is 799,069, and the R^2 = 0.219.

tive and significant (with t-statistics ranging from 2.6 to 14.4) and increase in magnitude with own age from roughly −.010 for ages less than 60 to −.030 for ages greater than 65. These coefficients confirm the hypothesis that at all ages men with wives not yet eligible for Medicare are less likely to retire the younger are their spouses. We might also expect the magnitude of the coefficients to increase with age as spouse's lack of Medicare eligibility should have a greater absolute effect on the retirement hazard for men who themselves have a greater likelihood of retiring. The β_3 and β_4 coefficients in table 4.5 show no strong patterns, change in sign, and are generally insignificant (only 6 of the 30 coefficients have t-statistics exceeding 2 in magnitude). These results suggest that the retirement hazard is roughly constant with respect to wife's age once the wife is 65 or older and eligible for Medicare.

4.4.2 Alternative Explanations

Although the lack of a slope in the retirement hazard with respect to spouse's age greater than 65 is consistent with Medicare eligibility's playing an important role in retirement decisions, it is not, as mentioned earlier, completely inconsistent with a joint retirement story. This explanation for the patterns in the retirement hazard, however, relies on the premise that the wife is or at one time was working. If the effects presented in table 4.5 derive only from the financial rewards associated with the wife's collection of social security and/or pension benefits before age 65 or other joint retirement considerations, they should be confined to those men who have wives who have a history of labor force participation and there should be no effect among men whose wives have never worked. That is, in the specification of the retirement hazard in equation (4), the function $\beta(\cdot)$ will have no differential impact by spouse's age.

Because the census collects data on work history, this comparison is possible. Fortunately, a large enough fraction of the cohorts of men aged 55–69 in 1980 and 1990 had wives who reported never having worked (about 8 percent), so the comparison is feasible as well. Table 4.6 gives the retirement hazards shown in table 4.4 for the subsample of men whose wives never worked. As before, the hazards for those with spouses older than 65 tend to be greater than the hazards for those with spouses younger than 65. The wife older than 65 hazard and the differential (last column) is somewhat more noisy for those whose spouses have never worked because this stratification breaks even the census into somewhat small cell sizes for those at young ages who have Medicare-eligible spouses. For the older ages, however, the results suggest that even among those who have never worked, having a Medicare-eligible spouse increases the retirement hazard. The differential is on average smaller for those whose spouses have never worked than for those whose spouses have worked, suggesting that some of the effects in table 4.4 can perhaps be attributed to joint retirement or other considerations associated with having a spouse older than oneself.

Table 4.7 presents the regression coefficients of table 4.5 for the subsample of men whose wives never worked. The baseline retirement rate, β_1, is slightly higher for this subsample of men than for the full sample. The effect of having a spouse not yet eligible for Medicare (β_2) is, as in table 4.5, always negative, although at younger ages the coefficients are not significant. This is due in part to a significantly smaller sample, and to the fact that the coefficient estimates bounce around a little more. The overall pattern of coefficients, however, is very similar to that in table 4.5—increasing and becoming more significant

Table 4.6   Retirement Hazard by Age and Wife's Medicare Eligibility if Spouse Never Worked

| | Wife's Age | | |
Age	Below 65 (1)	65 or Older (2)	Difference (1) − (2)
55	0.0656	0.0517	−0.0139
56	0.0713	0.1045	0.0332
57	0.0784	0.0722	−0.0062
58	0.0772	0.0598	−0.0174
59	0.0861	0.0943	0.0082
60	0.1092	0.1759	0.0667
61	0.1295	0.1368	0.0073
62	0.2582	0.2914	0.0332
63	0.2582	0.3152	0.0570
64	0.2447	0.2764	0.0317
65	0.3579	0.3931	0.0352
66	0.3708	0.3721	0.0013
67	0.3135	0.3530	0.0395
68	0.3269	0.3515	0.0246
69	0.3505	0.3778	0.0273

Source: Authors' calculations using data from the 5 percent public use samples of the 1980 and 1990 censuses and the 1980–94 March Current Population Survey. Sample is all married men aged 55–69 who worked at least one week in the previous calendar year and whose spouses are not more than 15 years older or 20 years younger than themselves.

with age. Similarly, the vectors of β_3 and β_4 coefficients are also similar to those in table 4.5: they jump around in magnitude, they change sign, and they are generally insignificant. Restricting the sample to men whose wives have never worked thus yields results very similar to those obtained from the full sample of men.

4.5   Conclusions

While we hesitate to draw strong conclusions about the effect of Medicare eligibility on retirement behavior because the census data used in the analysis are less than ideal, we think that the results presented in the paper are suggestive that Medicare may indeed influence the retirement decisions of men. Our main findings are as follows: (1) 55–69-year-old men with Medicare-eligible spouses have a higher retirement hazard than men without Medicare-eligible spouses. (2) The retirement hazard exhibits a pattern with respect to spouse's age that is consistent with what would be expected if Medicare were an important consideration in the retirement decision. It is inconsistent with a story that other factors more generally related to spouse's age, such as a spouse's health status, are strong determinants of retirement as the retirement hazard appears to be roughly constant after the spouse reaches age 65 rather than generally

Table 4.7   **Effect of Spouse's Age and Medicare Eligibility on Retirement if Spouse Never Worked**

Age	Constant (β_1)	ln(65 − Wife's Age) if Wife < 65 (β_2)	Wife ≥ 65 (β_3)	Wife's Age − 65 if Wife ≥ 65 (β_4)
		Independent Variable		
55	.0815	−0.0063	−.0130	−.0114
	(.0351)	(.0138)	(.0781)	(.0338)
56	.0970	−.0105	.0620	−.0253
	(.0338)	(.0137)	(.0770)	(.0242)
57	.0839	−.0023	−.0238	.0053
	(.0309)	(.0129)	(.0648)	(.0187)
58	.1169	−.0177	−.0642	.0028
	(.0274)	(.0120)	(.0581)	(.0146)
59	.1078	−.0101	−.0361	.0080
	(.0248)	(.0113)	(.0516)	(.0121)
60	.1199	−.0053	.0219	.0141
	(.0215)	(.0103)	(.0422)	(.0107)
61	.1502	−.0110	−.0251	.0045
	(.0189)	(.0096)	(.0362)	(.0083)
62	.3236	−.0377	−.0219	−.0040
	(.0167)	(.0091)	(.0309)	(.0069)
63	.2899	−.0200	−.0112	.0149
	(.0161)	(.0094)	(.0278)	(.0061)
64	.2790	−.0238	.0080	−.0050
	(.0144)	(.0089)	(.0244)	(.0058)
65	.3856	−.0208	−.0161	.0115
	(.0144)	(.0094)	(.0213)	(.0047)
66	.3943	−.0195	−.0266	.0022
	(.0151)	(.0104)	(.0210)	(.0045)
67	.3655	−.0441	−.0418	.0130
	(.0180)	(.0137)	(.0229)	(.0042)
68	.3490	−.0200	−.0059	.0032
	(.0195)	(.0143)	(.0239)	(.0037)
69	.3976	−.0434	−.0294	.0031
	(.0232)	(.0173)	(.0271)	(.0034)

Source: Authors' calculations using data from the 5 percent public use samples of the 1980 and 1990 censuses. Sample is all married men aged 55–69 who worked at least one week in the previous calendar year and whose spouses are not more than 15 years older or 20 years younger than themselves. The sample size equals 59,731 and $R^2 = 0.263$.

increasing. (3) The pattern of effects is approximately the same when the sample is confined to men whose wives have never worked. This latter group of men cannot be affected by any financial considerations inducing their wives to retire. Furthermore, having a nonworking spouse cannot differentially impact the retirement hazard with respect to spouse's age of this group because their wives have never worked. The most plausible explanation for the pattern of retirement effects exhibited by this latter group is the Medicare eligibility of their wives. Because the effects are similar for the whole population of men regardless of spouse's work history, it is likely that Medicare is also an important determinant of retirement for all men.

References

Blau, David M. 1994. Labor force dynamics of older married couples. Chapel Hill: University of North Carolina. Mimeograph.
————. 1995. Social security and the labor supply of older married couples. Chapel Hill: University of North Carolina. Mimeograph.
Employee Benefit Research Institute. 1990. *Employee benefit notes.* Washington, D.C.: Employee Benefit Research Institute, November.
Gruber, Jonathan, and Brigitte C. Madrian. 1995. Health insurance availability and the retirement decision. *American Economic Review* 85:938–48.
————. 1996. Health insurance and early retirement: Evidence from the availability of continuation coverage. In *Advances in the economics of aging,* ed. David A. Wise. Chicago: University of Chicago Press.
Gustman, Alan L., and Thomas L. Steinmeier. 1994a. Employer provided health insurance and retirement behavior. *Industrial and Labor Relations Review* 48:124–40.
————. 1994b. Retirement in a family context: A structural model for husbands and wives. NBER Working Paper no. 4629. Cambridge, Mass.: National Bureau of Economic Research.
Headen, Alvin E., Robert L. Clark, and Linda Shumaker Ghent. 1995. Retiree health insurance and the retirement timing of older workers. Raleigh: North Carolina State University. Mimeograph.
Hurd, Michael D. 1990. The joint retirement decision of husbands and wives. In *Issues in the economics of aging,* ed. David A. Wise. Chicago: University of Chicago Press.
Hurd, Michael D., and Kathleen McGarry. 1996. Prospective retirement: Effects of job characteristics, pensions, and health insurance. Mimeograph.
Karoly, Lynn A. and Jeanette A. Rogowski. 1994. The effect of access to post-retirement health insurance on the decision to retire early. *Industrial and Labor Relations Review* 48:103–23.
Lumsdaine, Robin L., James H. Stock, and David A. Wise. 1994a. Pension plan provisions and retirement: Men and women, Medicare, and models. In *Studies in the economics of aging,* ed. David A. Wise. Chicago: University of Chicago Press.
————. 1994b. Retirement incentives: The interaction between employer-provided pensions, social security, and retiree health benefits. NBER Working Paper no. 4613. Cambridge, Mass.: National Bureau of Economic Research.
Madrian, Brigitte C. 1994. The effect of health insurance on retirement. *Brookings Papers on Economic Activity* 1:181–252.
Rust, John, and Christopher Phelan. 1997. How social security and Medicare affect retirement behavior in a world of incomplete markets. *Econometrics* 65:781–832.
Samwick, Andrew A. 1993. Retirement incentives in the 1983 Pension Provider Survey. Hanover, N.H.: Dartmouth College. Mimeograph.

Comment James H. Stock

This paper addresses a question at the intersection of two important areas of economic and policy research, the economic effects of health insurance and the retirement behavior of older workers. Because health care use increases with age, it makes sense that the particulars of a worker's health care situation will have a substantial impact on his or her retirement decisions. Moreover, to the extent that Medicare eligibility affects the timing of retirement, policy proposals that would change the age of Medicare eligibility could have significant effects on the ages of retirement. Quantifying these interactions is of evident importance both to those interested the economics of aging and to Medicare policy analysts.

Before proceeding to the particulars of Madrian and Beaulieu's empirical analysis, it is useful to lay out the central economic issues of the effect of Medicare on retirement. As discussed by Madrian and Beaulieu, there is now a well-developed literature on the retirement behavior of individuals. It is well established that economic incentives have significant and, importantly, predictable effects on retirement rates. For example, defined benefit plans typically induce spikes in retirement hazards at ages of eligibility and at ages in which the present value of benefits increase sharply. Because Medicare can be thought of as another retirement benefit, in light of this literature it would be quite surprising were Medicare eligibility *not* to have an effect on retirement. Rather, the relevant economic and policy question is whether Medicare is valued by potential retirees at more than its marginal cost to the government, or at more than its private replacement cost were retirees instead to purchase health insurance on the private market. This is not implausible if individuals are risk averse about changing medical coverage or if they are unable to obtain suitable coverage because of exclusions on preexisting conditions. If a dollar of government spending on Medicare is valued more on the margin than a dollar of government spending on social security, then it would be welfare improving to reduce social security expenditures and increase Medicare expenditures.

Results already in the literature can be used to obtain a rough estimate of the effect of Medicare on retirement rates at age 65. Consider a couple with employer-provided health insurance, and suppose that private insurance for the couple costs $6,500 in 1995 dollars. If the couple values Medicare at this private replacement cost, then the availability of Medicare corresponds to an accrual of retirement benefits of $6,500 when the couple becomes eligible for Medicare. Although the estimates of the effects of a $6,500 accrual on retirement differ depending on the couple's other benefits and on the model used, a typical estimate can be obtained from the retirement models in table 4 of

James H. Stock is professor of political economy at the John F. Kennedy School of Government, Harvard University, a research associate of the National Bureau of Economic Research, a fellow of the Econometric Society, and chair of the board of editors of the *Review of Economics and Statistics*.

Lumsdaine, Stock, and Wise (1993), which predicts an increase in the retirement hazard by between 3 and 6 percentage points. This corresponds to approximately one-fifth to one-third of the jump in retirement hazards observed at age 65, depending on the data set. One question thus is whether Medicare eligibility in fact produces an increase in retirement rates greater than those predicted by current structural models of retirement. If so, this would be evidence either that the models are misspecified or that individuals value Medicare at more than its private replacement cost.

With these general remarks in mind, now turn to the particulars of Madrian and Beaulieu's paper. In contrast to the parametric, structural model approaches pursued by most papers on retirement, Madrian and Beaulieu take a more nonparametric approach. The thought experiment is to find two otherwise identical couples, one who will bear costs of medical insurance and one who will be eligible for some Medicare coverage. To implement this strategy empirically, one would like to have data on pensions, wages, and social security benefits, by individual. However, these variables are not observed in Madrian and Beaulieu's data set, so additional assumptions are needed to identify the effect of Medicare.

To examine the identification strategy more precisely, it is useful to refer to the authors' initial equation linking the retirement hazard to demographic characteristics, the man's financial incentives, his spouse's financial incentives, and other determinants (the error term). As Madrian and Beaulieu point out, if the spouse has never worked, then the spouse's financial incentives will be restricted to Medicare, which is strictly linked to her age. Present value calculations suggest a particular functional form for the effect on the man's retirement of this benefit as a function of spouse's age. If, furthermore, the difference between husband's age and spouse's age is uncorrelated with any of the man's (unmeasured) financial incentives, then estimation of hazard functions involving this spouse's age effect should reveal the effect of Medicare.

This is a clever idea, and surely some of what it measures is related to the effect of Medicare. One unmeasurable effect is, however, the benefits a couple would get from joint retirement, both financial (possibly some cost reductions, or from moving) and, arguably more important, nonfinancial. It stands to reason that, all else equal, the older the spouse the more likely the husband is to choose retirement, simply so the couple can enjoy their retirement together. Presumably this effect is also nonlinear in both of their ages, although the precise form of the nonlinearity is presumably hard to determine.

It is useful to contemplate a hypothetical data structure that would permit controlling for this joint retirement effect. One would be if some spouses were randomly assigned to be Medicare eligible, while some spouses were randomly denied eligibility; this random assignment would need to be done far enough in advance for the couple to incorporate it into their retirement planning. Thinking of this approach makes it clear that Medicare eligibility has two effects: the direct subsidy at a certain age, but also the disincentive effect on savings, so that in a world without Medicare individuals would have different preretirement asset profiles. Both these effects will impact the decision to retire.

In summary, Madrian and Beaulieu's idea of quantifying the effect of Medicare eligibility using nonparametric comparisons is appealing, and the evidence they present is consistent with the view that Medicare provides a significant incentive for retirement. Some of the challenges to achieving identification arise from data limitations in the census, and these will be reduced with new data sets with greater information about retirement decisions that will soon become available. However, some of these difficulties are inherent in the nonfinancial issues surrounding joint retirement.

The set of issues surrounding health insurance and retirement are of central importance for analyzing the impact of current policy proposals such as postponing the date of Medicare eligibility and cutting back Medicare and/or social security funding. Related is whether individuals value the marginal Medicare expenditure at more than it costs the government to provide, in which case a dollar taken out of social security would arguably be more acceptable to the elderly than a dollar taken out of Medicare, all else equal. I look forward to seeing further work by Madrian and Beaulieu and others addressing these important problems.

Reference

Lumsdaine, R. L., J. H. Stock, and D. A. Wise. 1993. Why are retirement rates so high at age 65? Cambridge, Mass.: Harvard University, Kennedy School of Government. Manuscript.

Reverse Mortgage Choices: A Theoretical and Empirical Analysis of the Borrowing Decisions of Elderly Homeowners

Michael C. Fratantoni*

Abstract

This research seeks to explain the determinants of reverse mortgage product choice. Reverse mortgages can potentially be a great benefit to an aging population, but it is important that products be structured to meet the needs of this group.

The simulation model developed in this article shows that if the elderly are primarily concerned with the impact of unavoidable expenditure shocks on their standard of living, they are likely to be better off with a line-of-credit plan, which gives them access to a large sum of money, rather than adding an additional fixed component to their income. Support for the theoretical results is given by multinomial logit regressions based on a data set of Home Equity Conversion Mortgages. The empirical results are highly supportive of the predictions from the theoretical model.

Keywords: Reverse mortgages; Elderly housing; Economics of aging; Stochastic dynamic programming

Introduction

Reverse mortgages provide a means for elderly homeowners to access their home equity while continuing to live in their homes. This could be an effective means for reducing poverty among the elderly if this group has no other means for accessing its home equity. Despite this potential benefit, consumer interest in reverse mortgages has been relatively modest to date. Estimates of the potential market for this product have varied widely, but these estimates are generally much larger than current volumes. Whether this is because of resistance to reverse mortgages generally or more specific difficulties with the products that are available is unclear at this point. Given this, it is important to understand which types of reverse mortgage products would be most beneficial to each subset of the elderly population. Ideally, products would add to elderly homeowners' current well-being and help to build their liquid asset bases to cushion future economic shocks.

Most often a reverse mortgage is described as an annuity payment to the homeowner for the length of time that she remains in the house (Kutty 1996). However, evidence from the U.S. Department of Housing and Urban Development's (HUD's) Home Equity Conversion Mortgage (HECM) program provides a different picture. The HECM offers five different payment options: an annuity payment for the remainder of the borrower's tenure in the home, a payment for a fixed term, a line of credit, or a combination of a line of credit and

---

*Michael C. Fratantoni is a Senior Economist at Fannie Mae. The author thanks Gordon Crawford, Mike Goldberg, and several anonymous referees for helpful comments on earlier drafts of this article.

either a tenure or term payment plan. Interestingly, the majority of borrowers to this point have opted for the line-of-credit plan. Other researchers have noted that for most borrowers the annuity payment associated with a reverse mortgage is quite small. However, these same borrowers could gain immediate access to a substantial portion of their equity if they selected the line-of-credit option. The typical reverse mortgage borrower is house rich but income poor and thus would not qualify for a conventional home equity line of credit because she would not be able to meet income requirements. It is likely that such a borrower would gain more from a line of credit where she has immediate access to a large sum, rather than a continuing small payment over a long horizon.

This article is composed of four sections. In the first section the HECM program and a selection of previous research on reverse mortgages are reviewed. The second section develops a stochastic dynamic programming model of reverse mortgage product choice, based on borrowers maximizing the expected discounted value of utility. The third section presents summary statistics from a data set of HECM loans. This data set consists of approximately 17,000 HECM loans purchased by Fannie Mae. These loans were originated between 1993 and 1997. The final section presents estimates from logit regressions of reverse mortgage product choice using the HECM data set. These results closely match the results from the simulation model.

Overview of the HECM Program and Literature Review

HECM Program Overview

The HECM program provides mortgage insurance for reverse mortgages originated by Federal Housing Administration– (FHA) approved lenders. Reverse mortgages are secured only against the value of the home and become payable when the borrower moves, sells the house, or dies. Borrowers must be 62 or older, own their homes free and clear (or be able to subordinate any existing mortgage into the HECM), attend counseling before closing, and live in a single-family property that meets HUD's minimum property standards. For each of the HECM payment plans, the size of the loan is based on the principal limit factor, which is a function of the age of the youngest borrower, the expected average interest rate, and the adjusted property value.[1] Borrowers cannot be forced to sell or move out of their home, even if loan balances rise above the current house values.

Literature Review

Most research on reverse mortgages has focused on their potential market and the technical and financial difficulties in their management. The HECM program is detailed in *The Journal of the American Real Estate and Urban Economics Association's* 1994 special summer issue on housing finance for the elderly.

---

[1] The expected average interest rate is a forecast of future short-term rates based on current long-term rates. The adjusted property value is the minimum of the appraised value and FHA's mortgage limit for one-family houses, which varies by geographic area. In January 1995, this limit ranged from $67,500 to $124,875. As of April 1999 this range had increased to span $115,200 to $208,800 ($313,200 in Alaska, Guam, Hawaii, and the Virgin Islands).

Mayer and Simons (1994) used the 1990 Survey of Income and Program Participation (SIPP) to show that more than six million elderly homeowners have high levels of home equity and could increase their monthly incomes by obtaining reverse mortgages. Although the reverse mortgage payment, as a percentage of monthly income, is small for most households, they showed that it would raise income for almost 1.5 million elderly persons above poverty level. This is due to the fact that most elderly homeowners own their homes free and clear and thus have substantial amounts of untapped home equity. However, since most elderly home-owners have little or no current labor income they cannot qualify for a conventional home equity loan or line of credit. Mayer and Simons point out that the majority of HECM bor-rowers have chosen the line-of-credit option. They attribute this to the fact that many elderly households also have very little liquid wealth. They suggest that the availability of a lump-sum payment to protect against various financial shocks that might be related to housing, health care, or automobile care could be very valuable to many elderly homeowners. They use data from the SIPP to illustrate that drawing the full line of credit available in a lump sum could increase liquid wealth by 200 percent or more for many elderly homeowners.

Merrill, Finkel, and Kutty (1994) showed that the potential ratio of annuity payment to income is greatest for households with low incomes. They argued that houses valued below $100,000 would result in annuity payments too small to be worthwhile, while those valued above $200,000 would likely indicate their owners have other assets and would not need to tap into home equity.

Weinrobe (1985) showed that the great majority of homeowners in a Buffalo reverse mort-gage program chose a lump-sum payment over an annuity, even though the lump-sum pay-ment had a smaller expected present value.

Case and Schnare (1994) evaluated HECM borrower characteristics, including the deter-minants of product choice, using a sample of approximately 2,500 loans. They calculated the probability of a borrower choosing each payment option as a function of age, family compo-sition, property value, property location, and other characteristics. Their findings included the following: 1) younger borrowers were more likely to elect tenure payments; 2) there was not a strong relationship between income and product choice; 3) single men were less likely than women or couples to choose the line-of-credit option; 4) borrowers with higher-valued properties were much less likely to choose the line-of-credit option; and 5) rural borrowers were more likely to choose the line-of-credit option than suburban or urban borrowers.

Rasmussen, Megbolugbe, and Morgan (1995) analyzed the potential size of the reverse mort-gage market. They note that there are two motives for obtaining a reverse mortgage: to draw down wealth as one ages (life-cycle motive) and to diversify illiquid housing wealth (asset-management motive). They note that for many households the annuity value may not be large, but the addition to liquid wealth is substantial.

Rasmussen, Megbolugbe, and Morgan (1997) explored the importance of investment motives for obtaining a reverse mortgage and noted how certain expenditures, such as long-term care insurance, mid-career human capital investments, and children's college costs, may be better financed with a reverse mortgage. The ability of a reverse mortgage to make housing equity more readily accessible allows homeowners more flexibility in financing large expen-ditures. The availability of a line-of-credit or lump-sum option is necessary for this expanded flexibility. They also note that for some borrowers the term, rather than the tenure, duration better fits financial needs.

Theoretical Model

In this section, a simple theoretical model of the reverse mortgage borrower's product choice is developed using stochastic dynamic programming techniques. The elderly face what amounts to a reversal of the standard consumer's optimization problem.[2] Nonelderly consumers optimize consumption expenditures, given an uncertain labor income. By contrast, the elderly have fixed incomes but may face large and, to some extent, unpredictable expenditure shocks related to medical and other crises.[3] Some elderly may choose line-of-credit plans, which could better meet these unpredictable crises, rather than adding an additional fixed component to their income.

In this model, the borrower chooses the product that yields the highest expected present discounted value of utility. It is assumed that there are only two types of reverse mortgage products: a line of credit (LOC) and a tenure duration annuity payment plan (AP). For the moment, it is further assumed that the borrower stays in the house for life, that she has no bequest motive,[4] and that there is no length-of-life uncertainty (the borrower lives until age 90).[5] At mortgage inception, the borrower has home equity equal to H and maximizes the sum of expected discounted lifetime utility subject to a budget constraint as follows,

$$Max E_0 \sum_i^T \beta^i \cdot U(C_i) \tag{1}$$

$$\text{subject to } X_{t+1} = (X_t - C_t - \pi M_t)(1 + r) + \bar{Y} \tag{2}$$

where E_0 is the expectation operator evaluated at mortgage inception, β is the discount factor, X is cash on hand, C is nonemergency consumption expenditures, $\bar{Y}$ is the fixed level of income, M is an expenditure shock, r is the interest rate, and π is a (0,1) dummy variable. π takes a value of 1 with probability p, and a value of 0 with probability $1-p$. The expenditure shocks are proportional to $\bar{Y}$, $M = \gamma \bar{Y}$, and are independent across time. The borrower's

---

[2] An example of a more standard problem relating to homeownership and risky asset choice is found in Fratantoni (1998). The solution method for this article is similar to the method found there.

[3] Social security payments include a cost-of-living adjustment, which means that real income rather than nominal income is fixed, but this does not change the central intuition.

[4] The addition of a bequest motive would not qualitatively change the results of this exercise. Assuming that there is no bequest motive forces last-period consumption to equal last-period cash on hand. A bequest would shift down consumption at each point in time, so that last-period consumption plus the bequest would be equal to last-period cash on hand. More complex bequest behavior would be needed for wealthy households, but the relevant population for the reverse mortgage problem is the low- to moderate-income elderly population, so this simple solution would suffice.

[5] Length-of-life uncertainty is introduced at the end of this section.

preferences are modeled using Constant Relative Risk Aversion (CRRA) utility, that is $U(C) = C^{1-\rho}/1 - \rho.$[6] Given this, the first-order condition for this problem is

$$C_t^{-\rho} = \beta(1+r)E_t(C_{t+1})^{-\rho} \tag{3}$$

The marginal utility of current consumption is set equal to expected marginal utility from future consumption properly discounted. Since agents have no length-of-life uncertainty and no bequest motive, in the final period of life they consume all of their assets, $C_T = X_T$. Thus

$$C_{T-1}^{-\rho} = \beta(1+r)E_{T-1}(X_T)^{-\rho} \tag{4}$$

and substituting from equation 1,

$$C_{T-1}^{-\rho} = \beta(1+r)E_{T-1}((X_{T-1} - C_{T-1} - \pi M_{T-1})(1+r) + \bar{Y})^{-\rho}. \tag{5}$$

This expectation can be written as

$$C_{T-1}^{-\rho} = \beta(1+r)\{p \cdot ((X_{T-1} - C_{T-1} - M_{T-1})(1+r) + \bar{Y})^{-\rho} \\ + (1-p) \cdot ((X_{T-1} - C_{T-1})(1+r) + \bar{Y})^{-\rho}\} \tag{6}$$

Given values for each of the parameters and the assumptions listed above, this equation can be solved numerically for optimal consumption expenditures at time $T - 1$. A similar equation can be solved for each period of life, working recursively back to the mortgage inception date. This will yield optimal consumption rules as a function of initial cash on hand, income, and the specified parameter values.

The next step is to model how each reverse mortgage product would affect the problem above. Up to this point home equity has not played a role. Assuming that a reverse mortgage will draw home equity down to zero, and ignoring any home price or interest rate uncertainty that would affect the lender's payout calculations, the discounted sum of the annuity payments, AP, and the line of credit at origination, LOC, are equal to the principal limit. The principal limit increases with borrower age and with the amount of home equity. A borrower who chooses an annuity payment plan faces the following problem:

$$C_{T-1}^{-\rho} = \beta(1+r)\{p \cdot ((X_{T-1} - C_{T-1} - M_{T-1})(1+r) + \bar{Y} + AP)^{-\rho} \\ + (1-p) \cdot ((X_{T-1} - C_{T-1})(1+r) + \bar{Y} + AP)^{-\rho}\} \tag{7}$$

With this product, the borrower's current income will always be increased by AP. With the line-of-credit plan, a borrower has the option of drawing on the line at any point from mortgage inception until the end of life. Case and Schnare (1994) noted that 94 percent of borrowers had made at least one draw on their line at the time of their study. In this study, the simplifying assumption is made that the borrower takes out 100 percent of his or her line at closing. Thus, in this model, cash on hand in period one is equal to initial cash on hand plus the line of credit, $X' = X_0 + LOC$, where LOC is equal to the principal limit. From this point, the consumption expenditures are chosen as above,

---

[6] It is important to note that borrowers get no utility from expenditures on M. These emergency expenditures presumably are caused by some incident that has considerable disutility. Any utility brought about by M (say a hospital stay) is negated by the disutility of the event (the illness).

$$C_{T-1}{}^{-\rho} = \beta(1+r)\{p\cdot((X'_{T-1}-C_{T-1}-M_{T-1})(1+r)+\bar{Y})^{-\rho}$$
$$+(1-p)\cdot((X'_{T-1}-C_{T-1})(1+r)+\bar{Y})^{-\rho}\} \tag{8}$$

The third option for elderly households is to do nothing; that is, not to obtain a reverse mortgage. Assuming that these households have no other means of getting equity out of their property, this option will always be inferior to either product previously discussed and, therefore, will not be formally modeled.

Given these consumption rules, 1,000 different paths are simulated where agents face a probability of an expenditure shock in each period of life and set nonemergency consumption expenditures accordingly. Using these data, expected utility at each point in life is calculated, and the discounted sum of utility over the mortgage duration is determined. The borrower chooses the product with the greatest expected utility.

The output from the simulations includes the expected discounted value from choosing the annuity payment plan, $E_0(AP)$, and the expected discounted value from choosing the line-of-credit plan, $E_0(LOC)$. The baseline parameter values are borrower age = 75, income = $15,000, home equity = $100,000, cash on hand (wealth) at closing = 0, subjective discount rate = 0.05, risk aversion parameter = 4, interest rate = 8 percent, and a 10 percent probability that an expenditure shock equal to one-half of income will arrive each period. Figure 1 shows the median paths for consumption and cash on hand for the two products from the simulations. For the AP product, cash on hand is slightly greater than consumption across most of the mortgage. For the LOC product, cash on hand in the first year is much greater than consumption, because the entire line is drawn immediately but diminishes quickly over time. In the final year of life, consumption and cash on hand are equal for both products. For the baseline parameter values, $E_0(AP) = -0.00064$, $E_0(LOC) = -0.0005$ and $\phi = E_0(LOC) - E_0(AP) = 0.000132$. If ϕ is positive, the borrower should choose a line-of-credit plan. If ϕ is negative, the borrower should choose an annuity payment. Thus, under the baseline parameter values, the borrower would be better off choosing the LOC product.

Figures 2 through 5 show the sensitivity of these results to different parameter values, with ϕ plotted over a range of values for each parameter *ceteris paribus*. Figure 2 graphs ϕ by income. The model predicts that a borrower is less likely to choose the line-of-credit plan as income increases, but that ϕ is positive over the range shown, $0 to $40,000. Figure 3 shows a negative predicted relationship between ϕ and age over most of the range, but a slight increase as age approaches 90. The model predicts that a borrower between ages 79 and 85 would choose an annuity payment product, while a borrower outside this age range would choose the LOC product. Figure 4 graphs the predicted relationship between wealth (initial cash on hand) and ϕ. This relationship is monotonically decreasing, with the model predicting that a borrower with about $50,000 in liquid wealth at closing would be indifferent between the two products. Figure 5 shows an interesting predicted relationship between home equity and ϕ, which first increases, then decreases, in a quadratic relationship. The prediction is that a borrower with $50,000 to $60,000 of home equity is most likely to choose the line-of-credit plan, while a borrower with more or less home equity would be less likely to choose this plan. The model results are sensitive to other parameter values as well. Representing the ratio of the expenditure shock to income, as γ increases, the model predicts that a borrower is more likely to choose the line-of-credit plan. ϕ is monotonically increasing in the probability of an expenditure shock, p. A borrower who expects more frequent expen-

Figure 1. **Simulation Output: Baseline Parameter Values**

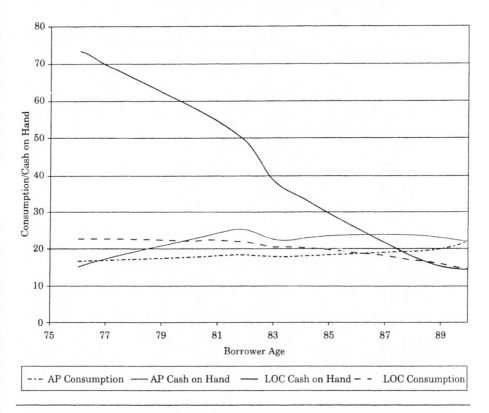

diture shocks is more likely to choose the line-of-credit product. The borrower's level of risk aversion is also an important factor in product choice. A relatively risk-averse borrower is more likely to choose the payment plan, rather than the line-of-credit plan. A borrower who draws the full line of credit available at mortgage inception immediately increases his consumption expenditures since he has a higher level of cash on hand; this can mean lower levels of consumption at the end of life compared with those under the annuity payment plan. The annuity payment plan results in a much smoother consumption path, which is preferable for a more risk-averse borrower.

A final sensitivity check is to determine whether length-of-life uncertainty would qualitatively affect these results. In order to do this, an age-dependent discount rate is introduced. This rate is the product of a constant discount factor and an age-dependent mortality probability; later years are discounted at an increasing rate.[7] With this added age-dependent

---

[7] The mortality probabilities are taken from Hubbard, Skinner, and Zeldes (1995).

discount rate, another analysis is carried out. Figure 6 displays the relationship between φ and age, given this length-of-life uncertainty. Comparing this with figure 3, one sees that qualitatively the relationship remains the same. The model without length-of-life uncertainty predicted that a borrower between ages 79 and 85 would choose the annuity payment product, while a borrower outside this age range would choose the LOC option. With length-of-life uncertainty, the annuity is preferred if the borrower is between ages 81 and 87, while a borrower outside this age range would choose the LOC option.

Comparisons across other variables and parameters also show that adding length-of-life uncertainty to the model does not qualitatively affect the results, although there are some small quantitative changes.

Data and Summary Statistics

The sample used in the empirical analysis of this article is discussed in this section. This data set consists of approximately 17,000 HECM loans originated between 1993 and 1997 and purchased by Fannie Mae. Because Fannie Mae is the only secondary market purchaser of HECMs, this represents a substantial portion of the population of loans. Table 1 presents summary statistics from my sample, and table 2 shows a comparison between this sample and the Case and Schnare (1994) sample. Although my sample includes more loans, it has very limited information on other household characteristics. The explanatory variables include borrower age, household income, borrower type, the appraised value of the house, the

Figure 2. φ **versus Income**

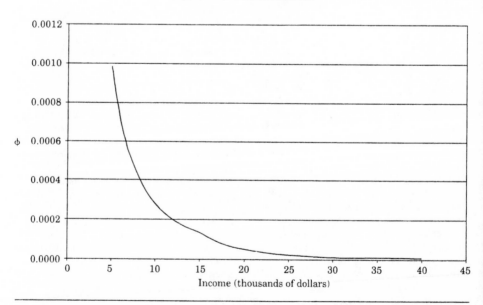

Figure 3. φ **versus Age**

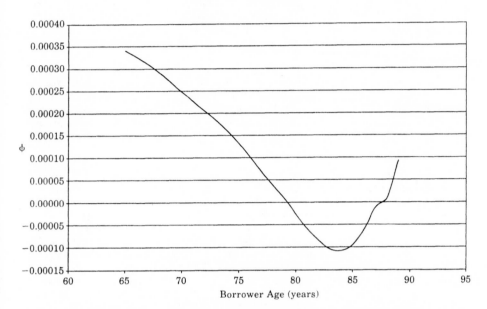

Borrower Age (years)

number of bedrooms, the age of the house, and the type and origination date of the mortgage. There are three borrower types: single females, single males, and couples, where couples include any household where there is more than one borrower. For couples, the age referenced is that of the youngest borrower.

The total sample results in the first column of table 1 show that the average reverse mortgage borrower lives in a house of modest size that is relatively old. The elderly bear significant psychological as well as financial costs of moving, so the fact that they tend to live in older houses is expected. Elderly households that have recently moved have had the opportunity to adjust their housing consumption, and possibly withdraw some of their housing equity if they traded down. The remaining columns of table 1 present this information by product type. The mean estimates show that line-of-credit borrowers are younger, have higher incomes, and have houses with a lower appraised value. Borrowers who opt for a combination of line of credit with a term or tenure payment are generally older with lower incomes and have houses that are older and worth more. Borrowers who opt for a term or tenure payment have the highest mean appraisal values but fall in between combination and line-of-credit borrowers for the other variables. Each of these estimates has a relatively large standard deviation associated with it, so none of these differences are statistically significant.

The sample used here has several differences from that used in the Case and Schnare study. The median age in this sample is 75, compared with Case and Schnare's 76.7; the median nominal income is $11,160 compared with $7,572. The change in median income is important because it shows that reverse mortgages are becoming more attractive to elderly house-holds at the upper edge of the poverty line. The median appraisal value is larger in my sample, and the median house is older than in Case and Schnare's sample. My sample has a larger proportion of single females, a smaller proportion of single males, and an equal proportion of couples.

In my sample, 63.8 percent of reverse mortgage borrowers chose the line-of-credit plan, 22.3 percent chose a term or tenure payment in combination with a line of credit, and 13.9 percent chose a plan that provides only a term or tenure annuity payment. For payment duration, modified and regular term borrowers are grouped together, as are modified and regular tenure borrowers. A term duration is chosen by 55.1 percent of borrowers who elect to receive an annuity payment of some sort, while a tenure duration is chosen by 44.9 percent.

Reverse mortgage borrowers in the HECM program must own their home free and clear or be able to subordinate any existing mortgage into the HECM. In fact, most elderly home-owners in the United States have no mortgage on their property. Table 3 presents evidence to this effect from the 1995 *American Housing Survey*, listing homeownership rates and mortgage holdings by age group. With the homeownership rate higher than 80 percent for the 61 to 70 and 71 to 80 age groups and almost 70 percent for the group 81 and older, the majority of each group has no mortgage attached. In fact, 91.8 percent of homeowners older than 81 own their house free and clear. This suggests that the potential pool of reverse mortgage borrowers is quite large, since most elderly have no mortgage obligations. It is

Figure 4. ϕ **versus Wealth**

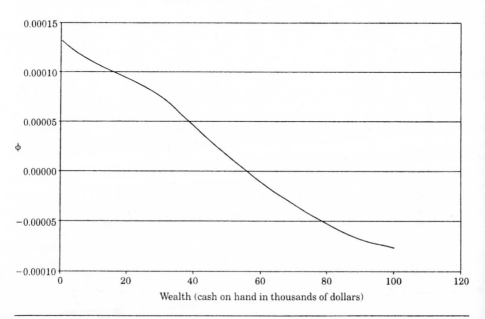

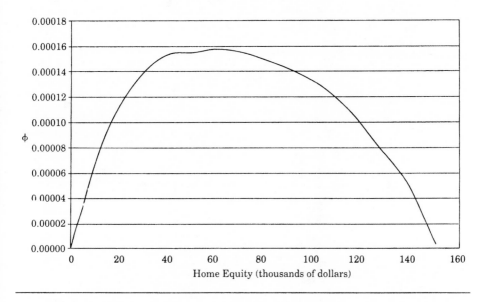

Figure 5. φ **versus Home Equity**

unclear whether the reason they have not already drawn down their home equity is because they were unable to or because they did not want to (see Venti and Wise 1990).

To what extent are the elderly homeowners who obtain reverse mortgages representative of all elderly households? Or, to put it another way, is there something unusual about households who decide to draw down their home equity rather than doing nothing (i.e., keeping their housing wealth in an illiquid form)? Ideally, this question would be answered with a data set of elderly homeowners where only a subset had taken out a reverse mortgage. A two-step procedure could then be used: first, to determine the likelihood that a household would take out a reverse mortgage, and second, to determine which reverse mortgage product they would choose. Unfortunately, such a data set does not yet exist, primarily because so few households have obtained reverse mortgages. Thus there will be a form of selection bias in my empirical results. It is unclear what the effect of this bias will be. One would think that only those borrowers who expect to be better off would use this product, but this sort of selection bias is hardly unique to reverse mortgages. In any event, the difficulty of assessing the representativeness of this sample is a call for future research as more data become available.

Empirical Model

In this section, results from logit regressions are examined to determine the impact of each of several variables on product and payment duration choice and to compare the predictions from the simulation model with the empirical results.

Table 1. **Summary Statistics of Explanatory Variables, Fratantoni 1997 Sample**

	Total		Line of Credit		Combination		Payment	
	Mean	Standard Deviation	Mean	Standard Deviation	Mean	Standard Deviation	Mean	Standard Deviation
Number of bedrooms	2.75	0.97	2.78	0.97	2.73	0.94	2.68	1.01
Appraisal value of the house ($)	121,371.76	66,556.45	116,103.31	64,294.84	128,930.79	65,001.36	133,449.21	75,893.10
Age of the house (years)	42.29	23.22	41.84	23.65	45.43	22.78	39.33	21.37
Age of the youngest borrower (years)	75.61	7.18	74.47	6.98	78.10	7.16	76.80	6.91
Household income ($)	13,160.38	18,896.64	13,929.09	22,723.35	11,416.07	7,318.43	12,431.03	10,234.86

Figure 6. **Length-of-Life Uncertainty Model: φ versus Age**

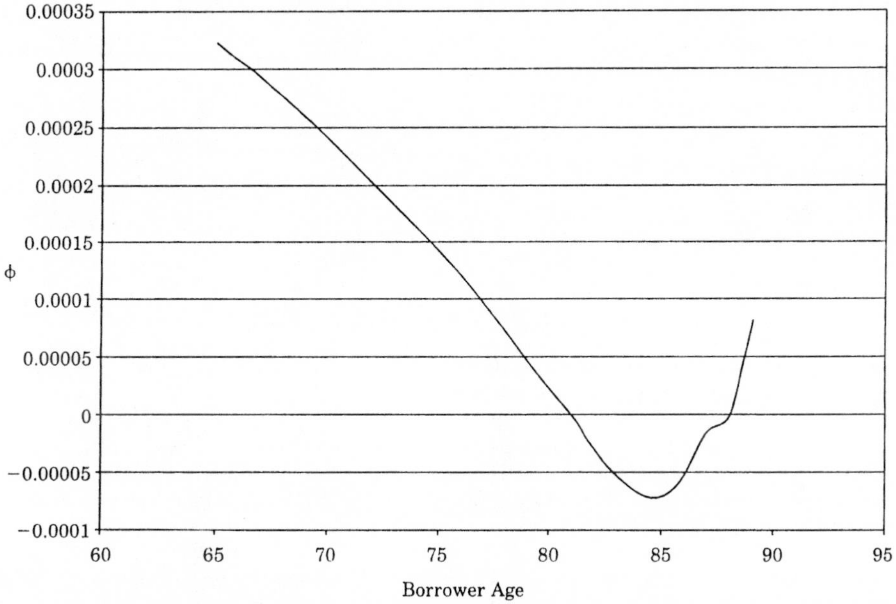

Determinants of Reverse Mortgage Product Choice

In order to estimate the determinants of product choice empirically, a multivariate logit framework is used. This estimation method is best if none of the products are strictly preferred to all of the others. For example, if it were the case that a line-of-credit plan is the most flexible product, and hence would be preferred by everyone, an ordered probit estimation would be preferable. However, I am assuming that because of transaction costs, taking out a line of credit and purchasing an annuity would yield a smaller payment than choosing the annuity option. It would also be possible to estimate a nested logit model where first the product is chosen, then, conditional upon the product, the payment duration is chosen. However, the payment duration decision is only applicable to borrowers who choose the annuity payment option, and this led to a decision to model these choices independently.

In order to simplify the estimation, borrowers are grouped into three general products: a line-of-credit plan, a combination of a line of credit with a term or tenure payment, and a term or tenure payment plan without a line of credit. The explanatory variables include the age of the youngest borrower, household income, the appraised value of the property, origination year, borrower type, borrower closing costs, and the census region where the property is located. The simulation model predicted a negative relationship between income and line-of-credit choice, and quadratic relationships between home equity, age, and line-of-credit choice. Other variables are included in the estimation to capture variation due to factors not controlled for in the simulation model. In particular, borrower closing costs capture variable

Table 2. **Comparison of Fratantoni Sample with Case and Schnare Sample**

	Fratantoni (1997)	Case and Schnare (1994)
Number of households	17,478	2,522
Median values		
Appraisal value of the house ($)	108,000	103,000
Age of the youngest borrower (years)	75	76.7
Household income ($)	11,160	7,572
Age of house (years)	40	36.5
Percent of borrowers who are		
Single females	58.1	56.5
Couples	29.6	29.2
Single males	12.3	14.3

transaction costs that would be difficult to incorporate in a simulation model. Origination-year effects could be important if there were changes in the marketing practices or underwriting standards of HECMs since the program started, or if transaction costs have changed over time, as reverse mortgages become more widely accepted. If men, women, and couples have different life expectancies, different expected future incomes, or if the uncertainty around these variables is different for different types of borrowers, then capturing borrower type effects is necessary. It is also possible that there are geographic region effects.

Table 4 presents results from three specifications of the multinomial estimation. The dependent variable in these regressions is categorical and can take on one of three values: "line of credit," "annuity payment," and "combination." The first specification includes age, income, appraisal value, the squares of these three variables, borrower closing costs, and origination year; the second specification adds borrower type; and the third specification adds regional dummies. The table includes parameter estimates, Chi square values for individual parameters and for categories, the p-values associated with these values, and the log likelihood for each specification. The missing parameters from each category form the excluded group. The "combination intercept" is the factor used to capture the effect on the probability of the third choice, the combination of a line of credit and an annuity pay-

Table 3. **Mortgage Holdings by Age Group**

Age Group	Homeownership Rate	Percent of Owner Households with Number of Mortgages		
		0	1	2+
30 or younger	29.3	15.4	80.7	3.9
31–40	59.7	14.4	77	8.7
41–50	72.2	19.5	69.1	11.4
51–60	78.3	36.2	55.1	8.6
61–70	81.3	64.3	32.6	3.1
71–80	80.3	83	16.1	0.8
81 or older	68.3	91.8	8	0.2

Source: American Housing Survey (1995).

Table 4. **Parameter Estimates for Product Choice Model**

Category	Model 1 Estimate	Model 1 Chi Square	Model 1 P-Value	Model 2 Estimate	Model 2 Chi Square	Model 2 P-Value	Model 3 Estimate	Model 3 Chi Square	Model 3 P-Value
Intercept	19.61	177.38	0.0001	19.67	178.24	0.0001	19.62	176.68	0.0001
Age	−0.41	120.34	0.0001	−0.41	120.08	0.0001	−0.41	118.97	0.0001
Age squared	0.00	92.99	0.0001	0.00	92.77	0.0001	0.00	91.94	0.0001
Income/1,000	0.02	101.98	0.0001	0.02	82.31	0.0001	0.02	69.99	0.0001
(Income/1,000) squared	0.00	32.68	0.0001	0.00	29.49	0.0001	0.00	23.75	0.0001
Appraised value/1,000	−0.01	94.65	0.0001	−0.01	94.70	0.0001	−0.01	71.05	0.0001
(Appraised value/1,000) squared	0.00	46.82	0.0001	0.00	46.88	0.0001	0.00	35.58	0.0001
Origination year									
1993	−0.69	140.94	0.0001	−0.69	140.11	0.0001	−0.69	141.53	0.0001
1994	−0.51	102.02	0.0001	−0.51	101.54	0.0001	−0.51	100.69	0.0001
1995	−0.28	62.32	0.0001	−0.28	61.81	0.0001	−0.27	61.88	0.0001
1996	−0.28	19.00	0.0001	−0.28	18.86	0.0001	−0.27	17.42	0.0001
1997	−0.29	21.01	0.0001	−0.29	20.91	0.0001	−0.28	20.45	0.0001
Borrower type									
Single female				−0.07	2.86	0.2389	−0.08	3.25	0.1969
Couple					1.69	0.193		1.89	0.169
Single male				−0.08	2.83	0.0923	−0.09	3.22	0.0726
Region									
Midwest							−0.11	76.80	0.0001
Northeast							−0.24	5.70	0.0169
South							0.16	35.69	0.0001
West								10.97	0.0009
Borrower closing costs	0.00	26.77	0.0001	0.00	26.63	0.0001	0.00	26.37	0.0001
Combination intercept	1.33		0.0001	1.33		0.0001	1.33		0.0001
Log likelihood	−15,008.81			−15,007.37			−14,968.82		

Notes: For the categorical variables (origination year, borrower type, and region) the Chi-square statistic and P-value for the variable across all categories are given first. The omitted categories represent the reference group, i.e. 1997 origination, single male, and from the West. The "combination intercept" is the factor used to capture the effect on the probability of the third choice, the combination of a line of credit and an annuity payment.

ment.[8] Each specification determines the effect of the explanatory variables on the probability that the borrower would choose a line-of-credit product. Examination of the Chi-square statistics shows that appraisal value is the most important determinant of product choice, followed by origination year, age, and income. The second specification shows that the borrower type category is not significant, even at the ten-percent level, although the individual parameter for single females is significant at that level. The third specification shows that region is significant as a category.

Table 5 presents the mean probability that a borrower would choose each of the three products broken down by category. The probabilities sum to one hundred percent across the three products. This table shows several interesting results. The first is that the younger elderly borrowers are more likely to choose a line-of-credit plan than the older elderly borrowers. This fits the prediction from the simulation model. Second, contrary to what was predicted in the simulation model, the empirical finding is that borrowers with higher income are more likely to choose the line-of-credit plan. Finally, the empirical model shows that borrowers in houses with lower appraised values are more likely to choose the line-of-credit product, consistent with the simulation results. Table 5 shows that there are no large differences in the probabilities of different product choices across borrower types. Couples and single males are more likely to choose a line-of-credit plan than single females, but there is not a large difference. In fact, there are larger differences in mean probabilities across regions than across borrower types in model 3, where both region and borrower type are included in the specification. Borrowers from the South have the greatest probability of choosing a line-of-credit plan, while borrowers from the Northeast are more likely than those from other regions to choose a combination or a payment plan.

These results generally agree with the predictions from the simulation model with regard to age and home equity, but differ with respect to household income. They also show surprisingly that origination year and region are more important determinants of product choice than borrower type. I was unable to capture the effect of these variables in the simulation model, so this could explain why the results for income are different from those found in the empirical model.

Determinants of Payment Duration Choice

Although the simulation model in this article only yielded predictions regarding product choice, in this section the same explanatory variables are used to estimate the determinants of payment duration choice. Of borrowers who received an annuity payment, 55.1 percent chose term over tenure duration.

Table 6 presents parameter estimates from a bivariate logit model of the term/tenure choice. The dependent variable in these regressions is again categorical and can take on one of two values: "term" or "tenure." Three specifications are estimated: the first specification includes only age, income, appraisal value, the squares of these three variables, borrower closing costs, and origination year; the second specification adds borrower type; and the third

---

[8] In this formulation of the multivariate logistic model, the probabilities are calculated as follows: P(annuity payment) = $F(X\beta)$, P(combination plan) = F(combination intercept + $X\beta$) − $F(X\beta)$, P(line of credit) = $1 − P$(annuity payment) − P(combination plan).

Table 5. **Estimated Mean Probabilities by Product**

Category	Model 1			Model 2			Model 3		
	Line of Credit	Combination	Payment	Line of Credit	Combination	Payment	Line of Credit	Combination	Payment
Age group									
70 or younger	0.767	0.156	0.077	0.767	0.156	0.076	0.767	0.156	0.076
71 to 80	0.634	0.229	0.137	0.634	0.229	0.137	0.634	0.229	0.137
81 or older	0.525	0.275	0.200	0.525	0.275	0.200	0.526	0.274	0.200
Income									
0–$15,000	0.620	0.232	0.148	0.620	0.232	0.148	0.620	0.232	0.148
$15,001 or more	0.694	0.195	0.111	0.694	0.195	0.110	0.694	0.196	0.110
Appraised value									
0–$60,000	0.703	0.193	0.104	0.703	0.193	0.104	0.706	0.192	0.102
$60,001 or more	0.635	0.225	0.141	0.635	0.225	0.141	0.635	0.225	0.141
Borrower type									
Single female	0.617	0.234	0.150	0.614	0.235	0.151	0.614	0.235	0.151
Couple	0.692	0.196	0.111	0.692	0.197	0.111	0.692	0.197	0.111
Single male	0.637	0.224	0.139	0.652	0.217	0.131	0.652	0.216	0.131
Region									
Midwest	0.662	0.213	0.126	0.662	0.213	0.126	0.653	0.218	0.129
Northeast	0.614	0.234	0.152	0.614	0.234	0.152	0.572	0.253	0.175
South	0.663	0.212	0.125	0.663	0.212	0.125	0.702	0.193	0.105
West	0.641	0.222	0.138	0.641	0.221	0.138	0.656	0.215	0.129

Table 6. **Parameter Estimates for Term versus Tenure Payment**

Category	Model 1			Model 2			Model 3		
	Estimate	Chi Square	P-Value	Estimate	Chi Square	P-Value	Estimate	Chi Square	P-Value
Intercept	11.63	21.66	0.0001	11.71	21.96	0.0001	11.06	18.66	0.0001
Age	−0.25	15.16	0.0001	−0.24	14.91	0.0001	−0.23	12.35	0.0004
Age squared	0.00	12.25	0.0005	0.00	12.12	0.0005	0.00	9.60	0.0019
Income/1,000	0.02	9.40	0.0022	0.01	4.87	0.0273	0.01	0.85	0.3572
(Income/1,000) squared	0.00	0.05	0.8163	0.00	0.01	0.9425	0.00	0.58	0.4476
Appraised value/1,000	−0.01	33.07	0.0001	−0.01	33.59	0.0001	0.00	13.40	0.0003
(Appraised value/1,000) squared	0.00	21.60	0.0001	0.00	21.90	0.0001	0.00	12.11	0.0005
Origination year		30.89	0.0001		31.36	0.0001		24.37	0.0001
1993	0.33	9.31	0.0023	0.33	9.42	0.0021	0.30	7.65	0.0057
1994	0.49	20.37	0.0001	0.49	20.56	0.0001	0.44	15.55	0.0001
1995	0.28	6.69	0.0097	0.29	6.78	0.0092	0.26	5.26	0.0219
1996	0.55	22.50	0.0001	0.55	22.94	0.0001	0.51	18.46	0.0001
1997									
Borrower type					7.18	0.0276		11.63	0.0030
Single female				−0.21	6.52	0.0107	−0.26	9.29	0.0023
Couple				−0.11	1.41	0.2349	−0.10	1.04	0.3088
Single male									
Region								276.27	0.0001
Midwest							−0.55	46.14	0.0001
Northeast							−0.39	22.72	0.0001
South							0.83	71.41	0.0001
West									
Borrower closing costs	0.00	34.07	0.0001	0.00	33.54	0.0001	0.00	18.51	0.0001
Log likelihood	−4,210.73			−4,207.12			−4,053.62		

Note: For the categorical variables (origination year, borrower type, and region) the Chi-square statistic and P-value for the variable across all categories are given first. The omitted categories represent the reference group (i.e., 1997 origination, single male, and from the West).

specification includes regional dummies. Each specification determines the effect of the explanatory variables on the probability that a borrower would choose a term payment. The Chi-square values for the different categories show that appraised value, origination year, and age are the most important determinants of the payment duration decision. Income and borrower type also are significant but have a smaller impact. The third specification shows that region is in fact the most important determinant of the payment duration decision and that including regional dummies reduces the importance of appraisal value.

Table 7 presents the estimated mean probabilities by category. In this table, subtracting the given probability from one yields the probability that a borrower would choose a tenure payment plan. There are two main results shown in this table: younger borrowers and borrowers with less home equity are more likely to choose a term payment. These results are intuitive: Because younger borrowers and borrowers with less home equity would receive smaller tenure payments, they choose to increase the size of their payments by selecting a term plan.

Conclusion

This research seeks to explain the determinants of reverse mortgage product choice. Reverse mortgages can potentially be a great benefit to an aging population, but it is important that products be structured to meet the needs of this group. This article contributes to an understanding of this market by showing the importance of unavoidable expenditure shocks on the well-being of elderly households. Products such as line-of-credit plans allow house-

Table 7. **Estimated Mean Probabilities of Term Payment Choice**

Category	Model 1	Model 2	Model 3
Age group			
70 or younger	0.637	0.637	0.638
71 to 80	0.556	0.556	0.556
81 or older	0.504	0.504	0.503
Income			
0–$15,000	0.543	0.542	0.543
$15,001 or more	0.579	0.581	0.577
Appraised value			
0–$60,000	0.660	0.660	0.674
$60,001 or more	0.544	0.544	0.543
Borrower type			
Single female	0.540	0.530	0.530
Couple	0.582	0.589	0.589
Single male	0.548	0.587	0.587
Region			
Midwest	0.589	0.589	0.785
Northeast	0.522	0.522	0.482
South	0.582	0.581	0.611
West	0.544	0.544	0.461

holds to protect against these shocks at a relatively low cost while continuing to live in their homes. The theoretical and empirical findings in this article show that for a large subset of elderly homeowners, the line-of-credit plan is the preferred product.

Practical implications can be drawn from this research for business and policy purposes. On the business side, this research can advise lenders on a marketing strategy. If the prevailing perception among consumers is that the annuity plan is synonymous with a reverse mortgage, then an aggressive marketing strategy to educate consumers about the availability of the line-of-credit plan could result in origination volume increases. On the policy front, this research suggests that small additions to an elderly household's income result in very small increases in well-being, while forms of insurance to guard against expenditure shocks can have larger effects.

Further research on this topic could proceed along two fronts. As new data become available, additional empirical research could further address the potential sample biases present in these results. Additional theoretical and simulation research could more realistically model the income and expenditure experiences of elderly households. Finally, application of similar stochastic dynamic programming techniques to other areas within mortgage finance could prove quite fruitful.

References

Case, Bradford, and Anne B. Schnare. 1994. Preliminary Evaluation of the HECM Reverse Mortgage Program. *Journal of the American Real Estate and Urban Economics Association* 22(2):301–46.

Fratantoni, Michael. 1998. Homeownership, Committed Expenditure Risk, and the Stockholding Puzzle. Working Paper No. 406. Baltimore: Johns Hopkins University.

Hubbard, R. Glenn, Jonathan Skinner, and Stephen Zeldes. 1995. Precautionary Saving and Social Insurance. *Journal of Political Economy* 103(2):360–99.

Kutty, Nandinee. 1996. Reverse Mortgages: A Solution to Elderly Poverty. Working Paper. FEN Real Estate Series.

Mayer, Christopher J., and Katerina Simons. 1994. Reverse Mortgages and the Liquidity of Housing Wealth. *Journal of the American Real Estate and Urban Economics Association* 22(2):235–55.

Merrill, Sally R., Meryl Finkel, and Nandinee K. Kutty. 1994. Potential Beneficiaries from Reverse Mortgage Products for Elderly Homeowners: An Analysis of AHS Data. *Journal of the American Real Estate and Urban Economics Association* 22(2):257–99.

Rasmussen, David W., Isaac F. Megbolugbe, and Barbara A. Morgan. 1995. Using the 1990 Public Use Microdata Sample to Estimate Potential Demand for Reverse Mortgage Products. *Journal of Housing Research* 6(1):1–23.

Rasmussen, David W., Isaac F. Megbolugbe, and Barbara A. Morgan. 1997. The Reverse Mortgage as an Asset Management Tool. *Housing Policy Debate* 8(1):173–94.

Venti, Stephen F., and David A. Wise. 1990. But They Don't Want to Reduce Housing Equity. In *Issues in the Economics of Aging*, ed. David A. Wise, 13–32. Chicago: University of Chicago Press.

Weinrobe, M. 1985. HELP Comes to Buffalo: A Review and Analysis of the Initial Equity Conversion Experience. *Housing Finance Review* 4(1):537–48.

Copyright 1994 by
The Gerontological Society of America

The Gerontologist
Vol. 34, No. 4, 491–496

Aging and health care are the emerging policy issues in the Third World. However, we currently do not have the data to address these issues because economic status and health have not been integrated into a single survey design. This article discusses the rationale for the principal features of an emerging new international survey design which includes integration of younger and older families; reliance on retrospective data; intensive measurement of economic status, health outcomes and utilization and intergenerational transfers; and the combination of a household and community survey.
Key Words: International data, Health and economics, Intergenerational transfers, Retrospective data

Measuring Health and Economic Status of Older Adults in Developing Countries[1]

James P. Smith, PhD[2]

The central research questions on aging cross national boundaries. Even more so than in the United States, however, inadequate data have been the major limitation on aging research in developing countries. In most Third World countries, research and data collection has focused on the other end of the life-cycle: fertility and family planning or infant nutrition and mortality. The major multinational surveys — the World Fertility Surveys (WFS) and the Demographic and Health Surveys (DHS) — provide little information about what life is like for older people in these countries. Unfortunately, the policy issues of the next decades will reflect a very different time bomb than the one for which policy makers have been preparing. The loud ticking that they should now be hearing is the count of the aging of their populations. However, they have little data to prepare themselves for that demographic reality.

In light of this reality, a growing number of researchers have been involved in significant new data collection efforts in many developing countries. While these efforts have been unrelated administratively, they have been linked by a common set of themes and concerns. First, they all strive to have adequate samples of the elderly population. More importantly, they have learned the painful lessons of the earlier U.S. surveys of the elderly by integrating health, social support, and economic modules into a single survey design. For this integrative objective, these surveys have been explicitly designed to parallel the two new major social science aging surveys in the United States — the Health and Retirement Survey (HRS) and the Assets and Health Dynamics of the Oldest Old (AHEAD). Finally, they do not repeat another earlier mistake by recognizing that the elderly do not live in isolation and that the generations

[1]This research was supported by grant P-01-AG08291 from the National Institute on Aging.

[2]Address correspondence to Dr. James P. Smith, RAND Corporation, 1700 Main Street, Santa Monica, CA 90407.

Vol. 34, No. 4, 1994

must be linked. While there are a number of such efforts, the character of these surveys will be illustrated herein with the RAND Indonesian Family Life Survey (IFLS).

Policy Framework

These new surveys were guided by a specific policy framework. Most governments are trying to effect some outcome — improved health status or reduced mortality are only two of many I could mention. For example, they can open new health centers, change user fees, promote an immunization program, and so on. But between those policy instruments and goals lies the behavioral reaction of households and service providers. Well-intentioned policy often fails because we do not anticipate or understand these important behavioral reactions. To put it most simply, if individuals don't respond to policy changes, no social goal will be achieved.

The implication is that our surveys must strive for state-of-the-art measurement of the final outcomes of interest (health, income, schooling, etc.), the proximate determinants of those outcomes (health care utilization), the attributes of the individuals and families who make these decisions, and the programmatic determinants of these behaviors, including the price variables emphasized by economists. As I will discuss later, these factors should be measured at both the individual and community levels.

One of the departures of these surveys from the current norm is that equal weight is given to the health and economic modules. Disciplinary specialization has meant that health and economic surveys have been fielded separately in developing countries with little substantive overlap. The consequence of this separation has been that neither the health nor economic surveys have been able to fully achieve their own stated objectives. The key risks to successful aging rest in a complex two-way interaction between wealth and good health and the social and financial support networks set up within families. If anything, the potential impact of health on income is even more direct and immediate in developing countries. When physical labor is most important, poor health means that energy levels are difficult to sustain, bouts of sickness are more frequent, and crop output falls. But causation may well run in the other direction. Better-off farmers have better diets, and their nutrition levels are higher. Both directions of influence are plausible and both may well be quantitatively large. However, unless surveys of the elderly give sufficient weight to both the health and economic domains, neither the determinants of health outcomes nor those of economic performance will be well understood.

I will highlight four innovative features of these new emerging international aging surveys using the IFLS as a prototype. These four features are its sample design, use of retrospective data, substantive instruments, and its dual reliance on community and household data.

The Indonesian Context

One point that should not be controversial is that aging and health is the emerging issue in the Third World. The demands placed on health care systems in developing countries will grow dramatically in the coming decades. Not only will the capacity of their systems have to expand dramatically, but the type and mix of services will have to change to serve an older population with a markedly different pattern of diseases.

This point can be illustrated with one developing country, Indonesia, but it applies to many others.

One reason for their increased concern about the elderly is purely demographic. As in many other developing countries, Indonesian birth rates have been declining rapidly and will continue to do so for the foreseeable future. At the same time, mortality risks at all ages have been falling rapidly. The demographic consequence is certain — a dramatic tilt in the age structure toward the old. In Indonesia, the size of the population of those age 60 and over will quadruple over the next 30 years, while that of younger people will stabilize. These shifts in Indonesia's age structure combined with other likely demographic trends — increased urbanization and rising incomes — foretells a need for a very different public health system than the one that exists there today. As demonstrated in Figure 1, health risks will shift dramatically from the acute infectious diseases of the young — diarrhea, respiratory infections, and measles — toward the more chronic noninfectious diseases of the old — heart disease and cancer.

Figure 2 highlights the pressures that are being placed on the Indonesian medical system by the aging of their population. Inpatient admissions will almost quadruple among those age 60 and over. With this dramatic shift in patient mix, the Indonesian health system may well have to be revamped from top to bottom. Both the existing personnel and the physical facilities are geared for a much different population of patients than that which will exist tomorrow. Moreover, this tomorrow is not in some distant future — a problem safely put aside for the next generation. Mortality rates for acute infectious diseases fell by a third between 1985 and 1990, and chronic disease mortality may well outrank deaths due to infectious disease by 1995.

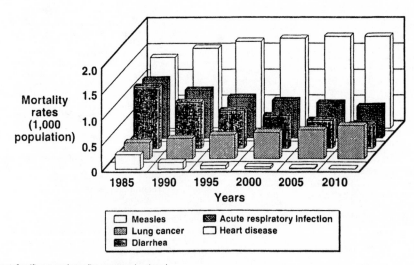

Figure 1. Specific causes of mortality, present and projected.

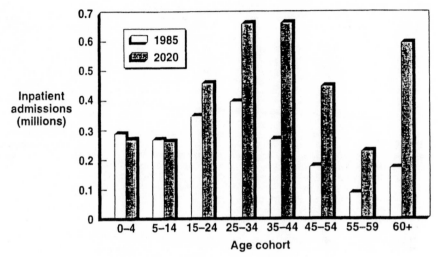

Figure 2. Inpatient admissions by age cohort; Indonesia, 1985 vs 2020.

Sample Design

One unique feature of these new international aging surveys rests on their sample design. Too often, surveys of the elderly are treated as isolated samples in which only people above a given age are eligible. For both substantive and cost reasons, this is a mistake. Surveys of the elderly population are much more cost-effective when they are combined with the more traditional demographic surveys that continue to dominate scientific work in these countries. The substantive argument is even stronger because it is impossible to understand the behavior of the elderly population unless their mutual dependency with the younger adult generation is monitored.

My point is illustrated in Table 1, which lists household sample sizes in the RAND IFLS. The first row mimics the conventional demographic survey of the 1970s and 1980s, the World Fertility Surveys or Demographic and Health Surveys being the most important prototypes. Their primary sampling units are currently married or ever married women (EMW). In the case of IFLS, our sample consists of 5,173 such ever married women less than age 50. This conventional demographic sample was to be fielded anyway, but we decided to augment it with a sample geared to the older population. Many of them were not difficult to find.

For example, 1,835 of these households contained a senior member (an individual over age 50). While these older persons were there for the asking, they are always ignored in fertility-oriented demographic surveys. In fact, a randomly selected elderly person and spouse were interviewed so that there were more than 2,500 elders present in the households with an EMW less than 50. Since a large fraction of

Table 1. Sample Design, Indonesian Family Life Survey

Households	With Person Aged > 50	Without Person Aged > 50	Total
With an EMW*	1835	3338	5173
Without an EMW	1287	540	1827
Total	3122	3878	7000

*EMW = ever married woman.

survey costs involve preparing the instruments and contacting households, the marginal costs of including these older people were low.

To obtain a random sample of persons over age 50, we only had to contact 1,287 additional households not part of our normal demographic sample. These were households with seniors who did not live with an ever married woman less than 50. Many of these seniors were married and both spouses were interviewed. Thus, at a cost of less than 1,300 new households, a sample of more than 4,300 seniors was obtained. More than 2,000 of these people were over 60 and more than 800 will be more than 70 years old. One reason this sample design is appealing is its cost-effectiveness. The cost of conducting these two samples separately was 75 percent higher than combining them. The marginal cost of the elderly subsample was one-fourth of the cost of a stand-alone elderly sample.

This design was not driven by convenience alone, but it is important for substantive reasons as well. In most Third World countries, the lives of the generations are so intertwined that one cannot speak coherently about the welfare of the older generation without reference to their substantial interaction with the younger generations. The scope of these interactions spans living arrangements, shared economic resources including extensive remittances and transfers, and time and care during episodes of poor health or bad economic times. We have already seen that a large fraction of the senior sample lives in a household with a young married woman. However, even when the generations live apart, they often behave as a geographically extended household, assisting each other with life's vagaries. Surveys of the elderly that ignore these generational links may be flawed.

Retrospective Data

Perhaps the most controversial feature of our approach is its extensive reliance on long-term retrospective data. Until recently, such data had a poor reputation with doubts cast on the ability to recall events two months ago, much less a decade or more in the past. While memory decay is a legitimate concern, the potential gains from retrospective data are also large. Long-term prospective panel data are simply not currently available in these countries, and even in the best of circumstances, will not be for a decade or two in the future. In addition, the success of the original RAND Malaysian survey and the current waves of DHS have reopened the issue of the quality of retrospective data. Most demographers now accept that complete fertility and marital histories are both feasible and desirable. But what about less salient aspects of people's lives?

Questions about events decades ago are unlikely to yield as reliable a response as asking what happened last week or last year. Unfortunately, while opinions are often strongly held, there exists little scientific evaluation of the quality of retrospective questions. The two RAND Malaysian Family Life Surveys give us the potential of quantitatively evaluating the quality of long-term recall data. The first wave, MFLS-1, collected information on about 1,200 women and 900 of their spouses during 1976–77. As part of the second wave, which took place in 1988–89, updated information was gathered on the households originally surveyed 12 years earlier. The degree of correspondence between these two histories for the pre-1977 time span allows us to evaluate the quality of the retrospective data. This evaluation can be conducted on any of the life histories contained in the data, but I will summarize here the results of a recent study of the migration histories (Smith, Thomas, & Karoly, 1993).

In the Malaysian surveys, respondents were asked to recall the date and location of all migrations that lasted 3 months or more. Our evaluation simultaneously illustrates the problems and potential of long-term recall questions. The type of memory decay that raises concern about recall data with time is certainly evident in the data. For example, the longer ago the migration occurred, the less likely a respondent reported both a month and year. When the move took place more than 40 years ago, only one in seven respondents told us the month and year. In contrast, for migrations within the last five years, over 70% gave

a specific month and year. Similarly, 61% (68%) of all male (female) migrations reported in the original survey were also remembered in the follow-up. At first blush, the statistics in the last paragraph give credence to a pessimistic verdict on the usefulness of long-term recall data. This verdict is premature because we were able to isolate which migration events people remember and which they forget. Respondents remembered salient moves, those linked with other important life events such as the start or breakup of a marriage, the birth of a child, or moves that lasted for a long time. In contrast, migrations that dim in memory as time passes were short duration or short distance moves often made by the young before they were married. This kind of mobility is not successfully retrieved by retrospective data. But for many purposes these may be less important moves for analysis, especially for the older population.

How useful then are retrospective migration data? A summary index involves the fraction of time respondents report themselves in the same location in both surveys. This fraction is 86% for all respondents and more than 90% among those over age 50. These positive summary evaluations are not meant to imply that long-term recall data are an easy panacea, for we have already seen that they certainly are not perfect. In addition, less positive bottom lines will surely be made for other outcomes of interest. However, until recall data for other outcomes are scientifically tested, the current presumption against long-term retrospective questions is premature.

Measurement Issues

These new international aging surveys face many complex questions about how to appropriately measure the concepts. While these issues are present in every part of the survey instrument, I will briefly discuss here our approach to three of the more central and least settled — health, income, and intergenerational transfers.

Because health is multidimensional and inherently difficult to measure, we pursued a multidimensional measurement approach. One common set of questions that proved not to be useful were probes about the past or current prevalence of specific diseases, such as cancer, heart disease, or the like. Because of limited physician contact, such diagnoses are rare. Even when physicians were visited, there was a cultural bias not to inform seriously ill patients about specific diseases. Instead, we asked about symptoms of illness such as headache, coughs, nausea, fever, or diarrhea during the last month. In measuring current health conditions, we rely heavily on self-reported health measures — overall health status, activities of daily living (ADLs), and limitations on daily activities. ADLs have been extensively tested for validity and reliability in the United States (Ware, Davies-Avery, & Brook, 1980) and have been shown to be strongly correlated with self-assessed health and economic status. These functional measures were extensively tested. With appropriate sensitivity to the different cultural contexts, both the physical and emotional measures appear to be equally useful

The Gerontologist

402

in Third World settings. Especially in developing countries, anthropometric measurement has been particularly useful in predicting economic performance. In the IFLS, height and weight are measured for all children younger than 5 and for the biological parents of these children.

Our health module concludes with extensive detail on the principal behavioral proximate determinant — outpatient and impatient utilization. Our instruments are comprehensive and span type of health care — physician, nurse, traditional practitioner, hospital, local health clinic, self; time and money costs of treatment; and type of treatment. While we experimented with other options, a 4-week recall period for outpatient and one year for inpatient care did as well as any other.

I argued earlier for the critical importance of income and wealth for behavioral analysis of the elderly. In spite of this, most demographic and health surveys have not collected adequate income data. While the reasons are varied, an often cited one is the difficulty of measuring income in settings where markets are informal and most income is not received in monetary forms. We are following three approaches: The first relies on a detailed questionnaire about labor supply, occupation, and wages on all jobs in the month prior to the survey. A persistent finding by economists is that current income is often a very inadequate measure of the long-term economic status of households. Based on extensive pretesting, retrospective questions were asked about occupation and work for the first full-time job after school completion, the job held 10 and 20 years ago, and for each of the 5 years preceding the survey. Because a substantial fraction of Indonesian households still work in agriculture, our second approach measured gross revenues and costs for the enterprise as a whole. A similar approach was followed for all households who owned nonagricultural enterprises.

Most economists now argue that the best income measure in developing countries is aggregate household consumption. Unfortunately, such data are difficult to collect. Many government expenditures surveys take 3 hours or more to administer, and the best current alternative, the World Bank Living Standard Measurement Surveys (LSMS), took 50 minutes. Neither is a practical alternative in surveys with other priorities. Fortunately, while we were in our design phase, the World Bank was simultaneously conducting an experiment on the periodic consumption module of SUSENAS (National Social and Economic Survey) a well-established government survey in Indonesia. This consumption module contained more than 300 individual items, and took one and one-half hours on average to administer. The Bank wanted consumption as part of the regular core. To evaluate the feasibility, the Bank conducted a pilot study of 8,000 households in which both the current long form and a shorter form (25 items and 15 minutes to administer) were tested. The results were remarkable. The mean of the two consumption distributions were within one percent of each other, and one

could not reject the hypothesis that the two distributions were identical. The most important implication was that one could obtain adequate measures of household consumption at reasonable survey time cost. Our consumption module is a compromise between the short and long forms (50 items) and takes about 24 minutes to administer to the average household.

There are two problems that have bedeviled measurement and interpretation of transfer data — their episodic nature and the opportunity set over which the transfers are defined. Most surveys in the United States, as well as in developing countries, collect demographic data only on those family members who currently live in the household. When they deal with non-coresident kin, often only the attributes of those who actually gave or received transfers are recorded. This partial recording of the opportunity set of people who can give transfer can make the eventual transfer data uninterpretable. For example, a large transfer of help in the form of hours of time from a highly educated male sibling is more unusual if there are four low-schooled sisters close by. Since it was essential that at least the full household opportunity set was defined, our roster includes a basic set of demographic data for all children, parents, and siblings whether they reside in the household or not. A very detailed set of characteristics is available for all relatives living in the household. For those outside the household, the detail varies by the relationship. We ask for non-coresident parents, their age, schooling, work status, occupation, location, health status, and degree of contact; for children, we ask their age, sex, schooling, location, and marital status; and for siblings, we ask their age and sex. Hours of time and money transfers in and out of the household were then asked about as a subset of this complete list of potential relations. This subset included up to four non-coresident children and siblings, for whom a more complete list of attributes was obtained. The additional attributes for children were their work status, occupation, extent of contact, health status, and land ownership. The corresponding added sibling characteristics were schooling, marital status, work status, occupation, location, health status, and extent of contact. To select the four children or four siblings, interviewers asked about the oldest and youngest and the two closest in age to the respondent. While other reasonable selection algorithms exist, it is essential that they not be selected based on the outcome of interest. In particular, while it might seem tempting to do so, relatives should not be selected based on the existence or size of the transfers. In addition to this one-on-one recording of transfers, the total amount of transfers for all nonlisted children and siblings was recorded. Transfers are also difficult to measure given their episodic character. Many transfers are triggered by other catastrophic events, such as an illness in the extended family, a severe economic shock, marriage, or death. In the IFLS, we opted for a two-track approach to this problem. The first relied on capturing all time and money transfers that took place within a recent time period (the last year). This track has the advantage of completeness and places the least strain on recall. The second track attempted to capture "domain specific" transfers associated with other salient events: marriage (dowry and bride prices), divorces (assets at separation), migration (remittances and job help), illness, death of a parent (inheritances), and economic shocks. Not only are significant transfers associated with these events, but imbedding transfer questions inside these salient events is the best aid in prompting memory of these transfers.

Community Level Data

The last dimension of the survey involves its dual emphasis on household and community level data. Measurement of community characteristics is critical, because they contain the instruments that can be manipulated by public policy, e.g., the prices, availability, and quality of the services provided at health facilities and the kind of environment the people live in. Since health is a stock that reflects current as well as past investments, it is not only the kind of current community that respondents live in, but what their communities were like in the past. We started with a detailed review with our Indonesian colleagues and the relevant ministries of the major parameters of public policy programs and how they have changed over time. This review shaped all our attempts to measure characteristics of the community. To measure the key community level variables, we have followed three complementary approaches.

The first step involved a community questionnaire given to the village head or "informed" leader. This questionnaire describes a number of key dimensions of the community, including its history and economic base, characteristics of public programs (agricultural aid and loans), infrastructure (electricity, water supply, irrigation, transportation, and financial institutions), the number and type of education and health facilities available, average housing quality and rent, the prices of stable crops, and wages of daily workers. Second, we conducted a major survey of all family planning clinics, schools, and health facilities that were mentioned by respondents in the household

survey. Among other things, this health facility survey measures such critical variables as distance and transportation cost from the village, type and date of disease epidemics, and the history and type of immunization and other public health programs.

In addition, a comprehensive description of the quality of the facility and its staff was obtained. This description included a list of all medical services provided at the facility; numbers, specialty, and training of staff; type, price, and quality and availability of specific services provided; medical equipment present; and specific drug prices and availability. Finally, the household data will be linked with other secondary Indonesian data that have been measuring community characteristics. Indonesia has conducted a number of studies over time at the community level, i.e., PODES (Village Infrastructure Survey) and SAKERNAS (National Workforce Survey).

Conclusion

Because of their rapidly changing age structures, aging is fast becoming the emerging policy concern in developing countries. However, these countries will have even less time than was available in the U.S. to adapt their institutional structures to the health and income problems of their elderly. Fortunately, there are a number of new aging surveys in several developing countries that have the potential of filling the gap. In many ways, these surveys match or are superior to the best aging data sets in this country. This article highlighted some of the more innovative features of these new international surveys in order to increase their visibility across the gerontological community.

References

Smith, J. P., Thomas, D., & Karoly, L. A. (1993). *Migration in retrospect: Differences between men and women.* Unpublished paper.
Ware, J., Davies-Avery, A., & Brook, R. (1980). *Conceptualization and measurement of health status for adults in the health insurance study: Volume VI. Analysis of relationships among health status measures.* R-1987/6-HEW. Santa Monica, CA: RAND.

Received January 5, 1994
Accepted May 8, 1994

ELSEVIER

Journal of Health Economics 20 (2001) 169–185

JOURNAL OF
**HEALTH
ECONOMICS**

www.elsevier.nl/locate/econbase

Health and endogenous growth

Adriaan van Zon[a,b,*], Joan Muysken[a,b]

[a] *MERIT, Maastricht Economic Research Institute on Innovation and Technology,
P.O. Box 616, 6200 MD Maastricht, The Netherlands*
[b] *Faculty of Economics and Business Administration, Maastricht University,
P.O. Box 616, 6200 MD Maastricht, The Netherlands*

Received 9 April 1998; received in revised form 19 June 2000; accepted 6 September 2000

Abstract

The focus of endogenous growth theory on human capital formation and the physical embodiment of knowledge in people, suggests the integration of the growth supporting character of health production and the growth generating services of human capital accumulation in an endogenous growth framework. We show that a slow down in growth may be explained by a preference for health that is positively influenced by a growing income per head, or by an ageing population. Growth may virtually disappear for countries with high rates of decay of health, low productivity of the health-sector, or high rates of discount. © 2001 Elsevier Science B.V. All rights reserved.

JEL classification: I1; O3; O4

Keywords: Health; Endogenous growth

1. Introduction

These days total health costs in Western economies are roughly 8–9% of GDP, whereas expenditures on education account for another 6–7%. [1] The expenditures on education are generally motivated by the insight that education provides a strong contribution to economic growth. Health expenditures on the other hand, have been a cause of general concern for some time now, especially because of the seemingly autonomous and permanent character of rises in the corresponding costs. This is due to the fact that a significant part of total health costs are associated with care rather than cure. The former costs have shown a tendency

---

* Corresponding author. Tel.: +33-43-3883890; fax: +33-43-3884905.
E-mail address: adriaan.vanzon@merit.unimaas.nl (A. van Zon).
[1] See OECD (1999) and The Economist Yearbook (1998), respectively.

to rise, largely due to the ageing of the population.[2] However, one should not forget that health is also a very important factor in economic growth.

The impact of education on economic growth has been recognised for more than a decade now in economic theory. In his pioneering endogenous growth model, Lucas (1988) underlines the principal importance of human capital formation for growth and development in a relatively straightforward manner.[3] But, paradoxically, in this and subsequent growth models, it is generally overlooked that human capital formation as a source of growth is quite literally embodied in people.[4] Nonetheless, people can provide effective human capital services only if they are alive and healthy. Therefore, the general acceptance of human capital formation as a source of growth also warrants a closer look at how changes in the health-state of the population may influence growth and hence total welfare.[5]

As observed by Grossman (1972, p. xiii), health contributes to well-being and economic performance in several ways. From a growth perspective, the positive contribution of a 'good health' to labour productivity is particularly important. However, the provision of health requires resources. As a consequence, there seems to be a direct trade-off between health and human capital accumulation: an expansion of the health sector may promote growth through increased health of the population, while a contraction of the health sector could also free the resources necessary to promote growth by means of an increase in human capital accumulation activities.[6] Moreover, this trade-off is complicated because of the asymmetries in the productivity characteristics of health generation and the accumulation of human capital. Baumol (1967), for instance, takes the health sector as an example of a sector which permits "... only sporadic increases in productivity" because "... there is no substitute for the personal attention of a physician ... ", as opposed to human capital accumulation activities, which give rise to "... technologically progressive activities in which innovations, capital accumulation, and economies of large scale make for a cumulative rise in output per man hour".[7]

---

[2] For instance, according to Polders et al. (1997, p. xii), roughly 50% of the total rise in health costs between 1988 and 1994 in the Netherlands was due to both an ageing population and factors like technical change and demand shifts. And according to Centraal Planbureau (1999, p. 5), more than one-third of total health expenditures in 1997 in the Netherlands was directly associated with care for the elderly and the (mentally) handicapped. This does not include cure expenditures for these groups of patients.

[3] See also Romer (1990) and Aghion and Howitt (1992) for examples of human capital formation or knowledge generation as the source of economic growth.

[4] A notable exception is Ehrlich and Lui (1991), who focus on the way in which subsequent generations and the trade between them influence human capital formation, longevity and growth in an overlapping generations setting.

[5] In Muysken et al. (1999) we show how this point has been recognized in many empirical growth studies, in particular on economic convergence — see for instance Knowles and Owen (1997) — but not in theoretical growth models.

[6] This provides an interesting contrast to microeconomic analysis that suggests the existence of complementarity between health and education. Fuchs (1982), for instance, argues that increases in health investment would lengthen one's life span, ceteris paribus, and hence increase the returns on investment in education. An alternative explanation would be that a higher level of education would go hand in hand with increases in the preference for health (possibly due to the rise in the opportunity costs of not being healthy).

[7] Baumol (1967, pp. 416, 423, 415, respectively). It is these differences in productivity that are the cause of Baumol's disease.

In terms of the growth model, this implies that we assume that the generation of health services is characterised by decreasing returns, whereas human capital accumulation is generally modelled using increasing returns.[8] Another asymmetry between health and human capital which should be recognised in the analysis is that health directly affects welfare and therefore should be included in the utility function next to consumption — at least in Western economies. As a consequence, there is also a direct trade-off between resources used in the health sector and the final goods sector.[9]

In order to analyse both trade-offs and their consequences for economic growth, we extend the endogenous growth framework of Lucas (1988).[10] We take into account that health influences intertemporal decision-making in three different ways. First, it serves as the 'conditio sine qua non' to the provision of human capital services. Second, the provision of health services directly competes with the provision of labour services allocated to the production of output and time spent on human capital accumulation. The third way in which health influences intertemporal decision-making follows from the observation that health can generate positive utility of its own. In addition to this, we take account of the intertemporal welfare effects of providing health services through the positive impact on longevity.

Our model shares some features with Barro (1990), who looks at the contribution of government expenditures to welfare directly and through government expenditures induced productivity growth in an AK-setting.[11] However, unlike Barro (1990), we focus on the embodiment of human capital in people, and the role of the provision of health services in enabling society to reap both the productive effects and the direct welfare effects of having a healthy population. The 'labour augmentation framework' of the Lucas (1988) model therefore provides a 'natural' point of departure for our analysis.

In our model, we distinguish between the active part of the population and the inactive part. The latter may increase with longevity because of increased health — but this also expands the demand for health services. We assume that the provision of labour services by the active part of the population depends both on the average level of health of the work force and on the amount of human capital per (health-) worker. The idea is that a deterioration of health reduces the number of effective working days embodied in a person and hence in the population. From that perspective, health and human capital are complements, in that a low health status will lead to a low supply of human capital services, ceteris paribus. However, from the perspective of the generation of effective human capital services, the

---

[8] Decreasing returns in health services are used in Forster (1989), Ehrlich and Chuma (1990) and Johansson and Lofgren (1995), increasing returns in human capital generation appear in the growth models mentioned above.

[9] This is reflected for instance in the fact that, in Western economies at least, a significant part of total health costs are associated with care rather than cure — mainly because of the ageing of the population. See also Footnote 2.

[10] Grossman (1972), followed up by, for instance, Muurinen (1982), Forster (1989) and Ehrlich and Chuma (1990) have concentrated on the provision of health services from a micro economic demand perspective. Meltzer (1997), using 'intertemporal cost effectiveness analysis' at the micro-level, even goes as far as defining a lifetime utility maximization problem that internalizes all future costs (medical and non-medical) of medical interventions, through changes in survival probabilities. Our analysis integrates both costs (in terms of consumption foregone) and benefits (in terms of productivity and longevity effects) at the macro-level.

[11] The AK-model is the simplest endogenous growth model that exhibits the key property underlying endogenous growth, namely the absence of diminishing returns to capital. This property is implied by the use of the linear production function $Y = AK$, where Y is output, K capital and A (fixed) capital productivity. See further Barro and Sala-i-Martin (1995) for an extensive discussion of the AK-framework.

provision of health services is also a direct substitute for the generation of human capital. We show that our model defines an optimal mix of the provision of health and human capital accumulation that depends on the parameters describing the characteristics of the entire economy, including the health sector.

Our approach has three distinct features. First, following Lucas (1988), we concentrate on the 'social planner solution' of the model. In the absence of externalities, this solution coincides with the 'market solution' where agents are consuming, producing and accumulating in response to market prices. However, in this model several externalities are present which would be ignored in individual decision making. [12] We therefore, concentrate on the 'social planner solution'.

The second feature of our approach is that we only analyse steady-state situations with balanced growth. That is, we show how the trade-offs mentioned above lead to a situation in the long run in which growth and health depend on the fundamental parameters reflecting technology and taste. The emphasis on differences in steady-state situations is in line with a quite impressive history of comparative growth studies that taught us that conditional convergence — in which different steady-state situations can occur — is much more plausible than absolute convergence. [13] The transition to the steady-state situation is not part of our analysis. This is analytically impossible without resorting to numerical methods, whereas the insights gained from such an exercise will contribute very little to our present analysis of the consequences of the trade-offs. [14]

Finally, and in line with the second feature, we assume that in the steady-state both the average health and the age of population are constant. However, they are generated by the model and depend on the fundamental parameters that reflect technology and taste. We can then analyse how differences in technology or taste lead to differences not only in growth performance, but also in the health-state and age of population. As a consequence, exogenous productivity increases in the generation of health services, next to the endogenous efficiency increases in human capital accumulation, or an exogenous rise in the preference for health, can be used to explain long-term changes in the health-state and age of population. At this stage, however, we leave the endogenisation of the processes underlying these parameter changes for further research. [15]

The remainder of the paper is organised as follows. Section 2 introduces our model of population growth and longevity, while Section 3 describes the health generation process that we want to integrate with the Lucas (1988) model. Section 4 provides an overview of the extended Lucas (1988) model and presents the steady-state solution, while Section 5 shows how changes in the fundamental parameters of the model would affect the steady-state

---

[12] The generation of health services have an impact on productivity that would tend to be ignored in individual decision making.

[13] For an overview, see for instance, Barro and Sala-i-Martin (1995).

[14] In a much simpler model, Muysken et al. (1999) analyze the impact of health generation in an exogenous growth model. They use numerical methods to obtain the market solution. With respect to the dynamics of the model, their main finding is that, depending on the initial sizes of the stocks of physical capital and health, during the transition process optimal expenditures on health are lower or higher than in the steady-state.

[15] An example is the explanation of the observation of Lapre and Rutten (1993, p. 32) that the value share of expenditures on health in national income rises with national income per head. This can be 'explained' by means of a positive relation between the preference for health and GDP.

solution. In Section 6 some (policy) implications of the model are discussed, while Section 7 provides a summary.

2. Longevity and population size

We introduce longevity in the model since this enables us to mimic the impact of ageing on growth and welfare by increasing the share of old people in the population. The population model we present here is designed in such a way that longevity can be introduced in the basic Lucas (1988) framework as simply as possible.

The population is subdivided into two parts: a part that is actively engaged in producing output, health services and human capital ('the young'), and a part that only consumes output and health services ('the old'). People live up to age T, but are actively involved in productive activities till age A. In order to simplify things even more, we assume that each year n persons are born that live for T years with health $g(t)$ and human capital $h(t)$, where t is a time index. At age T, people leave the population through sudden death. Consequently, the population is uniformly distributed over T year-classes with n persons in each year-class — and with identical health level $g(t)$ and human capital $h(t)$ per person over the whole population.

We now assume that the age A at which persons will retire from active participation in productive activities is fixed. Moreover, it seems reasonable to assume that longevity T is proportional to the average health level g of the population. [16] We therefore have

$$T = \mu g \tag{1}$$

where μ is a constant factor of proportion.

From the above, it follows that the number of inactive people is equal to $(T - A)n$. A rise in longevity will therefore increase the number of inactive people in the economy, thus leading to a rise in the consumptive uses of the health sector, ceteris paribus. Consequently, the total population will increase with longevity. However, when the health level of the population stabilises, the number of births per period exactly matches the number of deaths, so that the population remains constant in the steady-state.

A good health may be also be expected to influence utility directly. [17] In our case, this happens through the link between health, longevity and the size of the total population, using the following CIES (Constant Intertemporal Elasticity of Substitution) utility function: [18]

$$U = \int_0^\infty e^{-\rho \tau} \left(g^\gamma \left(\frac{C}{L} \right)^{1-\gamma} \right)^{1-\theta} \frac{L}{(1-\theta)} d\tau, \quad 0 < \theta < 1 \tag{2}$$

---

[16] Since we concentrate on problems associated with an ageing population, we abstract from the impact of wealth or health on the birth rate. Therefore, the number of births per period does not depend on the health-state of the active population, nor on Malthusian economic circumstances.

[17] This is noted by Grossman (1972, p. xiii), who says ". . . what consumers demand when they purchase medical services are not these services per se but rather 'good health'".

[18] In the context of the CIES function, we ignore the possibility that $\theta = 1$, in which case we arrive at Eq. (2). Others have used a utility function like this too. See, for instance, Barro (1990, p. S117) and Barro and Sala-i-Martin (1995, p. 323) where government consumption services and leisure, respectively, take the place of health.

where ρ is the rate of discount, and $1/\theta$ is the intertemporal elasticity of substitution, $0 \leq \gamma \leq 1$ measures the relative contribution of health to intertemporal utility, compared to per capita consumption. Time $t = 0$ refers to the present, total private consumption is C, while $L = nT$ is the size of the population.

Since $(C/L)^{(1-\gamma)(1-\theta)}L = C^{(1-\gamma)(1-\theta)}L^{1-(1-\gamma)(1-\theta)}$, longevity T is an implicit argument (through L) of the utility function that contributes positively to utility (cf. Eq. (1)), next to the direct contribution of health in case $\gamma > 0$. [19]

3. The generation of health services

Because we want to integrate health and growth in an endogenous growth framework, we use a specification of the production characteristics of the health sector and its impact on health, that is as simple as possible. In order to integrate the notion of productivity increases due to human capital accumulation and decreasing returns, it is instructive to link up with some of the features of the Romer (1990) model. We describe our model of the generation of health services in dynamic terms. Since in the steady-state health will be constant, however, we will just use the implied steady-state relationship between health services inputs and health output as an implicit health production function. This paragraph provides the notions underlying that production function.

As mentioned above, we assume that the labour force consists of active people, and measured in physical units, it is constant. We assume furthermore that the amount of effective labour services that a person can supply is directly proportional to his average health level and human capital. Therefore, the supply of labour measured in efficiency units equals $hgnA$.

In the medical profession, there are two kinds of productivity gains: those from specialisation and those associated with individual specialisations becoming more productive due to increased knowledge within the field, or improved medical practices. Let us assume that the number of relevant specialisations Ω grows with the same rate as the human capital index, i.e. $\Omega = \pi h$. Knowledge within the field is assumed to grow with the rate of growth of human capital per person. However, the provision of health services takes place under conditions of decreasing returns — see, for instance, Forster (1989), Ehrlich and Chuma (1990), and Johansson and Lofgren (1995). Hence, the average health level of the population rises less than proportionally with the amount of health services rendered per person.

Let a fraction v_i of effective labour services be used as the sole input into the health generation process for specialisation i. Then $v_i hgnA/(nT)$ will measure the number of healthy hours spent on providing health services for specialisation i per person. Then, following the specialisation argument put forward in Romer (1990), the gross increase in the average health level of the population is given by [20]

---

[19] Because $0 < \theta < 1$ and $0 <= \gamma <= 1$, it follows that $1 - (1 - \gamma)(1 - \theta) >= 0$.

[20] Note that this specification assumes that the demand for health services is the same for all age-classes, which is generally not true in practice. However, as long as the distribution of the population across age-classes is relatively stable, the mechanism described here also applies to a population that is heterogeneous (by age-class) in terms of its demand for health services. In order to simplify matters, we stick to Eqs. (3) and (4), however.

$$\frac{dg}{dt} = \int_0^{\pi h} \psi \left(h g v_i \frac{nA}{nT} \right)^\beta di = \psi \pi h \left(\frac{h g v A}{\pi h \mu g} \right)^\beta = \psi \left(\frac{A}{\mu} \right)^\beta \pi^{1-\beta} v^\beta h \qquad (3)$$

where ψ is a productivity parameter and v represents the share of total effective labour supply employed in the health sector. The condition $0 < \beta \leq 1$ reflects the assumption of decreasing returns in health generation.

Technological change does not only have positive effects on health, though. It is quite conceivable that increases in the technological content of an average workers' job has led to higher incidences of burn-out due to stress, etc. Moreover, demand for medical care, i.e. the perception of health deterioration, will increase with the average level of medical technology in a society. [21] We take this into account by assuming that the percentage loss of labour time due to these technology related factors is proportional to the level of technology πh with factor of proportion ς. The net increase in the average health level is now given by

$$\frac{dg}{dt} = \left[\psi \left(\frac{A}{\mu} \right)^\beta \pi^{1-\beta} v^\beta - \varsigma \pi g \right] h \qquad (4)$$

An interesting feature of the health generation process is that it is inherently stable in the long run. It can easily be observed that for any given positive value of the share of the health sector in total employment v, the health level g will converge to g^*. The latter can be obtained by setting $dg/dt = 0$ in Eq. (3), which yields

$$g^* = \frac{\psi}{\varsigma} \left(\frac{A}{\pi \mu} \right)^\beta v^\beta = z_0 v^\beta \qquad (5)$$

where z_0 is implicitly defined by the equivalence of the right most part of Eq. (5) and its middle part. As one might expect, a higher share of employment in the health sector will result in a higher equilibrium health level g^*, while human capital formation as such increases the speed of adjustment towards that equilibrium level.

4. Health and the Lucas model

As we mentioned earlier, health enters the intertemporal decision framework in three different ways. *First*, a fall in the average health level of the population may be expected to cause a fall of the amount of effective labour services that the population can supply. [22] *Second*, the generation of health takes scarce resources that have alternative uses (like the production of output or human capital), while *third*, a good health may be expected to influence utility directly. As we have discussed above, the latter includes the link between health, longevity and the size of the total population.

---

[21] This argument is also used in Fuchs (1982).
[22] Grossman (1972, p. xiii) states: "... the level of ill-health measured by the rates of mortality and morbidity, influences the amount and productivity of labour supplied to an economy".

Using the description of the health sector as given in the previous sections, the Lucas (1988) framework can be extended in a straightforward manner. The production structure is represented by

$$Y = B\left[(1 - u - v)hgnA\right]^{\alpha} K^{1-\alpha} \tag{6}$$

where Y measures total output, K the capital stock and B is a constant productivity parameter. Note that a fraction $(1 - u - v)$ of the supply of labour in terms of efficiency units is used in final output production, and the remaining fractions u and v are spent on human capital accumulation and health services production, respectively.

The human capital accumulation process has the same properties as in Lucas (1988) — the only difference is that we take health explicitly into account. Hence

$$\frac{dh}{dt} = \delta ugh \tag{7}$$

where δ is a productivity parameter. Finally, the accumulation of physical capital is given by

$$\frac{dK}{dt} = Y - C \tag{8}$$

As we explained in the introduction, we follow Lucas and concentrate on the so-called 'social planner solution'. To solve the model, intertemporal utility (2) should be maximised with respect to C, the allocation of consumption over time, and u and v, the allocation of labour over its different uses, subject to the conditions (6), (7), (8) and (4). [23] Using the method of optimal control, it turned out to be impossible to find a closed form solution to the optimisation problem. In order to simplify matters therefore, we use the insight presented above that, for a constant steady-state allocation of effective labour services as we find in Lucas (1988), the health generation process is inherently stable in the long run. This implies that the health level will always converge to g^* defined in Eq. (5). We therefore replace the constraint of Eq. (4) by that of $g = g^*$ defined in Eq. (5). This is consistent with the focus of our analysis on long-term developments and balanced growth situations. Consequently, the out of steady-state behaviour of the health-state of the population will not be analysed, as stated in the introduction. And although the revised system still doesn't allow us to obtain a closed form solution, we can rearrange it in such a way that we can employ a graphical solution method instead.

The first order conditions that the steady-state growth solution of the revised model has to obey can now be condensed into the following simultaneous equation system: [24]

$$f = c^2 - \alpha c \tag{9.A}$$

$$v = \frac{f + \alpha(1 - \alpha)(1 - \theta)(1 - \gamma)/(\theta + (1 - \theta)2\gamma)}{f + ((1 + \beta)/\beta)\alpha(1 - \alpha)(1 - \theta)(1 - \gamma)/(\theta + (1 - \theta)2\gamma)} \tag{9.B}$$

---

[23] We simplify the original Lucas model somewhat by dropping the knowledge spill-over effect, which is not an essential ingredient of endogenous growth. The original Lucas model (without the knowledge externality) can be obtained by dropping (4) and setting $v = 0$, $g = 1$ and $A = L$ in (6) and (7).

[24] See the Technical Annex for more details.

$$c = 1 - \frac{(1-\alpha)r}{(\theta + \gamma(1-\theta))r + \rho} \qquad (9.C)$$

$$r = \frac{\delta(1-v)z_0 v^\beta - \rho}{\theta + \gamma(1-\theta)} = \frac{\delta g^*(1-v) - \rho}{\theta + \gamma(1-\theta)} \qquad (9.D)$$

$$u = \frac{1-c}{1-\alpha}(1-v) \qquad (9.E)$$

where c is the average propensity to consume and r is the balanced growth rate of the system.

It should be noted that Eq. (9.D) is completely comparable to Lucas' growth results, i.e. $r = (\delta - \rho)/\theta$, for $g = 1$, $v = 0$ and $\gamma = 0$. From Eq. (9.D) it follows that the rate of growth rises with the productivity of both health generation and the human capital accumulation process. It also rises with the value of the intertemporal elasticity of substitution, which indicates the willingness of people to wait for their 'consumption' returns on investment (i.e. postponing current consumption until later). Likewise, a rise in the rate of discount indicates a decline in the valuation of future consumption possibilities, and hence reduces the rate of growth of the system.

Finally, Eq. (9.E) implies that in order to ensure $1 - u - v \geq 0$, we need $\alpha \leq c$. The steady-state savings rate therefore needs to be smaller than $1 - \alpha$. This is similar to the result found by Lucas for $v = 0$. [25]

4.1. A graphical solution

Eqs. (9.A)–(9.D) need to be solved simultaneously, and u would then follow immediately from (9.E) and the simultaneous solution to (9.A)–(9.D). Unfortunately, that cannot be done in an analytical way. We use a graphical analysis instead. The analysis is based on the observation that Eqs. (9.A)–(9.C) define a relation between r and v, just like Eq. (9.D) does. Combining these two relations in the r, v-plane, and seeing how changes in the system parameters then shift these relations about in that plane, will give us information how the steady-state growth solution depends on those parameters.

In Fig. 1, we present a four-quadrant diagram to derive the relationship between r and v that follows from Eqs. (9.A)–(9.C). Eq. (9.A) is presented in the first quadrant as a relation between f and c, where we concentrate on the range $\alpha \leq c \leq 1$. It increases from $f = 0$ at $c = \alpha$ to $f = 1 - \alpha$ at $c = 1$. Similarly, Eq. (9.C) is represented in the fourth quadrant as a relationship between r and c, which decreases from $r = \rho/(1-\gamma)(1-\theta)$ at $c = \alpha$ to $r = 0$ at $c = 1$. Finally, in the second quadrant Eq. (9.B) is represented as a relationship between f and v. It increases from $v = \beta/(1+\beta)$ for $f = 0$ to $v = v'$ at $f = 1 - \alpha$, while for f goes to infinity, v would asymptotically approach a value of 1. [26] The relevant range for v is therefore $\beta/(1+\beta) \leq v \leq v'$, while the relevant range for r is given by $0 \leq r \leq \rho/(1-\gamma)(1-\theta)$. Any point within the latter range corresponds with a unique point in the former range by 'going round' in Fig. 1 in a counter-clockwise direction — mapping r onto c, c onto f and then f onto v. The resulting curve $v'r'$ in the third quadrant of

---

[25] Cf. Lucas (1988), p. 10.
[26] Here $v' = \{\theta + (1-\theta)(\alpha(1-\gamma) + 2\gamma)\}/\{\theta + (1-\theta)(\alpha(1-\gamma)((1+\beta)/\beta) + 2\gamma)\} \leq 1$.

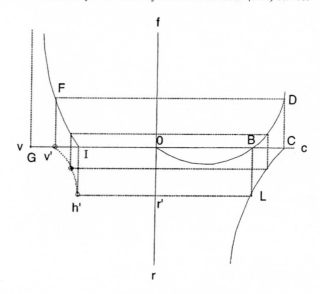

Fig. 1. A four quadrant diagram.

Fig. 1 summarises Eqs. (9.A)–(9.C). This curve can now be confronted with (9.D) to obtain the simultaneous solution of (9.A)–(9.D).

Eq. (9.D) describes r as a function of v. It is represented in Fig. 2, which corresponds to the south-west quadrant of Fig. 1. The curve has the same orientation as in Fig. 1. Eq. (9.D) is concave — it decreases from is maximum at r^* for $v = \beta/(1+\beta)$ to $r = 0$ at $v^* < 1$.[27] The solution of the model is obtained at the point of intersection E of Eq. (9.D) and the curve $v'h'$. A unique solution exists if the curve $v'h'$ is convex and if $r^* < \rho/(1-\gamma)(1-\theta)$, $v^* > v'$.[28] We conclude that in the steady-state Y, C, K and h will grow at the equilibrium rate r_E, while health and longevity are constant at g^*_E and T_E, respectively. The latter are found by substituting v_E into Eqs. (5) and (1), respectively.

4.2. The trade-offs in the model

The trade-offs mentioned in the introduction that follow from the incorporation of health in the analysis, are now clearly reflected in the results we have obtained so far. The trade-off between health and human capital accumulation can be seen in Eq. (9.D). As we mentioned above, this equation is comparable to Lucas' growth results, i.e. $r = (\delta - \rho)/\theta$, for $g = 1$, $v = 0$ and $\gamma = 0$. The presence of the term $(1 - v)$ in Eq. (9.D) reflects the fact that a fraction

---

[27] The way in which r^* and v^* depend on the parameters of the model can be summarized by $r^* = r[\delta(+), z_0(+), \beta(+), \rho(-), \theta(-), \gamma(-)]$ and $v^* = v[\delta(+), z_0(+), \beta(+), \rho(-), \gamma(+)]$, where the sign within brackets denotes the sign of the partial derivative with respect to the parameter in question. These results follow directly from Eq. (9.D) and the requirement that $r(v^*) = 0$.

[28] In van Zon and Muysken (1997) we show that for plausible values of the parameters of the model, these constraints are likely to be satisfied. We assume this to be the case in the remainder of the analysis.

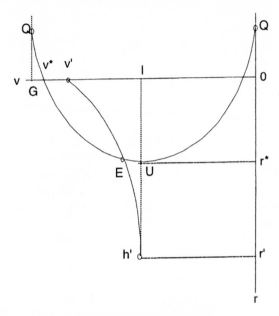

Fig. 2. The south-west quadrant again.

$(1 - v)$ of the labour force is not available for the generation of output or human capital, since its task is to maintain the average health level of the population at its steady-state value g^*. This lowers the maximum rate of growth attainable in the extended model as compared to the original Lucas model. The trade-off between consumption and health follows from the observation that, as is shown in the Technical Annex, disregarding the contribution of health to welfare by setting $\gamma = 0$ and treating the impact on longevity as a pure externality, leads to a growth maximising choice of v, i.e. $v = \beta/(1 + \beta)$. But if we do take account of the direct welfare effects of health generation also through its impact on longevity, Fig. 2 shows that the point of intersection between the two curves implies a value of r that is lower than r^*, while in that case $v > \beta/(1 + \beta)$. Hence, the incorporation of the direct contribution of health to welfare (also through longevity) increases the level of health services at the expense of growth (but not of welfare), ceteris paribus.

5. A comparison of steady-states

As we mentioned in Section 1, we want to analyse how the steady-state characteristics of the model depend on the fundamental parameters that represent technology and taste. The relevant technology parameters are δ and z_0, i.e. the productivity of human capital accumulation and health generation, respectively, while the relevant taste parameters are $1/\theta$ and ρ, reflecting the intertemporal elasticity of substitution and the discount rate, respectively.

In order to illustrate what happens to health, growth and to the size of the health-sector for various constellations of the parameters of our model, we have used a graphical analysis

Table 1
Parameter changes and health and growth responses

Parameter	$c = 1 - s$	v	u	r	g^*
θ	+	+	−	−	+
ρ	+	+	−	−	+
δ	−	−	+	+	−
z_0	−	−	+	+	?(+)
γ	+	+	−	−	+

based on Fig. 2.[29] We summarise the results in Table 1, in which positive and negative influences of a positive change in a parameter are indicated by a + sign and a − sign, respectively. Ambiguous reactions are indicated by a question mark followed by a sign within brackets, which indicates the sign we would expect.

The first thing to notice from this table is the negative correlation between the effects of a parameter change on growth and on the propensity to consume. This is due to the fact that there is a positive correlation between the saving rate s and the rate of growth itself. The reason is that for a stable value of the capital output ratio, a rise in the saving rate is required in order to sustain a higher rate of growth. Secondly, v and u are negatively correlated, instead of positively as suggested by micro economic analysis.[30] In our model, the negative correlation exists because both health production and human capital accumulation compete for the same scarce labour resources, for a fixed size of the active labour force measured in physical units. Thirdly, there is in most cases a negative correlation between the level of health and the rate of growth. This follows from the positive impact of increased health on longevity, which in its turn increases the demand for health care, at the expense of growth.

Let us now turn to the interpretation of the individual results. A rise in θ implies a fall in the value of the intertemporal elasticity of substitution. This means that people become more reluctant to wait for their return on investment, and consequently they are inclined to increase current consumption of goods, but also of health services. This is reflected in a rise in the steady-state values of c, v and g^*, accompanied by a fall in r itself, but also in u. Note that a rise in θ also implies an increase in the relative contribution of longevity to welfare, as we discussed in Section 2.

The results for a rise in θ are very similar to those obtained for a rise in the rate of discount ρ.[31] This is to be expected since a rise in ρ reflects the decrease in the subjective valuation of the utility derived from the consumption of a certain package of goods and health-services in the future relative to the valuation of the utility of that same package when it would be consumed today. Hence, one would expect people to spend more resources on fulfilling

---

[29] Basically, the analysis consists of calculating the shifts of the two relations between v and r in Fig. 2 due to a change in one of the parameters, in order to see how the new equilibrium would be affected. These shifts can be calculated directly by differentiating $r = r(v)$ as given by (9.D) with respect to the various parameters, or by differentiating the 'chain' of relations $c = c(r)$, $f = f(c)$, and $v = v(f)$ as given by (9.A)–(9.C) with respect to those parameters to obtain the shift in v for a given value of r. For the full technical details, see Annex F of van Zon and Muysken (1997).

[30] Cf. Fuchs (1982), for instance, as is elaborated in Footnote 5.

[31] There are differences though, as explained in more detail in Annex F of van Zon and Muysken (1997).

current needs, by redirecting labour input to activities that increase present consumption possibilities, rather than future ones. Consequently, c, v and g^* rise, while r and u fall.

A rise in the productivity of human capital accumulation, i.e. δ, has quite different effects. Since the latter increases the marginal benefits of investing in human capital accumulation, a reallocation takes place of labour from activities that increase current utility to activities that increase future utility. Consequently, growth is positively affected. In order to make this possible, c and v fall, while u and r increase. Also g^* falls because of the reduction in v.

The previous results are very similar to those obtained for an increase in the productivity of the health sector, i.e. ψ, which corresponds to an increase in z_0 (see Eq. (5)). This corroborates the 'engine-like' features of the health sector that we pointed out in Section 1. Because an increase in ψ would tend to increase g^* for a given v, it would also permanently increase the productivity of the human capital accumulation process. The productivity increase in the health sector then enables a contraction of the allocation of labour resources to that sector (v falls). The net effect on g^* is therefore ambiguous, but one would expect g^* to rise, [32] which in turn makes investment in human capital accumulation more profitable because of its intertemporal spill-over effects. Hence u rises, and so does r. Similar results are readily obtained for the other structural parameters that define z_0. We do not repeat them here.

A rise in the direct impact of health on utility γ has all the expected effects. It reduces growth and raises average health by changing the allocation of human capital in the direction of health production. In addition to this, the average propensity to consume can rise, because of the slow down in growth.

Finally, it is worth mentioning that the effective productivity of the health sector may be that low (either due to a high value of ς or low values of β, ψ or A/μ), that the curve given by Eq. (9.D) describes just a few instances of v that generate (moderately) positive growth. [33] Such parameter constellations may be relevant for the poorer developing countries, for example. In that case, aid aimed at changing the system parameters mentioned above, may well help growth to take off. Growth may even become self-sustaining if medical aid succeeds in raising life expectancy, and lowering the rate of discount which, by shifting Eq. (9.D), would lead to more promising growth potentials. It should be noted that for the richer countries too, a rise in γ would result in a reduction in growth performance. However, in the latter case that would be choice rather than fate.

6. Model implications

The model has a number of interesting implications. Before pointing these out, however, we would like to stress again that our analysis applies to long-term developments

---

[32] In the decreasing returns setting we have defined, one would expect a reaction to an exogenous shock not to be able to wipe out all the effects of such a shock, because such a reaction would involve the re-allocation of resources which were initially allocated in such a way as to generate maximum overall benefits for a given stock of scarce irreproducible labour resources. In fact that is exactly what we found during exploratory simulations with our model using 'reasonable' parameter values, where we observed a fall in g^* despite the rise in v which is required to counter the effects of a rise in ς. Note that a rise in ς would have the same effect as a fall in ψ. See van Zon and Muysken (1997) for more details.

[33] This might also be caused by a high value of the rate of discount ρ or a high value of the relative contribution of health to welfare γ.

and balanced growth situations. The phenomena we discuss here — like the productivity slow-down — could be interpreted to occur in the transition to a steady-state growth situation, in which case they would have to be explained from the transitional dynamics of the growth model. However, they could also be explained as the outcome of a process of balanced growth, where different situations correspond to different parameter constellations regarding technologies and tastes. We present the latter explanation in this analysis.

First of all, the fact that we have a decreasing returns health sector which level of activity defines the effective availability of human capital within the economy, makes the efficiency of this sector one of the central determinants of economic performance. Indeed, the notion that effective inputs of human capital and labour into the various production processes depend on one's health status, makes health a complement to growth from a supply perspective. Moreover, a change in ψ or ς (and to a lesser extent A and μ depending on the value of β (cf. Eq. (5)) is as important for growth as an equal proportional change in δ. This stresses the importance of health as a determinant of both the level and the growth of labour productivity, quite apart from the direct positive welfare effects induced by changes in the productivity of the health sector.

Second, the influence of the decreasing returns nature of the health sector on growth provides an interesting alternative explanation for the productivity slow-down. If, as seems reasonable to assume, the preference of people for a good health rises with the standard of living, i.e. γ rises with output per head, then growth would automatically slow down in the process.

Third, the average age of the population in Western European economies has shown a tendency to rise during the last decades. This introduces a wedge between the two functions of the population in our model. It is the active population that determines labour supply, and hence the scale of all economic activities which rely on the use of labour services, while the total population determines the scale of the demand for health-services. Hence, technological breakthroughs in medicine could be expected not only to boost overall productivity, but also to provide a brake on productivity growth, although not necessarily on the growth of welfare, through rises in longevity.

Fourth, in the case of high values of the rate of decay of health, due to malnutrition for instance, people may have such a high preference for consumption now, reflected by a low value of the intertemporal elasticity of substitution (i.e. a high value of θ), that they could become stuck in a 'no growth', 'low health' situation because there are only very few, if any, instances of v with positive growth. This suggests that policies aimed at furthering growth by means of reducing ς, or increasing δ_H, through direct aid in the form of technology or income transfer, may induce growth which is sufficiently high to lower the rate of discount ρ and increase the intertemporal elasticity of substitution $1/\theta$ to such an extent, that savings will arise that will allow growth to take-off and become self-sustaining.

7. Summary and conclusion

In this paper, we have presented a simple model of endogenous growth based on the Lucas (1988) model, in which a good health functions as a necessary condition for people to be able to provide labour services. At the same time, health is produced under conditions of decreasing returns, whereas human capital is produced under conditions of increasing returns. If we regard the impact of health on longevity as an externality, we find that the health sector has a size that is consistent with maximum economic growth. In that case, health is a pure complement to growth, and any re-allocation of labour from the health sector towards human capital accumulation activities would cause a decline in growth.

In our model, however, we internalise the impact of health on longevity, because part of total welfare at the population level comes in the form of longevity itself. In order to solve the resulting steady-state values of growth and health, we devised a graphical procedure that enables us to show that increases in the demand for health services caused by an ageing population, will now adversely affect growth; next to being complements, as mentioned above, health and growth have also become substitutes. This provides a dynamic version of Baumol's disease with respect to the health sector — in particular when the preference of people for a good health rises with the standard of living.

We also concluded that, since the steady-state growth rate rises linearly in the average health-level of the population, the productivity of the health-sector is as important a determinant of growth as the productivity of the human capital accumulation process itself.

Finally, we have arrived at the conclusion that there may be circumstances regarding the provision of health-services and life expectancy, in which it may be hard for growth to take place at all. Aid meant to improve the productivity of the health-sector or the net availability of human capital resources for non-health activities in the poorer developing countries, could actually lead to growth taking off on its own. Growth can even become self-sustaining if the rate of discount would fall and the intertemporal elasticity of substitution would rise in the face of structural gains in life expectancy.

Appendix A. Technical annex

The Hamiltonian of the revised system can be written as

$$
\begin{aligned}
H &= e^{-\rho t} C^{\gamma_1} (n\mu)^{\gamma_2} (g^*)^{\gamma_3} / (1 - \theta) \\
&\quad + \lambda (B((1 - u - v)g^* hnA)^\alpha K^{1-\alpha} - C) + \xi \delta u g^* h
\end{aligned}
\tag{A.1}
$$

where C, u and v are the control variables, and K and h are the state variables that grow with the balanced growth rate in equilibrium. $g^* = z_0 v^\beta$ is a 'quasi'-state variable, since it must be constant in the steady-state. Moreover, $\gamma_1 = (1 - \gamma)(1 - \theta)$, $\gamma_2 = 1 - \gamma_1$ and $\gamma_3 = 1 - (1 - 2\gamma)(1 - \theta)$. Note that for a value of $\gamma \geq 1/2$ we have $\gamma_3 \geq 1$.

The first order conditions with respect to the control variables are

$$
\frac{\partial H}{\partial C} = (1 - \gamma)e^{-\rho t} C^{\gamma_1 - 1}(n\mu)^{\gamma_2}(g^*)^{\gamma_3} - \lambda = 0
\tag{A.2}
$$

$$
\frac{\partial H}{\partial u} = -\frac{\lambda \alpha Y}{(1 - u - v)} + \xi \delta g^* h = 0
\tag{A.3}
$$

$$
\frac{\partial H}{\partial v} = \frac{\gamma_3 \beta e^{-\rho t} C^{\gamma_1}(n\mu)^{\gamma_2}(g^*)^{\gamma_3}}{(1 - \theta)v} - \frac{\lambda \alpha Y}{1 - u - v} + \frac{\lambda \alpha Y \beta}{v} + \frac{\xi \delta u \beta g^* h}{v} = 0
\tag{A.4a}
$$

If we would ignore the direct influence of health on welfare as well as the influence through longevity, i.e. treat L as given in the welfare function and not substituting (1) in the welfare function while setting $\gamma = 0$, Eq. (A.4a) is reduced to

$$\frac{\partial H}{\partial v} = -\frac{\lambda \alpha Y}{1 - u - v} + \frac{\lambda \alpha Y \beta}{v} + \frac{\xi \delta u \beta g^* h}{v} = 0 \tag{A.4b}$$

Substituting (A.3) into (A.4b) and then solving for v, gives us $v = \beta/(1 + \beta)$. But if we do take account of (1) and substitute $C = (1 - s)Y$, where s is the saving rate, as well as (A.2) and (A.3) into (A.4a), we get

$$\frac{(1 - s)\gamma_3 \beta}{(1 - \gamma)(1 - \theta)v} - \frac{\alpha}{1 - u - v} + \frac{\alpha \beta}{v} + \frac{\alpha u \beta}{(1 - u - v)v} = 0 \tag{A.5}$$

Substitution of (A.3) in the first order condition $\partial H/\partial h = -d\xi/dt$ leads to the following result

$$-\hat{\xi} = \delta g^*(1 - v) \tag{A.6}$$

Assuming the existence of a steady-state, we can use (A.6), (A.2) and the underlying production function in order to obtain

$$r = \hat{Y} = \hat{K} = \hat{h} = \hat{C} = -\frac{(\hat{\xi} + \rho)}{\theta + \gamma(1 - \theta)} = \left(\frac{\delta g^*(1 - v) - \rho}{\theta + \gamma(1 - \theta)}\right) \tag{A.7}$$

which is the same as Eq. (9.D). The rate of growth of human capital accumulation is given by

$$\hat{h} = \delta u g^* \tag{A.8}$$

Moreover, from the condition that $\partial H/\partial h = -d\lambda/dt$ and (A.2) in combination with the definition, $s = (dK/dt)/Y = \hat{K}(K/Y)$ and $\hat{C} = \hat{K}$, it follows directly that

$$s = (1 - c) = \frac{(1 - \alpha)r}{(r(\theta + \gamma(1 - \theta))} + \rho \tag{A.9}$$

which is equivalent to Eq. (9.C). Substituting (A.8) into the numerator of (A.9) and (A.7) into the denominator of (A.9), we have

$$(1 - c) = \frac{(1 - \alpha)u}{(1 - v)} \Rightarrow u = \frac{(1 - c)(1 - v)}{(1 - \alpha)} \tag{A.10}$$

(A.10) is the same as Eq. (9.E). Substitution of $c = 1 - s$ and (A.10) into (A.5) and solving for v, results in

$$v = \frac{c(c - \alpha) + \alpha(1 - \alpha)(1 - \theta)(1 - \gamma)/(\theta + (1 - \theta)2\gamma)}{c(c - \alpha) + ((1 + \beta)/\beta)\alpha(1 - \alpha)(1 - \theta)(1 - \gamma)/(\theta + (1 - \theta)2\gamma)} \tag{A.11}$$

which is the same as Eq. (9.B) after substituting $f = c(c - \alpha)$. The latter relation between f and c is the same as Eq. (9.A).

References

Aghion, P., Howitt, P., 1992. A model of growth through creative destruction. Econometrica 60, 323–351.

Barro, R.J., 1990. Government spending in a simple model of endogenous growth. Journal of Political Economy 98, S103–S125.

Barro, R.J., Sala-i-Martin, X., 1995. Economic Growth. McGraw-Hill, New York.

Baumol, W.J., 1967. Macroeconomics of unbalanced growth: the anatomy of urban crisis. American Economic Review 57, 415–426.

Centraal Planbureau, 1999. Ramingsmodel Zorgsector. Eindrapport tweede fase, Den Haag.

Ehrlich, I., Chuma, H., 1990. A model of the demand for longevity and the value of life extension. Journal of Political Economy 98, 761–782.

Ehrlich, I., Lui, F.T., 1991. Intergenerational trade, longevity, and economic growth. Journal of Political Economy 99, 1029–1059.

Forster, B.A., 1989. Optimal health investment strategies. Bulletin of Economic Research 41, 45–57.

Fuchs, V.R., 1982. in: Fuchs, V.R. (Ed.), Time Preference and Health: An Exploratory Study, Economic Aspects of Health. Conference Report NBER, University of Chicago Press.

Grossman, M., 1972. The Demand for Health: A Theoretical and Empirical Investigation. NBER, Occasional Paper 119, Columbia University Press.

Johansson, P.O., Lofgren, K.G., 1995. Wealth from optimal health. Journal of Health Economics 14, 65–79.

Knowles, S., Owen, D.P., 1997. Education and health in an effective-labour empirical growth model. The Economic Record 73, 314–328.

Lapre, R.M., Rutten, F.F.H., 1993. Economie van de Gezondheidszorg, Leerboek voor universitair en hoger beroepsonderwijs, tweede herziene druk. Uitgeverij Lemma BV, Utrecht.

Lucas, R.E., 1988. On the mechanics of economic development. Journal of Monetary Economics 22, 3–42.

Meltzer, D., 1997. Accounting for future costs in medical cost-effectiveness analysis. Journal of Health Economics 16, 33–64.

Muysken, J., Yetkiner, I.H., Ziesemer, T., 1999. Health, Labour Productivity and Growth. MERIT Research Memorandum, 99-030.

Muurinen, J.M., 1982. Demand for health: a generalised grossman model. Journal of Health Economics 1, 5–28.

OECD, 1999. Health data 1999: A Comparative Analysis of 29 Countries. OECD, Paris.

Polders, J.J., Meerding, W.J., Koopmanschap, M.A., Bonneux, L., van der Maas, P.J., 1997. Kosten van Ziekten in Nederland 1994. Instituut Maatschappelijke Gezondheidszorg, Instituut voor Medische Technology Assesment, Erasmus Universiteit, Rotterdam.

Romer, P.M., 1990. Endogenous technological change. Journal of Political Economy 5, 71–102.

van Zon, A.H., Muysken, J., 1997. Health, education and endogenous growth. MERIT Research Memorandum, 97-009.

Acknowledgments

Schulz, J. H. (1995). "What we have learned about the economics of aging: ratings for the past years of research." *The Journals of Gerontology* B50(5): 271–3. Reprinted with the permission of Gerontological Society of America.

Aaron, H. J. and R. D. Reischauer (1999). "Paying for an aging population." *Setting National Priorities: The 2000 election and beyond.* H. J. Aaron and R. D. Reischauer, Washington, D.C., Brookings Institution Press, 167–209. Reprinted with the permission of Brookings Institution Press.

Bass, S. A. (2000). "Emergence of the Third Age: toward a productive aging society." *Journal of Aging and Social Policy.* 11 (2–3): 7–17. Reprinted with the permission of Haworth Press, Inc.

Fuchs, V. R. (2001). "The Financial Problems of the Elderly: A Holistic Approach." *National Bureau of Economic Research Working paper*: 8236. Reprinted with the permission of National Bureau of Economic Research.

von Weizsacker, R. K. (1996). "Distributive implications of an aging society." *European economic review.* 40(3–5): 729–747. Reprinted with the permission of North-Holland.

Barton, L. (1995). "Aging and Economics: A comparative examination of responses by the United States, Great Britain, and Japan." *The International Journal of Sociology and Social Policy.* 15(1–3): 120–134. Reprinted with the permission of Barmarick Publications.

Guest, R. (2001). "The Impact of population aging on the socially optimal rate of national saving: A comparison of Australia and Japan." *Review of Development Economics.* 5(2): 312–327. Reprinted with the permission of Blackwell Publishers Ltd.

Yashiro, N. (1997). "The economic position of the elderly in Japan." The economic effects of aging in the United States and Japan. M. D. Hurd and N. Yashiro. *National Bureau of Economic Research Conference Report Series.* Chicago and London, University of Chicago Press: 89–107. Reprinted with the permission of National Bureau of Economic Research.

Ron, A. (1998). "Social Security financing policies and rapidly aging populations." Choices in financing health care and old age security: proceedings of a conference sponsored by the Institute of Policy Studies, Singapore, and the World Bank, November 1997. N. Prescott. *World Bank Discussion Paper*, No 392, Washington, D.C., World Bank: 51–61. Reprinted with the permission of World Bank Group.

Kemnitz, A. (2000). "Social Security, public education, and growth in a representative democracy. *Journal of Population Economics* 13(3): 443–62. Reprinted with the permission of Springer-Verlag.

Schieber, S. J. and J. B. Shoven (1997). "The consequences of population aging on private pension fund saving and asset markets." *Public policy toward pensions.* S. J. Schieber and J. B. Shoven. A Twentieth Century Fund Book. Cambridge and London, MIT Press: 219–45. Reprinted with the permission of MIT Press.

Broer, D. P. (2001). "Growth and Welfare Distribution in an Aging Society: An Applied general equilibrium analysis for the Netherlands." *De Economist* 140(1) 81–114. Reprinted with the permission of Kluwer Academic Publishers Group.

Benjamin, D. L. Brandt, et al. (2000). "Aging, Wellbeing, and Social Security in Rural Northern China." *Population and Development Review* 26(Supplement): 89–116. Reprinted with the permission of the Population Council.

Burtless, G. and J. F. Quinn (2000 or 2001). "Retirement Trends and Policies to encourage work among older Americans." The Brookings Institution, Working paper, (see web site), 1–38. Reprinted by permission of the Brookings Institution Press, Washington D.C.

Clark, R. L., E. A. York, et al. (1999). "Economic Development and Labor Force Participation of Older Persons." *Population Research and Policy Review* 18(5): 411–32.

Venne, R. A.(2001). "Population Aging in Canada and Japan: Implications for labor force and career patterns." *Revue Canadienne des Sciences de L'Administration* 18(1): 40–49. Reprinted with the permission of Dalhousie University.

Madrian, B. C. and N. D. Beaulieu (1998). Does Medicare eligibility affect retirement? *Inquiries in the economics of aging.* D. A. Wise. NBER Project Report Series. Chicago and London, University of Chicago Press: 109–28. Reprinted with the permission of the University of Chicago Press.

Fratantoni, M. C. (1999). "Reverse mortgage choices: A theoretical and empirical analysis of the borrowing decisions of elderly homeowners." *Journal of Housing Research* 10(2): 189–208. The copyrighted material is used with the permission of the Fannie Mae Association.

Smith, J. (1994). "Measuring health and economic status of older adults in developing countries." *The Gerontologist.* 34(4): 491–496. Reprinted with the permission of Gerontological Society of America.
VanZon, A., J. Muysken. (2001). "Health and Endogenous Growth." *Journal of Health Economics* 20(2): 169–185. Reprinted with the permission of North-Holland.